Building Highly Scalable Database Applications with .NET

Wallace B. McClure and John J. Croft IV

Wiley Publishing, Inc.

Best-Selling Books • Digital Downloads • e-Books • Answer Networks
e-Newsletters • Branded Web Sites • e-Learning

Building Highly Scalable Database Applications with .NET

Published by Wiley Publishing, Inc., Indianapolis, Indiana

www.wiley.com

This book is printed on acid-free paper.

Library of Congress Control Number: 2001092936

ISBN: 0-7645-3640-0

Printed in the United States of America.

10 9 8 7 6 5 4 3 2 1

1B/RR/QW/QS/IN

About the Authors

Wallace B. (Wally) McClure is the owner of McClure Development in Knoxville, Tennessee. Wally has Bachelor's and Master's degrees in Electrical Engineering specializing in Computer Architectures and Digital Signal Processing from the Georgia Institute of Technology (Georgia Tech) in Atlanta, Georgia. While in school, Wally was involved with the development of a package to perform symbolic signal processing routines within a package called Mathematica. McClure Development specializes in building applications that scale to a large number of users, either on the Web or using client/server technologies. Some of McClure Development's customers include Lucent Technologies, the State of Tennessee, and a major Internet portal. Wally has been a programmer involved with some type of programming since 1988. McClure Development uses the Microsoft suite of development tools to tie in to SQL Server, Oracle, DB/2, and MySQL.

Wally is married to a loving wife, Ronda; they have two children. He enjoys golf on a regular basis, physical fitness, and *really* enjoys programming and development.

John J. Croft IV is president of AtlantaProgramming.com in Atlanta, Georgia. He graduated from Georgia Institute of Technology in 1991. He did consulting work for several Fortune 100 companies before founding his own company in 1995. AtlantaProgramming.com focuses on custom database solutions for medium to large enterprises with brief forays into satellite telemetry, car wash control, and lithotripter control, for the treatment of kidney stones. Database applications have included inventory control, performance evaluation, production management, and executive information systems. These systems have been implemented on a variety of proprietary and open-source databases, including SQL Server, Oracle, Interbase, and MySQL. These systems have been both single location and distributed, but most have been client/server-oriented. Platforms have varied from Windows NT to Solaris and Linux.

John is married with two kids. He sometimes runs on a regular basis, managing to enter some 10K races. He coaches soccer, tries to play golf, and can periodically be found woodworking.

Credits

SENIOR ACQUISITIONS EDITOR
Sharon Cox

PROJECT EDITOR
Elizabeth Kuball

DEVELOPMENT EDITOR
Erik Dafforn

TECHNICAL EDITOR
Mike MacDonald

COPY EDITOR
Elizabeth Kuball

EDITORIAL MANAGER
Mary Beth Wakefield

VICE PRESIDENT AND EXECUTIVE
GROUP PUBLISHER
Richard Swadley

VICE PRESIDENT AND EXECUTIVE
PUBLISHER
Bob Ipsen

VICE PRESIDENT AND PUBLISHER
Joseph B. Wikert

EXECUTIVE EDITORIAL DIRECTOR
Mary Bednarek

PROJECT COORDINATOR
Dale White

GRAPHICS AND PRODUCTION
SPECIALISTS
Beth Brooks
Melanie DesJardins
Kristin McMullan
Jacque Schneider
Erin Zeltner

QUALITY CONTROL TECHNICIANS
Laura Albert
John Greenough
Carl Pierce

PROOFREADING AND INDEXING
TECHBOOKS Production Services

Preface

We wanted to write a book with a focus on building scalable applications. Many books focus only on a particular language or database product, and these same books often lack context. The language books provide syntax and examples based on common algorithms. They start with, "Hello, World!" and work their way up. The database books tend to cover basic SQL, move on to proprietary DDL and DML extensions, and finish up with how to use the management tools that ship with the product. Although these books are useful (our shelves are full of them), their focus on a single subject often leaves some shortcomings for the more experienced developer. Experienced developers generally don't need a whole book to pick up a new language because they already have a sufficient knowledge of algorithms. Most developers have a working knowledge of SQL and a good idea of the type of tools that will be provided.

Of course, there is always the documentation, but documentation will not explain how to build scalable applications with .NET. Documentation explains the specific techniques or details related to the language or environment. Documentation shows how not why. If the topical books suffer from not seeing the forest for the trees, documentation itemizes the leaves. Scalability results from a broad strategy, and scalability results from selecting the right techniques to implement the strategy.

We have both had experiences with large systems where large performance problems existed because of bottlenecks that could have been anticipated. These problems arose, however, because techniques that are adequate for 10 or 100 records fail miserably when dealing with tens or hundreds of thousands of records. So with the arrival of Microsoft's latest development environment, we thought a new type of book would be useful — a book that would cover the technology in the context of solving a particular problem (in this case, the problem is building scalable databases). The material is presented in a manner that we hope is beneficial to the experienced programmer by providing broad groundwork for addressing the issues and coding required to build a large database system.

We would also like to present an idea in this book that scalable systems are engineered. That is, scalable systems are achievable without a hit-or-miss design strategy. Highly scalable systems are achieved through a steady evaluation of requirements and implementation of solid solutions to meet these requirements. This means that the primary goals of a system must be understood, because some performance requirements may be at odds with other requirements. A single system will not scale in all directions at once. So, priorities must be set or the two competing requirements must be isolated from each other. The common circumstance for this is the isolation of OLTP systems from data mining or OLAP systems. When building a large system, these tradeoffs between design options must be considered.

For situations in which hard choices must be made, it is important to consider the different design tradeoffs *in advance*. Generally, there is more than one way to skin a cat or retrieve or update data. In isolation, the different methodologies may seem equivalent, but in a real system, one technique may impact another objective.

Also important to remember is that some decisions are wrong. In these days, when people eschew passing judgments, or pass things off as a matter of opinion, there are still some database-design decisions that we can deem wrong under a given set of circumstances. We can say this because we can watch response time increase by orders of magnitude when the wrong approach is used.

So, having said all that, we have some expectations for our readers. We hope anyone who reads the book will understand the concepts of scalability and what scalability implies. We hope the reader understands the tradeoffs involved with different designs and how to compare them; and that some designs do not scale at all. So, although some designs are worth considering, some designs are not.

We hope this book achieves this goal.

In addition, we also had to make some technical choices about the languages and databases to use, and we want to give you some background for our choices in the following sections.

Databases

In the final chapters of this book, we cover four databases:

◆ **SQL Server:** SQL Server was chosen for the obvious reasons. It allows a demonstration of a Microsoft end-to-end solution, it is one of the top three enterprise databases, and it is what the .NET code was primarily developed against.

◆ **Oracle:** Oracle, too, is a straightforward choice, given that it is the number one database server in the client/server arena. Many places that use Microsoft tools will use them against an Oracle server.

◆ **DB/2:** Although DB/2 may not be as popular in the client/server realm as Oracle or SQL Server, the importance of IBM's flagship database should not be underestimated. A vast amount of corporate data is held in DB/2 systems from micro servers to minicomputers and mainframes.

◆ **MySQL:** Some people in the enterprise may think that MySQL is an open-source buzzword, to be used to demonstrate open-mindedness. However, in the real world of open source, MySQL has long established itself as a robust and reliable data-storage system. It was built with the Web in mind and currently supports some very large Web sites, so its ability to scale has been proven and its popularity continues to grow.

Although other good database systems exist, we cannot discuss all of them here. We're confident that we're covering the four most important at this time. Other technologies, such as OODBMSs or the newer XML databases, are oriented to particular niches; when people want to manage millions of records, they will opt for relational database systems.

Languages

In this book, almost all the code is written in Visual Basic .NET or C#. Why do we focus on Visual Basic .NET and C#? Visual Basic .NET is the next extension of VB, which is the most popular tool at the moment for RAD and client-side applications. C# provides C-style syntax with VB RAD capabilities and a very robust object library. This gives it RAD capabilities in a format that most advanced programmers are used to. And what about managed C++? With managed code there is no benefit of compiled versus interpreted code as in the world of unmanaged code. Also, managed code makes it easier to do many things. Managed code limits the functionality of C++. Thus we feel that most people will not opt for managed C++. And what about using JScript? Similarly, JScript does not seem to have much of a solution niche anymore, especially when writing scalable enterprise apps.

How This Book Is Organized

This book is divided into three parts, outlined in the following sections.

PART 1: INTRODUCTION

Part I lays out the architecture of the .NET Framework and how that architecture can be used to build a highly scalable application. Chapter 1 covers current development requirements and leads into how the .NET Framework can help resolve those problems. Chapter 2 covers the general concepts of the .NET Framework.

PART II: DESIGNING DATABASES AND MIDDLE-TIER COMPONENTS FOR MAXIMUM SCALABILITY

Part II has general information about how to develop applications that work with databases. Chapter 3 provides general information about databases along with strategies on how to best store and retrieve data in a database. Chapter 4 provides a general discussion about how databases provide support for transactions along with the impact of different types of transactions and locking levels. Chapter 5 covers general database access with ADO.NET with some information on using Classic ADO 2.x within the .NET Framework. Chapter 6 discusses how to write components that can be used in a reusable fashion. Chapter 7 covers how to integrate COM components with .NET applications and vice versa. Chapter 8 discusses how to properly implement threads within your applications and how to properly write Windows Services using the .NET Framework. Chapter 9 focuses on how to access MSMQ through the .NET Framework. MSMQ is a part of COM+ Services. It allows messages to be sent back and forth by applications in an asynchronous fashion.

PART III: SPECIFIC DATABASE SCALING ISSUES

Part III covers how to access and use the SQL Server, Oracle, DB/2, and MySQL databases from within the .NET Framework. We include coverage of issues such as accessing the database, inserting data into the database, different ways of getting a primary key back, and other database optimizations.

APPENDIXES

The appendixes contain general background information on our programming. Appendix A contains an overview of our example application. Appendix B contains an overview of the standards used in our code. Appendix C contains a list of some of our favorite online resources for the .NET Framework and ASP.NET.

Conventions Used in This Book

Each chapter in this book begins with a heads-up of the topics covered in the chapter and ends with a summary of what you should have learned by reading the chapter. Throughout this book, you'll find icons in the margins that highlight special or important information. Keep an eye out for the following icons:

 Notes provide additional or critical information and technical data on the current topic.

 The Tip icon indicates tidbits that we've picked up along the way and want to share with you.

 This icon indicates where in the book you can find more information on the topic at hand.

In addition to the icons, the following formatting and typographical conventions appear throughout the book:

◆ Code examples appear in a `fixed width font`.

◆ Other code elements, such as data structures and variable names, appear in `fixed width`.

◆ File, function, and macro names as well as World Wide Web addresses (URLs) appear in a `fixed width font`.

◆ The first occurrence of an important term in a chapter is highlighted with *italic* text. Italics are also used for placeholders in file and directory names, which may be different on each computer, depending on where the product was installed.

◆ Menu commands are indicated in hierarchical order, with each menu command separated by an arrow. For example File → Open means to click the File command on the menu bar and then select Open.

◆ Keyboard shortcuts are indicated with the following syntax: Ctrl+C.

Acknowledgments

Wally McClure: Thanks to all those people who have given me the opportunity to work on this book. Thank you to the folks at Wiley for working with me, including Sharon Cox, Elizabeth Kuball, Neil Romanosky, and others; a bunch of folks at Microsoft who answered my questions and didn't laugh at me too much; my wife Ronda and my family (who gave me the time to work on this); my co-author, John Croft, for working with me; several customers who were patient and understood that I sometimes needed to spend time on this book instead of doing development for them; and my friends, who put up with my grumpiness over some of the dumbest things and still helped get me through working on this book.

John Croft: Thanks to Wally McClure for including me on this project. Thanks also to Sharon Cox and others at Wiley for their endless patience allowing us to write this book. Thank you to Elizabeth Kuball for her patience and editing. Many thanks to my parents and to my father, in particular, for my first job as a professional programmer. Thank you to all of my teachers. Thanks to my kids for behaving on Saturdays when I had to write, and, most of all, thanks to my wife, Valerie, for everything.

Contents

xvi   **Contents**

Part I

Introduction

Chapter 1

Current Development Issues

IN THIS CHAPTER

◆ Understanding current challenges in software development

◆ Identifying the advantages and disadvantages of Visual Studio 6

◆ Recognizing how some features of the .NET Framework will assist developers

IN TODAY'S SOFTWARE-DEVELOPMENT ENVIRONMENT, developers commonly work on several types of applications simultaneously. Consequently, the tools used for these applications all need to be supported. Depending on the project you're working on, you may be developing client/server applications; Web site applications; distributed N-Tier applications with COM+ Services in the middle tier; data interchange technology with XML; applications that need to communicate with other platforms, such as the AS/400, mainframe, or Unix-based systems; or any combination of these.

Microsoft's Visual Studio 6 is the most popular suite of development tools available. These tools are widely used to develop many of these databases. The tools are very good, yet each seems to lack some critical feature that limits it. The problem is that Microsoft's Visual Studio 6 suite of development tools makes developing the aforementioned applications in one environment difficult. It's not that this development can't be done with Visual Studio 6; it's merely that the development of these types of applications is harder than it could be.

In this chapter, we take a look at the previous Visual Studio 6 environment and see how Visual Studio .NET and the .NET Framework can be used to allow developers to satisfy new development requirements.

Visual Basic 6

Visual Basic 6 is the jack-of-all-trades in Visual Studio 6. Through VB, developers have been able to quickly and easily create client/server and front-end applications, middle-tier COM+ applications, and distributable components. VB has allowed developers to create applications for customers quickly and easily. These applications have been easy to develop because of the rapid application development (RAD) environment. Developers are not required to know or understand how to place a button or textbox on a screen or even to understand the intricacies of actually starting the GUI application and launching an initial form. All the knowledge

3

that is required is how to click and drag a user interface (UI) element onto a form. Developers can start writing code, implementing an application after the design and business rules are decided on.

Because of these qualities, VB is widely seen as the most productive programming language currently in use. In addition to being productive, VB is a very widely used language. Approximately 3.5 million VB programmers worldwide use the product on an almost daily basis. In addition, a tremendous amount of third-party support exists. You can go out on the Web and see a large number of third parties that have created components to assist developers in VB-based applications.

However, several potential problems with applications developed with VB. One problem is due to a feature included in VB that is often incorrectly used: data-bound controls. Data-bound controls allow a programmer to very quickly and easily hook into the records contained within a database. Although this is a great feature for developers, the use of data-bound controls can greatly affect the performance of a database. When most developers create an application with data-bound controls, they use a string to create a connection. For each set of data-bound controls that is loaded, a different connection to the database is made. An application that uses five different sets of data-bound controls can create five different connections to your database. Attempting to run 10, 50, or 100 instances of this program can very easily bog down your database server. Depending on whether updates are allowed, the potential for locking other users out from records exists. Programmers can quickly get into trouble by using data-bound controls.

 Are data-bound controls all bad? Absolutely not. You can get around these problems by using ActiveX Data Objects (ADO) disconnected recordsets. The problem is that most programmers don't know about disconnected recordsets and, therefore, don't use them.

Another drawback of VB has to do with its feature set, which lacks two important features that are included in other development languages: multiple threads and visual inheritance. Multiple threads allow an application to divide the workload of an application. This allows a programmer to improve the end user experience by allowing long-running tasks to run on a separate thread. By supporting multiple threads of execution within an application, the executable can be more responsive to user input. By not supporting multiple threads, applications written in Visual Basic are not as responsive as applications written in languages that do support multiple threads. Visual inheritance allows a programmer to create either one or several standard forms for an application. These standard forms can then be connected to the forms in an application to provide a standard and consistent look to an application's user interface. By supporting visual inheritance, a language makes the maintenance of an application easier and the user interface more consistent.

This is not to say that not having threading and visual inheritance is always a bad thing. For example, threading is a relatively simple concept, but the complexity of debugging a multi-threaded application can be overwhelming. What do you do when you start several threads that each perform the same type of function and these threads must all access the same variable within the starting thread? Access to that variable must be locked, the variable must be updated, and then access to that variable must be unlocked. Once again, this is not a complex concept, but unfortunately not many VB programmers are familiar with it. Threading and inheritance are merely features of a programming language. In this case, they are complex features of a programming language. These features can take programmers a great deal of time to properly master. With the .NET Framework and Visual Studio .NET, most issues with threading are actually hidden from the programmer. If there is a need to create an application that uses threading with Visual Basic .NET, the Visual Studio .NET IDE provides full design, development, and debugging support.

Developing middle-tier COM+ applications is very easy with Visual Basic 6. Middle-tier business logic can quickly and easily be developed, debugged, and deployed with COM+ Services enabled. The problem with using Visual Basic 6 for development of COM+ applications is that the VB6 runtime does not provide support for object pooling. Object pooling is a mechanism to have objects available and in memory ready to be called by an application. Because of the VB6 runtime's lack of support for the appropriate threading model, support for object pooling is not available. By not supporting object pooling, performance of VB6 COM+ components may be between 30 and 50 percent worse than for languages that support object pooling.

In spite of the lack of support for object pooling, VB allows components to quickly and easily be created and debugged. In general, this will offset the problems down the road with the lack of object pooling. With the .NET Framework, components developed with the Visual Basic language have complete access to COM+ Services, including support for object pooling.

Components written in VB6 are easy to create and distribute. The problems are that these components must be installed, along with upgrades to existing components. The initial installation of these components is easy most of the time. However, there are times when the umbrella application must be stopped to perform these upgrades. Users don't like this, but they can live with a small amount of downtime. The other problem is that the upgrade to a component might introduce an incompatibility, which users really don't like. The .NET Framework provides a relatively easy application install mechanism. For example, ASP.NET applications that are written with the .NET Framework and do not make use of features outside of the .NET environment, such as COM+, may be copied into a directory and run without the need to install the components or run any registration utility to register the components.

Visual C++ 6

C and C++ development for DOS, Windows, OS/2, and other environments have been around for a long time. Microsoft's Visual C++ continues in the tradition of high-end Microsoft development tools. Visual C++ 6 is the high-end development language of Visual Studio 6. With VC++, developers can create the highest performing applications in any point in the development process compared to the other tools available in Visual Studio 6. In addition, C/C++ development is considered to be the top of the development ladder. With VC++, developers can take advantage of multiple threads in their front-end applications and object pooling in the middle tier with COM+ Services. With these two features, VC++ developers can create high-performing applications on Windows 2000 today. The problem with C/C++ development has been the added development time over a rapid application development tool, such as VB, Delphi, or PowerBuilder. Plus, the lack of a high number of talented C/C++ developers has kept many projects from being implemented in C/C++.

Why are there fewer talented C/C++ developers? Two reasons jump right out: confusion over *pointers* (variables that contain the address of another variable in memory) and the fact that Windows development with C/C++ is just plain hard, lowering the number (and raising the price) of qualified developers. Although commercial application developers can justify the cost of using a C/C++ approach to development based on spreading out additional development costs to potentially hundreds of thousands of customers, internal line of business applications have a hard time justifying that expense. In general, these applications are only distributed to a few thousand users at most. In addition to the cost, time to build and deploy an application must be considered. By the time a business unit starts looking for a solution, the problem is most likely out of control. Businesses want and need immediate solutions to their problems. By developing and deploying solutions as quickly as possible, businesses can gain advantages over competitors.

Microsoft is providing Visual C++ .NET for programmers who are currently developing with Visual C++. For those programmers who prefer the C-style syntax, yet do not want the complexity of pointers and having to learn the Windows development methodology, Microsoft is providing a new programming language based on C/C++ syntax. This language is called C# (pronounced "C Sharp"). C# provides RAD-style application development while at the same time allowing programmers to use the C-style syntax that they desire. In addition to providing support for C-style programming in a RAD environment, C# is very similar to the Java programming language and should allow programmers proficient in Java to quickly and easily make the jump to C#.

Visual Interdev and Active Server Pages

Visual Interdev is Microsoft's development tool for Active Server Pages (ASP). ASP is Microsoft's development platform for building Internet applications. ASP creates a scripting environment whereby Web applications are built. With ASP, practically any type of HTML, DHTML, XML, WAP, or other Web-based interface can be developed and deployed to run underneath Microsoft's Internet Information Server (IIS). Although this is the most exciting part of Microsoft's development strategy, it is the least mature and causes the most problems for developers. Some of the problems include the following:

- ASP is interpreted.

- There are no good prebuilt sets of user interface elements that scale to a large number of users.

- Development with ASP/VI is not really up to the development standards of a Visual Basic environment or other RAD tool.

Visual Interdev ships with a set of prebuilt user interface controls called the *design-time controls*. Through the design-time controls, programmers can easily create UI elements to add, edit, delete, and query data. However, much like the data-bound controls in VB, the design-time controls do not scale to large numbers of users. The controls also make extensive use of session variables within the global.asa file. Applications that make extensive use of the global.asa file tend not to scale as well as applications that store state within browser-based cookies.

Active Server Pages are interpreted by the ASP.dll script processor within IIS. Although there is caching of the ASP files, ASP files are still interpreted each time that they are called by a web browser. Although being interpreted during each execution is not necessarily bad, the problem is that it isn't as efficient as if the application was compiled during the first run and the compiled version was run during each request.

Developers love environments like VB and Delphi. These environments have spoiled developers, because they come with many GUI elements that they can easily manipulate to their hearts' content. These GUI elements provide you with text boxes, drop-down lists, and other pieces of functionality. Although Visual Interdev has attempted to provide developers with prewritten pieces of code, the problem is that these pieces of code do not scale to lots and lots of users. To scale to a large number of users, developers must manually write the code to draw text boxes and drop-down lists, populate those elements, and provide other necessary management tasks. The end result is that developers have come up with ways around these issues. However, these mechanisms rarely work from one project to the next.

Today, ASP developers must write code that captures browser events and sends commands to the web server to process those events. For example, updating a row in a database involves clicking on a button. This verification will be performed by client-side JavaScript routines. If the JavaScript routines allow processing to continue, the web browser then sends processing commands to the server. The ASP code will then process the commands using a series of parsing commands to discover the intent of the developer. When this is done, data is sent back to the client browser. This is much different from the development process in a traditional RAD/GUI development tool. In those worlds, the client events and the processing are tied together much more closely. Traditional development tools make this development much easier than it is with ASP.

The .NET Framework, ASP.NET, and Visual Studio .NET have improved the development and performance of Web-based applications. The .NET Framework provides a number of prebuilt controls that provide the RAD-style development methodology necessary for rapidly developing applications without the scalability limitations of the design-time controls included with Visual Interdev. These prebuilt controls include support for text boxes, data grids, list boxes, calendar controls, and many other form elements that developers need. ASP.NET is not an interpreted environment. ASP.NET applications are compiled into Microsoft Intermediate Language (MSIL) and then compiled into machine code as needed. While the first request to an ASP.NET application results in the compilation, requests made after the compilation is completed are run through the compiled ASP.NET application. This results in all requests after the first request having improved performance over an interpreted ASP application.

Components and Deployment

The holy grail of development is reusability. By creating software code and packaging it into reusable objects, developers and development teams can build on previous work and package business rules into consistent and repeatable packages. Over the last ten years, developers have had several mechanisms to package their code: dynamic link libraries (DLLs), VBx and OLE controls, and Component Object Model (COM) components.

DLLs were the original mechanism to package reusable code. Unfortunately, they have suffered from several problems. Originally, DLLs were developed in C. Due to certain issues in how C compilers loaded code, DLLs written with one compiler could not be used easily by an application written with a different compiler. Although not necessarily a problem for development teams inside of a company working on company-specific applications, this issue limited their broad distribution and use. Even when they were used, DLLs were limited in their use by the Windows API `LoadLibrary` function. By using the system path to load the external code, `LoadLibrary` was at the mercy of a DLL with the same name that was in a file location in front of the required DLL within the path. Personally, we spent more than one sleepless night trying to unearth why an application wouldn't work correctly on some machines before we tracked down this issue. For example, under Windows 3.1, when we logged into our Novell Network, several directories were put into the front of the path. In one directory was a DLL (nwipxspx.dll) that had the same name but was an older and buggy version of the exact same DLL that we needed to use. Systems that had this older DLL in the path would not communicate with the database server reliably.

VBx components were the first mechanism to make reusable code easily available to developers. VBx components worked very well. Unfortunately, they were only 16-bit. As developers moved into the 32-bit world starting with Windows 95 and Windows NT, they needed a component model that would fully support the 32-bit world.

COM components have been with developers in some form since 1995. COM components work very well, until it becomes time to distribute them. Components must be registered into the Windows registry. This is done through the use of a utility called regsvr32.exe. Regsvr32.exe allows for the registering and unregistering of components. Most of the time, these components and their upgrades work very well. There are times, however, when the global nature of COM makes deployment onto a machine hazardous if incompatibilities are undetected. The updating of one component could break other applications. This update could break what is referred to as *binary compatibility*. Binary compatibility is an option for programmers creating components that allows components to keep the class and interface ID that already exists for existing clients while generating new class and interface IDs for new versions of a class. Although binary compatibility sounds easy enough to maintain, in practice it is harder. When business logic changes, the result is often that the interfaces into a component will change, and the parameters that are passed to a component will change. Because these parameters are changed, an application that is expecting to use the original calling parameters may generate an error with this updated component. Although there are ways around these issues, the problem is that the global nature of the COM can make life hard for programmers as business rules change. One of the great features of the .NET Framework is the ability of multiple versions of a component to be installed and running at the same time, without affecting other running versions of the component. The .NET Framework not only incorporates naming schemes into its loading of components, it also uses the version number that an application requests to be loaded with. By using the version number, the .NET Framework is able to track multiple versions of a component on disk and loaded into memory that differ only by the version number.

Database Operations and Scalability Issues

Businesses have invested significant time, money, and other resources to be able to understand their customers better. Spreading that information over a sales force, allowing customers to place orders directly through an order-entry Web site, distributing the information to management, and making information work for a company are very important for a company to satisfy the needs of its customers. Building database applications to support the largest number of users possible and being reliable over a long period of time is very important to any business. Writing a sales force automation tool that will only scale to five users is not the best idea. Over the last several years, Microsoft has provided developers with tools to greatly increase the scalability of applications when used correctly. The other side of the coin is that the incorrect use of these tools will also cause a number of problems and can greatly limit the scalability of applications.

ActiveX Data Objects

ActiveX Data Objects (ADO) is Microsoft's mature data-access technology. ADO is based on the Microsoft COM architecture. It supports connecting to many types of databases, such as client/server databases like Oracle and SQL Server along with file-based databases such as Access or dBase files. It has developed over the years to add several important options, such as updateable scrollable recordsets, disconnected records, and XML support. In the hands of a developer familiar with the many options that are available through ADO and how to use them, ADO provides many opportunities. Unfortunately, these many options can also get developers into trouble. Support for scrollable recordsets has gotten developers into more issues than anything else. Two of the features that support updateable scrollable recordsets are cursor support and locking support. Here we use SQL Server as an example. Assume that you're going to iterate through data. Many times a programmer will create a recordset that is much more powerful than is needed with support for scrolling and updating. Look at an example in VB and Microsoft SQL Server in Listing 1-1.

Listing 1-1: Title Retrieve Data

```
Dim rs as ADODB.RecordSet
Dim cn as ADODB.Connection
Dim strCn as String
Dim strSql as String
strCn = "database connection string"
strSql = "select * from table where ....."
Set rs = CreateObject("ADODB.Recordset")
Set cn = CreateObject("ADODB.Connection")
cn.open strSql
rs.open strSql, cn, adOpenDynamic, adLockPessimistic
while not rs.eof
    'Do something to read the data and perhaps perform an update
using the updateable recordset.
    rs.MoveNext
wend
if rs.State <> adStateClosed then
    rs.Close
```

```
end if
set rs = Nothing
if cn.State <> adStateClosed then
    cn.Close
end if
set cn = Nothing
```

When this recordset is opened, a query is issued to a table and data is copied from the table and placed into tempdb. By writing your code this way, a data structure is created in your database that holds the data, and during the update process a significant amount of communication occurs between the client application and the database. A more efficient way to handle the update and meet the program's needs would be to a perform a SQL `update` command and to provide an `adReadOnly` lock. If there is no need for locking the data during the read process, a forward-only cursor of type `adForwardOnly` in combination with a client-side cursor would lighten the load on the database even more.

Although there is a need for these options, way too many programmers out there are using these types of operations and don't realize that their code is not running as efficiently as it could. A good rule of thumb is to use the options that are necessary. If locks are needed on tables, then by all means use them. If locks are not needed, don't use them. Listing 1-1 can cause too many unnecessary locks on a database table. The locks in turn slow down operations. By not running efficiently, the application is using too many processor cycles and hard-disk operations. The end result is an application that is too slow.

With the .NET Framework, Microsoft provides ADO.NET. ADO.NET is designed to solve several of the problems that have cropped up as developers have used ADO. ADO.NET does not have support for server-side updateable cursors. Without support for server-side updateable cursors, it is harder for developers to get into trouble by inadvertently creating resultsets that use too many resources on the database server. ADO.NET also supports the ability to define insert, update, and delete commands for those operations.

Distributed transactions

Microsoft's Transaction Server and COM+ have given the development community the ability to do many things, including object brokering, DCOM encapsulation within COM, and distributed transactions. In addition, they bring a relatively easy-to-use API to developers. The biggest problem is with distributed transactions. Because most applications are running on a single database, there is little need to set up a distributed transaction environment. Most applications simply do not need to update multiple databases through a two-phase commit. Creating an environment to support distributed transactions takes time – time that might be better spent in processing a client's order or running a report for senior management. For an application that doesn't need distributed transactions, the time to set them up can be a significant percentage of the processing time for a component.

Object pooling

Object pooling is the mechanism whereby objects are already created and available in memory for calling applications. Object pooling is a service provided by COM+. When a pool of objects is created, there is no need for a calling application to wait on an object to be created. Object pooling is best used when the initialization of an instance of a component is significant. For example, if the initialization of an object requires 100 milliseconds, that object is a good candidate for object pooling.

Initially, there was confusion, because many folks thought that NT4 provided object pooling. This was not the case. NT4 with the Option Pak did not support object pooling. When Windows 2000 shipped, there was much excitement because now developers would get object pooling. Although VC and VJ (Visual J++) developers could now take advantage of object pooling, VB6 developers were not able to support object pooling, because the VB6 runtime does not support the necessary threading models (multi-threaded apartment, neutral-threaded apartment, or the both-threaded model) to provide object-pooling support to components written in it. With the .NET Framework, all .NET languages, including VB, VC++, and C#, that are used to produce objects that use COM+ Services may take advantage of object pooling.

Summary

The Visual Studio 6–based development environment is a very good development environment. The tools contained within it are top notch and fit nicely into different development needs. Developers are constantly confronted with new requirements within applications: more performance, support for XML, more responsiveness, and other features. Your customers need you to make them more profitable. In turn, you need Microsoft to deliver development tools with new features that allow you to solve your customers' problems easier and quicker. With the .NET Framework and Visual Studio .NET, Microsoft has provided a foundation for building highly scalable and high-performing database applications.

The next chapter takes a look inside the cover of the .NET Framework and Visual Studio .NET and shows you how to build applications that successfully scale to a large number of users and to a large number of operations.

Chapter 2

The High-Performance .NET Architecture

- ◆ Understanding the .NET Framework and Architecture
- ◆ Executing .NET applications
- ◆ Understanding durability
- ◆ Working with ASP.NET

THE .NET ARCHITECTURE contains many performance and durability improvements over the Visual Studio 6/COM–based solutions that developers have been working with. Some of these enhancements are built in so that programs running within the .NET environment will automatically get this support; your code must be written in order to take advantage of other enhancements; and nearly all of these enhancements are welcomed by the development community. Some of these new features are:

- ◆ **Threading:** Applications that take advantage of multiple threads of execution are more responsive to the user.

We will take a quick look at threading in this chapter, but you can find more information on threading in Chapter 8.

- ◆ **Garbage collection:** Garbage collection automates the destruction of allocated objects used by managed applications in the .NET environment. By building in garbage collection to the .NET Framework, the system is now responsible for destroying .NET objects managed.

You can find more on garbage collection later in this chapter.

◆ **Object pooling:** COM+ components written with one of the .NET languages gets support for object pooling. COM+ Services has supported object pooling since Windows 2000 shipped. Unfortunately, support for object pooling was not available to developers using Visual Basic 6. With the .NET Framework, languages that support the .NET Framework support the necessary threading models for object pooling.

◆ **Managed providers:** Microsoft has provided SQL Server developers with a high-performance data-access technology that is optimized for data operations (select, insert, update, and delete).

◆ **ASP.NET:** Although ASP.NET is a new development tool, it has many enhancements over the existing ASP in IIS 4/5. These enhancements will be discussed later in this chapter.

In addition to performance enhancements, the .NET runtime offers several new features that programmers, especially Visual Basic programmers, have desperately needed. These include:

◆ Structured exception handling

◆ Improved access to COM+ Services

◆ Visual Inheritance for development of Windows GUI applications

Historically, Microsoft has provided the development community with high-quality tools. The .NET Framework and Visual Studio .NET continue that tradition. They provide developers with the features and services necessary for producing highly scalable database-oriented applications along with the development environment necessary to produce these applications in a short amount of time.

The .NET Framework

In the second half of 1999 and throughout the first half of 2000, the developer community began to hear about some new items coming out of Microsoft. Some of these items were called a term used to describe the C# language (COOL), Next Generation Windows Services, the Simple Object Access Protocol (SOAP), and other terms. These items referred to something that would be a piece of the .NET Framework or a code name referring to the .NET Framework. In July 2000, at the Professional Developers Conference in Orlando, Florida, a bunch of these items came into focus as Microsoft made its first public announcement of its .NET Framework along with the release of an alpha copy of the .NET Framework and Visual Studio .NET. *.NET* is an umbrella term for a number of new and interesting items coming from Microsoft. One of these items is the .NET Framework.

So what is the .NET Framework? To a developer, the .NET Framework is a redesign of Microsoft's development strategies, taking into account lessons learned from COM, Java, VB, and other environments. This redesign includes a common runtime, a better approach to server development for the masses of Windows programmers, and easier deployment than COM. At a high level, the .NET Framework looks like Figure 2-1.

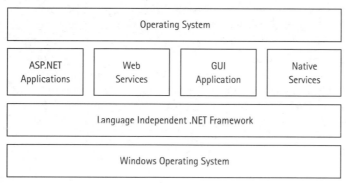

Figure 2-1: The .NET Framework

The .NET Framework provides a number of features and functions. Back to the original question. What is the .NET Framework? It is a number of things. First, we'll look at what it is conceptually:

♦ **Object-oriented and Hierarchical API to access Windows and the services that Windows provides.** In some cases, the functionality of the base class libraries depends on features provided by the Windows operating system. For example, the `System.Data.OleDb` namespace depends on OLE-DB providers included with the Windows operating system. In other cases, the base class libraries are implemented entirely within the managed environment provided by the .NET Framework. For example, the `System.Data.SqlClient` namespace does not directly depend on the other data-access features of OLE-DB, ODBC, or the Windows libraries that talk with SQL Server. It is believed that, at some time in the future, .NET will form the preferred API for development, much like Microsoft's movement away from the DOS-based Windows 9*x* platform to the Windows NT/2000 platform with Windows XP.

♦ **Integration of a number of Internet features into the Windows platform, including XML, SOAP, and cross-platform communications into a**

number of items. For example, within Classic ADO 2.x, data in a record-set is stored in a binary format in memory. Within the .NET Framework, data within a dataset is stored in an XML format in memory.

◆ **A unification of the GUI development layer for desktop applications into an item called Windows Forms.** With this feature, building form-based applications will be consistent across .NET languages.

◆ **A redesign of the Web-development experience.** This redesign makes the development of Web-oriented applications similar to the development of GUI applications. By redesigning the development, the resulting product is called ASP.NET.

◆ **A common development methodology between development in Windows and Web.** Controls in the Web and Windows GUI environments provide a more consistent calling scheme across the two platforms than is available between Visual Basic 6 and ASP 2 or 3. For example, to get at the text in a text box in an ASPX page and a WinForm application merely requires the use of the .Text property of the control. In both environments, setting the .Text property allows the contexts of the text control to be read and set. Previously, in the Web environment, getting the value of a text box required the use of `Request(text box name)` to read the contents of the text box.

Now that you have seen what the runtime provides at a high level, take a closer look at what the .NET Framework provides. The runtime within the .NET Framework provides the following features and functions:

◆ **Language independence.** Programs written in Visual Basic .NET, C#, JScript .NET, or any other .NET-compatible language will be able to run against the exact same runtime.

◆ **Managed environment.** The .NET Framework provides memory management and security automatically to all .NET applications. Included within the memory management features is garbage collection. As needed, the .NET Framework will eliminate any objects that are currently allocated that it's okay to deallocate.

◆ **Compilation into machine code.** The Framework compiles the input code, which is a language-independent format called Microsoft Intermediate Language (MSIL, or just IL), into the format necessary to run on the installed machine. The .NET Framework may either compile methods within executable code as needed, through just-in-time compiler, or may compile it all at once at install-time, through a utility called the native image generator (ngen.exe).

♦ **Verification.** The Framework verifies that the code has the necessary security privilege to perform the operations that it needs. If it does not, it halts execution.

♦ **Base class libraries (BCL).** The .NET Framework provides a set of classes to perform operations such as file I/O, database operations, client-side GUI creation, and server-side GUI creation (ASP.NET). The BCL are an important part of the .NET Framework.

Execution

With the introduction of the .NET Framework, several new terms have appeared with regards to the execution of code. The.NET Framework provides the ability to manage the execution process. It checks the safety of the code to run. The Framework verifies that the running code has the proper security to perform the operations. The Framework provides memory management, security checking, and other features. In other words, the Framework manages the execution of a program. Unmanaged code is code that does not have services provided to it by the Framework. For example, COM objects written in VB6 are unmanaged code. Those objects written in unmanaged code can be called from managed code written in the .NET Framework; however, the Framework does not provide any services to the unmanaged objects.

Just-in-time compilation

Before code in the IL format can be executed, it must be converted to native code. This compilation is performed by a .NET just-in-time (JIT) compiler. JIT compilation does not compile all the code in an executable at one time. It merely compiles methods within the code as those methods are requested to be executed by the runtime. After the code is compiled, the executable code is stored in a native format in the native image cache of the system. Subsequent calls to the previous compiled routines are handled by the compiled routines stored in the native image cache, not by the JIT compiler.

One of the important operations that occurs when the MSIL code is compiled to machine code is to verify that objects are safely isolated from one another and that security restrictions on the code can be enforced and are safe from corruption. One of the ways that this is done is through verification of type safety. The verification process makes sure that code can access memory locations and call methods only through defined types.

The .NET Framework supports a three-step execution process:

1. Compile code to the Microsoft Intermediate Language (MSIL) format. Technically, this is the job of the language compiler.

2. Compile MSIL to native code. This step is handled by compiler built into the .NET Framework called the just-in-time (JIT) compiler or a native image generator (ngen.exe).

3. After code is compiled to native machine code, the native machine code is subsequently called. The MSIL code is not interpreted again and executed.

During execution of code through the .NET Framework, managed code receives services such as garbage collection, security, interoperability with unmanaged code, cross-language debugging support, and improved deployment and versioning support.

Intermediate Language (IL)

Much like a traditional two-step compilation process where there is a compile of the source code and then a link to verify that external dependencies are resolved, there is a two-step compilation process in the .NET environment with a source code compile to the Microsoft Intermediate Language (MSIL, or just IL) format. Once in that format, an application can be distributed. This format is much like a pseudo (or p) code system with an imaginary environment to run in. In this case, the imaginary environment is the .NET Framework Upon execution of the MSIL code on a system. In the second compile step, the MSIL code is compiled through just-in-time compilation or through the native image generator (ngen.exe).

If you would like to view the MSIL code, Microsoft provides a tool called the IL DisASseMbler (ILDASM.EXE). ILDASM allows you to view the IL code that is created by your compiler. ILDASM and resulting IL code are shown in Figure 2-2.

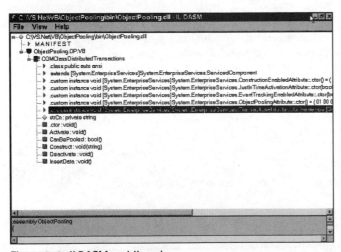

Figure 2-2: ILDASM and IL code

One interesting feature that is lacking in the .NET Framework is easy access to pointers. Pointers, pointer arithmetic, and other features commonly associated with

C/C++ can be a double-edged sword. Although pointers and their associated features provide many good features, including the ability to directly manipulate memory locations, a program that does not correctly use pointers can easily crash or gobble up memory. C# removes the ability to easily use pointers. Therefore, C#, VB, JScript, and other .NET languages are said to be safer. C# does allow a programmer to directly use pointers. However, the program must clearly mark the section of code that uses pointers as unsafe. This allows a programmer to program C in C#.

Why would you want to program C in C#? Although most of what you can do with pointers in C you can do with reference types in C#, the accessing of items outside of the Framework will most likely require the use of pointers. Working with advanced Platform Invoke (P/Invoke) and COM issues may require the use of pointers. In general, writing unsafe code involves directly accessing memory locations. Another problem with unsafe code is that the Framework moves objects around in memory. During the garbage-collection process, the small memory heap is compacted as needed. This could easily make pointers invalid because it would not be safe to believe that an object will stay at the same location between calls. Here's an example using C#:

```
 unsafe static void incInt (int* p) //by marking the function as
//unsafe, we are telling the compiler that the function incInt
//contains unsafe code.
{
    *p += 1;
}
```

 If you're using the command line C# compiler, you will need to add the /unsafe option to the call to the compiler.

In addition to the using the unsafe keyword for your method declarations, to keep objects from moving around in memory, you might need to fix, or pin, a pointer to a given location. There are currently two ways to do this. By using the fixed keyword, the garbage collector will not moved the contents of memory around while the code within the fixed() method call is being done:

```
fixed(int* p1 = &p.x)
```

The second option is to allocate elements, as follows:

```
string* strArray = stackalloc string[100];
```

By allocating elements from the stack, these elements are not moved around in memory because they are not under the control of the garbage collector.

Both methods can only be performed within a method that is marked unsafe. When you write code that is specified as fixed, you are instructing the Framework to keep objects within that section of code in the same locations and not move them around. The memory management part of the .NET Framework may move an object around at any time. By marking the object as fixed, the memory management routines will not move that object around in memory.

.NET Runtime Architecture

The .NET Architecture borrows heavily from what has been learned regarding software development. The .NET runtime is based on a Microsoft-developed standard called the Common Language Specification (CLS). The CLS (along with C#) has been presented to the ECMA standards body for consideration as a standard. The CLS is a minimum standard for language interoperability in .NET. Some of the items it implements include the following:

◆ **Compilation done at runtime/install.** By compiling an application at either install or at runtime, it is easier for the resulting code to be better optimized for that platform. Multiple compilations do not have to be distributed.

 The 1.0 version of the runtime for the 32-bit x86 processors will not provide much optimization beyond the standard features of the 32-bit architecture as defined by Intel's x86-based processors.

◆ **Language independence.** By allowing the runtime to be language independent, multiple languages can be designed to work together. Cross-language inheritance is possible through the use of metadata.

◆ **Metadata and versioning.** .NET applications can specify the acceptable version of the components and runtime, thereby reducing the possibility of "DLL Hell." This is enabled through "metadata."

◆ **Processor and Operating System independence.** By being processor independent, applications developed for the runtime are "mostly" portable across Windows environments that have the .NET runtime. (We use the term *mostly* because there are several unknowns regarding this. For example, Microsoft has not released a public viewing of CLR for 64-bit Windows systems.) In addition, there may be the ability to run applications across platforms, but there has been no official word on that at the time of the writing of this book. The ability to target Win9x, WinNT/2k, Windows on I-64, and Windows CE with the same source code will be very attractive. Microsoft has released the source code of the CLI and C# for BSD Unix under the Microsoft shared source license.

.NET languages

One of the design goals of the .NET Framework is to be language independent. In other words, all the languages that support the .NET Framework will have basically the same set of features. Some languages might implement things differently, but all in all, they have the same feature set with regards to the .NET platform. Obviously, there might be features implemented by one language that do not exist in other languages, such as the ability to author unsafe code. Out of the box, the .NET Framework provides five compilers:

- ◆ C#

- ◆ Visual Basic

- ◆ JScript (Microsoft's implementation of JavaScript for .NET)

- ◆ C++ with Managed Extensions

- ◆ Visual J#

In addition to the included compilers, several third parties are creating languages that integrate with Visual Studio .NET. Some of these languages include RPG, Perl, Python, XSLT, Fortran, COBOL, Pascal, and others.

TIP For a current list of current Visual Studio .NET partners, check out http://msdn.microsoft.com/vstudio/partners/language/default.asp.

One interesting side effect of the architecture of .NET is that, because a compiler generates IL code and not machine code, if two different compilers generate the same machine code, the performance of the two sections of code will be identical.

C#

C# appears to be the crown jewel of the languages supplied with the Framework. It appears that C# is C/C++ minus pointers plus the easy to use RAD development features of VB and Java. C# provides many of the features of C/C++ and will be almost instantly recognizable to C/C++ programmers. C# provides one interesting feature that the neither Visual Basic .NET nor JScript .NET have: the ability to produce unsafe code. With this ability, C# developers can access and use pointers within their applications. Although the ability to use pointers is not on by default, the inclusion of that ability is important because it does allow developers to do things that they might not be able to do otherwise.

VISUAL BASIC .NET

Of all the languages supplied with the Framework, Visual Basic has undergone the most changes from the previous version. Visual Basic .NET now provides support for multiple threads, inheritance, and structured exception handling. Also, a multitude of features have been dropped. For a complete discussion of the features that have been dropped and their various values, go to news://news.devx.com.

JSCRIPT .NET

JScript is Microsoft's implementation of the JavaScript language that has been standardized by ECMA. Microsoft has tweaked its implementation of the language to make it work with .NET. For example, the JavaScript language as defined by ECMA is not thread safe. Microsoft has made some changes, and the Microsoft implementation is threadsafe. Other than client-side web browser development, there does not appear to be tremendous interest in developing applications with JScript .NET.

C++ WITH MANAGED EXTENSIONS

C++ with Managed Extensions (MEs) allows developers who are already writing their code in Microsoft's Visual C++ to have their cake and eat it, too. Developers using C++ with MEs can develop native applications that run directly against the operating system without the Framework. They can still develop COM objects directly. Developing in C++ with MEs allows them to continue on with their existing applications and slowly migrate to the .NET Framework over time. Unless, you are currently developing with C++, you probably won't move to that as your new development environment. Developers currently developing with C++ will most likely stay with that environment, though some may move to C#.

With over 3 million developers having done some kind of development with Visual Basic, it is clear that the language chosen by those 3 million developers will most likely become the dominant language for development with the .NET Framework. It is our belief that Visual Basic .NET will garner the largest initial share in terms of immediate development in the .NET platform. Why? Because there are more VB developers than any other language, and there will be more possible developers who can use Visual Basic .NET to get their feet wet. Another thing that must be remembered is that developers want to move up the ladder in terms of expertise. The C family of languages is considered to be higher on the ladder than VB. Therefore, given the opportunity, some developers with VB experience will want to use, develop with, and move on to C#. Because this is the general way of thinking, we have decided to have as many examples as possible in both the Visual Basic .NET and C# languages.

VISUAL J#

Visual J# is Microsoft's implementation of the Java language running on the .NET platform. It enables programmers fluent in the Java language to target the features, functions, and services of the .NET Framework. J# allows developers to create applications that are targeted at the .NET Framework, such as WinForms applications, ASP.NET applications, and components, without having to learn a new language. It is not intended for programmers who are attempting to exploit a Java Virtual Machine.

Components

Today, software is built using the concept of reusability. Libraries of code are fashioned into a format that allows them to be used by multiple applications. Developers have had this type of reusability for several years. DLLs are examples of code libraries.

Through the use of the Windows API `LoadLibrary()` function, you have had the ability to call external code modules for years. Although you can still directly call DLLs, most code written today for the Microsoft Windows environment conforms to the Common Object Model (COM) specification. COM allows developers to call prewritten pieces of code. Assuming that the components follow the rules of being a COM component, these components can be called regardless of their location and the language that the component is written in.

The problem with COM is versioning. However, with Windows 2000 and Windows Me, there is an ability to allow COM objects to be installed "side-by-side," so that applications can choose the version of the component that the application needs. Unfortunately, using the "side-by-side" versioning in COM has not been very accepted in the marketplace.

In general, the installation of an updated COM component means that the older COM component is usually overwritten and almost always becomes the default installation of the component. This forces the application to call the updated COM object instead of the object that the application previously called. For example, assume that you have a COM component with `ProgId McClureDev.Expenses`. Within the component is the method `SaveExpense( ByVal strDescription as String, ByVal decAmount as Decimal )`. This method saves an expense amount and a description into a database table somewhere. Being the smart programmer that you are, you're using late bounding so that changes to the objects don't always affect you. Your company grows and now it needs to add the ability to save the expense information so that it can be charged back to a specific department. You then change your object so that the method is now `SaveExpense( ByVal strDescription as String, ByVal decAmount as Decimal, ByVal strDepartmentId as String )`. You put this into your component and bang — your Web application no longer works — the interface has changed. To resolve some of the issue, you could redefine you method so that it is defined as `SaveExpense( ByVal strDescription as String, ByVal decAmount as Decimal, Optional ByVal strDepartmentId as String )`. By making the last parameter optional, the

Web application would continue to run. If your application uses early binding of COM components, the situation is probably even worse because the application will most likely not even run. With early binding, it is important for the unique identifier (GUID) of the component to be constant. This would be enabled by setting the Binary Compatibility radio button, as shown in Figure 2-3.

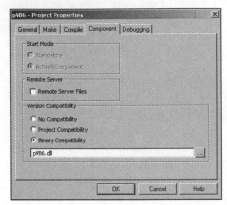

Figure 2-3: Setting a component's compatibility to binary

With the .NET Framework, the component system is much more advanced. Namespaces and the version information contained within the calling application control the specific components that are used. For example, an application can ask the Framework to load a specific version of a component into memory and run it alongside a different version of the same component. To facilitate this side-by-side running of components, the Framework implements two storage locations for components, the global assembly cache (GAC) and a private application assembly cache. The GAC is a cache of assemblies that are available to all applications running within the Framework. The private application assembly cache is just that, private to an application. Components with the private assembly cache are not viewable by the outside world of applications. In addition to this private assembly cache, .NET components are loaded by version number. If an application requests that an assembly that is version 1.7.4.0 be loaded, the Framework will attempt to load that version. However, it will not attempt to load version 1.9.6.4, because the version number is not the one that the application has listed within its manifest of components. It should be noted that the version number within the manifest can be overridden and a later version loaded, if a user with the appropriate authority does so.

Components are discussed in detail in Chapter 6.

Deployment

Deploying an N-Tier application is a really difficult job. Applications must be installed onto desktops and web servers. Components must be registered and possibly installed into COM+ Services. During the time that an application is being upgraded, users most likely cannot access the application. The .NET Framework allows for the installation of ASP.NET applications through what has been termed *XCopy deployment*. With XCopy deployment, an application is literally copied into place. The .NET Framework literally transitions users from one instance of an application to the new instance of the application.

One word of warning with XCopy deployment: XCopy deployment will not result in middle-tier components being automatically registered when a remote user makes a request against that component. The registration of that component can only be done by someone who is an administrator on that physical system.

Distributed transactions

What are transactions? Transactions are the smallest logical unit of work that a database can either accept or reject in whole. Most client/server databases support transactions. ADO.NET provides support for what are termed *manual transactions*. Manual transactions are transactions that are managed within the database. Distributed transactions are transactions in which the management of the transactions is not done by the database, but by an outside agent. This outside agent communicates with an item within the database called a *resource manager*.

Let's assume that there is a Web-based music-ordering application that must communicate with two separate databases on two different databases (A and B). For our example, Database A has the online store while Database B has the inventory of music in our physical warehouse. In our hypothetical application, we would like to either allow the user to download the music or to ship the music to them through an offline delivery service. If there is a failure in some part of our application, we want all the changes to be rolled back. We don't want a customer to be charged for a product that he doesn't receive, and we don't want a customer to receive a product that he is not going to be charged for. Data in both databases must be processed by adding to, updating, or deleting from these databases. An error in updating one database means that the other database either must not occur or must be stopped before it can be done. The application goes out and gets product data from Database A. A user inputs new data into a Web form and clicks Submit. The application must then go to database A to record that an order has been made for Motley Crue's album *Generation Swine*.

The second step in this process to go to the inventory system on Database B and reserve one of the albums in the warehouse. Unfortunately, Database B reports back that the *Generation Swine* album is not in stock. Using the business rules of the application, an error is generated. Without a distributed transaction, you would be required to manually manage the rollback of the transaction on Machine A. With a distributed transaction, after you call for the rollback in the transaction, the distributed transaction handles the rollback of the information in Machine A. In the

Microsoft world, the outside agent that manages distributed transactions is the Microsoft Distributed Transaction Coordinator (MSDTC), which is a part of MTS and COM+. The MSDTC works based on a 2-Phase Commit. In a 2-Phase Commit, the MSDTC sends a message to each resource manager telling it to prepare to commit a transaction. The messages are sent from the MSDTC to the resource managers at the same time. At this stage it is assumed that all commands have been sent to the resource manager for processing. Once the prepare message is sent, a second message is sent telling the resource manager to commit the transaction.

Code examples for using Distributed Transactions in the .NET Framework are available in the section on object pooling, later in this chapter. More detailed discussion on a Two-Phase Commit is included in Chapter 4.

At this point, you're probably thinking that distributed transactions are great and glorious and should be used for everything possible – but this is not the case. Distributed transactions require time to process and communicate over a network. Distributed transactions under MTS/COM+ place locks on data with an isolation level of serializable on the data within the database. If distributed transactions are needed, then they should be used. If distributed transactions are not needed, they should not be used. For example, embedding a routine that only returns data (such as a select statement) and performs no other updates would most likely perform better without being managed by a distributed transaction. The time required to set up, manage, and either commit or rollback can be significant. Locking the rows of your table with a serializable isolation level can severely limit the ability of your database to scale to a large number of users when used incorrectly. Database operations with a single database can often be better managed by the internal transaction mechanisms of that database. In this case, the transaction management is closer to the data and the isolation level of the transaction can be controlled more programmatically. Table 2-1 displays the time to insert 1,000 records with Manual Transactions and with Distributed Transactions where each insert is wrapped within its own transaction. The database and application were running on the same physical machine (1GHz Pentium III with 512 megabytes of RAM and 100,000 records already in the table). The SQL Server managed provider was used to connect to the database. No specific times are reported. The numbers that are reported are relative to each other.

COM+ 1.0, included in Windows 2000, only supports the serializable isolation level. COM+ 1.5, included in WindowsXP, allows for a more granular isolation level.

TABLE 2-1 A COMPARISON OF USING MANUAL AND COM+ TRANSACTIONS

Time to Complete 1,000 Inserts	0 Additional Clients Beyond the Test Application
Manual Transactions	1 (base)
Distributed Transactions	2.38 X

The interesting question about this type of test where we are trying to look at the performance effect of distributed transactions instead of using manual transactions, is what is the performance effect in the application that your team is working on? Are distribute transactions really 2.38 times slower in all situations? The answer is no. What we are showing here is that there is a price to be paid for using distributed transactions. Use distributed transactions wisely.

Message queuing

Typically, applications are tightly coupled. Applications talk to databases. When a database is not online, the client application cannot communicate directly with the database and the application is no longer functioning. What if an application, instead of communicating directly with a database, could send instructions to the database in a way that would allow the client application to believe that it had sent a command to the database, yet allow the database to process it when it received the command? For example, message queuing would allow a laptop user to "send" several commands to a database while the laptop is not connected. When the user gets back in his office and attaches to his network, the commands are sent and processed on the database.

In another use, let's assume that you're communicating over an unreliable link. A front-end client and a back-end database are separated by an unreliable link, such as the Internet. With a standard application, if the link is not up, your application cannot communicate. With message queuing, the front-end application can drop the message to the database in a queue. When there is a connection available, Microsoft Message Queue (MSMQ) transfers the message across the link. On the database side, a service picks up the message from the queue and processes the message. The front-end user never knows what had to happen in order for the application to do this. The data was just sent to the server and good things happened. Once again, you've seen another glorious technology. Much like distributed transactions, message queuing introduces its own problems. The problem with message queuing is that it is impossible to guarantee when a message will be delivered or the order that messages are delivered in. For some applications, this can be a problem. Use message queuing wisely.

MSMQ is Microsoft's application to perform message queuing. To effectively use message queuing, there must be a front-end application and a back-end application to process the message. The front-end application can be a standard Visual Basic, C#, C++, or other application that can communicate through the MSMQ COM interfaces. The back-end application is a little different. Typically, the back-end application is a service that constantly waits for data to appear in one of the queues it processes. Until now, it was not really possible to write a Windows service in VB without help from some third-party tools. With the .NET Framework, not only can you as a developer connect to and put data into a message queue, but you can also process it on the other end — and you can do it in any .NET language, not just C++!

More information on Message Queuing and MSMQ in particular is available in Chapter 9.

Object pooling

Objects running within the COM+ environment of Windows 2000 and later can be prebuilt and available in memory to calling applications. This ability to have COM+ objects available to calling applications is called *object pooling*. This is one of the services that COM+ provides. Object pooling is most useful in the business-logic tier. The problem with object pooling is that, in the COM world of VB5/6, object pooling on Windows 2000 was not supported. VB5/6 did not support the necessary thread model (multi-threaded apartment). Object pooling was only available to VC++/VJ++ components running under Windows 2000. Visual Basic developers were not able to take advantage of object pooling because the Visual Basic 6 runtime did not support the necessary threading models for COM+ to provide object pooling support. NT4 with Option Pak 4 did not support object pooling. Now, with the .NET runtime, components written in Visual Basic .NET support object pooling just like the other languages. Object pooling will provide the most benefit to an application when the objects that are pooled require a relatively long startup time. Instead of going through some type of startup processing that takes time, the application can be handed a reference to a pre-built object.

If you decide to use the AutoComplete attribute and a `Try-Catch` error handling routine, it is still necessary to raise an error so that the AutoComplete mechanism can fire. AutoComplete will not fire unless an error is raised within the component. When AutoComplete does fire, a call to `ContextUtil.SetAbort()` is automatically done so that all pending database work is rolled back.

Listing 2-1 contains the Visual Basic .NET code for an object that supports distributed transactions and object pooling. Listing 2-2 contains the C# code for an object that supports distributed transactions and object pooling.

 Components running with object pooling must be installed into the Global Assembly Cache (GAC) and be installed within a server package in COM+ for object pooling to work correctly.

Listing 2-1: Visual Basic .NET with Object Pooling and Distributed Transactions

```
Option Explicit On
Option Strict On

Imports System
Imports System.Runtime.CompilerServices
Imports System.EnterpriseServices
Imports System.Reflection
Imports System.Data
Imports System.Data.OleDb

<Assembly: ApplicationName("SimpleCOMTransactions")>
<Assembly: AssemblyKeyFileAttribute("KeyFile.snk")>
<Assembly: AssemblyVersion("1.1.0.3")>
<Assembly: ApplicationActivation(ActivationOption.Server)>

Namespace OP.VB

<Transaction(TransactionOption.Required), _
ObjectPooling(MinPoolSize:=1, MaxPoolSize:=100,
CreationTimeOut:=10000), _
EventTrackingEnabled(True)> _
Public Class COMClassDistributedTransactions : Inherits
ServicedComponent

Public Sub InsertData()
Dim strCn As String = "......connection string......"
Dim strSql As String = "insert into tblValue (tblValue) values
(getdate())"
Dim oledbCN As New OleDbConnection(strCn)
Dim oledbCM As New OleDbCommand(strSql, oledbCN)
Try
```

Continued

Listing 2-1 *(Continued)*

```
        oledbCN.Open()
        oledbCM.ExecuteNonQuery()
        ContextUtil.SetComplete()
        Catch e As Exception
            ContextUtil.SetAbort()
            Throw( new Exception( e.Message ) )
        Finally
            If oledbCN.State <> ConnectionState.Closed Then
                oledbCN.Close()
            End If
            oledbCM = Nothing
            oledbCN = Nothing
        End Try
End Sub

Public Overrides Sub Activate()
End Sub
Public Overrides Sub Deactivate()
End Sub
Public Overrides Function CanBePooled() As Boolean
    Return True
End Function
End Class
End Namespace
```

Listing 2-2: C# with Object Pooling and Distributed Transactions

```
using System;
using System.Data;
using System.Data.OleDb;
using System.EnterpriseServices;
using System.Reflection;
using System.Runtime.CompilerServices;

[assembly: ApplicationName("SimpleCOMTransactionsInCs")]
[assembly: AssemblyKeyFileAttribute("..//..//KeyFile.snk")]
[assembly: AssemblyVersion("1.1.0.7")]
[assembly: ApplicationActivation(ActivationOption.Server)]

namespace ObjectPoolingCS
{
/// <summary>
///Example component to be placed within the COM+ Services.
/// </summary>
```

```
[Transaction(TransactionOption.Required),
ObjectPooling(true, MinPoolSize=1, MaxPoolSize=100 ),
EventTrackingEnabled(true),
JustInTimeActivation(true),
ConstructionEnabled(Default="Provider=SQLOLEDB;Data
Source=......;Initial Catalog=DotNet;User
Id=......;PassWord=......")]
public class cCOMDistributedTransaction : ServicedComponent
{
private string strCn;
public void InsertData()
{
string strSql = "insert into tblValue (tblValue) values
(getdate())";
OleDbConnection oledbCn;
OleDbCommand oledbCm;
oledbCn = new OleDbConnection( strCn );
try
{
     oledbCm = new OleDbCommand( strSql, oledbCn );
     oledbCn.Open();
     oledbCm.ExecuteNonQuery();
     ContextUtil.SetComplete();
}
catch ( Exception exc )
{
     ContextUtil.SetAbort();
     throw( new Exception( exc.Message ) );
}
finally
{
     if ( oledbCn.State != ConnectionState.Closed)
     {
     oledbCn.Close();
     }
     oledbCm = null;
     oledbCn = null;
}
}

public override void Construct(string strConstructString)
{
     strCn = strConstructString;
}
```

Continued

Listing 2-2 *(Continued)*

```
public override void Activate()
{}
public override void Deactivate()
{}
public override Boolean CanBePooled()
{
      return true;
}
}
}
```

WHAT IS SCALABILITY?

When a computing solution is built, it must provide results within a certain time-frame and be durable. If a user cannot access a program, service, or database for whatever reason, that user needs to perform his job, and then there is some type of problem that must be resolved. *Performance* is a term used to describe either the amount of time necessary to complete a sequence of steps or the number of commands that can be performed within a given amount of time. *Durability* is the ability of a computing solution to provide access to its services over time. For example, a database application, middle-tier server, or web server that requires a reboot every few days would not be considered durable.

Scalability can be measured in several ways. It can be measured as:

◆ **The total number of users that a solution can support.** The measurement is based on an upper limit number.

◆ **The time to complete a command based on a given number of users currently running commands.** This measurement is usually based on a two-dimensional (x-y) graph. The x-axis is the number of users running on the system and the y-axis is the amount of time to complete a command. In general, this is considered to be the most important item when discussing scalability within the context of programming.

◆ **The ability of a solution to grow as additional processing resources are made available (for example, the addition of processors, memory, and systems to effectively use additional resources).** Within this scenario, there are two sub-areas:

■ Scaling up is the ability to add additional processors to improve the performance and availability of a solution.

■ Scaling out is the ability to add additional systems to improve the performance and availability of a solution.

How do you measure scalability? Measuring the time to complete a command based on the number of users currently running is a common measurement. In general, the resulting time to complete a function can be closely approximated by a formula such as $T(N) = a * N^2 + b * N \log(N) + c * N + d * \log(N) + e$, where N is the number of active users. The numbers represented by $a, b, c, d,$ and e are constants that represent a weighting factor. Typically, the largest factor represented is used to describe the performance characteristics of the solution. For example, solution A is termed as an N^2 solution. The N^2 solution scales to a large number of users very poorly. The goal is to use algorithms, database design, and database access in such a way as to minimize the time required to complete a command as the number of users increases. Figure 2-4 demonstrates the effect of increasing users/requests on performance of applications based on N^2-, $N \log(N)$-, N-, and $\log(N)$-based applications. As you can see from Figure 2-4, N^2 applications are highly undesirable. Getting our application to perform based on a $\log(N)$-based algorithm is much more desirable. Unfortunately, this may not be possible. Just remember that it is very important to understand the performance characteristics of your application.

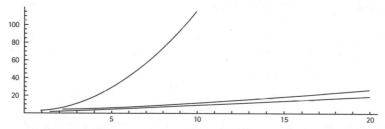

Figure 2–4: Performance plotted against increasing users and requests

One of the first things that we hear in regards to affecting performance is that the more processors in a system, the faster a solution is. For example, if one processor runs a command in X amount of time, two processors in the same system will run a command in X/2 amount of time. Unfortunately, this is not accurate. The ability to use multiple processors effectively is based on the amount of parallelism within an algorithm. If an algorithm is 90 percent serial and 10 percent parallel, the best performance boost that is possible by moving from one to two processors and multiple threads is 5 percent. The problem is that the algorithm does not support parallel operations very well.

We are often reminded of a story that one of Wally's professors told in a graduate-level class on computer architectures regarding parallelism. He was involved in research at IBM at one time, and he found an operating system function that was taking up to 80 percent of the system when a certain set of commands was running. He felt that this was not acceptable, so he spent about six weeks rewriting it. When he was done, he reran the test to see how much he had improved performance. The function continued to take up 80 percent of the system when the same set of commands was run. He explored a little deeper and found out that the system function was only called during a backup and that the reason the function took up 80 percent was because 99.9 percent of that time was taken up waiting on a write to tape, a serial operation. On the other hand, an algorithm to calculate a fast fourier transform (FFT), which is a signal processing algorithm, is highly parallel and does benefit greatly from the use of multiple threads and processors.

 TIP Understand what your algorithm is doing, where the bottlenecks are, the overall system design, and your application needs before you spend a significant amount of time working on the wrong part of your solution.

Performance and Durability

Microsoft's .NET platform contains several items that allow a computing solution to effectively use system resources better (scalability) and to provide a platform that will run under continual use (durability). They are:

♦ **Threading.** *Threading* is the ability to divide a workload into smaller units of work, perform those operations in parallel, and return results to the process or thread that manages everything else. (We discussed this a little earlier in this chapter and cover it in more depth in Chapter 8.)

♦ **Garbage collection and memory management.** The .NET Framework provides memory management and garbage collection services to managed applications.

♦ **Managed providers for high-speed connectivity to a database.** Managed providers are optimized for high-speed access to a database for data operations, such as select, insert, update, and delete. At this point in time, they do not provide all the functionality that ADO provides, such as ADOX. Managed providers are designed to access a database using standard database commands (select, insert, update, and delete) and provide performance as fast as possible. Within the basic .NET Framework, Microsoft has provided a managed provider that communicates with SQL Server. This managed provider is called System.Data.SQLClient. For compatibility with existing databases that do not currently have managed providers, Microsoft has provided OLE-DB and ODBC managed providers. These providers are called System.Data.OleDb and Microsoft.Data.Odbc. (This subject is discussed more in Chapter 6.)

♦ **Connection pooling.** Pooling database connections allows applications access to database connections that are already available within the computing system. When an application makes a request of the system to open a database connection, a connection can be used without having to go through the expense of creating a new connection.

♦ **Object pooling.** Object pooling is an automatic service provided by COM+ 1.0 and later systems to allow a component to have multiple instances of itself available in a pool, ready to be used by a calling application. For programmers who have written their middle-tier components in Visual Basic 6, there has not been the ability to perform this previously, as VB6 did not have the ability to create thread-neutral components.

ASP.NET's architecture includes a number of excellent features that provided increased performance and durability. ASP.NET architectural changes include the following:

♦ **Caching.** All or part of an ASP.NET page may be cached. Caching parts of an ASP.NET page allows those parts of the page to not need to be re-created on every view of that page. If the parts of that page require a relatively large amount of processing on the server, then caching may provide an improvement in performance.

♦ **Compiled.** By being compiled, ASP.NET pages no longer must be interpreted at each execution.

♦ **Increased reliability.** ASP.NET applications take advantage of the .NET Framework for services, such as garbage collection and the ability of the ASP.NET worker process to automatically restart based on various conditions.

♦ **Garbage collection.** Garbage collection assists programmers in keeping track of objects and effectively de-allocating them.

Threading in .NET

To understand threading, several other items must be defined first:

♦ **Multitasking:** Multitasking is the ability of an operating system to have multiple operations executing at once.

♦ **Preemptive multitasking:** Preemptive multitasking is multitasking whereby the operating system manages the time (time slice) that an application can run. When the time slice for an application to run is used up, another application is given the opportunity to run. Each application gets to share an amount of time with the operating system managing the time for each application. Windows NT is an example of a preemptive multitasking operating system.

◆ **Cooperative multitasking:** Cooperative multitasking is multitasking whereby the running applications manage the time slice(s) themselves. In this scenario, an application will not give up control of the processor until it is prepared to do so. Windows 3.x is an example of cooperative-multitasking operating system.

◆ **Processes.** Processes can be thought of as independent applications. SQL Server, IIS, and Microsoft Word are examples of processes.

◆ **Threads.** Threads are units of work within a process. For example, when a new web browser connects to an IIS system, a new thread is created and processes the work that the user requests. After a set amount of inactive time, that thread is removed from the system.

◆ **AppDomains.** An AppDomain is an independent execution environment whereby multiple applications and threads can execute within the .NET environment.

Operating systems that support preemptive multitasking create the effect of simultaneous execution of multiple threads from multiple processes.

Although creating and spawning multiple threads has been around since the beginning of 32-bit Windows development with Visual C++ and the Windows NT and Windows 9x platforms, controlling threads is a new concept to most Visual Basic programmers. To the user, an application that properly takes advantage of threading is more responsive. While a request is made to print or perform a long calculation, the application can respond to the user's actions. What are candidates for independent threads within an application?

◆ Network communications

◆ Database access

◆ Access to a middle-tier component

◆ System-level access across the network

◆ Long-running calculations

◆ Asynchronous operations

◆ Printing

◆ Algorithms that are highly parallel

For a complete discussion of threading, turn to Chapter 8.

Managed providers

Managed providers are the .NET equivalent of ADO and OLE-DB/ODBC drivers rolled up into one. Managed providers provide database access within the managed environment of .NET. Currently, there are three managed providers within the .NET environment: System.Data.SQL, System.Data.OleDb, and Microsoft.Data.Odbc. The SQL managed provider is a provider designed to communicate with SQL Server 7 and 2000. It uses the tabular datastream protocol to communicate directly with SQL Server and bypasses the ODBC and OLE-DB layers. The provider communicates with SQL Server directly through the .NET runtime and does not use the COM interop layer. The ADO managed provider is a provider designed to communicate with all databases that currently have either an OLE-DB or ODBC driver. The ADO managed provider communicates to the OLE-DB layer through the COM interop functionality of the .NET runtime.

Refer to Chapter 5 for more information regarding managed providers and ADO.NET.

Connection/session pooling

Connection pooling in ODBC provides a pool of available database connections. Resource pooling in OLE-DB provides an equivalent mechanism. These terms are used interchangeably in this section.

Connections to databases are expensive items to create. The overhead to create a connection over a network to a database server is a non-trivial amount of time. When several connections are created and destroyed per second, the overhead becomes a significant amount of time and processor utilization that applications could do without.

Connection pooling is the ability of a system to have a connection already created that is connected to the database server. Connection pooling is provided by the driver in the .NET managed provider and OLE-DB and by the driver manager in ODBC. Connection pooling is dependent on the environment of the application and the properties of the connection. For example, when using a connection in ASP.NET, if the connection that is made is dependent on the user who is making the connection, then connection pooling will not have a large effect on the performance of the system. However, if all connections are made with the exact same connection properties, then connection pooling will be helpful. The OLE-DB and ODBC managed providers support connection pooling. The underlying architecture of the OLE-DB and ODBC managed providers are OLE DB and ODBC, so connection pooling is already available. The SQL managed provider provides support for connection pooling within the driver, much like OLE DB.

It is important to explicitly call `.close()` on the connection object so that the connection is released back to the pool.

For additional information regarding connection pooling with ODBC and OLE DB, an excellent source of information is Microsoft's article at `http://msdn.microsoft.com/library/default.asp?URL=/library/psdk/dasdk/pool0y2b.htm`.

Error handling

The error handling available to VB and other languages within the .NET Framework is much improved over what has been available to VB programmers in the past. For VBers, the On Error Goto and On Error Resume Next have been replaced with a much more standard set of error handling referred to as structured exception handling (SEH). Although SEH is not strictly a new feature, it is still necessary to provide an overview of the error-handling procedures within .NET. First off, although we are all the greatest programmers on the face of the earth and our code will never have problems, there are times when we must plan for them.

What can cause these problems? There are two ways to cause these errors:

◆ **Business rule violations.** For example, what if you want to remove $200 from an account that only has $125? This is a business rule violation. Your logic could treat this as an error and raise that error to the calling routine.

◆ **Errors within the running environment.** What should happen in the case of a database application being taken offline for routine maintenance? Instead of a horrible error onscreen, how about a gentle message stating that the database is not currently available?

The .NET runtime supports a host of Exception types within the System namespace. These exceptions are thrown by the common language runtime when errors occur that are nonfatal and recoverable by user programs. The exceptions listed in Table 2-2 are derived from the `SystemException` class.

TABLE 2–2 EXCEPTIONS FROM THE SYSTEM.EXCEPTION CLASS

Exception	Description
AmbiguousMatchException	Caused by a call not being able to determine the exact class or overloaded class to utilize.
AppDomainUnloadedException	Attempt to access an unloaded application domain.
ArgumentException (base class)	Invoking a method with at least one passed value that does not match the parameter specified.
ArithmeticException (base class)	Error occurs in an arithmetic, casting, or conversion operation.
ArrayTypeMismatchException	Caused by attempting to store an incorrect datatype in an array element.
BadImageFormatException	Caused by the physical file containing a DLL or executable program being invalid.
CannotUnloadAppDomainException	Thrown when an application domain fails to unload after an attempt to unload.
ContextMarshalException	Thrown when an attempt to marshal an object across a context boundary fails.
CryptographicException	Thrown when an error occurs during a cryptographic operation.
DataException (base class)	Thrown when errors occur within ADO.NET components.
DBConcurrencyException	Thrown by a data adapter during the execution of an insert, update, or delete operation when the number of rows equals zero. This error is most likely due to a concurrency violation.
ExecutionEngineException	Thrown when there is an internal error in the common language runtimes.
ExternalException	The base exception type for all COM Interop exceptions and structured exception-handling exceptions.
FormatException	Thrown when the format of an argument does not exactly match the parameter specifications of the called method.

Continued

TABLE **2-2** EXCEPTIONS FROM THE SYSTEM.EXCEPTION CLASS *(Continued)*

Exception	Description
IndexOutOfRangeException	Thrown when an attempt is made to access an array element that is out of bounds of the array.
InstallException	Thrown by an error during the commit, rollback, or uninstall phase of an installation.
InvalidCastException	Thrown by an invalid cast or explicit conversion.
InvalidComObjectException	Thrown when an invalid COM object is used.
InvalidOleVariantTypeException	Thrown by the marshaler when it encounters an argument of a variant type that cannot be marshaled to managed code.
InvalidOperationException (base class)	Thrown when a method call is invalid for an object's current state.
InvalidProgramException	Thrown when a program contains invalid IL or metadata. This is most likely a bug in the compile process.
InternalBufferOverflowException	Thrown when the internal buffer overflows.
LicenseException	Thrown when a component cannot be granted a license.
ManagementException (base class)	Base class that represents management exceptions.
MarshalDirectiveException	Thrown when it finds a MarshalAsAttribute it does not support.
MemberAccesException (base class)	Thrown when an attempt to access a class member fails.
MulticastNotSupportedException	Thrown when there is an attempt to combine two instances of a non-combinable delegate type.
NotImplementedException	Thrown when a method or operation is not implemented.
NotSupportedException	Thrown when an invoked method is not supported, or when attempting to operate on a stream that does not support the invoked functionality.
NullReferenceException	Thrown when there is an attempt to dereference a null object reference.

Exception	Description
OutOfMemoryException	Thrown when there is not enough memory to continue the execution of a program.
PolicyException	Thrown when a policy does not allow code to run.
RankException	Thrown when an array with the wrong number of dimensions is passed to a method.
RegistrationException	Thrown when a component cannot be registered through the lazy registration process into COM+ Services.
ReflectionTypeLoadException	Thrown by the Module.GetTypes method if any of the classes in a module cannot be loaded.
RemotingException (base class)	Thrown when an error occurs during a remoting operation.
SafeArrayRankMismatchException	Thrown when an incoming SAFEARRAY does not match the rank specified in the managed signature.
SafeArrayTypeMismatchException	Thrown when the type of an incoming SAFEARRAY does not match the type specified in the managed signature.
SecurityException	Thrown when a security error is detected.
SerializationException	Thrown when an error occurs during the serialization or deserialization process.
ServerException	Thrown to communicate errors to the client when the client connects to a non–Univeral Run Time server that cannot throw exceptions.
ServicedComponentException	Thrown when an error has occurred within a serviced component.
StackOverflowException	Thrown when the execution stack overflows because there are too many method calls pending.
SqlException	Thrown when an error or warning is returned by SQL Server.
SynchronizationLockException	Thrown when a synchronized method is invoked from an unsynchronized block of code.

Continued

TABLE 2-2 EXCEPTIONS FROM THE SYSTEM.EXCEPTION CLASS *(Continued)*

Exception	Description
TimeoutException	Thrown when the specified timeout has occurred.
ThreadAbortException	Thrown when a call is made to the Abort method of a thread.
ThreadInterruptedException	Thrown when a thread is interrupted while it is in a waiting state.
ThreadStateException	Thrown when a thread is in an invalid ThreadState for the method call.
TypeInitializationException	Thrown as a wrapper around the exception thrown by the class initializer.
TypeLoadException (base class)	Thrown when the CLR cannot find an assembly or a type within an assembly, or cannot load the type.
TypeUnloadedException	Thrown when an attempt is made to access an unloaded class.
UnauthorizedAccessException	Thrown when the operating system denies access to a security or I/O error.
VerificationException	Thrown when the security policy requires code to be type-safe and the verification process is unable to verify that the code is type-safe.
WarningException	An exception that is handled as warning instead of an error.
XmlException	Returns detailed information about the last exception.
XmlSchemaException	Returns detailed information about the last schema exception.
XmlSyntaxException	Thrown when there is a syntax error during the XML parsing process.
XsltException	Returns detailing information about the last error involving the processing of an XSL transform.

There are two rules when throwing an exception:

1. Throw the most appropriate exception possible. For example, do not throw a `System.Exception` when it would be more appropriate to throw a `DivideByZeroException`.

2. Set *all* appropriate properties within the exception before performing the throw. Not setting all properties appropriately, such as the `.Source` property can affect tracking down the problem.

Take a look at some code that shows how errors may be handled. Listings 2-3 and 2-4 show some example error handling. In this example, you're looking at the error handling within that may be necessary if a divide by zero occurs.

Listing 2–3: Visual Basic .NET Error Handler

```
Dim I, a, b, c as Integer
Try
    ' perform some function
    I = a * b / c
Catch excDivide as System.DivideByZeroException
    'perform divide By zero handling
    excDivide.Source = "Method Name"
    Throw( excDivide)
Catch excOutOfRange as System.OverflowException
    'perform overflow handling
    excOutOfRange.Source = "Method Name"
    Throw( excOutOfRange )
Catch excS as System.Exception
    'perform generic error handling
    excS.Source = "MethodName"
    Throw( excS )
Finally
    'perform clean up work
End Try
```

Listing 2–4: C# Error Handling

```
int I, a, b, c;
Try
{
    I = a * b / c
}
catch ( System.DivideByZeroException excDivide )
{
    excDivide.Source = "Method Name";
    throw( excDivide);
```

Continued

Listing 2-4 *(Continued)*

```
}
catch ( System.OverflowException excOutOfRange )
{
    excOutOfRange.Source = "Method Name";
    throw(excOutOfRange);
}
catch ( System.Exception excS )
{
    excS.Source = "Method Name";
    throw( excS);
}
finally
{
//perform whatever cleanup work is needed
}
```

It is possible to define your own exceptions by deriving from the Exception class. Take a look at some code to define your own errors. Listings 2-5 and 2-6 show the classes necessary to create your own exceptions. StrMessage is merely the message associated with this exception. Inner is any previous exception that has bubbled up to this point.

Listing 2-5: Defining a Custom Exception in Visual Basic .NET

```
Public class AAAException Inherits Exception
    Public Function AAAException()
        'place any necessary code here.
    End Function
    Public AAAException( ByVal strMessage as String )
        'place any necessary code here.
    End Function
    Public AAAException( ByVal strMessage as String, ByVal Inner as
Exception )
        'place any necessary code here.
    End Function
End Class
```

Listing 2-6: Defining a Custom Exception in C#

```
public class AAAException: Exception {
    AAAException() { }
    AAAException(string strMessage) { }
    AAAException(string strMessage, Exception Inner) { }
}
```

ASP.NET Architecture

ASP.NET is a complete redesign when compared to ASP in IIS4/5. ASP.NET has a number of advantages over ASP code:

◆ Event handling

◆ Separation of the user interface and the server processing code through the use of a feature called code-behinds

◆ Caching

◆ Controls that can be optimized for the browser type

◆ Compiled

◆ Application/System automated restarts

◆ Stateful Web form controls

Event handling

Typically, when writing ASP with IIS, related code is spread across multiple pages. In addition, the top of each page tends to contain some type of state machine system. This is different from the way that applications are developed for the Windows environment with VB or C#. ASP.NET is designed to provide a more developer-friendly mechanism to produce code. User interface elements can now respond to events providing a more intelligent development environment, resulting in fewer ASPX pages that are necessary to maintain the same amount of functionality and fewer lines of code to support.

Caching

A *cache* is a small, fast, memory-storage system that is designed to speed up subsequent access to the same data. The first time that a request is made against the system for something, that data is not available. The system will go out and retrieve that data. Now that the data is available, all subsequent requests will be handled by the cached version instead of having to retrieve the data from its original location.

Why is caching important? Many times, drop-downs and listboxes are used in an application. In these types of applications, these list boxes are created based on data within a database. Many times, the data that fills the list boxes does not change quickly. In these situations, opening a connection and running a query against the database can be an unnecessary load. Caching the drop-downs would be an excellent choice. It would remove an unnecessary load on your database and the resulting processing on the web server.

ASP.NET supports several different kinds of caching:

◆ **Output caching.** ASP.NET has the ability to cache output for pages and user controls. With output caching, requests after the first request to an object are satisfied from the cache on the server so that the server does not have to create the same object on a continual basis. For output caching to be effective, it requires that all object requests contain the same `GET`, `HEAD`, and `POST` requests for the same object during the duration that the page is valid within the cache. After the object *expires* within the cache, the next request will cause the server to go through the complete process of generating the object output again. Figure 2-5 shows a visual example of output caching. The following settings control the output cache:

  ■ `<%@ OutputCache  %>`: The output cache directive contains several additional options. `Duration="# of seconds"` is the number of seconds that the object is cached. `VaryByParam` allows caching of requests by varying the name/value pairs in the specified parameter.

  ■ `Response.Cache`: For a more programmatic mechanism to cache output, you might want to use the `Response.Cache` properties. They contain the same basic set of features as the `OutputCache` directive.

◆ **Fragment caching.** It is possible to cache the output of portions of a page. Fragment caching allows a program to cache User Controls. These user controls could be something like the elements of a listbox or the output to a datagrid. Output caching accepts the following options:

  ■ `Duration="# of seconds"`: The number of seconds that the object is cached.

  ■ `VaryByParam`: Allows caching of requests by varying the name/value pairs in the specified parameter.

  ■ `VaryByControl`: Allows caching of requests by controls within the user control.

◆ **Application caching.** ASP.NET provides a caching engine that allows applications to store expensive objects in memory across HTTP requests. The cache is private to each application and its lifetime is tied to the lifetime of the application. When the ASP.NET application is restarted, the cache will require that it be re-created. The cache is treated like a dictionary.

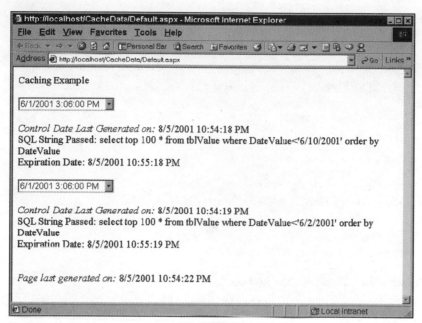

Figure 2-5: Caching using a drop-down list box

Listings 2-7, 2-8, and 2-9 are a complete caching example in Visual Basic .NET. This example creates a drop-down listbox with different parameters. In this example, two different drop-downs are created from a common User Control. The user control stays within the cache for up to 60 seconds.

Listing 2-7: ASPX Page

```
<%@ Page Language="vb" AutoEventWireup="false"
Codebehind="Default.aspx.vb" Inherits="CacheData.WebForm1"%>
<%@ Register TagPrefix="LB" TagName="DropDownWithDate"
Src="MenuControlWithParm.ascx" %>
<HTML>
<body>
Caching Example
<br>
<LB:DropDownWithDate runat="server" ID="Dropdown1"
NAME="DropDownCtl" EndDate="6/10/2001" />
<LB:DropDownWithDate runat="server" ID="Dropdownwithdate1"
NAME="DropDownCtl" EndDate="6/2/2001" />
<br>
<i>Page last generated on:</i>
<asp:label id="lblTimeMsg" runat="server" />
</body>
</HTML>
```

Listing 2-8: MenuControlWithParm.ascx Page

```
<%@ OutputCache Duration="60" VaryByParam="EndDate" %>
<%@ Control Language="vb" AutoEventWireup="false"
Codebehind="MenuControlWithParm.ascx.vb"
Inherits="CacheData.MenuControlWithParm" %>
<P>
    <asp:DropDownList id="ddlValues" runat="server">
    </asp:DropDownList>
</P>
<P>
    <i>Control Date Last Generated on:</i>
    <asp:label id="TimeMsg" runat="server" />
    <br>
</P>
```

Listing 2-9: MenuControlWithParam.ascx.vb Code Behind Page

```
'Import the SQL Client and Database Namespaces.
Imports System.Data
Imports System.Data.SqlClient

Public MustInherit Class MenuControlWithParm
    Inherits System.Web.UI.UserControl
    Protected WithEvents ddlValues As
System.Web.UI.WebControls.DropDownList
    Protected WithEvents TimeMsg As System.Web.UI.WebControls.Label

......Designer Code
'Get/Set the input EndDate Param
Private strDate As String
Property EndDate() As String
Get
    Return strDate
End Get
Set(ByVal Value As String)
    strDate = Value
End Set
End Property
'Perform the database lookup.
Private Sub Page_Load(ByVal sender As System.Object, ByVal e As
System.EventArgs) Handles MyBase.Load
Dim sqlCn As SqlConnection
Dim sqlDA As SqlDataAdapter
Dim ds As DataSet
Dim strSql As String
```

```
If strDate = vbNullString Then
    strSql = "select top 100 * from tblValue order by DateValue"
Else
    strSql = "select top 100 * from tblValue where DateValue<'" &
strDate & "' order by DateValue"
End If
sqlCn = New SqlConnection("Data Source=chakotay;Initial
Catalog=DotNet;User Id=sa;PassWord=kirsten;")
sqlDA = New SqlDataAdapter(strSql, sqlCn)
ds = New DataSet()
sqlDA.Fill(ds, "tblValue")
dllValues.DataTextField = "DateValue"
ddlValues.DataValueField = "DateValue"
ddlValues.DataSource = ds.Tables(0).DefaultView
ddlValues.DataBind()
If sqlCn.State <> ConnectionState.Closed Then
    sqlCn.Close()
End If
sqlCn = Nothing
sqlDA = Nothing
ds = Nothing
TimeMsg.Text = DateTime.Now.ToString() & "<br>SQL String Passed: " &
strSql & "<br>Expiration Date: " &
DateTime.Now.AddSeconds(60).ToString()
End Sub
End Class
```

CACHE OBJECT

The System.Web.Caching namespace contains the functionality to implement advanced caching routines within an ASP.NET application. The objects that are created from this namespace are global to the ASP.NET application. The cache class is a dictionary that allows data objects to be added and removed based on files and other cached entries.

Setting a value in the cache using Visual Basic .NET is as easy as calling Cache("dsData") = dsData. Getting the value is as easy as calling dsData = Cache("dsData"). Using C# is as simple as adding a ; (semicolon) to the end of each line.

Items may be modified in the cache based on their dependency on other items. The System.Web.Caching namespace contains a class called CacheDependency. This class allows items to be changed in the cache. The CacheDependency class may monitor changes in files, directories, or the keys to other objects that already exist in an application's cache.

When interacting with the cache, it's a good idea to check whether a value is already within the cache. You can do this by checking if the data returned from the cache is null:

```
cData = Cache("dsData")
if cData <> Null then
    'do something
end if
```

OPTIMIZED CONTROLS

Controls within a WebForm can be optimized for a specific browser. Currently, the controls that are included with ASP.NET can produce output for an HTML 3.2 browser or for IE 5 and later. By providing this capability, it is no longer necessary for a developer to design and develop applications for multiple browsers.

For developers writing applications to run on mobile systems, such as WAP devices, the problem is worse. Mobile devices tend to differ in their implementation of WAP.

By using the controls included with ASP.NET, such as the Internet Explorer WebControls, developers can write one application that will automatically detect the browser and output the appropriate display commands (HTML, DHTML, WAP, or other) for the requesting device. By having controls that can take advantage of the platform that they are running on, round trips from the web browser to the web server and back to the web browser can be minimized. The end result for the customer is a lower cost of development, quicker time to market, and in many cases, higher performance—a win for the developer and a win for the customer.

COMPILED CODE

In Classic ASP, ASP pages are loaded, interpreted, and executed on each request. While the ASP pages are cached so that there is not a continual request from the file system for each specific request for an ASP file, there is continual processing of the ASP pages as the files are interpreted and executed. When an .aspx page is requested by a Web user, the aspx engine goes through a several-step process in returning output to the browser:

1. If the current compiled code matches the current aspx page, the compiled code is executed.

2. The aspx page processor compiles the aspx code into IL.

3. If the application uses code behind pages, the code must be compiled by Visual Studio .NET or the command line compilers into IL in a DLL. The code behind page is combined with the aspx page.

4. The IL file is compiled and executed by the framework. The result is returned to the Web request.

By compiling an ASPX page into a machine executable, there is a compilation process that occurs during the initial request. After this initial request and the time the compilation product takes, the request is executed against the already compiled code. If there are hundreds of thousands or millions of requests against the ASPX page, this will most likely be an acceptable tradeoff of a longer initial request time on the first page request versus a shorter processing time on requests after the first request.

CODE BEHIND

ASP.NET code is developed with the goal of clearly separating the user interface and the server-side logic through the use of code behind pages. With a code behind page, the user interface design can be separated from the application logic. With this, there is little chance of the user interface tools destroying the server processing logic as there was with older versions of user interface Web tools (the FrontPage mangle of ASP code comes to mind).

STATEFUL WEB CONTROLS

Being stateful is not always a bad thing. If you've developed multi-tier solutions using Windows DNA architecture, you know that having a stateful MTS/COM+ tier or having a stateful IIS/ASP layer will result in an application that does not scale very well. An application built in this manner will also have problems when it comes to being deployed to a Web farm. Somewhere within this environment, you must store state information. Typically this is done by storing simple state at the client, such as userid information. Complex state, such as shopping cart information is stored within a back-end database. ASP.NET takes this one step further. By storing state at the client, only a small amount of resources are used on each client system. If these same resources were required on the IIS Server, the small amount of resources multiplied by the number of users making requests against the system during any defined timeframe could easily overwhelm the server.

First, think about how an ASP 3.0 application is typically structured. Ninety percent of all ASP pages contain a combination of state machine and display logic. The state machine logic allow the page to process whatever is needed. Typically, this involves one or more trips to the database involving operations such as insert, update, and delete. The display part of the page involves one or more trips to the database to display data. The result is two or more round trips to a database to display pages.

ASP.NET is somewhat different. ASP.NET provides a development metaphor much more like a classic client/server application. With this type of metaphor, a client application will only send the commands to the database to perform the state machine-style operations. There is no need to perform the display logic because the client/server front-end stores the data on its end. ASP.NET provides the same type of development metaphor. The interesting part about this statefulness in ASP.NET is that the stateful part of the form is stored client side. This state information is stored within a hidden form variable that is called __ViewState. No statefulness at the IIS layer or MTS layer is required. Better programming metaphor and better scalability — what a great combination!

Listing 2-10 shows the basic development methodology of ASP.NET. In this listing, the example is written in Visual Basic .NET and contains some commentary regarding the ASP.NET development experience. To re-create this example, create a WebForm and use a code behind page. On the WebForm, add a server-side text field called `txtFieldValue`, server-side button called `btnClickMe`, and a server-side label called `lblMessage`.

Listing 2-10: ASP.NET Code-Behind Page

```
Private Sub Page_Load(ByVal sender As System.Object, ByVal e As
System.EventArgs) Handles MyBase.Load
    If Page.IsPostBack Then
        'Executed on subsequent loads of the page.
        'Can be used to make page changes after a page reload.
        txtFieldValue.Text = "Subsequent page loads."
    Else
        'Executed on the first load of the page.
        'Initialization of the page occurs within the
        'Page.IsPostBack property is false.
        'For example, initial reading of values from a
        'database along with the setting of any appropriate
        'properties may be done here. No need to go back to
        'the database to re-read, except to verify that the
        'underlying database values have not changed.
        txtFieldValue.Text = "First page load."
        lblMessage.Visible = False
    End If
End Sub
Private Sub btnClickMe_Click(ByVal sender As System.Object, ByVal e
As System.EventArgs) Handles btnClickMe.Click
    'This code is execute after a page load when the btnClickMe
    'button is clicked.
    lblMessage.Text = "The 'Click Me in VB' button has been pushed."
    lblMessage.Visible = True
End Sub
```

APPLICATION/SYSTEM AUTOMATED RESTARTS

Applications running within the ASP.NET environment and controlled by the aspnet_wp.exe process can be restarted based on certain criteria. That criteria can be set on a global basis for all applications running on a system and on a local-application basis. These settings stored are within the processModel section of the system.web and machine.config configuration files. System.web and machine.web is an XML-formatted file that contains configuration information regarding your Web application.

Metadata and Versioning

Metadata is information regarding code that is stored within the .NET runtime's MSIL file. It provides many of the same functions as a COM-based type library. Figure 2-6 displays a look at the metadata displayed by the IL Disassembler product.

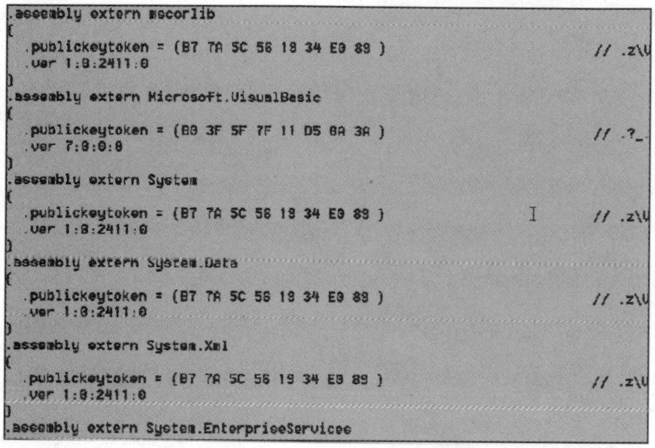

```
.assembly extern mscorlib
{
  .publickeytoken = (B7 7A 5C 56 19 34 E0 89 )                    // .z\V
  .ver 1:0:2411:0
}
.assembly extern Microsoft.VisualBasic
{
  .publickeytoken = (B0 3F 5F 7F 11 D5 0A 3A )                    // .?_
  .ver 7:0:0:0
}
.assembly extern System
{
  .publickeytoken = (B7 7A 5C 56 19 34 E0 89 )                    // .z\V
  .ver 1:0:2411:0
}
.assembly extern System.Data
{
  .publickeytoken = (B7 7A 5C 56 19 34 E0 89 )                    // .z\V
  .ver 1:0:2411:0
}
.assembly extern System.Xml
{
  .publickeytoken = (B7 7A 5C 56 19 34 E0 89 )                    // .z\V
  .ver 1:0:2411:0
}
.assembly extern System.EnterpriseServices
```

Figure 2-6: Metadata stored within an assembly listing external references

Metadata provides a common frame of reference that enables communication within the .NET environment. The information stored within the Metadata includes:

- Code name
- Code version
- Culture
- Public key
- Assemblies and components that this assembly depends on
- Security permissions needed to run
- Type information
- Name
- Visibility
- Base class
- Interfaces implemented
- Members of the assembly, such as methods and properties
- Attributes

Metadata provides enough detailed information to allow a component in one language to inherit from a component in another language. Most of that data is tucked away where mere mortals can't find it. It is viewable through ILDASM.EXE. Here is some example information. However, some of that information is configurable by a programmer through the use of attributes. The following items are available to describe an assembly within a .NET application. These attributes are used in the form `AssemblyAttribute("value")`:

- `AssemblyTitle`: Title of the assembly.

- `AssemblyDescription`: Textual description of the assembly.

- `AssemblyConfiguration`: Definition of an assembly configuration custom attribute within an assembly manifest.

- `AssemblyCompany`: Name of the company that produced the assembly.

- `AssemblyProduct`: Product name of the assembly.

- `AssemblyCopyright`: Copyright information associated with the assembly.

- `AssemblyTradeMark`: Trademark information associated with the assembly.

- `AssemblyCulture`: The culture associated with the assembly. For example, an assembly culture of `AssemblyCulture("de")` would be German.

- `AssemblyVersion`: Version number information for the resulting assembly. It is in the format of *major.minor.build.revision*.

- `AssemblyDelaySign`: Used with delayed signing of an assembly. It is a boolean value that indicates whether to reserve space for the strong name within the executable file while delaying the actual signing until sometime in the future.

- `AssemblyKeyFile`: The name of the file used for the strong name. This entry is very important for using your .NET component in COM, when using COM+ Services, and when installing a component into the GAC. Either this attribute or the `AssemblyKeyName` must be specified if a file is to be stored in the GAC.

- `AssemblyKeyName`: Refers to a Crypto Service Provider key that has been installed onto a system. A key must be specified for a file to be signed. Either this attribute or the `AssemblyKeyFile` must be specified if a file is to be stored in the GAC.

- `AssemblyBuildNumber`: The build number associated with the component. This is apart of the `AssemblyVersion` attribute.

- `AssemblyMajorVersion`: The major version number associated with the component. This a part of the `AssemblyVersion` attribute.

- `AssemblyMinorVersion`: The minor version number associated with the component. This is a part of the `AssemblyVersion` attribute.

- `AssemblyName`: The logical name of the assembly.

Garbage Collection

Garbage Collection (GC) is the mechanism within the .NET runtime environment that provides for the orderly destruction of all allocated objects within a computing environment. Why is this important? Let's look at the code in the following listings. In our examples, VB6 (Listing 2-11) and ASP VBScript (Listing 2-12) contain small memory leaks due to COM objects not being deallocated properly.

Listing 2-11: VB6 Example Where a Recordset Is Returned by a Function

```
Public Function ReturnData() as ADODB.RecordSet
Dim Cn as ADODB.Connection
Dim Rs as ADODB.RecordSet
Set Cn = CreateObject("ADODB.Connection")
Set Rs = CreateObject("ADODB.RecordSet")
Cn.open ". . . . . ."
Rs.CursorLocation = adUseClient
Rs.open 'sql statement', Cn
Set Rs.ActiveConnection = Nothing
ReturnData = Rs
End Function
```

The connection object is the root of the problem. Fixing this code will require that the connection object be closed and de-allocated by:

```
set Cn = Nothing.
```

Listing 2-12: ASP 2/3 Example Where a Data Is Retrieved from a Database and Some Type of Operation Is Performed on Each Row

```
Dim cn, rs
Set cn = Server.CreateObject("ADODB.Connection")
Set rs = Server.CreateObject("ADODB.RecordSet")

cn.Open ". . . . . ."
Rs.open "sql statement", cn

While not rs.eof
. . . . . . . . . . . . . . . . . . . . . . . . .
     rs.MoveNext
Wend
```

Both the connection object and the recordset object cause a problem here. Fixing this code will require that both the connection and recordset objects be closed and deallocated by:

```
If rs.State <> adStateClosed then
    rs.Close
end if
if cn.State <> adStateClosed then
    cn.Close
end if
Set rs = Nothing
Set cn = Nothing
```

The preceding code samples look fine, yet both will cause problems over time. The problem is that both code samples will open COM objects and not properly close and deallocate them. Although some developers think that when the objects go out of scope the system will automatically close and deallocate them, that is not the case. Although going out of scope closes the objects, there is a small memory leak associated with the non-deallocation. If the VB6 code is in a middle-tier object or the ASP code is in a Web page, both could be called several hundred thousand times in short order. That small memory leak multiplied by hundreds of thousand of calls can wreak havoc on an application's or Web site's stability.

A second issue in the world of COM appears with circular references. With a circular reference, Object A and Object B are holding references to each other. COM will deallocate an object when there are no references held to it. The issue with circular references is that neither object can be destroyed because the other is always holding a reference to it. The result is that neither object is deallocated. The resulting memory leak and the fact that, with the Internet, it is possible to have hundreds of thousands or millions of calls in a relatively short amount of time can result in an unstable server and the failure of an application in a small amount of time.

Garbage collection would assist in resolving these issues by managing the destruction process of objects. When an object is no longer needed by the system, the garbage-collection service will pause program execution and perform any cleanup of allocated objects that are no longer needed. How does garbage collection work? All objects in .NET are allocated from one of two central heaps. One heap is for objects that are smaller than 20,000 bytes; the other is for objects that are larger than 20,000 bytes. The only difference in the two is that the heap for smaller objects is compressed, while the large object heap is not. When an object goes out of scope or is closed, it is marked as not being needed.

When the garbage collector is called, program execution is halted. All objects in the stack are destroyed by the garbage collector that are not marked as still needed by a running application and memory is returned and made available to the system. All objects within the small object heap are moved together and objects are allocated from the next available location in the heap. Note that objects from the large object heap are not moved around. Moving objects of 20,000 bytes and larger places a load on the system that is not necessary and provides very little value when compared to the work done. Therefore, the reordering of objects only occurs within the small object heap.

With the .NET Framework, there is an additional concept within the GC called *generations*. An object of generation 0 has not had any attempt at garbage collection processing it. An object of generation N has survived N attempts at garbage collection. At this point in time, the Framework supports a maximum of two generations. Generations operate based on the idea that objects of the same generation have a relationship with each other and will many times call into each other. Because of this, the GC will attempt to place objects in the same generation next to each other in the heap. This will reduce processor cache misses and hopefully increase performance.

Several interesting methods that are exposed by the Garbage Collector are:

◆ `GC.Collect()`: Tells the GC to perform a collection.

◆ `GC.Collect(int32 intGeneration)`: Instructs the GC to perform a collection on the heap for objects up to `intGeneration`.

◆ `GC.MaxGeneration()`: Returns the maximum number of generations supported by the Framework. Currently, the .NET Framework supports a maximum value of 2.

WEAK REFERENCES

One interesting item that Microsoft has provided with the Garbage Collection in the .NET Framework is the concept of weak references. For Visual Basic developers, there is not really any thing that is analogous. Let's assume that you're developing an application that will use a large amount of memory and a large number of objects, but most of those objects are not going to be used at any one moment. Weak references might be a good mechanism to use, because they allow you to act as if you have a large number of allocated objects. Listings 2-13 and 2-14 show a simple example of using weak references. The basic idea is that there is an object, called `obj` in this example. A weak reference is created to it. When the garbage collector runs, the `obj` object is cleaned up. If there are no references to the weak reference of the object, then the weak reference is cleaned up by the garbage collector. If there is at least one reference, the garbage collector does not clean up the weak reference.

Listing 2-13: Weak References in Visual Basic .NET

```
Public Sub WeakReferenceMethod()
Dim obj as new Object()
Dim objWR as new WeakReference( obj )
obj = Nothing
obj = objWR.Target
if ( objWR <> Nothing ) then
' the object is available
else
```

Continued

Listing 2–13 *(Continued)*

```
'the object is not available
end if
End Sub
```

Listing 2–14: Weak References in C#

```
Public Void WeakReferenceMethod() {
Object obj as new Object();
WeakReference objWR as new WeakReference( obj );
obj = null;
obj = objWR.Target;
if ( objWR != null ) {
//the object is available.
}
else {
//the object is not available.
}
}
```

So, weak references are cool, but what good are they? Because ASP.NET applications are based on browsers coming in, connecting, and then disconnecting, the benefit of weak references is minimal. A properly designed client/server application also releases resources on the server, so the value of the weak references is most likely minimal. The biggest use for weak references is in any type of application that allocates a large number of objects for an extended period of time, such as a Windows Server. If a large number of objects are created, it can place a large drain on available memory. By using weak references, programs can have access to a large number of objects while at the same time respecting other programs that need to have access to memory.

Summary

The Microsoft .NET Framework provides a number of features and services that will enhance the scalability and durability of an application. The inclusion of Garbage Collection will make applications more durable by minimizing memory leaks. The addition of support for threads and COM+ Services will assist developers in creating more response and scalable applications. The overhaul of the ASP programming model by including support for a more traditional programming methodology will increase programmer productivity and performance. By packaging these features into the base .NET Framework, applications developed with the Framework will tend to be more reliable, more scalable, and easier to develop.

Part II

Designing Databases and Middle-Tier Components for Maximum Scalability

Chapter 3

Developing a Line of Business Applications

IN THIS CHAPTER

- ◆ Understanding database design
- ◆ Working with optimal queries
- ◆ Identifying database features that affect performance

WHEN A HOUSE IS BUILT, if the foundation is not put together well, there is a good chance that the house will develop problems over the course of its lifetime. These problems don't typically show up when the first homeowner moves in, but over several years, the house may have problems directly related to the poorly-put-together foundation. The same may be true of any application that sits on top of a database. If the database is not well designed, than any application — including those based on the .NET Framework, COM, or any other technology — may have problems running with acceptable speed.

This chapter, along with Chapter 4, covers building a solid database foundation for a business application. Taking a quick glance at this chapter, it would seem to have very little to do with Microsoft .NET. However, if you don't build your application on a solid foundation, your application will not perform up to the expectation of you and your customer. Not having a well-designed database schema that is geared to the needs of your customer and to providing a high-performance environment can be detrimental to your application. To borrow a great phrase from Bill Vaughn, formerly of Microsoft Corporation and now President of BetaV, "All data access technologies wait at the *same* rate." After a command is sent to a database, RDO, ADO, and ADO.NET will wait the same amount of time for a response. Although the situation is the same underneath the covers for all applications and databases, making sure that the database foundation for your application is as fast as possible is extremely important. It is significantly important in making sure that your Microsoft .NET–based application runs as fast as possible and has the foundation necessary for the highest performance possible. Without a solid and dependable foundation, applications will not successfully scale, customers will get angry, and if the situation is bad enough, money will be lost.

There is one other item besides performance that is very important to the design and development of a database application: transaction processing. Transaction processing is the lifeblood of many applications. A *transaction* is a unit of work that can be completed or undone as a unit. For example, the process of purchasing a product for cash is a transaction. If, during the process, the buyer decides not to purchase, the seller will (or at least *should*) return the money and the transaction is rolled back. After a buyer completes the purchase, leaves the store, and is satisfied with the work, the transaction is complete.

If your application cannot quickly and reliably perform its work, there is a problem. To assist in designing highly scalable database applications with Microsoft .NET, we will look at some design principles and suggestions used in developing the underlying database. By developing a database that will be highly scalable, programs will have the foundation necessary to provide a highly scalable application.

As you read through this chapter, you should think about how each item discussed would impact your application. Does a feature make sense for your application? Your application will not need to use every feature listed in this chapter. The decision to use or not use a specific feature is best left up to you, your system architects, and your development team.

Database Types

Two types of databases are commonly used: file-based databases and client/server databases. This choice of database type is very important and will greatly affect the scalability of your application.

File-based databases are popular tools for quick, small-scale development. In general, these databases provide little or no intelligent communications between the client application and the database. When a query is sent to this type of database, the database must read all rows from the file, match those rows to the query, and then send the data back to the calling client. Because there is no intelligence within the database, the time to process a query can be significant when compared to a client/server database. File-based databases tend to have fewer features than larger databases, such as SQL Server and Oracle. In addition, file-based databases do not scale to large numbers of users very well. When multiple users attempt to access the database, a significant slowdown occurs. The database is not really designed for multiple users accessing it at one time. Often, the database application will lock up and leave the database file in an unknown state; ultimately, file corruption and data loss can occur.

A client/server database is one in which communication occurs between the client and the server usually through some type of network protocol communications. The server sends data back to the client without the client having direct access to the database files. The client talks to the database service and the database service in turn talks to the files that it manages. By having this intelligent type of communication, the chance for a data loss is less than it is with a file-based database.

Unfortunately, there is a tradeoff between database types and cost. In general, after the initial application is installed, file-based databases do not have additional costs. Client/server databases such as SQL Server, Oracle, and DB/2 have licensing fees based on the number of users that connect. The more users that connect, the more money must be paid to the database vendor. The resulting tradeoff usually means that applications geared for a small number of users (five or fewer) are written on a file-based database. Applications geared toward a larger number of users, such as a corporate application or the Internet, are typically written with a client/server database. The two exceptions to this rule are Microsoft Database Engine (MSDE), also known as the SQL Server Desktop Edition, from Microsoft, and MySQL from MySQL AB. MSDE is a scaled-down version of SQL Server. It contains nearly all the features of SQL Server. It is scaled down in the number of connections that it can concurrently support and the amount of data that it can hold. Besides this throttling, MSDE is functionally identical to SQL Server. MySQL is an open source client/server database that has become very popular with programmers doing development in the open-source world. Unfortunately, MySQL does not currently support transactions or any locking level besides table locking for any operation that changes data. During any type of change operation within a table, such as insert, update, and delete, MySQL will lock an entire table. By locking the entire table, MySQL can guarantee that no other user will be making a change during that operation. Unfortunately, the other users are forced to wait for access to the table. This can severely limit the scalability of applications that perform a relatively high percentage of these data-change operations, such as those found in online transaction processing applications (OLTP).

Why is it important to know the difference between a file-based database and a client/server database? If you recognize some basic differences between file-based databases and client/server databases, it becomes easier to understand the type of database that should be used as the foundation for developing applications with the .NET Framework.

Locking Types

To get at data in a database and to add, update, and delete data, a database must support some type of mechanism to lock data. If not, it is entirely possible for two different users to attempt to update data at one moment. By locking data, a database can keep multiple users from overwriting the work that the other users are attempting to perform. This is also known as concurrency. Although most databases support more locking levels, the three most common types of locking that databases support are rows, pages, and tables. With row-level locking, a database will lock only a specific row in that specific lock mode. When a row is locked, all other rows within the table are available for all operations. With page locks, a group of contiguous rows is locked. In SQL Server 7 and 2000, a page is 8 KB of data. If a page lock is created in a SQL Server table, all rows contained within that 8 KB of the page are locked by the specified lock mode. With a table lock, all rows within a table are locked for use by that one connection's lock mode.

Row-level locking allows more users to access the different rows in a table, allowing what is called a higher concurrency. Unfortunately, row-level locking also requires greater resources on the database. Table locking requires the fewest resources on the database. However, it limits the concurrency of the application by not allowing multiple users to connect to the database. Databases attempt to strike a balance between the locking levels. For example, if a table has several row locks that would be better handled by a page lock, the database will most likely escalate the lock of those rows to a page lock. Typically, client/server databases implement row-level and page-level locking along with table-level locking. File-based databases may implement row-level locking, such as Microsoft Access, or table-level locking. The type of locking will depend on the database used.

Locking is an important feature to understand within the .NET environment. It can directly affect the number of users that may actively use an application at one time.

For more on Locking Types, check out Chapter 4.

Isolation Levels

Different applications need different *isolation levels* (modes of locks). These modes control the degree of concurrency that a database will allow. Much like the lock types, several isolation levels are commonly used. There are four typical isolation levels:

◆ **Read Uncommitted:** Read Uncommitted allows dirty reads. No locks are issued except during any actual updates.

◆ **Read Committed:** Read Committed allows shared locks on data. Dirty reads are avoided.

◆ **Repeatable Read:** Locks are placed on the data in a query. Other users are prevented from updating data held in Repeatable Read.

◆ **Serializable:** Other users are prevented from updating or inserting rows until the transaction is completed.

For a complete discussion of isolation levels, turn to Chapter 4.

Database Schema

The logical and physical layout and design of the tables in your database and the relationships among those tables is the first step in creating a successful application. A logical design maps what is occurring in the real world with the logical layout of your tables and where certain pieces of information are stored. If this step is not carried out correctly, there is little that can be done to improve the performance of an application.

Let's take an application that we once saw as an example. This manufacturing application allowed a user to control the entire manufacturing process from scheduling to final output. Within the plant, parts for each manufacturing step were stored in bins. Different bins of parts were available at each workstation in the plant, and there were several plants manufacturing this product for this company throughout the world. Logically, it would make sense for the application to have a BINS table. Within this BINS table, there would be a quantity field, a part field, a location field, and a plant field, as shown in Table 3-1. This setup would allow the plant managers and senior management to know current inventory levels as accurately as the application.

TABLE 3-1 TABLE DEFINITION FOR OUR BINS TABLE

Field	Data Type	Description
TBLBINID	integer/GUID	Primary key on the table TBLBIN. This field allows a row to be uniquely identified.
QTY	Integer	The number of units of the part within a specific bin.
TBLPARTID	integer/GUID	Foreign key to our tblPart table.
TBLLOCATIONID	integer/GUID	Foreign key to our tblLocation table.
TBLPLANTID	integer/GUID	Foreign key to our tblPlant table.

This setup would also allow for multiple simultaneous operations to occur on the same part at different locations, either within the same plant or outside of the plant and at different workstations within the plant. Unfortunately, the application that we saw was architected differently. The BINS table was laid out with a part field and a quantity field like that shown in Table 3-2.

TABLE 3-2 TABLE DEFINITION FOR OUR BIN TABLE WITHOUT THE LOCATION AND
          PLANT IDENTIFIERS

Field	Data Type	Description
TBLBINID	integer/GUID	Primary key on the table TBLBIN. This field allows a row to be uniquely identified.
QTY	Integer	The number of units of the part within a specific bin.
TBLPARTID	integer/GUID	Foreign key to our tblPart table.

The result was that the application would not scale to a large number of users. Why? Because the manufacturing operations at the plants used several common parts in nearly all operations. By continually selecting and updating the same small set of rows, the application would place varying sets of locks on a small set of rows. A call to select or update data will likely have to wait on pending operations. (This assumes that the database that is being used supports some type of locking besides table locking.) Taken together, these rows that are continually called over the course of our application running are termed a *HotSpot*. This means that the application is depending on a few rows within the table for a majority of its operations. By providing more detailed information within the table and using location and plant information, we are able to spread out the rows that are used from just a few to the actual rows appropriate for each part at each location and plant that is actually needed. By having these operations spread out over multiple rows in a table, concurrent operations can occur without the operations affecting each other severely.

Establishing Performance Goals

Establishing realistic performance goals for an application and knowing the location of potential bottlenecks will be very important for meeting the requirements of your customer's application. For a successful application, performance must be measured at many different levels:

◆ How long it takes for an operation to be performed by the database

◆ How long it takes to process query results

◆ How many users the database design can realistically support

◆ How long it takes the application to return user information to the client

◆ How many active users can be supported by the application

♦ How long the application runs without problems

♦ How durable the application is under load

Performance is an issue that needs to be considered from the beginning. As your application is designed and developed, all the choices made in designing your application somehow affect the performance of your application. If performance is not addressed upfront along with establishment of performance goals, the performance of your application will, in general, suffer. Database design issues along with application development issues will need to be addressed from the beginning if you want to meet application performance goals. Assuming that your database design is appropriate for a high-performance application, it would be good to know that the problem is most likely in your application logic. If there is a performance problem in your application, not only will you have to go into your database and change the database design, but you will have to change some code within the application layer above the database.

The most common mistake that is made in regards to database design is not designing for concurrency and not accurately making the database design fit the business rules. In our example with the BINS table, the table design in Table 3-1 will allow for multiple users to access a specific part from different locations within the same plant. The database table design in Table 3-2 will not allow multiple users to access the same part from different locations within the same plant or others. Why should our application limit two users from different locations from accessing the exact same part? By using the database table design listed in Table 3-1, our application will overcome this problem. In database design, the question that must be asked is, "How specific does our data need to be?" The more specific the data, the better it is to define our database tables so that the data may be separated out. The second problem of not making the database design fit the business logic rules is a much more subtle problem. This problem can crop up when all the business logic rules have not been defined before the database is developed. The problem with changing the database design to support additional rules and logic is that these changes require synchronizing with the application logic and the deployment of these changes from development to production database and client systems.

Considerations for Scalability

Now that we've gotten through the basics of databases and database design, let's take a look at database features and how to efficiently query our data. Looking at these items will allow us to create a .NET application that can scale as efficiently as possible. By creating a high-performance database table design and query strategy, your application will be able to execute to its fullest potential.

Set-oriented operations

SQL statements are optimized for set-oriented operations. Set-oriented logic borrows from mathematical theory. Take a look at the SQL `select` statement based on Tables 3-1 and 3-2:

```
select TBLBINId from TBLBIN where TBLPARTID=12345.
```

This command specifically asks for all the `TBLBIN` records where the `TBLPARTID` value is 12345. Logically, it asks for all the material BINs in a system with a certain type of material loaded in the BIN. By asking for data in this way, you can quickly and easily communicate queries to your database. Over the years, database companies have spent large sums of money to make sure that their products use and are optimized for SQL processing. Computer programming languages are based on a different type of logic, procedural logic. If a program were to use procedural logic to simulate the above query, it is entirely possible that the result would take longer to execute and would be much harder to read and understand. As a result, it is best to use set-oriented operations as much as the logic to perform a given function will allow.

Reduce data transmissions

Applications need to interact with the data stored in databases, so data will always need to be transferred between the client and database server layers in an application. The problem occurs when attempting to transfer too much data between the two layers, especially when the two layers are on separate machines and must communicate over a network. In general, companies spend a large amount of money on server hardware. These servers have a large amount of memory, fast processors, and are optimized for database-oriented operations.

Let's take a look at several example requests in an application. In the example application, we need to see the quantity of a specific part within one of the manufacturing plants. These examples use the tables defined in Table 3-1.

Example 1:

Issue the following SQL statement to the database:

```
Select Sum(Qty) from TBLBIN where TBLPLANTID=145 and TBLPLANTID=1567
```

Example 2:

Issue the following SQL statement to the database:

```
Select Qty from TBLBIN where PARTNO='CO145' and TBLPLANTID=1567
```

After the data is returned from the database, the client application will iterate through the rows and perform a summation on the QTY field.

Example 3:

Issue the following SQL statement to the database:

```
Select * from TBLBIN where PARTNO='C0145' and TBLPLANTIT=1567
```

After the data is returned from the database, the client application will iterate through the rows, find the appropriate row within the row, and perform a summation on the qty field.

Example 4:

Issue the following SQL statement to the database:

```
Select * from TBLBIN
```

After the data is returned from the database, the client application will iterate through the rows and check the row to see if it has the appropriate part number and plant number. If the row meets the criteria, the application finds the appropriate column and performs a summation on the qty field.

Let's analyze the difference between our four examples. Example 4 returns the entire contents of the table TBLBIN from the database to the client application. The result set is returned over the network from the database to the client application. It is the responsibility of the application to iterate through all the rows, decide the rows to use, and perform the summation. Let's look at the problems that performing the operation in Example 4 would cause:

◆ **Database load:** There would be a load on the database server to stream the entire contents of a table to an external client.

◆ **Network load:** All rows from the table are sent over the network. This would waste network bandwidth.

◆ **Client load:** The client would be responsible for performing the summation. If the client does not have adequate memory and processing capabilities, the client might not be the best place to perform these operations.

Example 3 returns only the rows within the TBLBIN table that are necessary. It is the responsibility of the application to search each row for the appropriate field and to perform the summation. Performing this operation will result in more fields being returned than are necessary and the client application being required to find the appropriate field and perform the summation. This example is not as bad as Example 4, but the returning of too many fields and requiring the client to perform the summation is probably not an acceptable use of client or database resources. If there are other operations that are to be performed, this might be an acceptable use or it might not be. The appropriateness of this solution will depend on the situation.

Example 2 returns only the rows within the TBLBIN table and only the qty field within the rows. The client application is responsible for performing the summation. Depending on the situation, this could be an inefficient use of client and database resources.

Example 1 returns only the one row and the one field that is requested. All processing occurred on the database server. Only a small amount of data is sent across the network from the server to the client. The client application only needs to display the result. This is most likely the optimal query. Why do we say "most likely"? Well, if your application already has a result set open at the client, it might be best to not perform a query against the database. If the application already has a result set that contains the needed data, instead of running a query against the database, it might be best to go ahead and perform a summation on the client. The best solution will depend on the scenario. The best solution? Know your application, and then you can decide the best course to take.

Although it seems comical to believe that a programmer would actually use the Example 4 scenario, we have seen one set of programmers actually do this. The programmers were trying to process some sales information. They were attempting to group sales information by region. They discovered a problem when this calculation was taking over 20 minutes. The 20 minutes broke down into 30 seconds of communications between the client and server, followed by 19 minutes and 30 seconds of processing on the client. By moving to an Example 1 scenario, the processing time was cut down to about five seconds of processing on the database. The time to transmit the data over the network was negligible and no additional processing was required at the client. In this example, the database has performed all the work and will return the one record with one field within that record to the client. All the client application needs to do is process the one record that is returned. In most scenarios, Example 1 will be the best option.

Avoid serialization when possible

Serialization is neither good nor bad. Like many things, it depends on how it is used.

For a complete discussion of serialization, check out the section in Chapter 4 on isolation levels.

Let's think about how an application's logic is implemented. In general, application logic can be either serial or parallel. If your application logic is parallel, multiple operations can occur at one time. If your application logic is serial, operations must occur in the order of one operation at a time. Within a database, there is a similar type of operations, termed isolation *levels*. Most developers will not encounter serialization until they begin to work with transactions. With both manual and automatic/COM+ transactions, isolation levels must be at the forefront of your mind. With database serialization, if access to a row, a set of rows, or a table is serialized, two operations can't occur on the serialized rows at one time. Although one operation is serializing a set of rows, any additional operations attempting to access those rows must wait until the currently running operation releases its hold on its set of rows.

With automatic/COM+ transactions, database access is automatically serialized, unless your SQL code resets the isolation level or the application programmatically changes the isolation level (this feature is available in COM+ 1.5). When a row is locked with the isolation level of Serializable, that row is locked with that isolation level until the connection on the database is dropped, or the code executes a `.SetComplete()` or `.SetAbort()`.

When access to a set of database rows are serialized, only one database connection may operate on those rows at a time. Other database connections will be required to wait on the connections that are already waiting. If those rows are not used heavily, serialization of those rows may not cause a significant performance bottleneck. If those rows are heavily used, then the serialization may cause anywhere from a small to a large performance bottleneck depending on the application. If at all possible, avoid serialization.

Prevent deadlocks

Within databases and other multi-user environments, there is a need to manage access to a single object at any one moment. This management of access is referred to as *locking*. Locking can occur within a database, multi-process environment when attempting to communicate with system resources, or when multiple threads in a multi-threaded application attempt to access the same object at the same time within the parent process.

Locking within a database is done to preserve the transactional integrity of operations. Locking in a database can be done at many different levels. Typically, database locking can be done based at the row, page, or table level (though other options are available). Locking done at the row level is typically the most resource-intensive for a database. However, a row level can continue to allow multiple users to continue to access other rows within the table normally, so it increases concurrency. A table-level lock is the opposite extreme. Locking done at the table level will disallow other connections for accessing the table completely. Table locking won't allow other users to make changes; thus, it is a highly limiting concurrency. One good thing about table locking is that it requires the fewest resources from the database. Between the row-level and table-level locking is page-level locking. Depending on the number of rows that are currently being locked by a connection, the database engine may decide to scale the locks up to the next available locking level depending on factors within the database.

Let's take a look at a complete list of what some databases can lock. SQL Server, Oracle, and DB/2 have the ability to lock various rows within a table. Typically, these locks are performed at one of the following levels:

- ◆ **Row:** Lock a single row in a table.

- ◆ **Page:** Lock a page of data or index page. Remember that the size of a page in the database is dependent on the version of that database. A database page can be sized from 2K of data and up.

- ◆ **Table:** An entire table.

- ◆ **Database:** An entire database.

The MySQL database is somewhat different. MySQL supports fewer types of locks. In addition, the Innodb file system will not support lock escalation. These types are:

- ◆ **Row:** Row locks are supported by the Innodb file type.

- ◆ **Page:** Supported by BDB tables.

- ◆ **Table:** An entire table. Supported by MyISAM, BDB, and Innodb tables.

The degree to which a database engine allows others to read data that is currently locked is termed the *mode*. The mode determines how a resource may be accessed concurrently.

SQL Server supports a number of different types of locks. These types of locks are:

- ◆ **Shared (S):** Used on resources that are accessed by read-only operations, such as a `Select` statement.

- ◆ **Update (U):** Used on resources that can be updated. Only one transaction is allowed to obtain an update lock.

- ◆ **Exclusive (X):** Used to prevent access to a resource by other transactions.

- ◆ **Intent:** A mechanism within SQL Server to state that the engine wants to acquire a shared or exclusive lock. Within Intent locks, there are Intent Shared (IS), Intent Exclusive (IX), and Shared with Intent Exclusive (SIX).

- ◆ **Schema:** Used when a schema modification is needed.

- ◆ **Bulk Update:** Used when data is being bulk copied into a table and either the TABLOCK hint is specified or the table lock on bulk load table option is set using `sp_tableoption`.

MySQL supports the following two locks:

- ◆ **Shared:** Used for reading data from a table.

- ◆ **Write:** Used for writing data to a table.

Between the row-level and table-level locking is page-level locking. Depending on the number of rows that are currently being locked by a connection, the database engine may decide to scale the locks up to the next available locking level depending on factors within the database. The algorithm to decide whether to scale up to the next lock is dependent on the database engine.

Let's look at an example. If a database engine decides that a page lock would be a much more efficient use of memory than ten row locks, the database engine might decide to use a page lock instead of the ten row locks.

Blocking occurs when Object A needs to access Resource B and Object B is currently accessing Resource B in a manner that does not allow other objects to access Resource B. Object A must wait on Object B to release Resource B.

A deadlock is a special case of blocking. Deadlocks occur when two parallel operations are in need of resources owned by other operations. These operations are blocked by each other. Each operation is in need of another resource whose owner is currently stopped from operating due to its need for a blocked resource. Here is the typical deadlock condition. Operation A has locked access to Object A. Operation A is attempting to access Object B. Unfortunately, Operation B has locked access to Object B. Object B is attempting to access Object A. Unfortunately, Operations A and B can access the necessary objects because the other currently owns exclusive access to the necessary objects.

Let's assume that we have instances of the application. Both instances are currently running. Instance A needs to access a specific row in Table A of the database. Instance B needs to access a specific row in Table B. The problem is that Instance A is currently holding a lock on the specific row that Instance B needs in Table A. At the same moment, Instance B is holding a lock on the exact row that Instance A needs in Table B. Each application is blocked from getting the data that it needs by the other instance. Because each instance will be blocked because of the other, each instance of the application will appear to be locked up. Because each instance is blocked by the other, this is termed a *deadlock*.

How can you avoid a deadlock? Some databases have code within the database engine that will monitor connections for deadlocks. If a deadlock is found by the database engine, the database engine can close one of the connections and remove the deadlock condition. For programmers, deadlocks are hard to reproduce and are even harder to debug. There are two ways to minimize the possibility of deadlocks:

◆ Don't hold locks on database rows if there is no need to hold a lock.

◆ Within your application logic, attempt to access database tables in a consistent way. Do not randomly pick an order to access your tables. Many times, the database table order is going to be determined by the business logic, and there is nothing that may be done to change this. If it is possible to control the order of access, attempt to access the tables in a specific order.

Using a consistent order to querying tables and minimizing the number of locks within a table reduces the chances of having a deadlock.

Avoid long-running operations

Long-running database operations can destroy the performance of any application. Databases operate their best when the database does not have to manage a large number of connections and does not have to manage a large number of locks. Long-running operations tend to cause the number of connections and the number of locks to increase. Sometimes these connections and locks increase slowly, and sometimes they increase much more quickly. The ramping up in connections and locks depends on the database operations and the number of operations. Depending on the amount of data within your database and the type of operations that are occurring, you may want to separate out the online transaction processing operations (OLTP) from the offline reporting/decision support system (online analytical processing, or OLAP). We offer a more detailed discussion of OLTP and OLAP performance considerations later in this chapter.

Sometimes an operation will take a while to run. This is a simple fact of life. However, it is best for your application to avoid long-running and complex queries if at all possible.

Relations and defining relationships

A relational database is merely a set of related data. In a formal database, this data is stored in *tables*. Typically, there is some type of relationship between data in the different tables. For example, in our previous example, we have a TBLBIN table containing the current contents of all the product bins within our organization. There is a related table called tblPart. The tblPart table contains information about a specific part, such as the material that makes up the part and the unit of measure of that part. The TBLBIN table is related to the tblPart table. The tblPart table contains a primary key called tblPartId. This relationship is contained in a structure called a *foreign key*. Structured data like this is termed as *normalized*. There are three widely accepted forms of normalization within the database field. In First Normal form, repeated groups within individual tables are removed, a separate table is created for sets of related data, and each set of related data is identified with a primary key. Second Normal Form, creates separate tables for sets of values associated with multiple records, and these tables are related together through the use of foreign keys. With Third Normal Form, fields that do not depend on the key are removed.

What type of advantages do we achieve by normalizing our data this way? We save space within the system, and it is easier to manage the data.

Let's look at an example. We will be using the example database table shown in Table 3-3. Using the table TBLBIN as defined in Table 3-3, our application has 500 bins containing a part with a material information of 1245. With the table as described in Table 3-3, we would need to manage the material and unit of measure in 500 places. It could become fairly easy for the same part number to end up with a different material or unit of measure.

TABLE 3-3 AN EXAMPLE BINS TABLE

Column Name	Column Description
TBLBINID –	Primary key
MATERIAL –	Material information
UOM –	Unit of material information

By designing our system more along the lines of Figure 3-1, our application only has to manage the material and the unit of measure in one spot for a specific part number. In this figure, notice that the line connecting the TBLBIN table and tblPart table denotes a foreign key relationship. The column tblPartId in the tblPart table is a primary key. The column tblPartId in the TBLBIN table is a foreign key. The next section discusses primary and foreign keys in detail.

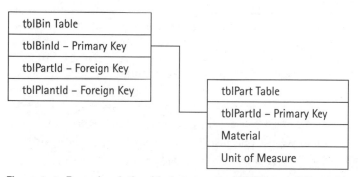

Figure 3-1: Example relationship between the TBLBIN and tblPart tables

A downside to using a normalized approach to data storage is that in order to get a complete view of the data, many times an operation to put this data together must be performed, which takes time. This type of operation is called a *join*.

A second downside to normalization is that it may be taken to an extreme at times. For example, zip codes may be used to describe a city and state. As a result, city and state may be pulled out of a table containing address information. Yet rarely is this done. For most applications, the cost and time of putting data together in a join is more than offset by the benefit of having multiple rows of data stored as fewer rows in a separate table using the foreign key relationship.

Keys

Database tables have multiple rows within them, otherwise they would not be of any use. How does the database engine uniquely identify a row within one of its tables? A primary key is a column, or set of columns, that will uniquely identify one row within a table. The value of that column is unique within that particular table. Different databases have different ways of generating a primary key. One method uses a data structure in a separate location in the database from which a program can receive unique values. A second method allows a table within a database to automatically fill a column within the database with a unique value – usually a numeric value.

Oracle uses the first method. This data structure in Oracle is called a *sequence*. A sequence is a numeric structure within a database. When you receive one value from the sequence, it will perform an autoincrement to the next available number. SQL Server allows a programmer to use both methods. Two column types are usually used as a primary key: `uniqueidentifier` and `integer/bigint`. When using a `uniqueidentifier` for your primary key, your program may use either method. A `uniqueidentifier` data type is what is known as a GUID within the Windows programming world. SQL Server 7 and later will allow you to retrieve a GUID that can be used in a `uniqueidentifier` through the command `select newid()`. After your code has this value, it can use this in an insert statement. SQL Server allows users to set up an integer column with the identity field attribute set on. This will automatically fill the value of the column with a unique integer value. MySQL uses the second method to automatically fill the primary key column.

With SQL Server, any of the integer style datatypes (tinyint, smallint, int, and bigint) may be used as an identity field. Typically only int and bigint are used due to the limited number of values available to tinyints and smallints.

By creating a primary key, a database engine will automatically configure an index on all columns contained within the key. For more information on indexes, take a look at the section on indexes in this chapter.

A second type of key within a relational database engine is a *foreign key*. A foreign key is a mechanism to associate data from two tables. For example, by placing the column tblPartId, which is a primary key in our tblPart table and creating a foreign key within TBLBIN, our column is limited in that it can only contain a certain set of values. These values are those that are defined within the column tblPartId in the tblPart table. In addition, the table TBLBIN is not required to contain information within the table as to what type of parts these products are. The TBLBIN table merely contains the foreign key. From the foreign key, it is possible to get information as to what type of part is contained within the physical bins. The information could be any data stored within the tblPart table. Attempting to insert an invalid value into the column tblPartId within the TBLBIN table will result in an error and the row will not be inserted.

Indexes

Now that your application runs, connects to your database, and returns a result, you are probably thinking your life is going to be pretty smooth sailing. Let's dig a little bit deeper into what the database engine is doing when it runs a command that you send it. Here's the command:

```
select tblPartId, Qty, TBLBINId from TBLBIN where TBLPLANTID=1567
```

First off, this is a query. It will return rows of data to the client application. The rows of data will contain three columns:

♦ **tblPartId:** The column containing the part number of our product in the Bin

♦ **Qty:** The Quantity within the specific bin container

♦ **TBLBINd:** The primary key and unique identifier within the table TBLBIN

When the query is sent to the database engine, the engine must analyze the query and create a plan to execute the query. This plan is based on the indexes available in the table. If there is no index on the column TBLPLANTID, then the database engine must look through every row in the table to see if that row meets the criteria. Performing a search where every row must be individually checked results in a *table scan*. A table scan is a very expensive operation in terms of computing resources. A table scan is a data-retrieval operation where the database engine reads in all the rows in a table to retrieve the rows that match the query. An index on the column TBLPLANTID would allow for a much faster lookup. How? An index is, in general, a separate object within a database. This object contains a sorted set of rows from its associated table. The set of rows in the index is sorted based on the columns(s) within the index. By having a sorted set of rows, the database engine can find the requested rows much more quickly and easily than without the query.

In general, databases support three types of indexes:

♦ **Primary keys:** An index that is created on the primary key. This is done by default with all databases.

♦ **Unique:** An index that is essentially like a primary key, except that it allows null values. With this type of index, a non-null value must be unique.

♦ **Column:** The type of index most often associated with speeding up search operations.

What kinds of rows are good candidates for indexes? You might think that anything that your program must search on would be a good candidate. If there is column mentioned within the `where` clause of your SQL statement, then the column can be a good candidate for an index. Many times, foreign keys are used to join between tables. Because of this, the columns that are listed as foreign keys are also good candidates. With each additional index associated with a table, there is more work that the database may potentially do behind the scenes whenever a row is added, updated, or deleted. So, while using a lot of indexes can be good at speeding up performance, it can also have a negative overall impact on performance if it is overused.

What type of operations are good for indexes? It depends on the column type and the operation. Let's look at the operations:

◆ **Equals (=):** When a query runs and looks for an equals, it is asking for rows that have a specific value.

◆ **Foreign Keys:** In general foreign key columns are good candidates for indexes. Typically, these columns are used for JOINs between tables. JOIN conditions contain conditions on the JOINs. By having these columns contained within an index, good performance can be contained within JOIN conditions and the VIEWs associated with them.

Having said this, what columns and operations are not good possibilities for indexes?

◆ **OR operations:** If a query has within it the OR operation, then depending on the database, the query may be forced to perform a table scan.

◆ **IN operation:** Similar to an OR operation, the IN operator may force a table scan to occur.

◆ **Columns where four or less distinct values exist:** If there are only a few distinct values within a table, adding an index may not be the best option.

◆ **Subqueries:** Typically, subqueries use the IN operation and can cause performance issues. Because database engines can typically perform a JOIN much faster, if a query can be rewritten to use a JOIN, it can speed up the query.

◆ **Operations on the left-hand side of a query:** In most `where` clauses, a complete column is compared against a value. In a few queries that I have seen, there has actually been a need to operate on the column before it is compared to a value. Although this might be a valid operation, it will most likely cause the query processor to not use an index. If possible, you could add a column to the table that holds the data within from the operation. This data could be kept current with a trigger on the appropriate table. Although this does remove some of the concept of normalized data, this might be an appropriate tradeoff for increased performance. You will need to decide based on the skills of your database admins and development group.

So now you just want to create an index on every column in all your tables. Depending on the activity of your database, this may not be a wise decision. We are often reminded of a line regarding paying for concessions that we used to hear when we were small children and were dragged to some college football games that went something like, "Please use exact change and please pay no more." We feel like indexing is the same way: "Please index the columns that you need, and please index no more."

Why can over-indexing be a problem? Think about what happens when a new row is inserted into a table. This row must be added to the table, and data must be inserted into the proper location in each and every index on that table. In an update, the update must be performed along with modifications to any indexes that need to be changed in relation to the update command. With an update, the delete from the table must be performed along with removal from any indexes required by the driving delete. By having too many indexes, the database may be required to make changes beyond those to the changed rows in the table.

As you can see, having a database with a proper indexing strategy is important to the performance of your application. Over the last several years, databases have included tools to assist your development team in finding and determining the proper indexing strategy. Microsoft includes a tool with SQL Server called the Index Tuning Wizard. Oracle includes the Oracle Tuning Wizard. DB/2 contains the Index Advisor.

JOINs

Now that you have structured your database tables such that there are relationships within your tables and your data is properly normalized, how do you typically pull this information together? At a very basic level, a `Select` statement is used. This `Select` operation will associate the related tables together through a `JOIN` operation that will relate the two tables together. In the earlier example with the tblPart and TBLBIN tables, the code below would perform the `Select` operation. The first select statement shows the explicit use of the `JOIN` statement. The second select statement is an example of the implied `JOIN`.

```
Select TBLBINId, Material, UnitOfMeasure from TBLBIN A JOIN tblPart
B on A.tblPartId=B.tblPartId
```

```
Select TBLBINId, Material, UnitOfMeasure from TBLBIN A, tblPart B
where A.tblPartId=B.tblPartId
```

 Different databases have different levels of support for the SQL standard. As a result, each database implements a slight variation of the SQL standard.

These two statements would return all the rows from both tables where there was a matching value for tblPartId in both tables. Each row returned will contain the TBLBINId from the TBLBIN table, the Material Column from tblPart, and the UnitOfMeasure from tblPart.

There are several types of JOINs:

◆ **Inner JOINs:** An inner JOIN is one in which data from multiple tables must match the JOIN conditions. If a table does not correctly match the JOIN conditions, it is not included.

◆ **Outer JOINs:** With outer JOINs, there are three subtypes. An outer JOIN is one in which data from multiple tables can match the JOIN conditions, with the acceptance of a row in one table not having a matching row in the other table.

  ■ **Left JOIN or Left Outer JOIN:** A left JOIN is one in which all the rows from the left table in the JOIN clause are included, even if there are no accompanying rows in the right table.

  ■ **Right JOIN or Right Outer JOIN:** A right JOIN is one in which all the rows from the right table in the JOIN clause are included, even if there are no accompanying rows in the left table.

  ■ **Full JOIN or Full Outer JOIN:** All rows from the left and right tables in the JOIN clause are included.

◆ **Cross JOINs or Cartesian Product:** All rows from both tables are included. Each row in the left table is associated with each row in the right table. For example, if one table has M rows and the other table has N rows, the resulting join will produce a result set that is M * N rows.

Views

Having to join tables with every query sent to the database could quickly become bothersome. There is a structure in most databases to allow a user to query an existing object and have the object then perform the join between the tables without the programmer needing to understand the appropriate JOIN syntax. This data structure is called a view. For a long time, views have only been prebuilt queries. The query merely goes off to the other tables and runs this query against those tables. There is no data that is associated with the view, and, therefore, not much performance benefit to using a view. The use of a view has only been of value as a way to simplifying data read access. If a view consisted of only a prebuilt query into an existing set of databases, it would not be very useful within this discussion. However, over the last several releases of Oracle and the last release of SQL Server, a feature has been added to both products to allow for the direct association of data with a view.

In SQL Server, an indexed view is one in which the result set is stored in the database. An indexed view will work best when the underlying data does not change often. An indexed view is not a good choice for caching data that is updated frequently due to the overhead of managing the caching of the data.

Oracle provides a type of index called material views. A *material view* is a view that actually stores the data associated with that view. The data associated with the view is physically stored with the view. The data within a materialized view must be updated to keep it as fresh as possible compared to the data in the associated tables. Due to this fact, the data within a materialized view is only truly up to date when the view is updated. After that, the data in the materialized view will tend toward being out of sync.

Although Microsoft and Oracle's solutions in regard to creating faster views have pluses and minuses, both work very well in regards to data warehousing/decision support where data changes relatively slowly over time.

Query planning

When a SQL statement is sent to a database, the database engine performs several actions:

◆ Parse the SQL statement.

◆ Check that the connected user has the appropriate security setting to perform the operation. For example, it is possible for a user to have select rights but not insert rights on a table.

◆ Divide the workload of the command so that the operation performed takes advantage of any optimizations within a database. For cxample, if an index will assist a query, the index will be used.

If the database engine already has an execution plan for a SQL statement, the database will use the existing query plan. If a SQL statement has no execution plan stored with the database engine, a query plan will be created before statement execution.

Let's look for a moment at how databases support the creation of query plans. Stored procedures have their query plans created when the stored procedure is created. All calls to the stored procedure use this query plan. This query plan is based on the status of table design and indexes at the time the plan is created. Changes to the database design or indexes can result in a query plan that is invalid. Changes in the table design and indexes often result in the need to re-create the stored procedure. Parameterized queries have their query plans created the first time the query is called. Subsequent calls through the parameterized query will use the query plan that already exists. With a SQL statement, which is not a stored procedure or parameterized query, created on the client and sent to the database, a query plan is created each time the statement is sent to the database.

Stored procedures

Stored procedures are pieces of prewritten code that are optimized for your database schema. When a stored procedure is created, a query plan is created. This query plan is saved with the stored procedure in the database. Typically, they are compiled. Unlike a SQL statement sent from an application, a stored procedure does not need to be parsed and a query plan created every time a call is made to the stored procedure. In addition, they should run faster, although the degree to which performance improves will vary greatly depending on the action within the stored procedure. The degree to which a stored procedure performs better than a SQL command will vary depending on the database and the functionality that is being performed.

One word of caution: If you choose not to use stored procedures, it is very easy to leave a security hole in your application. Here is an example scenario. If you have a Web application that accepts data through the URL, it is possible for a hacker to modify data within your database. The hacker would need to have knowledge about the schema of your database. Armed with that knowledge, if your application shows data to the user through a web browser with the URL www.yourserver.com/ShowData.asp?tblUserId=12345, a hacker could request the URL www.yourserver.com/ShowData.asp?tblUserId=12345;truncate%20 table%20tblUser. If there is no checking within the page ShowData.asp, it is possible for a hacker to literally truncate the table tblUser. Before passing commands to a database, it's a good idea to verify that the SQL statement that is sent to the database doesn't have any additional commands. For example, we use a routine to check for the existence of the words *delete* and *truncate*. If either of these words exists within the SQL statement, an error is raised and the command is not sent to the database. A call to a stored procedure would look something like execute sp_ShowData lngId, where the value lngId is defined as an integer. By being defined as an integer, the stored procedure will not accept the value of 12345;truncate table tblUser, because this is a string and the stored procedure is looking for an integer. An error occurs, the stored procedure does not execute the command, and the database never receives the truncate command.

There is a second advantage to using stored procedures beyond securing data operations. Many times, stored procedures are used to implement business logic. Stored procedures have an advantage over implementing business logic in an external component. When using an external component, data will be transferred out of the database to the component. Stored procedures won't require that data be moved out of the database. This assumes that the stored procedure only references data in the same physical database system. If the database references tables in another instance of a database on either the same machine or another system, this will result in data transfer, just like an external business component. This external business logic component may be on the same physical machine, or it may not be. In either case, there is a data transfer. This data transfer uses database, network, and component system resources. By implementing business logic in a stored procedure, there is no need to transfer data out of the database. This removes the time required to move data between the client and database system. The result is faster processing for the application.

Although stored procedures are usually considered to be transactional, it's possible for your ADO.NET application to control the commit/rollback of a stored procedure. For example, if a stored procedure commits a transaction, it is possible for ADO.NET to roll that work back to its previous state.

Another advantage of using stored procedures is that the query plan for executing a stored procedure is stored in the database engine. When a stored procedure is executed, the query plan doesn't need to be created each time that it is called.

Are stored procedures always better to use? Well, that depends on the expertise of your development team. If they are very database-oriented, stored procedures can be a very logical place to place application logic. However, stored procedures can be a very complex feature to learn. In addition, although each database language is marginally different from each other, each database's implementation of stored procedure functionality is dramatically different. Moving between SQL Server, Oracle, and DB/2 stored procedures would be enough to make a developer want to open a florist shop.

Stored procedures can assist in creating a high-performance application. Use them wisely.

Parameterized commands

A parameterized command is much like any other database command. When a SQL command is sent to a database, the command is interpreted/compiled, a query plan is created, and execution of the command is performed. If the same command is sent to the database more than once, the database must repeat the process each time the command is sent. With a parameterized command, the command is interpreted/compiled, a query plan is created, and execution of the command occurs on the first call. With subsequent calls, only the execution of the command occurs. The database stores a cached copy of the interpreted/compiled code and query plan. Parameterized commands are good to use when there is a loop that will perform multiple operations. The command can be created outside of the loop, then, within the loop, there can be multiple calls containing the parameterized query. Each call to the parameterized command will send the command to the database without having to create an execution plan with each command sent to the database.

Isolate OLTP and OLAP

Online Transaction Processing (OLTP) and Online Analytical Processing (OLAP) are two items that are very important to large business-centered applications. OLTP is the processing of operations that are running your business. They could be sales, CRM, or other types of immediate information. In this area of your application, there tends to be a relatively high percentage of insert, update, and delete operations to select operations. Typically, OLTP applications tend to have a large number of concurrent users.

OLAP is basically the historical part of your application. Data is continually added to the OLAP. Rarely is data removed from the historical portion of the application. OLAP may also be known by the terms *data warehousing, datamart,* and *decision support.* After this data is created, there are little to no additional operations to change its meaning. This is the information that is stored from yesterday, last week, last month, and last year. The only appreciable set of operations are the query/select operations.

Typically, OLAP datastores are highly indexed and optimized for queries. Everything that can be done to increase the performance of a query is done in an OLAP environment. Typically, this involves placing a large number of indexes on each table within the OLAP environment and making use of pre-filled views.

OLTP and OLAP have different needs and place different loads on the system. OLAP tends to have a high number of users performing a large number of operations. The large number of users and operations can create a significant load on the database server. Usually, these operations are relatively quick. OLAP systems must be able to provide high-speed access to all types of database operations, such as select, insert, update, and delete.

OLAP tends to have different needs to OLTP. After the data is in an OLAP system, in general it is queried in different ways and from different viewpoints. OLAP queries can run a long time and eat up database resources. Because the queries tend to be rather involved, a proper indexing strategy is essential. Due to the fact that OLAP data can be rather large, your queries are almost guaranteed to place a large number of locks on your data. The long-running nature of the queries and the fact that there is a large amount of data to potentially search tends to put the needs of these type of operations at odds with the needs of OLTP.

How do you design a system that meets the needs of both the current system users (OLTP) and the needs of those doing analysis of the running system (OLAP)? Separating OLTP and OLAP data into separate containers such as different databases running on the same machine is a first step. However, a load is still being placed onto the same system for OLTP and OLAP operations. It's best to separate OLTP and OLAP to completely different systems. Although this sounds expensive, it may not be as bad as possible. First, let's analyze the requirement. Does your application need to be separated? Does the application contain OLAP style data? Are there a large number of users hitting the system concurrently? Are the OLTP users receiving adequate performance? Are the OLAP users adversely affecting the OLTP users? What is the growth rate of the OLAP data? Does the business unit have funds for separate systems?

Although this is clearly not a book on funding your application development within your business, one thing that can be done to get the funds for an OLTP system is to use the OLTP system as part of the backup strategy for your OLAP system. For example, let's assume that you set up your OLAP and OLTP systems in some type of highly available cluster with common access to your database. If the main OLTP system goes down, your OLAP system would become your OLTP system and the OLAP part of your application could be turned off.

Summary

Designing a high-performing database involves properly implementing many pieces. Choosing the appropriate database type, properly designing your database schema, properly using database features, and properly designing a query/command plan are very important to creating a successful application. Unfortunately, there are no hard and fast rules regarding how these pieces can be made to work with your application. Each application is slightly different based on its performance characteristics. This chapter hits enough of the issues to allow you to build an application that can scale to almost any number of users, any number of transactions, and any amount of data.

Chapter 4

Transaction Processing

IN THIS CHAPTER

- ◆ Defining transactions and the ACID test
- ◆ Managing transactions in VB and C#
- ◆ Performing local and distributed transactions
- ◆ Setting transaction isolation
- ◆ Discussing scalability and performance

WHEN CONSIDERING DATABASE PERFORMANCE, the number and rate of transactions are the metrics that count. How many transactions will the database have to handle, and how fast will it have to handle them? Everywhere database vendors push their products, they are eager to talk about their Transaction Processing Performance Council (TPPC) benchmark performance or the transactions per minute (TPM) or transactions per second (TPS) they can handle.

With web servers widespread and application servers popping up all over, we now discuss transactions in terms that have meaning beyond database management systems. With the COM+ Services Compensating Resource Manager (CRM), a CRM object can be written to provide transaction support for file-system modification or e-mail messaging. But even in this new context, transactions still refer to sets of operations that must succeed or fail together. COM+ and .NET provide you with explicit means for handling transactions, both at the component-server and database-server level. This chapter covers how to manage and optimize these transactions.

Transaction Management

The transaction model was developed from research on relational database integrity performed during the 1970s and early 1980s. That is, the transaction model and the requisite transactions were, together, created as a mechanism to ensure the integrity of a relational database system. Transactions became a formal part of the SQL standard, and in 1992, the transaction isolation levels covered later in this chapter were formalized.

For a database transaction to effectively maintain system integrity, the model sets forth four qualities. A transaction must be:

◆ **Atomic.** Regardless of the number of operations contained in a transaction, together they must be handled as a single unit, and there can be no situation where one set of the operations completes and the others do not. A transaction must successfully complete (commit) or restore (rollback) all data to the original state.

◆ **Consistent.** A transaction must maintain the integrity of the database. When a transaction completes, successfully or otherwise, the system must be left in a defined state and all integrity constraints must be valid.

◆ **Isolated.** A transaction must not see the intermediate activity of other transactions. The results of a transaction must be seen completely or not at all.

◆ **Durable.** A transaction must exist until it completes, and the results of a transaction will be permanent when it completes. That is, even if the system fails while processing a transaction, upon restart the transaction must exist to enable rollback; and if failure occurs immediately following a request to commit or rollback, upon restart the system will have the desired state.

When a database supports transactions that meet these requirements, it has passed the ACID test. Passing the ACID test is an entry-level criterion for an enterprise-level database management system, and, today, all enterprise-quality database management systems support transactions that meet the SQL-92 standard.

From these requirements and the SQL standard comes an approach to managing transactions that are common to the databases and APIs that support them. This approach involves three steps:

1. Declare the start of a transaction.

2. Perform a database operation. This step may involve more than one operation and may involve more than one type of operation.

3. Terminate the transaction, either by committing the changes or by rolling back the changes that resulted from the operations in Step 2.

Listing 4-1 is Transact-SQL code that demonstrates this process. This example is used in a stored procedure for an online ordering system. This procedure is used to process a standard order only, which is an order that does not result in the generation of a back order. So, if the item is in stock, the transaction commits and the order is completed, but if the stock is not adequate to fill the order, an error is generated and the order is rolled back. Outside of the transaction, the user will be given an opportunity to decide whether to continue with the order knowing that part of the inventory is backordered.

Listing 4-1: Transact-SQL Code

```
CREATE PROCEDURE proc_order @order_num VARCHAR(6),
                            @order_err INT OUTPUT AS
```

```
-- Indicate start of transaction (Step 1)
BEGIN TRAN
-- Process records for the order (Step 2)
INSERT INTO ORDER
  (ORDER_NUM, ORDER_DATE) VALUES (@order_num,GETDATE())
-- Declare local cursor variable
DECLARE @line_items CURSOR
-- Select order line items from pending order table
SET @line_items = SELECT ITEM_CODE, ITEM_QTY FROM
  ORDER_PENDING WHERE ORDER_NUM = @order_num
OPEN @line_items
-- Loop through line items verifying and debiting inventory
FETCH NEXT FROM @line_items
    WHILE @@FETCH_STATUS = 0
BEGIN
      Check for adequate inventory for line item
    IF (@line_items.ITEM_QTY <=
        (SELECT CURRENT_QTY FROM INVENTORY
          WHERE ITEM_CODE = @line_items.ITEM_CODE) )
    BEGIN
        -- Debit inventory
        UPDATE INVENTORY SET CURRENT_QTY =
            CURRENT_QTY - @line_items.ITEM_QTY
            WHERE ITEM_CODE = @line_items.ITEM_CODE
        -- Process line item
        INSERT INTO ORDER_LINE_ITEM
            (ORDER_NUM, ORDER_LINE_NUM, ITEM_CODE,
             ITEM_QTY) VALUES
            (@order_num, @order_line_num,
             @line_items.ITEM_CODE, @line_items.ITEM_QTY)
    END
    ELSE
    BEGIN
        -- Set order_err
        @order_err = 1
        -- Rollback transaction since item would
        -- generate a back order
        -- (Step 3)
        ROLLBACK TRAN
    END
    FETCH NEXT FROM @line_items
END
-- Commit transaction since all items were processed successfully
-- (Step 3)
```

Continued

Listing 4-1 *(Continued)*

```
COMMIT TRAN
-- Set order_err
@order_err = 0
-- End of procedure
```

Although these steps always occur, where they occur may vary depending on the application. Within an N-tier application, the transaction management code will exist in one or more of the following places: the client, the database system, the web server, the application server, or the transaction processing system. Transactions may also vary by activity, operating in a distributed or local manner.

Local transactions

A *local transaction* is a transaction that occurs on a single database managed by a single connection. In the arena of N-tier computing, the term *local* can be somewhat ambiguous. In the case of local transactions, the meaning of local is the opposite of distributed, not the opposite of remote. To illustrate the difference, consider a typical Web site that has a guest registration page. The name and address information entered on the page needs to be stored into an individual database with a registered users table. Following the submit action on the Web page, a connection is opened to the database server, and a single registration record is stored in the table. This would be a local transaction even though the Web site user is not local, and the database server is not local. The transaction is considered local because the connection to the database is established and maintained locally at the web server.

The following examples demonstrate how to perform local transactions using either VB or C#. To begin a transaction, your program must call the `BeginTransaction()` method. This method instructs the database that all operations on this connection will be treated as a transaction and either committed or rolled back as a group. The `OleDbTransaction` object supports the following methods and properties shown using C# notation:

- `public void Commit();`: All the work has been completed successfully. Commit the transaction.

- `public void Rollback();`: A problem has occurred. Rollback the transaction and all associated changes.

- `IsolationLevel;`: `OleDbTransaction` object property that sets the isolation level of the transaction. The valid settings are `Chaos`, `ReadCommitted`, `ReadUncommitted`, `RepeatableRead`, `Serializable`, and `Unspecified`. Also, changing this property will have no effect until the next call to `BeginTransaction()`.

Table 4-1 provides a comparison between these settings and the ANSI isolation settings.

TABLE 4-1 OLEDBTRANSATION OBJECT ISOLATION COMPARISON TO ANSI ISOLATION LEVELS

OleDbTransaction Isolation Level	ANSI Isolation Level
Chaos	READ UNCOMMITTED
ReadCommitted	READ COMMITTED
ReadUncommitted	READ UNCOMMITTED
RepeatableRead	REPEATABLE READ
Serializable	SERIALIZABLE
Unspecified	NOT APPLICABLE

 The meaning and importance of the transaction isolation levels are discussed fully in the "Transaction Considerations" section later in this chapter. For now, in context of the following examples, all you need to know is that these transaction levels exist.

Here is an example of Visual Basic .NET code for using OLE-DB transactions:

```
Dim strCn As String = "Provider=SQLOLEDB;" & _
                      "DataSource=chakotay;InitialCatalog=DotNet; "
& _
                      "UserId=sa;PassWord=kirsten;"
Dim strSql As String = "INSERT INTO tblValue (tblValue) " & _
                      "VALUES (GETDATE())"
Dim oledbCN As New OleDbConnection(strCn)
Dim oledbCM As New OleDbCommand(strSql, oledbCN)
Dim oledbTrans As OleDbTransaction

Try
    oledbCN.Open()
    'Set the transaction Isolation level.
    OledbTrans =
      oledbCN.BeginTransaction(IsolationLevel.ReadUncommitted)
    oledbCM.Transaction = oledbTrans
    oledbCM.ExecuteNonQuery()
    oledbTrans.Commit()
Catch e As Exception
```

```
        oledbTrans.Rollback()
Finally
    If oledbCN.State <> ConnectionState.Closed Then
        oledbCN.Close()
    End If
    oledbCM = Nothing
    oledbCN = Nothing
End Try
```

The following is an example of C# code for using OLE-DB transactions:

```
string strCn = "Provider=SQLOLEDB;Data Source=chakotay;" & _
               "InitialCatalog=DotNet;UserId=sa;PassWord=kirsten";
string strSql = "INSERT INTO tblValue (tblValue) " & _
                "VALUES (getdate())";
OleDbConnection oledbCN = New OleDbConnection(strCn);
OleDbCommand oledbCM = New OleDbCommand(strSql, oledbCN);
OleDbTransction oledbTrans;
Try {
    oledbCN.Open();
    oledbTrans =
      oledbCN.BeginTransaction(IsolationLevel.ReadUncommitted);
    oledbCM.Transaction = oledbTrans;
    oledbCM.ExecuteNonQuery();
    oledbTrans.Commit();
}
Catch (Exception e) {
    oledbTrans.Rollback();
}
Finally {
    If (oledbCN.State != ConnectionState.Closed) {
        oledbCN.Close();
    }
    oledbCM = null;
    oledbCN = null;
}
```

The `SQLClient` provides native support for transactions through the transaction object `SqlTransaction`. The `SqlTransaction` object supports the following manual transactions method and properties beyond the `OleDbTransaction` object:

◆ `public void Commit();`

◆ `public void Rollback();`

◆ `public void Rollback(String transactionName);`

◆ `public void Save(String savePointName);`

◆ `int TransactionLevel {get;}`

ADO.NET provides the ability to manage transactions without using the distributed transaction facilities of MTS/COM+ and without the associated cost of using those services. When dealing with a single database, the control of transactions might be best handled within the application itself. These are termed *local* or *manual* transactions. Unlike the AutoComplete attribute of a COM+ application, local transactions are not automatically rolled back in the event of an error. An error must be trapped by a `try...catch` block by executing a call to `RollBack()` within the catch portion of the block.

Distributed transactions

As mentioned earlier in this chapter, there is a second category of transactions known as distributed transactions. Distributed transactions operate on multiple transactional systems. For instance, a production-monitoring system gathers daily data on an Oracle platform, and on a nightly basis this production data needs to be summarized and stored in an executive information system running SQL Server. While the nightly process runs, there will be two transactions: a transaction storing the data onto the executive system and a transaction marking the data as stored on the production system. Still, it would be desirable to have both of these transactions behave as a single transaction. In fact, with distributed transactions this is possible using a mechanism known as *two-phase commit*.

A two-phase commit system works by first corralling two or more transactions, each of which can commit or rollback individually. Secondly, each transaction is asked to perform its work. Following the transaction activity, as the first phase of the two-phase commit, each transaction is asked if it is ready to commit. If all the transactions respond that they are ready to commit their work, then, as the second phase of the two-phase commit, all of them are instructed to commit their work. If any one of the assembled transactions cannot commit its work, then all of the transactions are rolled back. On NT, this whole process is managed with Microsoft Transaction Server (MTS) and the Distributed Transaction Coordinator (DTC).

With Windows 2000, MTS became an integrated facility of COM+ Services, giving COM+ Services an inherent ability to manage distributed transactions. So, any COM+ object that supports transactions may become part of a distributed transaction, and the COM+ object does not even need to know whether it is part of a larger distributed transaction. Any COM+ object may specify one of five levels of transaction support, detailed in Table 4-2.

TABLE 4-2 COM+ TRANSACTION MODES

Transaction Mode	Description
Does Not Support Transactions	The component will not use a transaction, and if it is created by a transactional component, it will not inherit or pass on that component's transaction context.
Supports Transactions	The component does not require a transaction, but if it is created by a transactional component, it will inherit and pass on that component's transaction context.
Requires Transaction	The component must have a transaction, but the transaction can be new or inherited.
Requires New Transaction	The component must have a transaction, and it must be a new transaction.
Disabled	The component does not want any automatic transaction management, and if any transactional behavior is desired, the component will communicate directly with the DTC.

If the COM+ object uses transactions, then it simply needs to call one of two functions in response to Post(): SetComplete() or SetAbort(). These two functions work to handle the first phase of the two-phase commit. If the object successfully performs all its required activities, it calls SetComplete(), which indicates that it's ready to commit its work. If it doesn't successfully perform its work, then it calls SetAbort(), indicating that the work must be rolled back. The service that manages and responds to the SetComplete() and SetAbort() signals is the Distributed Transaction Coordinator (DTC).

The DTC manages the corralling of transactions and the associated two-phase commit operation by using a transaction ticket system. When a newly created COM+ object requires a transaction, COM+ automatically communicates with the DTC via the DtcGetTransactionManager function to retrieve a transaction identifier. This identifier is a 128-bit GUID and is stored in the object's context. If this object creates any objects that use transactions, then they will in turn inherit the transaction context of the parent object unless the newly created object specifies that it must have a new transaction. In the event that a new transaction is required, the DTC is again invoked to retrieve a new transaction that will become a root transaction context.

When all the transactional components have reported back to the DTC, the DTC will execute the second phase of the commit. If any of the components reported SetAbort(), then the DTC will notify all the databases involved that they need to roll back the required transactions. But if all the components reported `SetComplete()`, then the DTC instructs the databases to commit their transactions.

Although the previous discussion has referred to a single DTC, with distributed transactions there may be more than one DTC involved. In fact, the DTC supports Transaction Internet Protocol (TIP) which is an Internet Engineering Task Force proposed standard. This allows the DTC to communicate with other transaction processors that support TIP in a heterogeneous environment.

It is also important to note that a database must have a two-phase commit driver to support distributed transactions with the DTC. So, even if a database supports transactions, it cannot be enlisted in a distributed transaction with the DTC without a supporting driver. However, most of the major database vendors, particularly IBM and Oracle, provide drivers to support distributed transactions. Listing 4-2 outlines an object employing a distributed transaction. The code does not use `AutoComplete` and therefore uses `SetComplete` and `SetAbort` explicitly.

Listing 4-2: An Object Employing a Distributed Transaction

```
namespace TransactionalComponents
{
    [Transaction(Transaction.Required)]
    public class DistributedTransactionClass : ServicedComponent
    {
        public bool Post()
        {
            bool bSuccess = false;
            // Insert data modification code here
            // Set bSuccess appropriately
            ...
            // Test bSuccess
            if (bSuccess)
                SetComplete();
            else
                SetAbort();

            return bSuccess;
        }
    }
}
```

Stored procedures

Stored procedures are SQL procedures for databases that are held, or stored, within the database itself. A stored procedure allows a set of SQL instructions to be called through a reference to a single procedure name. Stored procedures provide great flexibility both in the variety of operations they can perform and in the data they can return. Stored procedures provide an excellent place to encapsulate business logic for the database. Stored procedures also have the capacity to manage their own transactions. For all of these reasons, there is a need to examine stored procedures in the context of transaction processing.

As a rule, when using stored procedures, transactions should be managed at the API level or the transact-SQL level but not both. For instance, if a component is managing a transaction and calls a stored procedure, there is no need for the stored procedure to invoke its own transaction. If the component calls `Commit()` or `Rollback()`, the work performed by the stored procedure will be committed or rolled back appropriately. However, if the component calls a stored procedure, which creates and commits a transaction, and the component calls `Rollback()`, the state of the work is indeterminate.

Does that mean that stored procedures should never manage their own transactions? No, just do not mix transaction control. Deciding where to put the transaction control code is a process of evaluating business and performance requirements. Transactions at the transact-SQL level will have better performance than manual or distributed transactions, but they will be isolated from the business logic contained at the client or the COM+ levels. So, database operations that are neither a part of distributed transactions nor a part of a more complex operation where the decision to commit or rollback is affected by something beyond the control of the database itself are good candidates for maintaining transaction control. Table 4-3 details the transaction control commands available in Transact-SQL.

TABLE 4-3 TRANSACT-SQL TRANSACTION-RELATED COMMANDS AND VARIABLES

Transaction Command	Description
BEGIN TRANSACTION or BEGIN TRAN or BEGIN TRAN[SACTION] NAME	Indicates the start of a transaction. The transaction may also be given a name.
COMMIT TRANSACTION or COMMIT TRAN or COMMIT TRAN[SACTION] NAME	Commits a transaction.
ROLLBACK TRANSACTION or ROLLBACK TRAN or ROLLBACK TRAN[SACTION] NAME	Rolls back a transaction.
SAVE TRANSACTION NAME or SAVE TRAN NAME	Creates a save point in the transaction. Any subsequent ROLLBACK will only affect statements following the save point.
@@TRANCOUNT	Indicates the transaction nesting level. @@TRANCOUNT is incremented with each BEGIN TRAN and decremented with each COMMIT TRAN and set to zero by a ROLLBACK.

Also, given that one stored procedure can call another stored procedure, it is worth noting that a hierarchy of transactions may be created. However, it is also important to know that when a rollback occurs, all activity from the first or outer-most BEGIN TRANSACTION will be rolled back. So, although SQL Server allows a batch or series of stored procedures to create a set of nested transactions, the individual transaction declarations do not carry any scope and will not effect the behavior of a rollback. In the event of a commit, only the final commit will have any effect. That is, only a commit that is associated with a @@TRANCOUNT of 1 will conclude a transaction. If the commit occurs when the @@TRANCOUNT is greater than 1, it will be ignored; and if the @@TRANCOUNT is 0, the commit will generate an error that indicates that there is no matching begin transaction.

If you do need to limit the effect of a rollback, SQL Server provides the SAVE TRANSACTION statement. SAVE TRANSACTION will limit the effect of a rollback to the statements that have been executed following the SAVE. However, the rollback will still set the @@TRANCOUNT to 0 and the transaction will be concluded. So, another BEGIN TRAN statement will need to be executed in order to group subsequent statements into a new transaction.

The following example shows a stored procedure that processes a set of records periodically saving the records in case an error occurs:

```
CREATE PROCEDURE proc_order @order_num VARCHAR(6),
@order_err INT OUIPUT AS
-- Indicate start of transaction (Step 1)
BEGIN TRAN
    -- Process records for the order (Step 2)
    INSERT INTO ORDER
        (ORDER_NUM, ORDER_DATE) VALUES
        (@order_num,GETDATE())
    -- Declare local cursor variable
    DECLARE @line_items CURSOR
    -- Select order line items from pending order table
    SET @line_items =
      SELECT ITEM_CODE, ITEM_QTY FROM ORDER_PENDING
      WHERE ORDER_NUM = @order_num
    OPEN @line_items
    -- Loop through line items verifying and debiting inventory
    FETCH NEXT FROM @line_items
    WHILE @@FETCH_STATUS = 0
    BEGIN
        FETCH NEXT FROM @line_items
    END
-- Commit transaction since all items were processed successfully
-- (Step 3)
```

```
        RAN
        /der_err
    _err = 0
- End of procedure
```

Transaction Considerations

In most engineering tasks, competing design goals exist. If an auto engine needs more power, it needs to be bigger and heavier; if an auto needs more fuel efficiency, it needs to be lighter. So, power and fuel efficiency become competing design goals when building an automobile. (You could use better technology to improve power without the penalty of fuel efficiency, but you'd then face the choice of technology versus cost.) Engineers exist to analyze these competing design requirements and to produce the best solution. With databases, two competing design goals are consistency and concurrency.

Data consistency and concurrency

As mentioned previously, *consistency* refers to the state of the data in the system. All data should agree, and if transactions are used properly, the database ensures that all data will agree. *Concurrency* refers to the ability of multiple users to access the data at the same time. Why are these goals competing? To illustrate, two people call an airline from their cell phones moments apart to book an earlier flight home from New York to Atlanta. Both contact separate agents who each find that one seat is available on the next flight. Both people request the seat, and the dilemma begins. Either the database design can enforce consistency, and inform the slower agent that there is no seat available; or the database design can yield to concurrency and allow the slower agent to overbook. We all know which design option the airlines chose.

There are four types of problems that concurrency introduces:

♦ **Lost updates:** Lost updates occur when the results of one transaction are overwritten by the results of a second transaction.

♦ **Dirty reads:** Dirty reads occur when a transaction is allowed to read the uncommitted work of another transaction.

♦ **Non-repeatable reads:** Non-repeatable reads occur when one transaction reads some data, a second transaction updates the same data, and the first transaction reads the data again and finds that it has changed.

♦ **Phantom reads:** Phantom reads are similar to non-repeatable reads, except phantom reads refer to records that have been inserted or deleted between successive reads of a transaction.

Isolation levels

The solution to different concurrency problems is found by setting the isolation level of the transactions preformed on the database. The isolation level refers back to the isolated requirement of the ACID test, but to what degree do the transactions require isolation? The answer is dependent on the type of concurrency problems that can be tolerated by the desired database solution. Table 4-4 lists isolation levels and their characteristics, which are covered in more detail in the following sections.

TABLE 4-4 ISOLATION LEVEL VERSUS CONCURRENCY ERRORS

Transaction Isolation Level	Allow Dirty Reads	Allow Non-Repeatable Reads	Allow Phantom Reads
READ UNCOMMITTED	Yes	Yes	Yes
READ COMMITTED	No	Yes	Yes
REPEATABLE READ	No	No	Yes (7.0)
SERIALIZABLE	No	No	No

READ UNCOMMITTED

This is the lowest level of transaction isolation. At this level, one transaction may see the uncommitted work of another transaction. This could result in any of the possible concurrency errors. However, this isolation level is one step below the default isolation level and the potential for dirty reads will only exist if this isolation level is set explicitly.

READ COMMITTED

READ COMMITTED is the default isolation level for SQL Server. At this level, you may encounter non-repeatable or phantom reads but never dirty reads. One transaction will only see the committed work of other transactions, but it does not preclude the possibility that the other transactions will commit changes in the midst of another transaction.

REPEATABLE READ

To ensure that a transaction will be isolated from the committed edits of another transaction, the read repeatable isolation level is required. This will not eliminate phantom reads, but it will ensure that once a transaction begins, the data in any row that exists at the start of the transaction will remain the same until the end of the transaction.

SERIALIZABLE

This is the highest level of transaction isolation. When this level of isolation is set, all transactions will occur as if they were performed in a serialized manner, one after the other. None of the concurrency problems will occur.

Scalability and performance implications

With a brief introduction to transaction isolation levels, it might seem that SERI-ALIZABLE is the best because it eliminates all the concurrency problems. To be clear, remember that all the problems caused by concurrent access are forms of inconsistent data; as discussed in the beginning of this chapter, concurrency and consistency are competing goals. So, if read serializable achieves the most consistency through the highest level of transaction isolation, it has done so at the expense of concurrency. The reason for this tradeoff is resource locking.

Resource locking is the mechanism for enforcing transaction isolation. Resource locking makes some database resource, from an individual record to the whole database, unavailable to any user who does not have a lock on the resource. As the transaction isolation level increases, the need for more and stronger locks increases. With the increase in the number and strictness of the locks, it's more likely a resource will be unavailable to another transaction, thereby negatively affecting concurrency.

Resource locking not only affects concurrency but also affects performance. The more locks the database has to maintain and enforce, the more performance will suffer. This is why read serializable is not the hands-down winner of the isolation-level game. Although it solves one set of problems, it creates another set that may, depending on circumstance, be worse. So, for each transaction isolation level, it is not sufficient to consider only the impact on concurrency; it is also necessary to consider the impact on database performance with performance and concurrency joining together to produce a measure of scalability.

To understand the impact of locking, it is important to know that locking occurs at different levels within a database. At each level, the relative impact on isolation, concurrency, and performance is altered. So, each locking level presents both decisions and opportunities for solving the problems of scalability. The six most common and important locks to understand are row, page, table, index-range, meta-data, and database locks. Many large databases also support intent locks, but this discussion will focus on the behavior and impact of these six locks:

- ◆ **Row lock:** A row lock provides the most granularity by locking only the individual rows within a table that are needed by a transaction.

- ◆ **Page lock:** A page lock isolates a whole page of data within a table. The page size can be adjusted, but the default for MS SQL 2000 is 8K.

- ◆ **Table lock:** A table lock restricts access to the whole table when it is involved in a transaction.

◆ **Index range lock:** This lock is applied against the index on a table and prevents updates that would impact the index for a given range including inserts and deletions.

◆ **Meta-data lock:** A meta-data lock restricts access to meta-data resources within a database, preventing updates to items such as data structures and index structures.

◆ **Database lock:** A database lock restricts access to a whole database.

When considering which locking strategy to implement, it is essential to determine how the database and the data in given tables will be used. For instance, if a database is used for data mining, and it is only updated once a day by a nightly data feed; an exclusive database lock may be entirely appropriate. So, by locking the database to all users while the nightly feed is running, the performance of the nightly feed will be optimized, and during the day, no locking will be required because the users only perform select operations and thus their access times will be optimized.

Conversely, if a call center uses a customer relationship management application to update customer information, row-level locking of customer records is probably most appropriate. With row-level locking, each operator will only impact the record of the customer with which they are working and will avoid impacting any other operator. However, there may be additional performance requirements for the database server if the database and number of operators is large because the database will have to maintain a large number of locked rows.

Although these two scenarios provide clear choices, most database applications are more complex and thus create more complicated choices. Nevertheless, most issues can be resolved through skillful database design that evaluates locking constraints prior to implementation. With that goal in mind, the following strategies should be implemented during the design phase:

◆ **Try to isolate frequently browsed data from frequently updated data.** For instance, if you need to track the last time you had contact with a customer in a customer relationship management system, it is often better to keep that timestamp data and contact information separate from basic customer information such as the customer name. Customer names are frequently browsed, and if the system must regularly lock records with customer names to update contact timestamps and lock records to browse consistent data, there will be a performance handicap.

◆ **Make sure your data has adequate granularity.** Remember the example from Chapter 3 where a manufacturing facility needed to track the number of available parts in different part bins. By adding plant and location fields to the BINS table, the granularity of the updated data, the number of parts, increased. This meant that it was less likely that two processes would need to update the same row at the same time, thus reducing the likelihood of a blocking delay.

◆ **Use compensating transactions with an additional table.** The most common example of this idea is in banking. Banks have customers who have balances, but the balance is a calculated value equal to the sum of the credits minus the sum of the debits. So, every time a customer has a transaction, the customer record does not have to be locked to update the balance. The only requirement is that a credit or debit be added to the customer's transaction history.

◆ **Separate data that needs to be current from data that is primarily historical.** On the macro scale, this refers to separating OLTP from OLAP as mentioned in Chapter 3. However, this idea can also be useful on a smaller scale and is similar to the idea of granularity. If data becomes less important or needed over time, try to have an indicator that allows the most relevant data to be easily grouped and queried.

◆ **Be aware of operations that require high levels of isolation.** If an operation does need to be performed at a serializable level of isolation, determine what procedures will be impacted. Then work to limit the impact locks will have by implementing one of the first two suggestions, or additionally, by performing the operations as a batch during times of low user activity. Finally, always use the lowest required level of transaction isolation. The lower the isolation level, the less the need for locks. The fewer locks, the fewer lock associated problems will exist.

Another important consideration with transactions is the unfortunate possibility of deadlocks. *Deadlocks* are possible in any system that supports concurrent processes, and they occur when a process has to wait for a resource held by another process that is itself waiting for a resource held by the first process. Neither process can proceed and the result is deadlock. In the database world, this situation can occur with concurrent transactions. For instance, Transaction 1 needs to lock Records A and B and gets a lock on A. Meanwhile, Transaction 2 needs to lock Records A and B and gets a lock on B. Because neither transaction can lock all the required records, neither transaction can complete and release the lock the other transaction needs. The result is deadlock.

In fact, in most systems, one or both transactions would eventually time out allowing processing to continue, but that is a huge performance penalty. The time-out period may easily be one or two orders of magnitude longer than the time required to complete the transaction. It is therefore worthwhile to follow some guidelines to avoid deadlocking transactions:

◆ **Use the lowest level of isolation required by the application.** Remember that locking is a byproduct of isolation enforcement, so if the current isolation level doesn't require a lock, then the problem will be avoided.

◆ **Keep transactions short.** If a lock is required, the longer the transaction runs, the more likely resource contention will be a problem and deadlocking along with it.

◆ **Access objects in the same order.** In a deadlock scenario, two transactions get locks on resources needed by each other. If the transactions locked resources in the same order, the second transaction would be blocked from establishing any locks because the first resource it required would already be locked. Also, in the situation where the second transaction uses a subset of the resources of the first transaction, the second transaction may temporarily block the first, but it would still complete and then allow the first to complete. Accessing objects in the same order requires team standards to managing transactions, but that in itself will provide benefits to the project.

Microsoft SQL Server and other major databases employ a feature known as *automatic lock escalation*. Automatic lock escalation prevents the overuse of a low-level lock when a higher-level lock would be more efficient. For instance, a user needs to update a large number of records in a table that implements row-level locking. Instead of individually locking several hundred rows of data, the database would instead use a page-level lock, or if numerous pages would be affected, a table lock. By implementing automatic lock escalation, Microsoft frees the DBA from having to manually tune the lock escalation level.

There are three modes for implementing transactions in MS SQL Server:

◆ **Autocommit:** Autocommit is the default mode for SQL Server, and each transaction is automatically committed when it is successful and rolled back when it isn't.

◆ **Explicit:** With explicit mode, the structure and results of the transaction are determined by the developer. So, the developer must declare the start of a transaction, and after executing one or more SQL statements, the developer must commit or roll back the transaction. Following the commit or rollback, SQL Server will return to the previously defined mode of operation.

◆ **Implicit:** When using implicit mode, SQL Server automatically opens a transaction, but the developer must terminate the transaction expressly with a commit or rollback. Caution must be exercised with implicit transactions, or a transaction may accidentally be left open and uncommitted because a developer did not expect a transaction to be opened or assumed that it would be committed.

When using transactions, there are some common guidelines to follow:

◆ **Avoid user interaction.** If you start a transaction and then prompt the user for information required to complete the transaction, the transaction could be open for a long time, especially if the user just left on vacation. If information is required of the user, gather it before opening a transaction so that it will be available as soon as it's needed.

◆ **Along the same line of thought, transactions should be as short as possible.** Even if user interaction is not required, creating a transaction that affects large amounts of data over an extended period of time will also be detrimental to concurrency and performance. If large batch operations are required, break them into a series of more manageable transactions.

◆ **Avoid mixing API and Transact SQL transaction calls.** If you're using an API to call a stored procedure, you can control the start and end of the transaction from either location, so pick one location and use it consistently.

Database-Specific Transaction Processing Issues

This chapter has been written with a focus on Microsoft SQL Server 2000, and how it handles transactions using either transact-SQL or the `OleDbTransaction` object available in .NET. So, a brief overview of the differences between these methods of transaction management on this system and some other major database systems and other common methods of transaction management is in order.

Microsoft SQL Server

Although everyone aspires to run the latest and greatest software, for a myriad of practical reasons not everyone does. So, it is worth noting a few implementation changes in locking and isolation levels that Microsoft has made over the last three major releases: 6.0, 7.0, and 2000.

The most notable change occurred between 6.0 and 7.0. With the release of 6.5, Microsoft supplied the distributed transaction coordinator, allowing SQL Server to support distributed transactions. From 6.5 to 7.0, Microsoft added support for the repeatable read isolation level. In versions prior to 7.0, this isolation level was escalated to serializable, which has a much greater impact on concurrency. In addition, 7.0 introduced row-level locking, which improved lock granularity over the page-level locks used in prior versions. SQL Server 2000 improves on the row locking scenario with dynamic locking that optimizes the lock level depending on the type of query being executed.

Oracle

Oracle is currently the most widely used enterprise-level database system in the world, and it has a distinct transaction– and isolation-level implementation. Oracle implements three isolation levels instead of the four ANSI levels, and only two of the three levels correspond to the ANSI specifications. This is mentioned merely to provide reference, not to make judgments about Oracle's level of ANSI compliance.

Remember that the point of isolation levels is to enable the optimal balance between consistency and concurrency among transactions. So, with three isolation levels and a number of other data-access and locking strategies, Oracle believes it can always provide that optimal balance for applications. After all, if market share is any indication, Oracle is right.

The three transaction modes Oracle supports are READ COMMITTED, SERIALIZABLE, and READ ONLY. As shown in Table 4-5, the first two isolation levels correspond to their ANSI counterparts and address the same problems. The READ ONLY isolation level is unique to Oracle. The READ ONLY isolation level does not allow transactions that contain INSERT, UPDATE, or DELETE statements. (The use for this transaction level is explained later.)

TABLE 4-5 ANSI ISOLATION LEVEL COMPARISON TO ORACLE ISOLATION LEVELS

ANSI Isolation Level	Oracle Isolation Level
READ UNCOMMITTED	N/A
READ COMMITTED	READ COMMITTED
REPEATABLE READ	N/A
SERIALIZABLE	SERIALIZABLE
N/A	READ ONLY

Oracle provides read consistency at two levels: statement-level read consistency and transaction-level read consistency. Statement-level read consistency is always maintained by means of a data snapshot. When a select statement is run in Oracle its results reflect a snapshot of the data at the time the statement was executed. So, only data that was committed at the time the statement was executed will be seen in the result set. If the data change while Oracle is executing a query, the database system will recognize that the data was altered after statement execution began and will look into its rollback segments to retrieve the data required for a consistent result set.

However, this can cause a problem. In the event that the query is long running and numerous changes have been made to the data, the required older data may not be available in the rollback segment. If this occurs, Oracle will issue a "Snapshot Too Old" error. This error can be handled either by increasing the size of the rollback segment or by running the query when less update activity is occurring.

As previously mentioned, Oracle also provided transaction-level read consistency. This level of read consistency is only available to SERIALIZABLE or READ ONLY transactions and works in a manner similar to the statement-level read consistency. But at the transaction level, all data is consistent with the moment in time that the transaction began as opposed to the execution time of individual statements.

This consistency is qualified by the fact that statements within the transaction will see changes made by other statements within the transaction.

Just as individual statements require sufficient rollback segments to guarantee consistent data, serialized transactions also require sufficient historical data to determine what data is serializable. The INITRANS parameter determines how much transaction history is available to a block of data and it may require adjustment on systems with high activity.

Following along with Oracle's transaction management strategy are two more important facts. By default, Oracle makes use of row-level locking and data reads never block data writes. In conjunction with the default locking level, Oracle does not perform either lock conversion or lock escalation. Both of these measures work to reduce the chance of a deadlock. When Oracle locks a row, it uses the most stringent locking available and therefore does not have to worry about a resource conflict that could be caused by a lower level lock needing to be converted to a higher level lock. Similarly, it eliminates the conflict potential of changing a number of row locks into a table lock that could happen with lock escalation.

This fact that data reads do not block data writes is particularly important. Other databases achieve serialized transactions by preventing access to any data a serialized transaction is using even if the data in question is only being read. This is pessimistic locking. Oracle presents an optimistic approach, allowing data to be written even if a serialized transaction is already reading the same data.

Of course, this could cause a problem if one transaction changes the same data that another serialized transaction needs to change. In this event, Oracle throws an error: "Cannot serialize access for this transaction." The developer must be prepared to handle this error either by rolling back the transaction or by ensuring that an alternate but equally valid set of statements is executed in light of the error.

Now we'll briefly return to the idea of the READ ONLY isolation level. Given that the READ ONLY isolation level provides transaction-level consistency and that data reads in Oracle do not block data writes, the READ ONLY isolation level can be seen as a useful tool. It can allow a developer to look at data consistent across multiple statements without fear of hampering transactional concurrency.

Developers have access to two commands to alter the current transaction isolation level. The first is SET TRANSACTION ISOLATION LEVEL, which alters the isolation level for a single transaction. If the developer needs to change the default behavior for the current connection, the ALTER SESSION command may be used.

DB/2

IBM's DB/2 is number two in the enterprise database arena. DB/2 is available on a wide range of platforms from microcomputers to mainframes. Although there are important differences between the micro server and AS/400 implementations, those will be covered in more depth in Chapter 12, which focuses strictly on DB/2. Here the focus remains on the micro server implementation of transaction isolation levels.

First, and not surprising, is the fact that IBM has its own verbiage for the ANS isolation levels. Table 4-6 matches the IsolationLevel values for the

OleDbTransaction object to the DB/2 isolation level. With the exceptions of the Unspecified and Chaos values, Microsoft uses the terminology of the ANSI/SQL standard. So, in effect, Table 4-6 matches the ANSI terminology to the IBM terminology. The most important item to note is that REPEATABLE READ in DB2 provides the same level of isolation as ANSI's SERIALIZABLE and does not correspond to ANSI's REAPEATABLE READ, as you might have concluded.

TABLE 4-6 OLEDBTRANSACTION OBJECT ISOLATION LEVEL COMPARISON TO DB/2
ISOLATION LEVELS

OleDbTransaction Isolation Level	DB2 Isolation Level
Unspecified	N/A
Chaos	UNCOMMITTED READ
ReadCommitted	CURSOR STABILITY
ReadUncommitted	UNCOMMITTED READ
RepeatableRead	READ STABILITY
Serializable	REPEATABLE READ

Also, the locking strategy used by the REPEATABLE READ isolation level is worth noting. If a transaction operating at the REPEATABLE READ isolation level scans a set of records in search of a subset of qualifying records, every record scanned will be locked for modification, not just the records that satisfy the match. So, it is important to consider the impact of this high degree of isolation prior to database implementation to avoid serious concurrency headaches.

By default, DB/2 runs at the CURSOR STABILITY isolation level which correlates with SQL Server's default of READ COMMITTED. Also, in a manner similar to the other database management systems, DB/2 provides the CHANGE ISOLATION LEVEL command to allow the user to set the desired isolation level for a batch or stored procedure operation.

MySQL

Unfortunately, transactions are not supported by all databases. MySQL, a popular open source database, does not provide support for transactions in all its configurations, and the differences are too numerous to cover here. Chapter 13 covers the topic fully.

Summary

Transactions are the crux of database scalability. The first and best way to ensure that your database will scale to handle large numbers of transactions is through solid design. Understanding how different data will be accessed and used is the first step in the decision-making process. After that understanding has been achieved, further decisions about isolation levels and locking strategies can be made reliably. Conversely, if that understanding is not achieved, the scalability of the database will only be discovered through a painful trial-and-error process at each point where the database is choked by data contention or user connections. So, build on the understanding of data usage with appropriate transaction isolation, strategic locking, and fast, effective stored procedures, and the result should be a highly scalable system.

Chapter 5

ADO.NET

IN THIS CHAPTER

◆ Understanding data access with `System.Data.Sql`, `System.Data.OleDb`, and `Microsoft.Data.Odbc`

◆ Selecting data

◆ Inserting, updating, and deleting data

◆ Identifying data types

COMPANIES LIVE AND RUN on the data that they have collected over the lifetime of their businesses. Sales, marketing, engineering, and manufacturing organizations create large amounts of data. Those data are stored into a number of different systems and environments (Oracle, SQL Server, DB/2, Access, Excel spreadsheets) and on a number of different platforms (Windows, Unix, AS/400, Mainframe). Software applications have been developed to access these data to allow users to make business decisions going forward.

Initially, applications were packaged as single-tier applications. Data was stored in the same environment as the front-end applications. You see these types of applications all the time. They're viewed through a 5250 or 3270 screen, or an Access/DBase front-end talking to data stored in that same database, or an Excel spreadsheet, or any number of other types of applications. As data requirements grew and the PC-based front-end started to have enough memory, processing power, and stability, client/server applications were developed to take advantage of the added benefits of having an intelligent client. Client/server is a mechanism for having an intelligent, protocol-based conversation between a system requesting something (the client) and a system responding to that request (the server). These applications typically run through some sort of database communications standard (like Open Database Connectivity, or ODBC) or some type of database specific communications protocol to send operations to a database and retrieve results. Within a client/server application, business logic tends to reside within the database as stored procedures, or in the client application as functions and subroutines, or as some combination of the two.

These applications were fine, until two new requirements hit the scene: large numbers of users, typified by a Web site displaying products and allowing users to order those products, and the need for multiple types of front-ends to view data. Databases are meant to handle data. They are not very efficient when it comes to managing a large number of open connections, because this tends to cause the database to bog down. Applications with multiple types of front-ends require that business logic not be placed within the front-end application but within some type of middle-tier business component. These two items lead you to a middle tier that can process business rules and manage database connections. This is commonly called the *3-Tier* (or *N-Tier*) world of application development. Microsoft has developed a product that was initially called Microsoft Transaction Server (MTS) and is now referred to as COM+ Services. COM+ Services manages database connections, manages distributed transactions, and allows applications to call custom-developed business logic in a clean package. The biggest problem that these products have is that they're tightly coupled to each other. They become very cranky when there is any type of communications problem between tiers. These tiers must be configured correctly to communicate with each other and they must be of the appropriate version.

Distributed and Web-based applications are no exception. In a distributed scenario, however, things are a bit more complicated due to the possibility of different hardware and software platforms or object models. Despite all this, data are just data and need to be exchanged and processed just about everywhere.

Now we're starting to see some new requirements. Applications must be loosely coupled. Applications that require guaranteed connectivity will not perform reliably over the Internet. Integration with other platforms is an absolute requirement in this day and age. You must be able to share information with business partners and customers no matter what platform your customers and business partners are using. These applications must have XML integration and be able to recover when communicating in an environment that may not have guaranteed availability, such as the Internet. ADO.NET is designed to assist in meeting this new requirement and as a simpler interface with fewer options than ADO. In addition, ADO.NET's integration with standard XML is better than Classic ADO 2.x's implementation, which is based on the XML Data Reduced (XDR) standard and Classic ADO 2.x's internal binary format.

A Quick Review of Terms

First, you need to be familiar with the terminology of ADO.NET in order for the discussion to proceed. The following list is a great place to start:

- ◆ **Fat server application:** A fat server application is one in which minimal processing occurs on the client. Most, if not all, processing is handled on the server, and communication with the user is handled through some type of terminal. This can be seen as a 3270, 5250, or other terminal-style application. All processing occurs on the remote server, and the user merely gets updated screen information.

- ◆ **Fat client application:** A fat client application is one in which most, if not all, processing is handled on the client. Think of a fat client as a

Microsoft Access application that contains the user interface information, the business logic, and the database within the same file. Typically, these applications will not run successfully with more than a few active users at any one moment.

◆ **Client/server application:** A client/server application is one in which a client application communicates through some protocol and has an intelligent conversation with another system that provides a service. Client/server applications may have their business logic stored within the client application or the server application. Typically, client/server applications are written in some type of Rapid Application Development (RAD) front-end tool, such as Visual Basic or Delphi. These applications typically communicate through some type of communications layer, such as ODBC or OLE-DB to a back-end database.

◆ **Browser/server applications:** Browser/server applications are applications in which the end client application is a web browser. Between the browser and the system providing the service is some type of web server, such as IIS.

◆ **Cursor:** A cursor is a set of data that is storing a result. In SQL Server 2000, a cursor is a mechanism for storing a set of rows.

◆ **Server-side cursor:** A server-side cursor is one in which the back-end server, typically a database, is required to store the results until those data are requested by the client application. Within ADO and SQL Server 2000, a server-side cursor containing data will only send that data as the client asks for the individual rows. This is the default setting for ADO. Within ADO.NET, there is currently no concept of an updateable server-side cursor. There are rumors that there will be updateable server-side cursor support in the `System.Data.SqlClient` namespace, however, there is no hard data with which to back up that information at this time.

◆ **Client-side cursor:** A client-side cursor is one in which all the results are transferred from the back-end server to the client application. The client system holds the results in some type of data storage engine. Within Classic ADO 2.x and SQL Server 2000, a client-side cursor can be created by setting the ADO recordset's `ActiveConnection`'s `CursorLocation` property to adUseClient before opening the recordset. Within ADO.NET, a client-side cursor is currently the default (and only) location for data storage.

◆ **Client-side disconnected cursor:** A client-side disconnected cursor is a client-side cursor in which the connection to the server has been cut. The data at the client are still in a form that can be used by an application. It is perfectly fine for the data to be disconnected and modified, and then for an update to be sent back to the server in a batch update.

◆ **Data island:** A data island is another form of a client-side disconnected cursor. In this scenario, data have been sent from a back-end server, through a middle processing tier, such as IIS, and to a front-end application, typically a web browser. The data are stored at the front end in XML.

What Is ADO.NET?

ADO.NET is the native data-access technology for the .NET environment. It is not a replacement for COM-based ADO — it is the latest implementation of Microsoft's data-access strategy that is called Universal Data Access (UDA). Microsoft's data strategies began with Open Database Connectivity (ODBC) and have led us into:

◆ **Data Access Objects (DAO),** which was typically used for connecting to file-based data sources, such as Access databases

◆ **Remote Data Objects (RDO),** which was Microsoft's first data-access technology to effectively work with client/server databases

◆ **ActiveX Data Objects (ADO),** which was a technology designed to provide access to databases through IIS and grew into the dominant way to access data in COM

◆ **OLE-DB,** which started as a refinement of ODBC and has grown into a replacement of ODBC

ADO.NET is a refinement of ADO. ADO.NET adds several new objects over Classic ADO 2.x. At the same time, ADO.NET removes a number of Classic ADO 2.x's options that caused some confusion among programmers, and at the same time ADO.NET allows for a streamlined system for accessing data. For example, ADO.NET does not support server-side updateable cursors. Server-side cursors are sometime misused by programmers. By minimizing what programmers can do during data access, Microsoft can focus on making the options that are left highly optimized and better performing. In the following sections, we take a look at the environment.

Managed providers

Managed Providers, also known as Data Providers, are the .NET native mechanism for database operations (select, insert, update, and delete). Data Providers consist of five classes: Connection, Command, DataReader, DataSet, and Parameter. At this point, there are two Data Providers included in the .NET Framework: the SQL Data Provider (`System.Data.SQLClient`) and the OLE-DB Data Provider (`System.Data.OleDb`). Support for ODBC is not included within the .NET Framework's RTM version. However, support for ODBC is included within a download from Microsoft's Web site. This download is an ODBC Data Provider (`Microsoft.`

`Data.Odbc`). At this point in time, Data Providers are not meant to be a replacement for OLE-DB or ODBC. OLE-DB and ODBC drivers provide much more functionality than Data Providers, such as ADOX functionality to read and write database structure information. Data Providers are optimized for data operations (select, insert, update, delete, and so on) and provide very little additional functionality.

The SQL Data Provider allows ADO.NET to communicate with a SQL Server 7.0 or later database. The SQL Data Provider uses a SQL Server protocol called *tabular data stream* (TDS) to communicate with SQL Server. TDS is an application-level protocol that is specific to SQL Server. TDS packets are encapsulated within network communication packets. The SQL Data Provider is written entirely within the .NET Framework. It does not use OLE DB, ADO, or ODBC. It does not go through any type of layer outside of the .NET Framework or the runtime callable wrapper used to communicate with COM objects. Because of this, the SQL Data Provider has the potential to run faster than using the ADO Data Provider or classic ADO when communicating with SQL Server 7.0 or later.

The OLE-DB and ODBC Data Providers are designed to communicate with databases that do not have a Data Provider optimized for that database. They should work with most OLE-DB and ODBC providers to provide an interface from an application using ADO.NET to your database.

 For most methods in ADO.NET, there are SQL, OLE-DB, and ODBC counterparts. As more Data Providers are added, there most likely will be more namespaces that programmers will be required to explicitly support. This is unlike ADO, where the connection string that is used is basically the only difference between changing code to support different databases, assuming that the SQL used is portable between the different databases.

First, we'll go through the basic steps of getting data before we dive into the specifics. These examples will use SQL Server 2000 as the back-end database. Connections will be made through the SQL Server Data Providers along with the more generic OLE-DB and ODBC Data Providers. The example database is given in the code examples that follow.

Establishing a database connection

To connect to a specific data store, you must use either the `SqlConnection`, `OleDbConnection, or OdbcConnection` object. The `SqlConnection` connects to Microsoft SQL Server databases. The `OleDbConnection` allows you to establish a connection through an OLE-DB provider. The `OdbcConnection` object allows a program to establish a connection through an ODBC driver. These connection objects are meant to serve as a bridge between an application and the data that the application is requesting.

To use the Data Providers that come with the .NET Framework, you need to include the following namespaces within your solutions:

◆ **SQL Data Provider:** `System.Data.SqlClient`

◆ **ODBC Data Provider.** `Microsoft.Data.Odbc`

◆ **OLE-DB Data Provider:** `System.Data.OleDb`

The following code demonstrates creating and opening a connection to a SQL Server Database using Visual Basic .NET:

```
Dim strCn As String = "server=your server name;uid=appropiate
userid;pwd=appropiate password;database=your database name"
Dim cnSQL As SQLConnection = New SQLConnection(strCn)
cnSQL.Open() 'The application now has an open connection
'               to the database.
```

The following code demonstrates creating and opening a connection to a SQL Server Database using C#:

```
string strCn = "server=your server name;uid=appropiate
userid;pwd=appropiate password;database=your database name";
SQLConnection cnSQL = new SQLConnection(strCn);
cnSQL.Open(); //The application now has an open
//               connection to the database.
```

The `OleDbConnection` and `OdbcConnection` objects allow a program to connect to databases that do not have a Data Provider but do have an OLE-DB or ODBC driver. We have successfully connected with the following OLE-DB and ODBC drivers while using MDAC 2.7 on Windows2000:

◆ Microsoft Driver for Oracle

◆ Oracle OLE-DB Driver 8.1.7.1 and 9i

◆ Microsoft OLE-DB Driver for SQL Server

◆ IBM DB/2 OLE-DB Driver

◆ MySQL ODBC Driver

In addition, Microsoft has successfully verified that the following drivers run under .NET:

◆ Jet OLE-DB Provider (JOLT)

◆ SQL Server ODBC Driver via OLE-DB for ODBC Provider (MSDASQL/SQLServer ODBC)

♦ Jet ODBC Driver via OLE-DB Provider for ODBC Provider (MSDASQL/Jet ODBC)

The following code shows how to create and open a connection with `OleDbConnection` using Visual Basic .NET:

```
Dim strCn As String = "Provider=OLEDB Provider;server=your server
name;uid=appropiate userid;pwd=appropiate password;database=your
database name"
Dim oledbCn As OleDbConnection = New OleDbConnection(strCn)
oledbCn.Open()
. . . . . . . . . . . . . . .
oledbCn.Close()
oledbCn = Nothing
```

The following code shows how to create and open a connection with `OleDbConnection` using C#:

```
string strCN = "Provider=OLEDB Provider;server=your server
name;uid=appropiate userid;pwd=appropiate password;database=your
database name";
OleDbConnection oledbCn = new OleDbConnection(strCN);
oledbCn.Open();
. . . . . . . . . . . . . . .
oledbCn.Close();
oledbCn = null;
```

The `OleDbConnection` and `SqlConnection` objects provide many of the properties that you are accustomed to with ADO, such as transaction control and connection timeouts.

COMMON OLE-DB PROVIDERS

Some of the more common OLE-DB providers are:

♦ **SqlOleDb:** Connects to Microsoft SQL Server.

♦ **MSDAOra:** The Microsoft driver for Oracle. This driver only supports Oracle 7 datatypes and features. It will connect to Oracle 8i and 9i but does not support the Oracle 8i and 9i featuresets.

♦ **OraOleDb.Oracle:** The Oracle OLE-DB driver for Oracle. OraOleDb supports Oracle 7, 8, 8i, and 9i datatypes.

♦ **IBMDA400:** The IBM driver to communicate with the native database on the AS/400.

♦ **IBMDADB2:** The IBM driver designed to communicate with DB/2.

◆ MSDASQL: The Microsoft OLE-DB driver for ODBC. This driver is used by Classic ADO 2.x to allow ODBC drivers to work. This driver is not supported within ADO.NET. For those databases that do not have a Data Provider or OLE-DB provider, the `Microsoft.Data.Odbc` namespace and objects should be used.

CONNECTION STRING FORMAT: ODBCCONNECTION

For the ODBC Data Provider, the connection string format is identical to the connection format used when calling Classic ADO 2.x and an ODBC driver to connect to a database. The connection string may contain an ODBC data source name (DSN) or a DSN-less connection string.

CONNECTION STRING FORMAT: OLEDBCONNECTION

For the OLE-DB Data Provider, the connection string format is identical to the connection string format used in ADO. In most of the examples in this chapter, we are using SQL Server 2000 for our database. If we were using Oracle, DB/2, or another database, these parameters would be different.

CONNECTION STRING FORMAT: SQLCONNECTION

The SQL Data Provider supports a connection string format that is a similar to the ADO connection string format. The basics of the format are the same as for the OLE-DB Data Provider and for ADO minus the `Provider=OleDb Provider Name` parameter.

Having established a connection, you next need to be able to execute statements against the database. The simplest and most direct route for this is through the Command objects. The Command object is used to insert, update, and delete data from a database table. In the code that follows, note that the connection objects were previously defined and not listed for brevity.

The following code demonstrates how to establish a connection with OLE-DB and Visual Basic .NET:

```
Dim strSql As String = "database command"
Dim cmOleDb As OleDbCommand = New OleDbCommand(strSql, oledbCn)
```

The following code demonstrates how to establish a connection with OLE-DB and C#:

```
string strSql = "database command";
OleDbCommand cmOleDb = new OleDbCommand(strSql, oledbCn);
```

The following code demonstrates how to establish a connection with SQLCommand and Visual Basic .NET:

```
Dim strSql As String = "database command"
Dim cmSQL As SQLCommand = New SQLCommand(strSql, cnSQL)
```

The following code demonstrates how to establish a connection with SQLCommand and C#:

```
string strSql = "database command";
SQLCommand cmSQL = new SQLCommand(strSql, cnSQL);
```

Executing a command against the database

At this point, a connection and command have been created. The next thing to do is to execute this command against the database. Here things become a little different, depending on whether a command that returns records is being returned and what you plan on doing with those returned records. Here are the three scenarios to work with:

- ◆ **Returning data that are disconnected from the database.** The data are stored in a DataSet. In ADO, this would be termed a client-side disconnected recordset.

- ◆ **Returning data that you will scroll through and use, while not disconnecting from the database.** The data are stored in a datareader. In ADO, this would be termed a server-side recordset.

- ◆ **Execute a command against the database that does not return data.** In Classic ADO 2.x, this would be equivalent to the execute method of the connection object or using a command object to call a stored procedure and setting it not to return any records.

In the following sections, we look at some examples as to how we get data from a database and execute commands that do not return any data, such as insert, update, and delete.

DATASET

A *DataSet* is merely a subset of data. It contains many of the features of a class-relational database. Think of a DataSet as an in-memory database or subset of data from a datasource, such as SQL Server. It consists of the following:

- ◆ **DataTables,** which map fairly well to a table in a database.

- ◆ **DataRelations,** which are a mechanism to manage relationships between tables in a standard relational database.

- ◆ **Constraints,** which manage the data values that are allowed into a column.

- ◆ **Dataviews,** which allow you to view data in the databases in a predefined way, much like a view. For example, a dataview could represent the data in a customer table and the orders for those customers.

◆ **Datarows,** which represent the rows of data within a DataTable.

◆ **Datacolumns,** which represent the columns of data within a DataTable.

Do not confuse a DataSet with a Classic ADO 2.x recordset. An ADO recordset is usually the result of a query to one or more tables in a database. A DataSet is a subset of data within a relational database. For example, let's assume that you had a customer table and a product order table. The customer's table holds information about your customers, and the product order table holds information about orders that a customer has made. How would you go about getting information about a customer? With a recordset, you could run a query that joins the customers table and the product order table. The problem with this is that, in order to get the information for one customer, you must join the two tables. Although joining the tables is not necessarily a bad thing, you are moving data out of its original format, because you are moving data from two tables and pushing it into one recordset. A DataSet allows you to have the same logical design as your permanent database and to use the same type of logic.

There is a larger problem with Classic ADO 2.x that ADO.NET attempts to solve: interoperability. As our applications have grown and are now available to a variety of business partners and organizations that we could not have dreamed possible a few years ago, being able to communicate without mandating the systems that partners use is an absolute requirement. To solve the job of interchanging data, a standard called the Extensible Markup Language (XML) was created.

Over the last couple of years, use of XML over HTTP has skyrocketed. Unfortunately, the existing ADO standard that exists in the Microsoft world does not fully address XML. The existing COM-based ADO stores data in an internal binary format. XML support has been built on top of ADO, but it uses an earlier XML standard called XML Data Reduced (XDR), which did not gain widespread support. ADO.NET provides much better support for XML than its predecessor did. ADO.NET's internal data storage format is XML.

In additional to interoperability, there are several other changes to ADO.NET from ADO:

◆ **Type:** Because Classic ADO 2.x must work with several different languages and environments, including VBScript and JScript, which do not support datatypes, all ADO fields are output as variants. Because ADO.NET does not have to work in a typeless environment, ADO.NET fields are stored as a specific datatype.

◆ **Record position:** ADO has the concept of a current record; ADO.NET does not have that concept. Instead, the rows of a DataTable are a collection.

The following code shows how to create a DataSet using OLE-DB and Visual Basic .NET:

```
DataSetDim strSql As String = "SELECT * FROM tableName"
Dim oledbDSA as New OleDbDataAdapter( strSql, oledbCn)
```

```
Dim dsData as New DataSet()
oledbDSA.Fill( dsData, "DataTable name" )
```

The following code shows how to create a DataSet using OLE-DB and C#:

```
string strSql = "SELECT * FROM tableName"
OleDbDataAdapter oledbDA = new OleDbDataAdapter(strSql,
oledbCnoledbCn);
DataSet dsData = new DataSet();
oledbDA.Fill(dsData, "DataTable name" );
```

The following code shows how to create a DataSet using SQL and Visual Basic .NET:

```
DataSetDim strSql As String = "SELECT * FROM tableName"
Dim sqlDA as New SQLDataAdapter( strSql, sqlCn)
Dim dsData as New DataSet()
sqlDA.Fill( dsData, "DataTable name" )
```

The following code shows how to create a DataSet using SQL and C#:

```
string strSql = "SELECT * FROM tableName";
SQLDataAdapter sqlDA = new SQLDataAdapter(strSql, sqlCn);
DataSet dsData = new DataSet();
sqlDSA.Fill(dsData, "DataTable name" );
```

DATAREADER

A DataReader is a forward-only, read-only stream of data. Data is stored on the server until they are requested by the client. Only a set number of records are retrieved at a time; this keeps the memory utilization of a DataReader solution at a minimum. A DataReader stores data within a cursor structure within the database and that connection must be left open while the data is being read from the database. Under load, this can cause a large number of connections to build up. A large number of active connections can potentially slow down the database server. It's not that a DataReader is a bad object; it's just that, as the programmer, you need to be aware of this potential problem. Note the "out" used in C#; this is because the DataReader is passed into the Command .Execute() method and then passed back, but not as a return value.

The following code shows how to create a DataReader using OLE-DB and Visual Basic .NET:

```
Dim oledbDr As OleDbDataReader
oledbDr = cmADO.Execute()
while ( oledbDr.Read() )
'perform operations
```

```
end while
oledbDr.Close()
'Not necessary to set the object to Nothing
'Garbage collection should handle it.
'Old habits die hard.
oledbDr = Nothing
```

The following code shows how to create a DataReader using OLE-DB and C#:

```
OleDbDataReader oledbDr;
oledbDr = oledbCm.Execute();
while ( oledbDr.Read() ) {
//perform necessary operations.
}
oledbDr.Close();
oleDbDr = null;
```

The following code shows how to create a DataReader using SQL and Visual Basic .NET:

```
Dim sqlDr as SqlDataReader
sqlDr = sqlCm.Execute()
while ( sqlDr.Read() )
'perform operations
end while
sqlDr.Close();
sqlDr = null;
```

The following code shows how to create a DataReader using SQL and C#:

```
SqlDataReader sqlDr;
While ( sqlDr.Read() ){
//perform operations
}
sqlDr.Close();
sqlDr = null;
```

When iterating through a DataReader, there is no need to explicitly increment. When using ClassicADO 2.x, it was the responsibility of the programmer to call the method .MoveNext. If a programmer forgot to use .MoveNext, the result could be an infinite loop while accessing the recordset. This caused more than one programmer to wonder why his application took control of his system. Taking that into account, incrementing to the next row of the datareader is handled automatically when .Read() is called. When a DataReader is filled with data, the DataReader structure does not point to any record. When a .Read() is first called, the DataReader object points to the first record within the structure, as follows:

```
While drReader.Read()
........
'Do something with the data.
.......
End While
```

The code for iterating through the data reader with C# would look as follows:

```
While (drReader.Read()) {
........
//do something with the data
........
}
```

When you would like to execute a command against the database that does not return data, you will want to use the .ExecuteNonQuery() method. Why would you want to execute a command against a database without returning data to the client? This is a simple way to perform inserts, updates, and deletes. The ExecuteNonQuery method is contained within the DataSetCommand class. This method requires an open database connection object to use.

Use .ExecuteNonQuery with OLE-DB and either Visual Basic .NET or C# as follows:

```
cmOleDb.ExecuteNonQuery()
```

Use .ExecuteNonQuery with SQL and Visual Basic .NET as follows:

```
drReader = cmSQL.Execute()
```

Use .ExecuteNonQuery with SQL and C# as follows:

```
drReader = cmSQL.Execute();
```

There are many times in an application, where it is necessary to only return one value from a database. For example, only one value will be returned during a select count(*) from table operation. There is no reason to setup a large and bulky structure to hold data, such as a DataSet. Instead of this, ADO.NET provides a command that returns the first row and the first column of a query. This command is a method of the Command object, so there is a SQL, OLE-DB, and ODBC version.

Here is a Visual Basic .NET example with the ExecuteScalar() method:

```
Dim strSql as String = "select count(*) from table"
Dim sqlCn as New SqlConnection(strCn)
Dim sqlCm as New SqlCommand(strSql, sqlCn)
Dim iCount as Integer
```

```
sqlCn.Open()
iCount = sqlCm.ExecuteScalar()
MessageBox.Show("The number of records within our table is: " &
iCount.ToString())
if sqlCn.State <> ConnectionState.StateClosed then
    'Make sure that you close the connection to return it to the
pool.
    sqlCn.Close()
end if
```

Here is a C# example with the ExecuteScalar() method:

```
string strSql = "select count(*) from table";
SqlConnection sqlCn = new SqlConnection(strcn);
SqlCommand sqlCm = new SqlCommand(strSql, sqlCn);
int32 iCount;
sqlCn.Open();
iCount = sqlCm.ExecuteScalar();
MessageBox.Show("The number of Records within our table is " +
iCount.ToString());
if ( sqlCn.State != ConnectionState.StateClosed ) {
    //Make sure that you close the connection to return it to the
pool.
    sqlCn.Close();
}
```

The ExecuteScalar() method provides a simple routine to return the first element in the first row of a query.

DATATABLES AND DATAROWS

A DataTable is roughly the ADO.NET equivalent of a recordset. It is the result of a query sent to a database management system. The DataTable is a client-side object that sits in memory on the system issuing the query. It is the equivalent of a client-side recordset in ADO 2.x and later. A DataRow is the ADO.NET representation of one row of a DataTable. Let's walk through all the steps involved in creating and using a DataTable and DataRow.

The following code shows how to create a DataTable and a DataRow using Visual Basic .NET:

```
Dim strSql = "SELECT * from tableName"
Dim strCn As String = "Provider=OLEDB Provider;server=your server
name;uid=appropiate userid;pwd=appropiate password;database=your
```

```
database name"
Dim oledbCn As OleDbConnection = New OleDbConnection(strCn)
oledbCn.Open()
Dim OleDbDA as New Oledbdataadapter( strSql, oledbCn)
Dim dsData as New DataSet()
Dim dtData as DataTable
Dim drRow as DataRow
OleDbDA.Fill( dsData, "Table1")
dtData = dsData.Tables("Table1")
for each drRow in dtTable.Rows
.............
'do something with the data.
'the data can be manipulated through drRow("field name").ToString()
or drRow(number).ToString()
.............
next
```

The following code shows how to create a DataTable and a DataRow using C#:

```
string strSql = "SELECT * from tableName";
string strCN = "Provider=OLEDB Provider;server=your server
name;uid=appropiate userid;pwd=appropiate password;database=your
database name";
OleDbConnection oledbCn = new OleDbConnection(strCN);
oledbCn.Open();
OleDbDataAdapter oleDbDA = new OleDbDataAdapter( strSql, oledbCn);
DataSet dsData = new DataSet();
DataTable dtData;
OleDbDA.Fill( dsData, "DataTable name" );
DataTable = dsData.Tables["DataTable name"];
DataTable dtTable;
dtTable = dsData[0];
foreach( DataRow drRow in dtTable[0].Rows ){
.............
'do something with the data.
'the data can be manipulated through drRow["field name"].ToString()
or drRow[number].ToString()
.............
}
```

Table 5-1 shows the types of methods and properties available from a row.

TABLE 5-1 METHODS AND PROPERTIES OF A ROW

Property/Method	Explanation
AcceptChanges	Method that commits changes made since the last `AcceptChanges`.
BeginEdit	Method that begins the editing of the specified row.
CancelEdit	Method that cancels the current editing of the specified row.
ClearErrors	Method that clears the current errors for the specified row.
Delete	Method that deletes the specified row.
EndEdit	Method that ends the edit on the row.
Equals	Method that returns a Boolean value indicating whether the current object is the same as the specified object. It is inherited from `System.Object`.
GetChildRows	Method that returns the child rows of the specific `DataRow` by using the `DataRelation` and `DataRowVersion`.
GetColumnError	Method that returns the error description of the specified `DataColumn`.
GetColumnsInError	Method that returns an array of columns with errors.
GetHashCode	Method that is hash function for a type. It is inherited from `System.Object`.
GetParentRow	Method that returns the parent row of the current row based on the `DataRelation` settings and the `DataRowVersion` value of the row.
GetParentRows	Method that returns the parent rows of the current row based on the `DataRelation` settings.
GetType	Method that returns the object type.
HasError	Property that returns a value indicating whether there are errors within the columns collection.
HasVersion	Method that returns whether or not arrow has a specific version associated with it.
IsNull	Method that returns a value stating whether a column within a row is null.
Item	Property that gets or sets data within a specific column.
ItemArray	Property that gets or sets all items within the row with an array.

Property/Method	Explanation
RejectChanges	Method that removes all changes on a row since the last set of changes made through AcceptChanges.
RowError	Property that gets or sets the custom error description for the row.
RowState	Property that gets the current state of a row. Has this row been changed or unchanged since it was created. Rows can have five states associated with them.

How many rows are within the DataTable? dtTable.Rows.Count returns the number of rows within the DataTable dtTable, and it is the same for C# and Visual Basic .NET.

The DataColumn is the schema building block for a DataTable. It is the equivalent of the columns within a database.

Table 5-2 lists the types of information you can get from a datacolumn.

TABLE 5–2 TYPES OF DATACOLUMN INFORMATION

Information Type	Explanation
AllowDBNull	A Boolean value detailing whether the column in the DataSet allows a null to be within the column.
AllowIncrement	A Boolean value detailing whether the column in the DataSet increments automatically when new rows are added to the table that this column is in.
AllowIncrementSeed	The value associated with the starting value for a column with AutoIncrement turned on.

Continued

TABLE 5-2 TYPES OF DATACOLUMN INFORMATION *(Continued)*

Information Type	Explanation
AllowIncrementStep	The stepping value associated with a column that has AutoIncrement turned on.
Caption	The Column caption.
ColumnMapping	The datatype mapping of the column when the DataTable is saved as XML. Some of the allowed values are None, Element, Attribute, Text, and Internal.
DataType	The type of data stored in the column.
DefaultValue	The value that is automatically assigned to the column when a DataRow is created.
Expression	An expression used to calculate the column's value. This can be used to create calculated columns.
ExtendedProperties	A mechanism to store custom information within the object.
NameSpace	Gets or sets the namespace of the DataColumn.
Ordinal	The position of the column within the DataTable.
Prefix	Gets or sets an XML prefix that aliases the namespace of the DataTable.
ReadOnly	A Boolean value used to determine whether a column allows changes once a row has been added to a DataTable.
Site	A read / write property that indicates the site of the component. This property is inherited from MarsByValueComponent.
Sparse	A Boolean value used to determine whether a column's data should be stored in a fashion optimized for sparse data patterns.
Table	The DataTable that the DataColumn belongs to.
Unique	A Boolean value used to determine whether the values in the column must be unique within the DataRows of a DataTable.

Mapping data from a database field to a DataColumn

Tables 5-3, 5-4, and 5-5 show the mappings that occur within ADO.NET.

TABLE 5-3 SQL SERVER COLUMN MAPPING TYPES

SQL Server DataType	DataColumn DataType
BigInt	Int64
Binary	System.Byte[]
Bit	Boolean
Char	System.String
DateTime	System.DateTime
Decimal	System.Decimal
Float	Double
Image	System.Byte[]
Int	Int32
Money	System.Decimal
NChar	System.String
NText	System.String
NVarChar	System.String
Numeric	System.Decimal
Real	Single
SmallDateTime	System.DateTime
SmallInt	Int16
SmallMoney	System.Decimal
Sql_Variant	System.Object

Continued

TABLE 5-3 SQL SERVER COLUMN MAPPING TYPES *(Continued)*

SQL Server DataType	DataColumn DataType
Text	System.String
TimeStamp	System.Byte[]
TinyInt	Byte
UniqueIdentifier	System.Guid
VarBinary	System.Byte[]
VarChar	System.String

TABLE 5-4 DATACOLUMN MAPPINGS WITH ORACLE 8I R3
AND THE ORACLE OLE-DB DRIVER

Oracle DataType	.NET DataColumn DataType
Char	System.String
VarChar2	System.String
Long	System.String
Number	System.Decimal
Raw	System.Byte[]
Date	System.DateTime
RowId	System.String
MlsLabel	Int32
Blob	System.Byte[]
Clob	System.String
NClob	System.String
BFile	System.Byte[]

TABLE 5-5 ORACLE 8I R3 WITH THE MICROSOFT OLE-DB DRIVER FOR ORACLE

Oracle DataType	.NET DataColumn DataType
Char	System.String
VarChar2	System.String
Long	System.String
Number	System.Decimal
Raw	System.Byte[]
Date	System.DateTime

Note: The Microsoft OLE-DB Driver for Oracle only supports a subset of the Oracle 8iR3 DataTypes.

Creating columns within a DataTable

Unlike ADO 2.*x*, ADO.NET provides the capability to add new DataColumns to an existing DataTable. ADO 2.*x* does allow a programmer to create a recordset, but this recordset must be in the closed state when it is created. Discussions in online newsgroups reveal that this is one of the most asked-for features within the ADO 2.*x* environment.

The following code is an example of creating DataColumns within a DataTable using Visual Basic .NET:

```
Dim dtData as New DataTable = dsData.Tables[0]
Dim dcData as DataColumn
dcData = New DataColumn("MiddleName")
dcData.DataType = System.Type.GetType("System.String")
dcData.Unique = false
```

The following code is an example of creating DataColumns within a DataTable using C#:

```
DataTable dtData = dsData.Tables[0];
DataColumn dcData;
dcData = new DataColumn("MiddleName");
dcData.DataType = System.Type.GetType("System.String");
dcData.Unique = false;
```

DataRelation

A DataRelation is used to relate two `DataTable` objects to each other through `datacolumn` objects. For example, in a Customer/Orders relationship, the Customers table is the parent and the Orders table is the child of the relationship. Relationships are created between matching columns in the parent and child tables. That is, the datatype value for both columns must be identical.

When a DataRelation is created, it verifies that the relationship can be established. After a relation is created, it is maintained by disallowing any changes that would invalidate this relation. However, before it is added to the Relations collection, this can change. So, every access of the object between construction and collection add verifies that the state is still valid, and throws an exception if it is no longer a viable relation. A DataRelation is the rough ADO.NET equivalent of the relationship used to create hierarchical recordsets in ADO 2.*x*.

The following is an example of a DataRelation in Visual Basic .NET:

```
Dim dctblCustomerCustomerId as DataColumn
Dim dctblOrderCustomerId as DataColumn
'Code to get the DataSet not shown here.
dctblCustomerCustomerId =
dsData.Tables("tblCustomer").Columns("tblCustomerID")
dctblOrderCustomerId =
dsData.Tables("tblOrder").Columns("tblCustomerId")
'Create DataRelation.
Dim drCustomerToOrder as DataRelation
drCustomerToOrder = New DataRelation("CustomerToOrder",
dctblCustomerCustomerId, dctblOrderCustomerId)
'Add the relation to the DataSet.
dsData.Relations.Add(drCustomerToOrder)
```

The following is an example of a DataRelation in C#:

```
DataColumn dctblCustomerCustomerId;
DataColumn dctblOrderCustomerId;
// Code to get the DataSet not shown here.
dctblCustomerCustomerId =
dsData.Tables["tblCustomer"].Columns["tblCustomerID"];
dctblOrderCustomerId =
dsData.Tables["tblOrder"].Columns["tblCustomerId"];
// Create DataRelation.
DataRelation drCustomerToOrder;
drCustomerToOrder = New DataRelation("CustomerToOrder",
dctblCustomerCustomerId, dctblOrderCustomerId);
// Add the relation to the DataSet.
dsData.Relations.Add(drCustomerToOrder)
```

Inserting data into a table

There are several ways to insert data into a database through ADO.NET:

◆ A SQL statement can be created that is a basic insert command into a
database table.

◆ A parameterized SQL statement can be created that contains a SQL
statement that is optimized by the SQL processor within the database.

◆ A stored procedure can be called. A stored procedure has several
advantages:

 ▪ It is pre-compiled.

 ▪ Depending on your database, network communications are more
 efficient.

 ▪ There is additional security over a created SQL string.

 ▪ The stored procedure can be optimized to run against a database table.
 In this specific situation, values can be returned from the stored procedure that can uniquely identify the added row(s).

◆ A new row can be added to a DataTable within a DataSet, and then that
DataSet is reconnected to the database table. The rows that have been
added in a disconnected state are then added to the table. This is nothing
new, because ADO has had the capability to add records through an open
and updateable recordset in the past. Within the ADO 2.x environment, a
generic SQL statement is created underneath the covers to interact with
the database. This is relatively inefficient because there is a large amount
of traffic between the system the recordset is located on and the database
server. Within ADO.NET, the problem has been resolved by allowing programmers to associate Insert, Update, and Delete commands with the
database. This is accomplished by using `.InsertCommandText`,
`.UpdateCommandText`, and `.DeleteCommandText`.

For this example, take a look at a simple database table that we've created. The
table itself, does not have much meaning beyond being a basic logging table.

```
CREATE TABLE [dbo].[tblValue] (
    [tblValue] [varchar] (50) COLLATE SQL_Latin1_General_CP1_CI_AS
NULL,
    [tblValueId]  uniqueidentifier ROWGUIDCOL  NOT NULL) ON
[PRIMARY]
```

In the following sections, we take a look at each mechanism.

INSERT THROUGH SQL

A SQL `Insert` statement takes the form of `insert into` `tblName (field1, field2, . . . , fieldN) values (value1, value2, . . . , valueN)`, where the fields and values match up directly against each other. The downside with this method is that the database must parse and create an execution plan for each call to `.ExecuteNonQuery()`.

The following is example code for performing an insert through a SQL statement using C#:

```
string strCN = "Provider=SQLOLEDB;server= martok;UserId=. . . . . .
;PassWord=. . . . . .;Initial Catalog=dbTest;";
string strSql = "insert into tblTest (value) values ('" + pstrString
+ "')";
OleDbConnection oledbCn = new OleDbConnection(strCN);
OleDbCommand cmOleDb = new OleDbCommand( strSql, oledbCn );
oledbCn.Open();
cmOleDb.ExecuteNonQuery();
cmOleDb = null;
oledbCn.Close();
oledbCn = null;
```

The following is example code for performing an insert through a SQL statement using Visual Basic .NET:

```
Dim strCN as string= "Provider=SQLOLEDB;server= martok;UserId=. . .
. . .;PassWord=. . . . . .;Initial Catalog=dbTest;"
Dim strSql as string = "insert into tblTest (value) values ('" +
pstrString + "')"
Dim oledbCn as new OleDbConnection(strCN)
Dim cmOleDb as new OleDbCommand( strSql, oledbCn )
oledbCn.Open()
cmOleDb.ExecuteNonQuery()
cmOleDb = Nothing
oledbCn.Close()
oledbCn = Nothing
```

Within ADO.NET, when a call is made to `.ExecuteNonQuery()`, that command *must* be bound to an open database connection. `.ExecuteNonQuery()` does not automatically open the bound connection as when using a DataSet.

USING PARAMETERIZED SQL

Parameterized SQL differs from a basic SQL statement in that the database engine parses and creates an execution plan on the first execution. After that, the parameterized SQL statement's execution plan is stored in the database until the command object associated with the parameterized SQL statement is closed and de-allocated on the database server.

The following code shows parameterized SQL using C#:

```
string strCN = "Provider=SQLOLEDB;server= martok;UserId=s. . . . .
.;PassWord=. . . . . .;Initial Catalog=dbTest;";
string strSql = "insert into tblTest (value) values
('@ValueToInsert')";
OleDbConnection oledbCn = new OleDbConnection(strCN);
OleDbCommand cmOleDb = new OleDbCommand( strSql, oledbCn );
oledbCn.Open();
cmOleDb.Parameters.Add( new OleDbParameter("@ValueToInsert",
OleDbType.VarChar, 50 ) );
cmOleDb.Parameters["@ValueToInsert"].Value = strValue;
cmOleDb.ExecuteNonQuery();
cmOleDb = null;
oledbCn.Close();
oledbCn = null;
```

The following code shows parameterized SQL using Visual Basic .NET:

```
Dim strCN as string= "Provider=SQLOLEDB;server=
martok;UserId=sa;PassWord=kirsten;Initial Catalog=dbTest;"
Dim strSql as string = "insert into tblTest (value) values
('@ValueToInsert')"
Dim oledbCn as new OleDbConnection(strCN)
Dim cmOleDb as new OleDbCommand( strSql, oledbCn )
oledbCn.Open()
cmOleDb.Parameters.Add( new OleDbParameter("@ValueToInsert",
OleDbType.VarChar, 50 ) )
cmOleDb.Parameters("@ValueToInsert").Value = strValue
cmOleDb.ExecuteNonQuery()
cmOleDb = Nothing
oledbCn.Close()
oledbCn = Nothing
```

One item in the above code samples that has not been discussed is the OLE-DB data type enumeration. The OLE-DB data type enumeration contains the data types that the OLE-DB standard supports. More information on data types is available later in this chapter.

CALLING A STORED PROCEDURE

A stored procedure is function within a database that has been optimized for use before it is to be used. Calling a stored procedure allows a database to perform the database operation without requiring that the database compile and optimize the statement before it is used.

The following code shows calling a stored procedure using C#:

```
string strCN = "Provider=SQLOLEDB;server=
martok;UserId=sa;PassWord=kirsten;Initial Catalog=dbTest;";
string strSql = "sp_InserttblTest";
OleDbConnection oledbCn = new OleDbConnection(strCN);
oledbCn.Open();
OleDbCommand cmOleDb = new OleDbCommand( strSql, oledbCn );
cmOleDb.CommandType = CommandType.StoredProcedure;
cmOleDb.Parameters.Add( new OleDbParameter("@Value",
OleDbType.VarChar, 50 ) );
cmOleDb.Parameters["@Value"].Direction = ParameterDirection.Input;
cmOleDb.Parameters["@Value"].Value = strValue;
cmOleDb.ExecuteNonQuery();
cmOleDb = null;
oledbCn.Close();
oledbCn = null;
```

The following code shows calling a stored procedure using Visual Basic .NET:

```
Dim strCN as string = "Provider=SQLOLEDB;server= martok;UserId=. . .
. . .;PassWord=. . . . . .;Initial Catalog=dbTest;"
Dim strSql as string = "sp_InserttblTest"
Dim oledbCn as  new OleDbConnection(strCN)
Dim cmOleDb as new OleDbCommand( strSql, oledbCn )
oledbCn.Open()
cmOleDb.CommandType = CommandType.StoredProcedure
cmOleDb.Parameters.Add( new OleDbParameter("@Value",
OleDbType.VarChar, 50 ) )
cmOleDb.Parameters["@Value"].Direction = ParameterDirection.Input
cmOleDb.Parameters["@Value"].Value = strValue
cmOleDb.ExecuteNonQuery()
cmOleDb = Nothing
oledbCn.Close()
oledbCn = Nothing
```

DataSet Insert

Within Classic ADO 2.*x*, a recordset creates a generic database statement (or statements) when the .Update method is called. This command is based on whether a row is added, deleted, or updated. Within ADO.NET, the DataSet has a set of properties that allow programmers to create an optimized SQL statement to perform inserts, updates, and deletes. The properties are .InsertCommand.CommandText,

`.UpdateCommand.CommandText`, and `.DeleteCommand.CommandText`. The actions of the whole update command are not wrapped within a transaction. Each individual row that is contained within the `.Update()` method call will be transactional, however, the complete operation is not contained within a transaction. To perform a transaction over multiple commands that are sent to the database, you will want to wrap the call to the DataSet's `.Update()` method with a transaction object as described in the section on local transactions in this chapter.

The following code shows a DataSet Insert using C#:

```
string strCN = "Provider=SQLOLEDB;server= martok;UserId=. . . . .
.;PassWord=. . . . . .;Initial Catalog=dbTest;";
string strSql = "select top 1 * from tblTest";
int i = 55;
DataRow drowNew = null;
OleDbConnection oledbCn = new OleDbConnection(strCN);
oledbCn.Open();
OleDbDataAdapter oledbDA = new OleDbDataAdapter( strSql, oledbCn );
DataSet dsData = new DataSet();
oledbDA.Fill(dsData, "Test" );
drowNew = dsData.Tables["Test"].NewRow();
drowNew["Value"] = i;
dsData.Tables["Test"].Rows.Add( drowNew );
oledbDA.InsertCommand.CommandText = "insert into tblTest (Value)
values ('" + drowNew["Value"] + "')";
oledbDA.InsertCommand.ActiveConnection = oledbCn;
oledbDA.Update( dsData, "Test" );
drowNew = null;
dsData = null;
oledbDA = null;
oledbCn.Close();
oledbCn = null;
```

The following code shows a DataSet Insert using Visual Basic .NET:

```
Dim strCN as String = "Provider=SQLOLEDB;server= martok;UserId=. . .
. . .;PassWord=. . . . . .;Initial Catalog=dbTest;"
Dim strSql as String = "select top 1 * from tblTest"
Dim drowNew as DataRow
Dim oledbCn as new OleDbConnection(strCN)
Dim oledbDA as new OleDbDataAdapter( strSql, oledbCn )
oledbCn.Open()
Dim dsData as new DataSet()
oledbDA.Fill(dsData, "Test" )
drowNew = dsData.Tables("Test").NewRow()
drowNew("Value") = 55
```

```
dsData.Tables("Test").Rows.Add( drowNew )
oledbDA.InsertCommand.CommandText = "insert into tblTest (Value)
values ('" + drowNew("Value") + "')"
oledbDA.InsertCommand.ActiveConnection = oledbCn
oledbDA.Update( dsData, "Test" )
drowNew = Nothing
dsData = Nothing
oledbDA = Nothing
oledbCn.Close()
oledbCn = Nothing
```

Performing the `update` and `delete` functions is the same as the insert mechanism, except the commands will be appropriate for the actions that are needed.

Assuming that there is an existing DataSet, there is a method to filter records within an existing DataSet, much like the rs.Filter method within Classic ADO 2.*x*. The `DataTable.Select()` method has additional features to search rows within a DataTable, as seen in the following Visual Basic .NET code:

```
Dim foundRows() As DataRow
sqlDA.Fill(dsData, "Test")
dtData = dsData.Tables("Test")
foundRows = dtData.Select ("Value='10'")
```

The `foundRows` structure now contains an array of DataRows that match the select method call.

Storing images, files, or BLOBs within a database

Many times, there are files that need to be associated with a database record that don't fit nicely into a standard char or numeric style column. Pictures of an item for sale on a Web site fall into this category. Why would you want to store a large item, such as file or picture, in a database? There are two options regarding associating a file or binary large object (BLOB). The first is to store the item in a directory on the file system. The filename is stored in an appropriate text column in the database table. The application stores some data pertaining to the directory that the files are stored in.

The other alternative is to store the file/BLOB within a column of the table. This alternative allows the data to stay very close to the data that it represents without having to keep track of the file location and name. Although image/file management is a concern with storing the filename in the database table, performance is a concern with storing the file/Blob in a column.

The following code is an example of how to save data into a BLOB column:

```
CREATE TABLE [dbo].[tblCompany] (
[tblCompanyId] [uniqueidentifier] NOT NULL ,
```

```
[CompanyPic] [image] NULL
) ON [PRIMARY] TEXTIMAGE_ON [PRIMARY]
```

To use this function correctly, you will need to pass in the contents of your BLOB that you would like to store in the table. How do you do that? Take a look at this example (in Visual Basic .NET) using an ASPX file to upload the value to a web server, where the ASPX file then uploads that data into the database:

```
    Dim imgStream as Stream
    Dim imgLen as Integer
    Dim imgName_value as string
    Dim imgContentType as String
    Dim imgUploadedName as String
    Dim iCompanyId as Integer 'Set to some value
    imgStream = UploadFile.PostedFile.InputStream
    imgLen = UploadFile.PostedFile.ContentLength
    imgUploadedName = UploadFile.PostedFile.FileName
    Dim imgBinaryData(imgLen) as Byte
    imgContentType = UploadFile.PostedFile.ContentType
    Dim n as Integer = imgStream.Read(imgBinaryData, 0, imgLen)
    Dim NumRowsAffected as Integer = SaveImageToDb(iCompanyId,
imgBinaryData)
    If NumRowsAffected > 0 then
        Response.Write ( "<BR> uploaded image " )
    Else
        Response.Write ( "<BR> an error occurred uploading the
image.d " )
    End if
```

The first thing is to get access to the file upload stream using the following:

```
imageStream = UploadFile.PostedFile.InputStream
```

Now that you have access to the image stream, you will need to convert the image stream into a byte array. This can be done by using the Read() method of the image stream:

```
Dim imageBinaryData as Byte()
Dim imageLen as Integer
imageLen = UploadFile.PostedFile.ContentLength
imageStream.Read(imageBinaryData, 0, imageLen)
```

With the preceding code, data is read into a Byte(). After that, the data is passed to the SaveImageToDb() routine. The SaveImageToDb(piCompanyId, pimgBinaryData) routine is used to save values to the database. The first input value is the value of the company identifier. The second input value is the byte stream containing the image data. The following code shows the main features of this routine:

```
Dim strCn As String = ". . . . . ."
Dim strSql As String = "INSERT INTO Image
(tblCompanyId,img_data) VALUES ( @CompanyId, @img_data )"
Dim sqlCn As New SQLConnection( strCn )
Dim sqlCm As New SQLCommand( strSql, sqlCn )
Dim inumRowsAffected as Integer
Dim sqlParm0 As New SQLParameter("@Companyid",SQLDbType.Integer
)
sqlParm0.Value = piCompanyId
sqlCm.Parameters.Add( sqlParm0 )
Dim sqlParm1 as New SQLParameter( "@img_data", SQLDbType.Image )
sqlParm1.Value = imgbin
sqlCm.Parameters.Add( sqlParm1 )
sqlCn.Open()
inumRowsAffected = sqlCm.ExecuteNonQuery()
if connection.State() <> ConnectionState.Closed then
  connection.Close()
end if
```

The information regarding getting data into and out of a database is available at : http://aspfree.com/authors/123aspx/imgupload.aspx and http://aspfree.com/authors/123aspx/imgfromdb/.

Reading the image from a table

Reading the table and displaying it in a browser is relatively simple. In the sample, the image is assumed to be a JPG image. Other image types will work. The only issue is that the line that sets the content type should be changed to support the appropriate type of data being sent to the client. The following code sample will extract a specific JPG image from a table and display it in a web browser:

```
Dim imgid as String = Request.QueryString("tblcompanyId")
Dim sqlText as String = "SELECT CompanyPic FROM tblCompanyId
WHERE tblCompanyId='" & imgid  & "'"
Dim strCn = "Provider=SQLOLEDB;........."
Dim dbRead AS OleDbDataReader
Dim oledbCmd AS OleDbCommand
Dim oledbCn as OleDbConnection ( strCn )
```

```
oledbCmd = New OleDbCommand(sqlText, oledbCn )
oledbCn.Open()

oledbCmd.execute(dbRead )
If dbRead.Read()
Response.ContentType = "Image/jpeg"
Response.BinaryWrite ( dbRead.Item("CompanyPic") )
End If
oledbCn.Close()
oledbCn = Nothing
oledbCmd = Nothing
```

Local transactions

A *transaction* is a change event within a database that either occurs or doesn't occur completely. Transactions are considered the smallest unit of work that is identifiable as a unit of work, much like atoms are the smallest amount of matter that are identified as having the chemical properties of a type of matter. It is this atomic type of activity that is most often tied to transactions. There are additional requirements for a transaction. These requirements are collectively referred to as the *ACID test*, which is as follows:

◆ **Atomic:** A transaction is either completed or rolled back completely. All the changes are made or none of the changes or made. In no situation are only *some* changes made.

◆ **Consistent:** A transaction is a correct transaction. All changes are done as described by the program code.

◆ **Isolation:** Transaction changes are isolated from other incomplete transaction statements.

◆ **Durability:** After a transaction is processed, its changes will exist after a system failure and restart.

ADO.NET supports transactions differently than Classic ADO 2.x does. With Classic ADO 2.x, transactions are controlled by the connection object through methods like .BeginTrans(), .CommitTrans(), and .RollBackTrans(). ADO.NET uses a separate transaction object. The OLE-DB, ODBC, and SQL Clients provide their own Transaction object (OleDbTransaction, OdbcTransaction, and SqlTransaction). The Connection objects are used to create to begin the transaction and are then associated with the transaction objects.

To begin a transaction, your program must call the BeginTransaction() method. This method instructs the database that all operations on this connection will be treated as a transaction and either committed or rolled back as a group. The OleDbTransaction object supports the following methods and properties:

- ◆ `public void Commit();` //: All the work has successfully been completed. Commit the transaction.

- ◆ `public void Rollback();` //: There has been some type of problem. Rollback all the changes by rolling back the transaction.

- ◆ `IsolationLevel;` //: The SqlTransaction, `OleDbTransaction`, and `OdbcTransaction` objects supports the setting of isolation levels for transactions. The valid settings are `Chaos`, `ReadCommitted`, `ReadUncommitted`, `RepeatableRead`, `Serializable`, and `Unspecified`. The `IsolationLevel` enumeration provides these values.

The following is example Visual Basic .NET code for using OLE-DB transactions:

```
Dim strCn As String = "Provider=SQLOLEDB;Data
Source=chakotay;Initial Catalog=DotNet;User Id=. . . . . .
;PassWord=. . . . . ."
Dim strSql As String = "insert into tblValue (tblValue) values
(getdate())"
Dim oledbCN As New OleDbConnection(strCn)
Dim oledbCM As New OleDbCommand(strSql, oledbCN)
Dim oledbTrans As OleDbTransaction

Try
    oledbCN.Open()
    'Set the transaction Isolation level.
    oledbTrans =
      oledbCN.BeginTransaction(IsolationLevel.ReadUncommitted)
    oledbCM.Transaction = oledbTrans
    oledbCM.ExecuteNonQuery()
    oledbTrans.Commit()
Catch e As Exception
    oledbTrans.Rollback()
Finally
    If oledbCN.State <> ConnectionState.Closed Then
      oledbCN.Close()
    End If
    oledbCM = Nothing
    oledbCN = Nothing
End Try
Example C# code for using OleDb Transactions:
string strCn = "Provider=SQLOLEDB;Data Source=chakotay;Initial
Catalog=DotNet;User Id=s. . . . . .;PassWord=. . . . . .";
string strSql = "insert into tblValue (tblValue) values
(getdate())";
OleDbConnection oledbCN = New OleDbConnection(strCn);
```

```
OleDbCommand oledbCM = New OleDbCommand(strSql, oledbCN);
OleDbTransction oledbTrans;

Try {
     oledbCN.Open();
     oledbTrans =
      oledbCN.BeginTransaction(IsolationLevel.ReadUncommitted);
     oledbCM.Transaction = oledbTrans;
     oledbCM.ExecuteNonQuery();
     oledbTrans.Commit();
}
Catch ( Exception e ){
     oledbTrans.Rollback();
}
Finally {
     If ( oledbCN.State != ConnectionState.Closed) {
      oledbCN.Close();
     }
     oledbCM = null;
     oledbTrans = null;
     oledbCN = null;
}
```

The SqlClient provides native support for transactions through the transaction object SqlTransaction. The SqlTransaction object supports the following manual transaction methods and properties beyond the OleDbTransaction object:

- public void Commit();

- public void Rollback();

- public void Rollback(String transactionName);

- public void Save(String savePointName);

- int TransactionLevel {get;}

ADO.NET provides the ability to manage transactions without using the distributed transaction facilities of MTS/COM+ and without the associated cost of using those services. When dealing with a single database, the control of transaction might be best handled within the application itself. These are termed local or manual transactions. Unlike the AutoComplete attribute of a COM+ application, local transactions are not automatically rolled back in the event of an error. An error must be trapped by a try...catch block by executing a call to .RollBack() within the catch portion of the block.

Transactions are not supported by all databases. MySQL, a popular open-source database, does not provide support for transactions in the current version. Transaction support is planned for MySQL version 4, but at the time of this writing, that version is not available.

ADO to ADO.NET and Back

Integrating between ADO and ADO.NET is going to be a requirement over the next several years. Many companies have invested in the development of N-Tier applications using the plumbing provided by COM. ADO provides a broad range of supported column types. These column types are contained within the ADODB. DataTypeEnum Collection. These ADO datatypes are more popularly recognized to COM programmers as `adVarChar`, `adGUID`, `adInteger`, and about 40 other datatypes. The problem is that the datatypes exposed by ADO.NET are much more limited in their scope, because there are only about 15 datatypes supplied. The problem is somewhat like the issues that have occurred with language translation. An English-to-Russian-and-back translation of the term "The spirit is willing, but the flesh is weak" had been translated into "The vodka is strong, but the meat is rotten." The same type of problem occurs with translating from ADO to ADO.NET and back. The problem is that the .NET datatypes are used for many types of database datatypes, whereas with ADO, there is basically a one-to-one correspondence between the ADO datatypes and the database column types.

The following is some example code to manually fill a DataTable from an ADO recordset using Visual Basic .NET:

```
Public Function AdoToAdoDotNet (ByVal prs As ADODB.Recordset) As
DataTable
        Dim dtData As New DataTable()
        Dim i As Integer = 0
        Dim j As Integer = 0
        Dim strColName As String
        Dim strValue As String
        Dim drData As DataRow

        For i = 0 To (prs.Fields.Count - 1)
            Dim dcData As New DataColumn()
            strColName = prs.Fields(i).Name
            dcData.ColumnName = strColName
            dcData.Caption = strColName
            dcData.AllowDBNull = False
            dcData.DefaultValue = ""
            Select Case (prs.Fields(i).Type)
```

```
                    Case (ADODB.DataTypeEnum.adVarChar)
                        dcData.DataType =
System.Type.GetType("System.String")
                        'end case
                    Case (ADODB.DataTypeEnum.adGUID)
                        dcData.DataType =
System.Type.GetType("System.String")
                        ' end case
            End Select
            dtData.Columns.Add(dcData)
        Next

        For i = 0 To (prs.RecordCount - 1)

            drData = dtData.NewRow()
            For j = 0 To (prs.Fields.Count - 1)
                strValue = CStr(prs.Fields(j).Value)
                drData(j) = strValue
            Next
            prs.MoveNext()
            dtData.Rows.Add(drData)
        Next


        Return dtData
    End Function
```

The following is some example code to manually fill a DataTable from an ADO Recordset using C#:

```
public DataTable AdoToAdoDotNet( ADODB.Recordset prs )
{
DataTable dtData = new DataTable();
  int i = 0;
            int j = 0;
            string strColName;
            string strValue;
            DataRow drData;
            for(i=0;i< prs.Fields.Count;i++)
            {
                DataColumn dcData = new DataColumn();
                strColName = prs.Fields[i].Name;
                dcData.ColumnName = strColName;
                dcData.Caption = strColName;
                dcData.AllowDBNull = false;
                dcData.DefaultValue = "";
```

```
                    switch (prs.Fields[i].Type)
                    {
                        case (ADODB.DataTypeEnum.adVarChar):
                            dcData.DataType =
System.Type.GetType("System.String");
                            break;
                        case (ADODB.DataTypeEnum.adGUID):
                            dcData.DataType =
System.Type.GetType("System.String");
                            break;

                        default:
                            break;
                    }
                    dtData.Columns.Add( dcData );
                }

                for( i=0;i<prs.RecordCount;i++)
                {
                    drData = dtData.NewRow();
                    for( j=0; j<prs.Fields.Count;j++)
                    {
                        strValue = (string) prs.Fields[j].Value;
                        drData[j] = strValue;
                    }
                    prs.MoveNext();
                    dtData.Rows.Add( drData );
                }
                return dtData;
            }
```

Now that you've seen a manual solution to converting from ADO to a DataTable, let's take a look at an in-the-box solution. Microsoft has recognized that there is a need to manually accept an ADO recordset and populate a DataTable with that recordset. Assuming that you have a recordset, here is a built-in way to go from ADO to a DataTable (using Visual Basic .NET):

```
Dim dsData as DataSet = new DataSet()
Dim oledbDA as OleDbDataAdapter = new OleDbDataAdapter()
oledbDA.MissingSchemaAction = MissingSchemaAction.AddWithKey
Dim count as Integer = oledbDA.Fill(dsData, rs, "ADODBRecordSet")
```

And here is a C# example:

```
DataSet dsData = new DataSet();
OleDbDataAdapter oledbDA = new OleDbDataAdapter();
```

```
oledbDA.MissingSchemaAction = MissingSchemaAction.AddWithKey;
int icount = oledbDA.Fill( dsData, rs, "ADODBRecordSet")
```

The result of the two code snippets above is that the Classic ADO 2.x recordset represented by rs is placed into a DataTable called "ADODBRecordSet". This datatable is within the dataset dsData.

Converting from a DataTable to an ADO 2.x RecordSet

Converting from a DataTable to an ADO 2.x recordset may be necessary for applications that are front-end applications calling a middle-tier application written in C# or Visual Basic .NET. There are several problems in converting from a DataTable to a recordset. A column in a database can have several datatypes that map to the same .NET datatype. For example, the SQL Server datatypes varchar, char, and text map to the .NET datatype string. That's fine when converting from ADO to a DataTable. The problem occurs when going in the opposite direction. Given a DataType of System.String, which ADO field type should be chosen? AdVarChar? AdLongVarChar? AdWChar? Or another field type? The solution implemented in the accompanying code merely takes all the fields and places them into a adVarChar field type with a size of lngSize.

There will be the potential for performance problems regarding the manual translation of DataTables to and from ADO 2.x recordsets:

◆ The time to manually move data from a recordset to a table or vice versa is directly proportional to the number of rows (M) times the number of columns (N).

◆ Because this is a manual conversion, processor utilization is very high during the conversion process.

◆ Due to the fact that the DataTable is in memory and a client-side recordset is in memory, memory utilization will be fairly high.

Having said this, we see that it's not that this approach is bad. Rather, this approach merely has the possibility of problems. It should be used wisely. It should be used when the amount of data is not too large. So what is too large? It depends on the available processing power of your systems, network bandwidth, and memory available on your systems. Choose wisely.

Here is an example using Visual Basic .NET:

```
Dim rs As New ADODB.Recordset()
Dim dcData As DataColumn
Dim drData As DataRow
```

```
            Dim i As Integer
            'The max size for our varchar field. This value is
            ' arbitrary.
            Dim iSize as Integer = 50
            'create the columns within our ADO recordset.
            For Each dcData In pdtData.Columns
            'to change the used datatypes, you will need to implement a
            'if-then-else or case statement for the different datatypes.
                rs.Fields.Append(dcData.ColumnName, _
                    ADODB.DataTypeEnum.adVarChar, lngSize)
            Next

            rs.Open()

            For Each drdata In pdtData.Rows
                rs.AddNew()
                For Each dcData In pdtData.Columns
                    rs.Fields(dcData.ColumnName).Value =
drData(dcData.ColumnName).ToString()
                    Application.DoEvents()
                Next
                rs.Update()
            Next
```

A second way to transfer data between a .NET component and a Classic ADO 2.x client is to use XML. In this scenario, the .NET component creates a DataSet containing the necessary information. The DataSet's XML representation is then returned to the calling COM client as a string. The COM client would load the string into an XML parser and then parse the XML for the appropriate values. The problem with this route is that it would require the rewriting of the COM client to support XML. The following code will demonstrate a simple .NET component that can be called from a COM component. The function (in Visual Basic .NET) retrieves data from a database and returns it to a calling COM component in a string:

```
Imports system
Imports system.data
Imports System.data.OLEDB
Imports System.Reflection
<assembly:AssemblyKeyFileAttribute("component.snk")>
namespace McClureDevelopment
        Public Class COMComponent
                public function ReturnDataXML() as System.String
                Dim strSql as string = "select top 100 * from
tblTest"
                Dim strOleDbCn as String = "Provider=SQLOLEDB;User
```

```
Id=sa;Password=kirsten;Data Source=martok;Initial Catalog=VSDotNet"
            Dim OleDbCn as new OleDbConnection( strOleDbCn )
            Dim OleDbDA as new OleDbDataAdapter( strSql,
OleDbCn )

            Dim dsData as new DataSet()
            OleDbDA.Fill( dsData, "Test")
            return dsData.GetXML
            end function
        End Class
End Namespace
```

In addition to the preceding code, you will need to register this component to be visible and viewable from COM. Covered in detail in Chapter 7, it is basically a two-step process:

1. Register the assembly using the regasm.exe utility.

2. Install the assembly in the global assembly cache using gacutil.exe.

ADOX Functionality in .NET

ADO.NET is optimized for database operations involving data, such as select, insert, update, and delete. ADOX is ADO Extensions for Data Definition Language and Security. ADOX provides functionality to manage a physical database. It includes objects for schema creation, schema modification, and security management. At this time, there is no functionality within .NET that is the equivalent of ADOX. However, using ADOX within .NET is perfectly acceptable. The performance penalties associated with going through the COM interop layer are mostly insignificant because ADOX is used to mostly manage a physical database. This is only needed to run from one or two systems and mostly likely not even at the same time. The functionality that is within the ADO.NET that is the equivalent of ADOX is based on managing the DataSet object.

Let's take a look at ADOX underneath .NET and see how its functionality can be used. Before you can run this code, you will need to run the files that contain ADO and ADOX through the type library importer. Currently, those files are called msado15.dll and msadox.dll and are located within `Program Files\Common Files\System\ado` directory.

The following is a Visual Basic .NET sample to list the tables available from a connection:

```
Dim strCn = "Provider=SQLOLEDB;User Id=sa;PassWord=kirsten;Data
Source=martok;Initial Catalog=dbTest"
Dim strSql = "select top 1000 * from tblTest"
Dim cn as new ADODB.Connection()
```

```
Dim adox as new ADOX.Catalog()
Dim item as ADOX.Table
cn.open( strCn )
adox.activeconnection = cn
for each item in adox.Tables
    Console.WriteLine("Table Name: " & item.Name.ToString())
Next
adox.activeconnection = Nothing
adox = Nothing
cn.Close()
cn = Nothing
```

The following is a C# sample to list the tables available from a connection:

```
string strCn = "Provider=SQLOLEDB;User Id=. . . . . . ;PassWord=. .
. . . .;Data Source=chakotay;Initial Catalog=dotnet";
ADODB.Connection cn = new ADODB.Connection();
ADOX.Catalog adox = new ADOX.Catalog();
cn.Open( strCn, string.Empty, string.Empty, 0 );
adox.ActiveConnection = cn;
foreach( ADOX.Table item in adox.Tables )
{
    Console.WriteLine("Table Name: " + item.Name.ToString());
}
adox.ActiveConnection = null;
adox = null;
cn.Close();
cn = null;
```

Server-side cursors and transaction processing

Server-side cursors are a mechanism to open data from a database query whereby those data are stored within a temporary structure on the database server. In general, a server-side cursor-based mechanism is the quickest way to open data. With a server cursor, a lock may be placed on the data within the database. This lock can be used to allow the cursor to be updateable. In .NET, you can continue to use classic ADO 2.*x*. It still provides the server-side functionality that you are used to. The DataReader in ADO.NET provides a server-side cursor, but it is not updateable. To simulate transaction processing and server-side cursors with a DataSet, you need a mechanism to lock the records that you're using. Here are the steps necessary to simulate this:

1. Create an open connection.

2. Begin a transaction on the connection object.

3. Associate that connection with a DataSet.

4. Send a query through the DataSet that contains necessary locking hints to tell the database to lock the necessary records.

5. Perform the necessary add/update/delete operations, and send them back to the database.

6. Commit the transaction.

7. Close the connection object.

Depending on your circumstance, this may or may not work. It is offered as an option.

Inserting data and getting a primary key back

Inserting data and getting a primary key back is one of the most important actions that is done in using a database. In Oracle, this is not a big issue, because there is a database object type called a sequence. A sequence appears as a table that can be selected from. This selection retrieves a value and increments the value stored in the sequence. The returned value can be used in a second SQL command to insert a row with the primary key already known. SQL Server 7/2000 provides two mechanisms for creating a primary key: an Identity field and a GUID/RowId. There are several ways to do an insert and get the primary key back:

◆ **Continue to use Classic ADO 2.x.** Using a server-side recordset with a keyset cursor and optimistic locking, performing an `rs.AddNew` and an `rs.Update` will return the primary key to the recordset. In .NET, this mechanism may run into scalability problems, because it requires that calls go through the COM interop layer of .NET.

◆ **Use a stored procedure to insert data and return the primary key.** The primary key can be created within the stored procedure as a unique Identity or GUID value. (A complete example of this is in Chapter 10 on Oracle and Chapter 11 on SWL Server.)

◆ **Perform a `select newid()` or other mechanism to get a unique Identity field,** take the returned value, and then perform a SQL-style insert. This is much like the Oracle sequence solution.

Although all of these options will work, your application's needs and the experience of your development team will determine which is the best method to perform.

Scalability of DataSets: An Analysis of the SQL and OleDb Data Providers

The SQL Data Provider communicates through TDS to SQL Server. It bypasses ADO, OLE-DB, and ODBC to provide a high-performance mechanism for transferring data between a client and database system.

The OleDb Data Provider is the Data Provider to communicate between .NET and database systems that do not have a Data Provider. It communicates through the OLE-DB driver to the database, either a native OLE-DB or ODBC driver, much like ADO communicates in the COM world.

When we first started to work with .NET, we kept listening to how people online were so fascinated with the SQL Data Provider. The SQL Data Provider provides faster access to the SQL Server database than either ODBC or OLE-DB Data Provider. Table 5-6 shows some relative performance numbers of the Sql, Odbc, and OleDb Data Providers.

TABLE 5-6 RELATIVE PERFORMANCE OF THE SQL, OLE-DB, AND ODBC DATA PROVIDERS

Data Provider	0 Clients (Test Application Is the Only One Running)	10 Clients
SQL Data Provider	1	1
Odbc Data Provider	1.30	1.02
OleDb Data Provider	1.47	1.14

Note: All times are relative to the SQL Data Provider.

 The results shown in Table 5-6 compare the relative performance of the SQL, OLE-DB, and ODBC Data Providers. The operation that was performed is a single insert command into a table. There is no transaction support except what is provided within the database for a single operation. The database server and clients were running on the same machine (Pentium III, 1 GHz, 512 MB of RAM).

Scalability of DataReaders and DataSets

DataReaders and DataSets, client-side and server-side recordsets – how do these items affect scalability? Let's go back to what these terms mean. In a server-side recordset, when a query is issued, the data is stored at the server in a cursor structure. As the recordset is looped through, there is a continual conversation between the client and the database to get data. Depending on the database, a lock may or may not be placed on the data in the tables. With each request of new data, a new set of data is sent to the client.

In a client-side recordset, when a query is issued, the data is moved to the client all at once so that there is minimal conversation between the client and server after the data is sent to the client. In addition, with a client-side recordset, you could disconnect the recordset from the database, thereby removing any locks on the database associated with that client-side recordset. This is called a *client-side disconnected recordset*. You can't do that with a server-side recordset. A server-side recordset requires an active connection, creates a cursor on the server, and cannot be closed without the recordset automatically being closed.

The DataTable within a DataSet is roughly equivalent to ADO 2.x's client-side disconnected recordset. A DataReader is roughly the equivalent of ADO 2.x's read-only forward-only server-side recordset. You would think that a client-side disconnected recordset/DataSet would be the best way to work with large volumes of data. This seems to work very well with the Microsoft OLE-DB drivers for Oracle and SQL Server. However, this may not always true. The best choice of a client-side versus server-side recordset will depend greatly on the database, the OLE-DB/ODBC drivers, the performance characteristics of the application, and network bandwidth. For example, to connect to DB/400 with Client Access Express (CAE), a server-side cursor is the best way to iterate through data. Connect to the same instance of DB/400 through the Microsoft Host Integration Server using its OLE-DB driver and the best way to iterate through data is to use a client-side disconnected recordset. How do you figure out the best approach to use? Test and try things out. Run these mechanisms under a continual load and see what the results are. There is code on the Web site to assist you in testing your database under load with .NET.

The effect of open connections on a database

Keeping database connection to a minimum will allow your database to operate as efficiently as possible. How do you minimize connections? These are the ways that we know of:

◆ **Explicitly create, open, and close Connection objects.** This gives you complete control over the number of connections and the parameters that those Connection objects used against a production database. Implicitly created connection objects (those created by passing a connection string to a Command object) will not be returned to the connection pool until after the Command object is de-allocated by the garbage collector.

◆ **Whenever you can, open a DataReader, use the resultset, and close the resultset before you use that connection for anything else.** DataReaders require their own connection objects. Two DataReaders using the same connection object can not be open at any time.

Using Classic ADO 2.x with .NET

Although .NET contains a new data-access technology, it does not require that you replace your existing ADO knowledge with ADO.NET knowledge. You can continue to use Classic ADO 2.x within your .NET applications. But you will need to be aware of several issues when using Classic ADO 2.x within .NET:

- ◆ **Access is through the Runtime Callable Wrapper.** There is a small performance penalty when going through the Runtime Callable Wrapper.

- ◆ **C# programmers will need to provide all parameters for all method calls.** Visual Basic .NET programmers get off easy, because they aren't required to provide the optional method call parameters.

- ◆ **The XML support is rather limited because the default XML produced is the XML Data Reduced (XDR) spec.** XDR is not widely supported.

Data Types

One of the issues that was touched on earlier is that, by default, the .NET Framework will convert data from a database into a native .NET datatype. Retrieving more specific column information (varchar(25) versus char(25) versus text) requires going back to the database using a separate operation. This is based on the need for highly optimized data access within ADO.NET. ADO.NET includes a set of data types for the SqlClient, OLE-DB, and ODBC Data Providers. These data types help prevent data type conversion errors.

SqlTypes

Included within the .NET Framework is a namespace that provides the datatypes associated with SQL Server. This namespace is called `System.Data.SqlTypes`. These data types are stored within the `SqlDbType` enumeration. Table 5-7 lists the SQL Server data types and their SqlTypes equivalent.

TABLE 5-7   SQLTYPES

.NET SqlTypes	.NET SqlDbType	Native Sql Server Data Type
SqlBinary	Binary	Binary
SqlBinary	Image	Image
SqlBinary	VarBinary	VarBinary
SqlByte	TinyInt	TinyInt

.NET SqlTypes	.NET SqlDbType	Native Sql Server Data Type
SqlDataTime	DateTime	DateTime
SqlDecimal	Decimal	Decimal
SqlDecimal	Numeric	Numeric
SqlDouble	Float	Float
SqlInt16	SmallInt	SmallInt
SqlInt32	Int (Integer)	Int (Integer)
SqlInt64	BigInt	BigInt
SqlGuid	UniqueId	UniqueIdentifier
SqlMoney	Money	Money
SqlMoney	SmallMoney	SmallMoney
SqlString	Char	Char
SqlString	NChar	NChar
SqlString	NText	NText
SqlString	NVarChar	NVarChar
SqlString	Text	Text
SqlString	VarChar	SysName
SqlString	VarChar	VarChar
Object	Variant	Sql_Variant

In addition to the base data types, these data types contain a set of methods that perform operations based on the data. For example, the numeric SQL data types expose an add method. Take a look at the following code, which shows how to add to SqlInt64 numbers together and place that result within a third SqlInt64 value:

```
SqlInt64 lngV1 = 100;
SqlInt64 lngV2 = 100;
SqlInt64 lngResult;
lngResult = SqlInt64.Add(lngV1, lngV2);
MessageBox.Show( Convert.ToString(lngResult) );
```

OLE–DB and ODBC types

The `System.Data.OleDb` namespace contains a set of data types similar to those included with the `System.Data.SqlTypes` namespace. These data types may be used to describe input parameters to stored procedures and other operations when calling a database where the parameter type is important. The enumeration for these values is stored within the `System.Data.OleDb.OledbType` enumeration.

The `Microsoft.Data.Odbc` namespace also contains a number of data types similar to those provided by the `System.Data.OleDb` and `System.Data.SqlTypes` namespaces. These data types are stored within the `Microsoft.Data.Odbc.OdbcType` enumeration. These data types are primarily used when creating parameter objects to be used when calling stored procedures and operations where parameter type is important.

Table 5-8 shows the data types provided by the `System.Data.OleDb` and Microsoft.Data.Odbc namespaces.

TABLE 5-8 OLE–DB AND ODBC DATA TYPES

OLE–DB Member Name	ODBC Member Name	.NET Data Type
BigInt	BigInt	Int64
Binary	Binary	Byte[]
Boolean	Bit	Boolean
Char	Char	String
Currency	N/A	Decimal
Date	Date	DateTime
DBDate	N/A	DateTime
DBTime	N/A	TimeSpan
DBTimeStamp	DateTime, SmallDateTime	DateTime
Decimal	Decimal	Decimal
Double	Double	Double
N/A	Image	Byte[]
Empty	N/A	Empty
Error	N/A	Exception
Filetime	N/A	Datetime
Guid	UniqueIdentifier	Guid

OLE–DB Member Name	ODBC Member Name	.NET Data Type
Idispatch	N/A	Object
Integer	Int	Int32
IUnknown	N/A	Object
LongVarBinary	N/A	Byte[]
LongVarChar	Text	String
LongVarWChar	N/A	String
N/A	NChar	String
N/A	NText	String
Numeric	Numeric	Decimal
N/A	NVarChar	String
PropVariant	N/A	Object
Single	Real	Single
SmallInt	SmallInt	Int16
N/A	Time	DateTime
TinyInt	N/A	SByte
N/A	TinyInt	Byte
N/A	Timestamp	Byte[]
UnsignedBigInt	N/A	UInt64
UnsignedInt	N/A	UInt32
UnsignedSmallInt	N/A	UInt16
UnsignedTinyInt	N/A	Byte
VarBinary	VarBinary	Byte[]
VarChar	VarChar	String
VarNumeric	N/A	Decimal
VarWChar	N/A	String
Wchar	N/A	String

Note: N/A does not necessarily mean that there is not a direct relationship between the OleDbType and the OdbcType listed. It means that the OleDbType and OdbcType description do not exactly match.

Summary

ADO.NET is Microsoft's data-access technology designed for the .NET Framework. It supports an optimized connection to SQL Server 7 and later along with connections to most OLE-DB and ODBC drivers. Using the Data Providers that implement these connections, programs are able to perform data operations within a database. ADO.NET can be used to send SQL statements to a database in addition to calling stored procedures. Microsoft has met is goal of designing a database access technology that integrates XML, easily supports the concept of being disconnected, and provides optimized connections.

Chapter 6

.NET Components

IN THIS CHAPTER

- ◆ Creating private components
- ◆ Installing components into the global assembly cache
- ◆ Accessing components from unmanaged code
- ◆ Accessing unmanaged code from components
- ◆ Using components in conjunction with COM+ Services

COMPONENT-BASED PROGRAMMING can be considered one of the most important innovations in software development. Microsoft brought component-based development to the masses of Windows users with Visual Basic and VBXs. The usefulness of the VBX was immediately apparent, and an industry supplying third-party VBXs sprang up overnight. As development advanced into 32-bit environments, the VBX model was falling short. So the model was updated and brought forward to the 32-bit world in the form of ActiveX controls. ActiveX had many improvements aside from its 32-bit nature, but as technology advanced and the Internet emerged as the dominant computer network, ActiveX also demonstrated shortcomings in its new environment.

ActiveX controls were created for use by the thick clients of the corporate, client/server development world, not the thin clients of the World Wide Web. Also, even though ActiveX is built on the component object model (COM), COM's distributed side, DCOM, is complicated and difficult to implement. So now Microsoft brings forth .NET components to address the needs of the newer, more distributed world of development. This chapter focuses on this most recent evolution of components for the Microsoft platform.

Defining Namespaces

Namespaces logically group together related objects, methods, and data structures, and namespaces can contain other namespaces. This sub-grouping of namespaces enables the creation of a hierarchy of related classes and data that Microsoft uses to great advantage in the realm of the Common Language Runtime. All managed code must exist within a namespace. This facilitates code reuse, and it ensures that no two data structures or classes will conflict. Conflicts are removed because code that exists in different namespaces is treated distinctly, even if it defines the same variables, structures, or methods; variables, structures, and methods cannot be redefined within a namespace. Thus, namespaces provide context to all code, and any dependent code must refer to the correct, desired namespace.

Microsoft has predefined many namespaces within the base class libraries that are available to code executed by the Common Language Runtime. The central namespace is the System namespace. The System namespace defines the top-level class, Object, as well as the other primary data types. The System namespace contains more than 20 other namespaces that are central to application development, including System.IO for I/O-related operations, System.Collections for data-collection structures like Queue and SortedList, and System.Net for network-related operations. Of course, this is not a comprehensive listing but an illustration of the central nature of the System namespace itself.

Given that namespaces are central to .NET development, the following code illustrates how namespaces are used and defined in C#:

```
using System;
using System.IO;

namespace MyNamespace
{
    ...
}
```

The preceding code listing shows that the developer is using the System and System.IO namespaces. These two statements allow the developer to reference all publicly available code defined in those two namespaces, directly, without qualifying the code with its namespace hierarchy. Also, the developer is defining a namespace called MyNamespace. All code that the developer makes publicly available in MyNamespace will be directly available to later code that employs that namespace in a using clause, as shown in the following fragment:

```
using MyNamespace;

namespace MyOtherNamespace
{
    ...
}
```

In addition, a namespace can be defined with an alias in the following manner:

```
using IO = System.IO;
```

Given that namespace hierarchies can be quite deep, using an alias can make qualified references much more efficient.

Creating Assemblies

In the world of managed code, the product package that results from a development effort is an *assembly*. An assembly may have either a .DLL or .EXE extension, but it has several properties that distinguish it from the DLLs and executables of the past that we now refer to as *unmanaged code:*

♦ **An assembly is dependent on Microsoft's Common Language Runtime (CLR) environment.** This is because the assembly does not contain machine instructions but Microsoft Intermediate Language (MSIL) code. At execution time, this MSIL code is passed to a Just-In-Time (JIT) compiler that compiles the IL code to machine code. The benefit of this is that the IL and the JIT allow for the software application to be abstracted from the hardware platform.

♦ **An assembly will run on any platform that supports Microsoft's Common Language Runtime specification.** This means that code developed for a PC will also run on a Windows CE platform using the CLR without recompilation.

♦ **The manifest allows an assembly to be self-describing.** This eliminates the need for an assembly to register with the operating system.

So, an assembly is a self-describing, platform-independent, intermediate language that does not require system registration. Together, these concepts represent a fundamental change from the components and shared libraries of the past. But after the change is made, another set of assembly concepts presents itself. These concepts include sharing, versioning, security, deployment, and side-by-side execution.

An assembly represents the smallest unit of deployable managed code. Each assembly has exactly one program execution point in the form of a `main`, `WinMain`, or `DllMain` function. An assembly maintains type and publication boundaries. That is, a type is unique to its assembly context in much the same way that, on a programmatic level, a type is unique to its namespace. Also, an assembly controls what data types and code are made available publicly.

In addition to making data and code publicly available, the assembly maintains a security context that inherently includes the concept of security roles. This allows the assembly to enforce security restrictions based on the role of the consumer of the assembly.

An assembly also contains versioning information. The versioning information is essential in creating code capable of side-by-side execution. Side-by-side execution allows two or more different versions of an assembly to run at the same time, or side-by-side. Side-by-side execution may simply involve different versions of an assembly running on the same machine, or it may involve different versions running in the same process.

An assembly may also be shared or private. A *shared assembly* is an assembly intended for shared usage, and the installation location will often be into the global assembly cache (GAC) located in the assembly directory below the Windows system directory (the directory where Windows is installed). If the shared assembly is in the form of a DLL, it will generally contain the manifest as a resource, but a separate manifest file may be installed into the target directory alongside the assembly. A *private assembly* is an assembly deployed into the directory of, and intended only for use by, the application with which it is deployed.

Assembly location

The runtime engine is responsible for locating and loading the assemblies used by other assemblies and applications. The process for locating an assembly can be complicated and may involve the runtime engine completing up to four steps:

1. The runtime engine examines the configuration files associated with the application or assembly attempting to load the new assembly.

2. The runtime checks to see if the assembly has been previously loaded.

3. The runtime checks the global assembly cache.

4. The runtime performs a search based on some additional heuristic criteria.

When the runtime engine resorts to these additional heuristics, it is said to be probing for the assembly. The probing process will first check for a codebase configuration parameter. If a codebase parameter exists for the desired assembly, that will be the only place that the engine looks for the assembly. If the assembly is not found there, the load request will fail and the probing will end. If a codebase parameter does not exist, the engine will probe the application base directory. It will look for the assembly in both the root of the application base and in a directory with the same name as the assembly. The engine will also search the culture and private binpath directories in the same manner. Additionally, if one assembly references another, the current location of the first assembly may be probed as well. This is the general probing process, and there are some additional details. However, if assemblies are deployed in a rational manner, this should be all that is required for an assembly to be located.

The location process is initiated by a reference to the desired assembly during execution. This reference is frequently static but may be dynamic. In the case of a static reference, the name, version, culture, and public key token of the desired assembly will be found in the manifest of the current assembly or application. In the event of a dynamic reference generated by a call to a reflection method, the same reference data will exist, but it will be produced at runtime. In any event, the location, or binding, of the assembly will begin following the previously described procedures.

Assembly version control

Although the deployment of components and DLLs in the past could lead to the version control nightmare of "DLL Hell," managed code provides relief for this. It should be noted that assemblies can now be distinguished not only by their name but also by their culture, public key token, and version number. However, among these distinguishing characteristics and for a developer developing a single assembly with the same culture and strong name, assembly version control is a critical innovation. Every component built with .NET has a four-level version number in the following format:

```
major.minor.build.revision
```

Table 6-1 describes the version levels and their meanings.

TABLE 6-1 .NET COMPONENT VERSION NUMBER BREAKDOWN

Version–Number Level	Description
Major product number	A change in this number indicates a major change in the product and will result in the CLR considering the component incompatible.
Minor product number	A change in this number indicates a minor change in the product and will result in the CLR considering the component incompatible.
Build number	Indicates a new, fully compatible build. Given multiple components with the same major and minor numbers, the CLR will, by default, select the highest available build number for use by an application.
Revision number	Indicates an engineering fix. Given multiple components with the same major, minor, and build numbers (but no higher build number), the CLR will, by default, select the highest available revision number for use by an application.

With a C# project, the version number, by default, is controlled by the following line in the AssemblyInfo.cs file:

```
[assembly: AssemblyVersion("1.0.*")]
```

This is the default line created with the project; the asterisk will result in default build and revision numbers. However, the developer should supply and maintain his own build and revision numbers, ideally with a revision-control tool that will update the text in case the developer forgets. If the developer is using Visual Basic .NET, then a similar line may be found in the `AssemblyInfo.vb` file that is created for all VB projects.

So, when an application is built, the version numbers of the components it is built with are stored in the application's metadata, thereby allowing the application to request, and the runtime engine to locate, a specific version of a component. The effect of version control is demonstrated with the components developed later in the chapter. For the moment, suffice it to say that a developer doesn't need to worry anymore that an application that uses a 2.x version of a component will be affected by the installation of either a 1.x or a 3.x version.

Assembly distribution

As mentioned earlier in this chapter, the platforms on which an assembly can be executed are only limited by the existence of the runtime environment for those platforms. However, from a more practical standpoint, this means that the .NET Framework must be installed on a given machine before .NET components can be executed on that machine. Assuming you now have a machine running the .NET Framework, the physical deployment of .NET components may commence.

Because managed code is not dependent on system registration, the deployment process is much simpler. In fact, if the assembly being deployed is a standalone application that uses only other private assemblies, deployment could be as easy as copying all the files to the desired directory. Microsoft does provide two common formats for assisting the deployment process: the traditional .CAB file and the newer .MSI file used by the Microsoft installer.

The .CAB file is merely a compressed file that makes the distribution more efficient but offers little else. The .MSI file provides the most flexibility by working with the Microsoft installer that is part of the runtime distribution. The installer can coordinate the installation of assemblies that are private or require installation into the global assembly cache. The installer also provides uninstall capabilities.

Manifests

Manifests contain the metadata required for an assembly. As mentioned earlier, an assembly may contain one or more files, and it may have external dependencies. So, all the content and dependency information is bound together in the assembly manifest. The manifest itself is an XML file described by a corresponding manifest file schema defined by Microsoft. The manifest may reside in one of three locations, but the preferred location is as a resource within a DLL. A manifest file must have a "manifest" suffix, but there are no other restrictions on the name. Again, however, the preferred method of naming the manifest is to use the same name as the DLL that contains the manifest as a resource but with the "manifest" suffix.

Alternate locations for the manifest file are as a separate file in the shared assembly directory or as a separate file in the private assembly directory that is generally the location of the program executable. In any case , the manifest and its assembly will always be together.

In Listing 6-1, a partial manifest is displayed from the Clock control sample shown later in the chapter. This listing was retrieved using ILDASM.EXE. ILDASM.EXE is the intermediate language dissembler, which can be run from the Visual Studio .NET command prompt. After the program loads, the user can open an assembly and view the manifest and the objects defined in the assembly. This listing was cut from the manifest view.

This listing does not include the portion of the manifest that describes the clock control, but it does show how the dependant assemblies are represented. The common name of the assembly is listed with its version and public key token.

Listing 6-1: Partial Manifest Taken from Clock Example

```
.assembly extern System.Windows.Forms {
    .publickeytoken = (B7 7A 5C 56 19 34 E0 89 )   // .z\V.4..
    .ver 1:0:3300:0
}
.assembly extern System {
    .publickeytoken = (B7 7A 5C 56 19 34 E0 89 )   // .z\V.4..
    .ver 1:0:3300:0
}
...
.assembly Clock {
    ...
    .ver 1:0:751:16366
}
...
```

So, using this information, the running assembly can make a request to the runtime engine for another required assembly. In Listing 6-2, a portion of the application manifest has been clipped from the ClockTestApp application that was written as a test container for the Clock component. Now, in turn, the Clock control assembly information can be seen as one of the assemblies that ClockTestApp is dependant upon.

Listing 6-2: Partial Manifest Taken from ClockTestApp Example

```
.assembly extern System.Windows.Forms {
    .publickeytoken = (B7 7A 5C 56 19 34 E0 89 )   // .z\V.4..
    .ver 1:0:3300:0
```

Continued

Listing 6-2 *(Continued)*

```
}
.assembly extern Clock {
    .ver 1:0:751:16366
}
...
.assembly ClockTestApp {
    ...
    .ver 1:0:751:16540
}
...
```

Another important item to note in this application assembly listing is that the listing for the Clock component does not have a `.publickeytoken` property. This is because, at this point, the Clock component has not been signed with a strong name key. A strong name is the name generated when an assembly is signed using the private half of a public key pair, and the strong name will be globally unique, or strong. This also means that the Clock component may only serve as a private component and cannot be installed into the global assembly cache. So, the method of signing an assembly is essential, because creating a globally available assembly is a good thing. Globally available assemblies allow the developer to easily share code between projects, and because assemblies now inherently support side by side versioning, global assemblies do not have the same issues as globally available unmanaged DLLs. With the Common Language Runtime, globally available assemblies and any associated components need to be installed into the global assembly cache (GAC), which is the standard repository for global assemblies.

The basic reason for requiring assemblies to be signed for use in the GAC is name uniqueness. That is, using the Clock control as a good example, the common name of the assembly (Clock) is not guaranteed to be unique. If this control were capable of being installed into the GAC, then another organization could create a control called Clock and could deploy it into the GAC. Then a problem would ensue. In the COM world, this problem was partially solved by the GUID and the requirement that the registry would only maintain unique common names for components. But the limits of this solution are easily demonstrated by registering a completely different object that has the same common name as an existing component.

So, by requiring that all globally deployed components are signed with a private key, the system ensures that there is a unique identifier for every .NET global component. To save on storage, the manifest does not store the whole public key required for verification or the signature itself; it simply stores the public key token, which is a hash of the public key used by the assembly.

A secondary, positive benefit of the strong name signature is that the origin and integrity of the component may be verified. This is important both from the standpoint of product control and product security. That is, after a component has been signed, you can verify that the component was distributed by your organization and that the component has not been modified since it was distributed. So, finally, how are components signed?

The first step in the signing process is to use the strong name tool, `sn.exe`, provided with Visual Studio .NET to generate a public/private key-pair as shown in the following example:

```
sn -k keypair.snk  // keypair.snk is the <outfile> parameter
                   // for this case and could be any filename
```

After the public/private key-pair has been generated, it needs to be referenced by the assembly for compile-time signing. By default, this reference is found in the project's assembly information file. For C#, the filename is AssemblyInfo.cs, and the `AssemblyKeyFile` attribute needs to be modified to refer to the key-pair file as follows:

```
[assembly: AssemblyKeyFile("..\\..\\..\\..\\keypair.snk")]
```

Similarly, if the project is Visual Basic .NET, then the corresponding file will be AssemblyInfo.vb, and the line with `AssemblyKeyFile` attribute will look like the following line:

```
<Assembly: AssemblyKeyFile("..\..\..\..\key.snk")>
```

In both of these examples, relative directories were used, and the relative directory is determined from the directory with the final compiled output, not the directory containing the source code, which is generally two levels up from the output. Also, there is no need to create a new key-pair for every project. You could create a single key-pair for use by a given organization, and all code could refer to it.

This leads to a discussion of key control and delayed signing. Because any person with your public/private key-pair could sign code, controlling this capability may be important to you. The way to control this capability is through the delayed signing process. With delayed signing, the key-pair file is separated into two files — one with the public key and the other with the private key. The private key is then kept secure and used for generating key signatures by a limited group of people; meanwhile, the public key is stored in a generally available location for the developers who need it.

To separate the key-pair, the sn.exe tool is employed in the following manner:

```
sn -p keypair.snk publickey.snk  // sn -p <infile> <outfile>
```

So, the public key is extracted from the key-pair and left publicly available while the key-pair file is secured. Then, in the assembly information files the `AssemblyKeyFile` attribute is changed to use the public key file, and a second attribute, `AssemblyDelaySign`, must now be altered to true. So, in the AssemblyInfo.cs file of a C# project, you would now have the following:

```
[assembly: AssemblyKeyFile("..\\..\\..\\..\\publickey.snk")]
[assembly: AssemblyDelaySign(true)]
```

Again, the corresponding Visual Basic .NET AssemblyInfo.vb file would contain the next two lines:

```
<Assembly: AssemblyKeyFile("..\..\..\..\key.snk")>
<Assembly: AssemblyDelaySign(true)>
```

When the assembly is compiled in this format, the public key is put into the manifest and space is left in the compiled assembly for a signature to be added at a later time. Until the signature is added, the assembly cannot be verified; therefore, verification must be turned off with the following sn.exe tool command:

```
sn -Vr <assemblyname>
```

Finally, when the code is ready to be signed, the person controlling the key-pair would issue the next command:

```
sn -R <assemblyname> keypair.snk
```

This results in a fully signed component. Looking at a signed version of the Clock assembly, two important changes can be seen. Public key and hash algorithm attributes now exist and are shown in Listing 6-3.

Listing 6-3: Partial Manifest Taken from Clock after Signing

```
.publickey =
(00 24 00 00 04 80 00 00 94 00 00 00 06 02 00 00 // .$..........
 00 24 00 00 52 53 41 31 00 04 00 00 01 00 01 00 // .$..RSA1....
 ...
 14 9D 1E EA 06 E2 78 B4 8B 22 72 85 D9 9A 78 ED) //......x.."r.
.hash algorithm 0x00008004
```

So, the public key is now in the manifest, and the algorithm used to hash the public key token is specified. The effect of this can also be seen in the manifest generated for ClockTestApp after Clock is signed. In Listing 6-4, the public key token is present.

Listing 6-4: Partial Manifest Taken from ClockTestApp after Signing Clock

```
.assembly extern Clock
{
  .publickeytoken = (0D A3 87 A7 FD 43 2E 43 ) // .....C.C
  .ver 1:0:756:26443
}
```

Building .NET Components

Having discussed the benefits of .NET components, let's turn to building and implementing components in applications. Creating a component in .NET is a much simpler undertaking than the same task in COM. In this section, we will build a component for a WinForm application and later build a component for a Web application.

WinForm Components

Listing 6-5 contains the code for the example Clock control mentioned earlier. This component inherits from the UserControl class that provides us with all the base functionality we expect for a form-based control.

Listing 6-5: Code for the Clock Component

```
using System;
using System.Collections;
using System.ComponentModel;
using System.Drawing;
using System.Data;
using System.Windows.Forms;

namespace Clock
{
    /// <summary>
    /// Summary description for UserControl1.
    /// </summary>
    public class ClockCtl : System.Windows.Forms.UserControl
    {
        private System.Windows.Forms.Label lblTime;
        private System.Timers.Timer tClock;
        /// <summary>
        /// Required designer variable.
        /// </summary>
        private System.ComponentModel.Container components = null;
        public ClockCtl()
        {
        // This call is required by the Windows.Forms Form Designer.
        InitializeComponent();

        // TODO: Add any initialization after the InitForm call
        }

        /// <summary>
```

```
/// Clean up any resources being used.
/// </summary>
protected override void Dispose( bool disposing )
{
    if( disposing )
    {
        if( components != null )
            components.Dispose();
    }
    base.Dispose( disposing );
}


#region Component Designer generated code
/// <summary>
/// Required method for Designer support - do not modify
/// the contents of this method with the code editor.
/// </summary>
private void InitializeComponent()
{
    this.lblTime = new System.Windows.Forms.Label();
    this.tClock = new System.Timers.Timer();
    ((System.ComponentModel.ISupportInitialize)
     (this.tClock)).BeginInit();
    this.SuspendLayout();
    //
    // lblTime
    //
    this.lblTime.Location = new System.Drawing.Point(8, 4);
    this.lblTime.Name = "lblTime";
    this.lblTime.Size = new System.Drawing.Size(64, 16);
    this.lblTime.TabIndex = 1;
    this.lblTime.Text = "23:00:00.00";
    //
    // tClock
    //
    this.tClock.Enabled = true;
    this.tClock.Interval = 10;
    this.tClock.SynchronizingObject = this;
    this.tClock.Elapsed += new
     System.Timers.ElapsedEventHandler(this.tClock_Elapsed);
    //
    // ClockCtl
    //
    this.Controls.AddRange(
     new System.Windows.Forms.Control[] {this.lblTime});
```

```
        this.Name = "ClockCtl";
        this.Size = new System.Drawing.Size(80, 20);
        ((System.ComponentModel.ISupportInitialize)
         (this.tClock)).EndInit();
        this.ResumeLayout(false);
    }
    #endregion
    private void tClock_Elapsed(object sender,
     System.Timers.ElapsedEventArgs e)
    {
        DateTime t = DateTime.Now;
        lblTime.Text = t.Hour + ":" +
        (t.Minute<10 ? "0" + t.Minute : "" + t.Minute) + ":" +
        (t.Second<10 ? "0" + t.Second : "" + t.Second) + "." +
         t.Millisecond / 10;
    }
}
}
```

This code was created in four steps:

1. A new Clock project was created using the Windows control library template. Figure 6-1 shows the creation of a new C# Clock project. The process is nearly identical to the creation of a new VB project, except that Visual Basic projects would be selected.

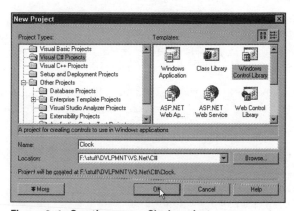

Figure 6-1: Creating a new Clock project

2. Label and timer controls were added to the form and given the name lblTime and tClock, respectively.

3. The tClock_Elapsed event was defined to handle the timer events occurring every 10ms.

4. AssemblyInfo.cs was updated to use an assembly key file, and the project was compiled.

At this point, development of the component is complete with no further action required for its use as a private component. That is, no registration or special installation is needed. If the component needs to be installed into the GAC, the component can be installed using the gacutil.exe command in the following line:

```
gacutil /i Clock.dll
```

The component can be removed from the GAC with the /u option as follows:

```
gacutil /u Clock
```

It bears repeating that, unlike COM registration, installing a component into the GAC is completely optional. In fact, installation to the GAC should only be done on the basis of necessity and not as a standard practice. For an individual application, installing a component into the GAC only has the negative effect of additional maintenance that results from having to keep up with updating or removing a component that is not in the application's directory. But, in the event that multiple applications will share a component and will take advantage of side-by-side versioning, installing into the GAC makes sense and provides benefits.

Some additional parts of the code are worth noting:

◆ The control ClockCtl inherits from UserControl, whereas the control in the next Web component example inherits from WebControl.

◆ There is no using Clock statement. The using keyword provides a syntax shortcut, and it is not the same as an include statement in C. The managed code equivalent of include is a reference, and references will be covered in the examples that implement the components.

◆ The Visual Studio environment provided all the initialization code in this example, which left only the tClock_Elapsed function to be declared and defined.

Web components

Having demonstrated the creation of a standard Windows-based component, let's examine the creation of a Web-based component in .NET. Again, the basis for the example is a clock mechanism, but this component derives from WebControl and it implements two interfaces — IPostBackEventHandler and IPostBackDataHandler — which are shown in Listing 6-6.

Listing 6-6: Code for the WebClock **Component**

```
using System;
using System.Web.UI;
using System.Web.UI.WebControls;
using System.ComponentModel;
using System.Collections;
using System.Collections.Specialized;

namespace WebClock
{
    /// <summary>
    /// Summary description for WebClock.
    /// </summary>
    [DefaultProperty("Text"),ToolboxData("<{0}:WebClockCtl
      runat=server></{0}:WebClockCtl>")]
    public class WebClockCtl : WebControl, IPostBackEventHandler,
      IPostBackDataHandler
    {
        private string time;
        [Bindable(true), Category("Appearance"), DefaultValue("")]
        public string Time
        {
            get
            {
                return System.DateTime.Now.ToString();
            }
        }
        /// <summary>
        /// Render this control to the output parameter specified.
        /// </summary>
        /// <param name="output">
        /// The HTML writer to write out to </param>
        protected override void Render(HtmlTextWriter output)
        {
          output.WriteLine("<body onload=\"StartClock()\">");
          output.WriteLine("<a href=\"javascript:StartClock()\">");
          output.WriteLine(Time);
          output.WriteLine("</a>");
          output.WriteLine("<script language='JavaScript'>");
          output.WriteLine("<!--");
          output.WriteLine("function StartClock()");
          output.WriteLine("{");
```

Continued

Listing 6-6 *(Continued)*

```
            output.WriteLine("timerID=setTimeout(\"UpdateClock()\",
              1000);");
            output.WriteLine("}");
            output.WriteLine("function UpdateClock()");
            output.WriteLine("{");
            output.WriteLine("timerID=setTimeout(\"UpdateClock()\",
              1000);");
            output.WriteLine("location.reload();");
            output.WriteLine(Page.GetPostBackEventReference(this,
              "UpdateClock") + ";");
            output.WriteLine("}");
            output.WriteLine("//-->");
            output.WriteLine("</script>");
        }
        public bool LoadPostData(String postDataKey,
                                 NameValueCollection values)
        {
            return false;
        }
        public void RaisePostDataChangedEvent() { }
        public void RaisePostBackEvent(String eventArgument) { }
    }
}
```

Because this is a WebControl, the control renders itself by producing HTML that will become part of the Web page served to the client. At runtime, communication with the server is conducted via HTTP and is initiated at the client by calls to `sub-mit()`. IIS receives the client call and invokes ASP.NET, which will dynamically produce a form and post-back function for the page. The name of the post-back function is retrieved via the call to the `Page.GetPostBackEventReference()` function found within the `Render` event. This post-back function will set two parameters on the form and then call `submit()`, which will allow IIS to pass the event back to the correct server-side control for a response.

Also, the clock does not have its own timer. The reason for this is that this component will be served via ASP.NET and IIS, and after the component reaches the client as part of a Web page, it will not be able to "hear" a server-side timer. That is, after the page is rendered, it is at the mercy of the user and the browser. The way this is solved here is by including JavaScript that will run on the browser to generate timing events. When the timing event occurs, the form is posted, IIS makes a callback to the `WebClock` component, and the control re-renders itself with the current server time.

Using a Component in an Application

With two components developed, it is time to actually implement the components. The common component based on `UserControl` will be implemented in a WinForm application, and the component based on `WebControl` will be implemented in an ASP.NET application. In both cases, the implementation of the managed component will be simpler than implementing previous, unmanaged components.

In order to implement a component in an application, the application must contain a reference to the component. There are two methods for adding a reference to an application. The first method is to use the Add Reference dialog. This dialog can be accessed from two locations: the Visual Studio application menu and the references window. Using the Visual Studio application menu, the user selects Project and then Add Reference on the menu. This brings up the dialog shown in Figure 6-2. This same dialog can also be accessed by right-clicking on the References window, which will provide a pop-up menu with an Add Reference menu item that leads to the same dialog shown in Figure 6-2.

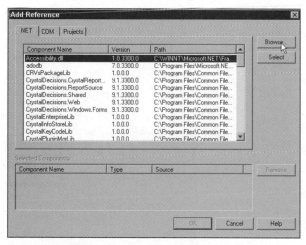

Figure 6-2: Adding a new reference

The other means of gaining a reference also involves adding the component to the form from the components toolbox. Again, there are two ways to reach the Customize Toolbox dialog. The first is by selecting Tools → Customize Toolbox from the Visual Studio application menu. The second option is via a pop-up menu that is shown by right-clicking on the toolbox. Either way, the dialog shown in Figure 6-3 appears. When the desired component is visually added to the form under development, Visual Studio will add the required reference to the project.

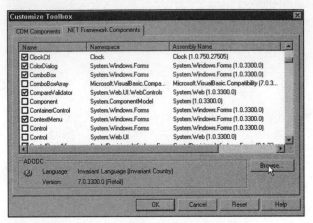

Figure 6-3: Adding a component to the toolbox

WinForm application

The first application is a WinForm application, and the code is shown in Listing 6-7. WinForm is the new term for the standard Windows, form-oriented application. In this application, the Clock component is used. The application was created by selecting File → New → Project and then selecting the Windows Application template. ClockTestApp was provided for the name of the project.

Three standard controls were added to the form; two command buttons were added to start and stop the clock, and a text box was added to allow the user to input the update interval for the clock. Finally, the ClockCtl was added to the form.

Listing 6-7: The Implementation of the Clock Component

```
using System;
using System.Drawing;
using System.Collections;
using System.ComponentModel;
using System.Windows.Forms;
using System.Data;

namespace ClockTestApp
{
    /// <summary>
    /// Summary description for Form1.
    /// </summary>
    public class frmClockTest : System.Windows.Forms.Form
    {
        private Clock.ClockCtl clockCtl1;
        private System.Windows.Forms.Button cmdStart;
        private System.Windows.Forms.Button cmdStop;
```

```
private System.Windows.Forms.TextBox txtInterval;
private System.Windows.Forms.Button cmdGC;
/// <summary>
/// Required designer variable.
/// </summary>
private System.ComponentModel.Container components = null;
public frmClockTest()
{
    // Required for Windows Form Designer support
    InitializeComponent();
    // TODO: Add any constructor code after
    // initializeComponent call
}
/// <summary>
/// Clean up any resources being used.
/// </summary>
protected override void Dispose( bool disposing )
{
    if( disposing )
    {
        if (components != null)
        {
            components.Dispose();
        }
    }
    base.Dispose( disposing );
}

#region Windows Form Designer generated code
/// <summary>
/// Required method for Designer support - do not modify
/// the contents of this method with the code editor.
/// </summary>
private void InitializeComponent()
{
    this.clockCtl1 = new Clock.ClockCtl();
    this.cmdStart = new System.Windows.Forms.Button();
    this.cmdStop = new System.Windows.Forms.Button();
    this.txtInterval = new System.Windows.Forms.TextBox();
    this.cmdGC = new System.Windows.Forms.Button();
    this.SuspendLayout();
    //
    // clockCtl1
    //
```

Continued

Listing 6-7 *(Continued)*

```
this.clockCtl1.Location =
  new System.Drawing.Point(24, 9);
this.clockCtl1.Name = "clockCtl1";
this.clockCtl1.Size = new System.Drawing.Size(100, 20);
this.clockCtl1.TabIndex = 0;
this.clockCtl1.TimerInterval = 0;
//
// cmdStart
//
this.cmdStart.Location =
  new System.Drawing.Point(140, 12);
this.cmdStart.Name = "cmdStart";
this.cmdStart.Size = new System.Drawing.Size(85, 25);
this.cmdStart.TabIndex = 1;
this.cmdStart.Text = "Start";
this.cmdStart.Click +=
  new System.EventHandler(this.cmdStart_Click);
//
// cmdStop
//
this.cmdStop.Location =
  new System.Drawing.Point(140, 43);
this.cmdStop.Name = "cmdStop";
this.cmdStop.Size = new System.Drawing.Size(85, 25);
this.cmdStop.TabIndex = 2;
this.cmdStop.Text = "Stop";
this.cmdStop.Click +=
  new System.EventHandler(this.cmdStop_Click);
//
// txtInterval
//
this.txtInterval.Location =
  new System.Drawing.Point(24, 48);
this.txtInterval.Name = "txtInterval";
this.txtInterval.TabIndex = 3;
this.txtInterval.Text = "";
this.txtInterval.TextChanged +=
  new System.EventHandler(this.txtInterval_TextChanged);
//
// frmClockTest
//
this.AutoScaleBaseSize = new System.Drawing.Size(5, 13);
this.ClientSize = new System.Drawing.Size(238, 120);
```

```
                this.Controls.AddRange(
                  new System.Windows.Forms.Control[] {
                    this.cmdGC,
                    this.txtInterval,
                    this.cmdStop,
                    this.cmdStart,
                    this.clockCtl1});
            this.Name = "frmClockTest";
            this.Text = "Clock Test";
            this.ResumeLayout(false);
        }
        #endregion
        /// <summary>
        /// The main entry point for the application.
        /// </summary>
        [STAThread]
        static void Main()
        {
            Application.Run(new frmClockTest());
        }
        private void txtInterval_TextChanged(object sender,
          System.EventArgs e)
        {
            int i = Convert.ToInt16(txtInterval.Text);
            clockCtl1.TimerInterval = i;
        }
        private void cmdStart_Click(object sender,
          System.EventArgs e)
        {
            clockCtl1.Start();
        }
        private void cmdStop_Click(object sender,
          System.EventArgs e)
        {
            clockCtl1.Stop();
        }
    }
}
```

IIS application

The next sample, shown in Listing 6-8, demonstrates the WebClockCtl implemented
in an IIS/ASP.NET application. The page is very simple, containing only a label and
the WebClockCtl. Every second the timer event on the Web page, provided by the
WebClockCtl, causes the form to submit the page. Upon submission, the form values
are read, and the WebClockCtl updates itself with the current server time.

Listing 6-8: The Implementation of the Clock Component in ASP.NET

```
using System;
using System.Collections;
using System.ComponentModel;
using System.Data;
using System.Drawing;
using System.Web;
using System.Web.SessionState;
using System.Web.UI;
using System.Web.UI.WebControls;
using System.Web.UI.HtmlControls;

namespace BookSamples
{
    /// <summary>
    /// Summary description for WebForm1.
    /// </summary>
    public class WebForm1 : System.Web.UI.Page
    {
        protected System.Web.UI.WebControls.Label lblWebClock;
        protected WebClock.WebClockCtl WebClockCtl1;
        private void Page_Load(object sender, System.EventArgs e)
        {
            // Put user code to initialize the page here
            lblWebClock.Text = "Hello, the time is ...";
        }
        #region Web Form Designer generated code
        override protected void OnInit(EventArgs e)
        {
        //
        // CODEGEN: This call is required by the ASP.NET Web Form
        // Designer.
        //
            InitializeComponent();
            base.OnInit(e);
        }

        /// <summary>
        /// Required method for Designer support - do not modify
        /// the contents of this method with the code editor.
        /// </summary>
        private void InitializeComponent()
        {
            this.Load += new System.EventHandler(this.Page_Load);
        }
```

```
    #endregion
  }
}
```

Transactions and Performance

Having demonstrated the fundamentals of .NET components, the focus now shifts to more sophisticated components that employ database access and transactions. Although non-transactional components are far more common, the transactional components are often critical to the performance of a large system.

When examining components and transactions, there are some considerations.

Here, consideration will be given to connection-based and distributed transaction components. Again, it is important to consider the costs and benefits of these two different solutions. The framework provided to perform distributed transactions to components within .NET incurs additional overhead, but in systems where distributed transactions are mandatory or the advantages of object pooling can be fully realized, then distributed will be the way to go.

Connection-based transactions

Components that perform transactions using connection objects and methods operate much as you might expect. The component can inherit from either UserControl or WebControl, and it then provides the connection-based data access capabilities within one of the component methods. In Listing 6-9, a typical UserComponent derived class is shown implementing connection-based data access.

Listing 6-9: Connection-Based Transactional Component

```
using System;
using System.ComponentModel;
using System.Data;
using System.Windows.Forms;

namespace CBComponent
{
    class CBDemo : UserControl
    {
        public void UpdateDatabase()
        {
            SqlConnection conn = new SqlConnection(connectString);
            SqlCommand cmd = new SqlCommand("CommandProc",conn);
            cmd.CommandType = CommandType.StoredProcedure;
```

Continued

Listing 6-9 *(Continued)*

```
            try
            {
                conn.Open();
                cmd.ExecuteNonQuery();
            }
            catch ( Exception e )
            {
                // store exception in error log
            }
            finally
            {
                conn.Close();
            }
        }
    }
}
```

This component shows a connection-based data access and transaction execution that would be effective for a client application but would not scale particularly well. The primary drawback of a connection-based component on the server side is the overhead imposed by repeatedly opening and closing the database connection. Opening a database connection is a high overhead activity, and if this component were used on a server-side application with high demand, the results would be average at best.

Within the scope of data-oriented components, the solution to this problem would be to use pooled components. This will be covered in conjunction with distributed transactions in the next section.

Distributed transactions

Components that need to make use of the distributed transaction framework can enlist the framework by deriving from `ServicedComponent`. A serviced component can be registered with COM+ Services and, therefore, can provide distributed transaction capabilities and object pooling, mentioned earlier. Object pooling can also be used to provide a form of connection pooling. There are other ways to provide connection pooling, but the other means involve specific data providers that have built-in connection pooling capabilities. Listing 6-10 demonstrates the use of the `ServicedComponent` class.

Listing 6-10: Distributed Transaction Component

```
using System;
using Microsoft.ComServices;
```

```
using System.Runtime.CompilerServices;

namespace DTComponent
{
    [Transaction(Transaction.Required)]
    public class DTDemo : ServicedComponent
    {
        // Set complete automatically called if no exception is
        // raised
        [AutoComplete]
        public bool Post()
        {
            // Add data code here
            ...
        }
    }

    // Registration details
    // COM+ Application Name to add the component
    [assembly: ApplicationName("DTComponent")]
    // Strong name for assembly
    [assembly: AssemblyKeyFileAttribute("keypair.snk")]
}
```

A ServicedComponent must carry a strong name. The reason for the strong name is that the component must have a unique name to be successfully registered with COM+ Services.

 The use of strong names and component registration is covered in more detail in Chapter 7, which covers managed components and COM integration.

This component requires a transaction context and is auto-completing. The transaction requirement means that if the component is not supplied with a transaction context by a calling component, the component will retrieve a transaction context on its own. Auto-completing means that the developer does not need to explicitly call SetComplete(). As long as the component does not raise an exception while performing its database operations, then SetComplete() will be called by the framework. Listing 6-11 shows code employing the DTDemo serviced component from Listing 6-10.

Listing 6-11: Implementation of the Distributed Transaction Component

```
using System;
using DTComponent;

namespace DTComponentTest
{
    class DTDemoClient
    {
        public static int Main()
        {
            DTDemo demo = new DTDemo();
            demo.post();
            return 0;
        }
    }
}
```

The ease of implementation is clear. All that the client requires is a reference to the DTComponent component. The client program then creates an instance of the component with the new operator, and the component is utilized as if it were the same as any other local component.

Summary

This chapter reviews the development of a broad range of components within the .NET Framework, including components for use by WinForm and ASP.NET applications as well as .NET components that do and do not use transactions. Whether a developer chooses to implement components in VB or C#, the managed code environment provides rapid application development for the components. The managed components do not require registration as COM did. The only requirement is that the application using the component contains a reference to the component. Aside from the reference there are no other constraints on where the component needs to be installed on a target system. Although the preferred location is to use components privately, installing them into the local application directory, the component can be installed into the GAC. In either case, nothing additional has to be done to the application that implements the component, because the runtime environment will locate the component for the application when it is needed.

Components are also a preferred location to consolidate business logic and database access. Depending on circumstances, components may make use of connection-based transactions or distributed transactions, via ServicedComponent inheritance. Although connection-based transactions are simple and efficient, some requirements will mandate the use of distributed transactions. In these cases, scalability can be increased through the use of object pooling.

Chapter 7

Integration with COM Components

IN THIS CHAPTER

◆ Knowing how COM and .NET interoperate

◆ Calling a COM object from .NET

◆ Registering a .NET object

◆ Calling a .NET object from COM

◆ Using COM+ Services from .NET

ALTHOUGH THERE ARE MANY benefits to .NET components, there is one significant drawback: newness. While the situation may be short lived, right now there are very few, if any, .NET components within any given enterprise, while a myriad of COM objects are already in place. Therefore, reality necessitates that COM and .NET interoperate in the enterprise. .NET components will need to call upon legacy COM objects to access established business rules. And, as .NET development progresses, the logical route to follow when extending COM-based applications will be to use new .NET components, which will mean that COM objects will need to call .NET components.

The Common Language Runtime provides classes that facilitate accessing COM and native APIs from .NET, and the Visual Studio .NET distribution provides tools to wrap managed code with a COM layer to facilitate access from the other direction. This chapter covers the interoperation of COM and .NET, including COM+ Services and native Windows APIs. After reading this chapter, you should understand the process of communication between the two technologies and how to address the differences that result from the different development paradigms that exist for COM and .NET.

COM and .NET Interop

Before exploring how to implement COM and .NET interoperation, we'll cover the underlying design for interoperation. First, what is meant by *interoperation*, or *interop,* as it is commonly called, and why is the interaction between COM and .NET considered interoperation when the interaction between COM and VB 6.0 is not? To answer this, it is necessary to define interoperation. *Interoperation* is two or more different systems working together. So, it's important to realize that COM and .NET are running as parts of two different systems even if they may be running on the same computer. COM facilities are available as part of the Windows operating system and are directly tied to the registry. Managed code developed in .NET, however, is running in the Common Language Runtime environment, which is a separate virtual system that, as shown in Chapter 6, does not need and is totally unaware of the Windows registry. When a COM object needs to communicate with a .NET component, or vice versa, the gap between these two systems must be crossed, and that is interop.

General principles

As you may expect, calling COM objects from .NET is more straightforward than calling .NET from COM. After all, COM objects are designed to provide a generic interface via a type library for any Windows application to use. In this case, the application happens to be the Common Language Runtime (CLR). Given that the CLR can load a COM object like any other application, the managed code simply needs a reference to, and type definition for, the COM object. These are provided by the `System.Runtime.InteropServices` namespace, which provides classes for accessing COM and the native APIs from .NET. The end result is that interoperation with COM can be accomplished with little effort and is nearly seamless.

Part of the additional complexity of calling a .NET component from COM involves the generation of type libraries and registration. That is, any system or COM object expecting to call another COM object expects a type library and a GUID with a common name entered into the registry. So, for a .NET component to appear as a COM object, a type library must be created and the component must be registered. In order for a component to be accessed from COM+ Services, it must be signed with a strong name and installed in the GAC. There are utilities to create a type library and effectively register the .NET component for use by COM. (This process is discussed in greater detail later in this chapter.)

Differences in paradigm

Although the general principles for interoperation are clear, additional problems arise from the differences in the paradigms that govern development in COM and .NET, respectively. Table 7-1 lists these differences.

TABLE 7-1 DIFFERENCES IN DEVELOPMENT PARADIGMS BETWEEN
           MANAGED AND UNMANAGED CODE

Characteristic	Unmanaged Paradigm	Managed Paradigm
Identification	GUIDs	Strong Names
Error handling	HRESULTs	Exceptions
Type compatibility	Binary Compatibility	Type Compatibility
Type definition	Type Library	Manifest
Type safety	Unsafe	Optionally Safe
Versioning	None	Inherent

So, to fully interoperate, these issues must be considered and addressed in the components that are developed for interoperation. Of the items in Table 7-1, error handling is probably the most obvious issue to be addressed by the developer of custom components. If a COM object returns an HRESULT, how should that be turned into a managed code exception for proper handling? Conversely, if a managed component generates an exception, how should that be turned into an HRESULT so that COM will handle the error? Other techniques will need to be employed as a result of these fundamental differences shown in the table; examples for handling them follow in the subsequent sections of this chapter.

Calling COM from .NET

The first topic to cover will be calling COM from .NET, because this will likely be the first hurdle to jump, given the existence of the myriad COM objects already in place. We cover C# and Visual Basic .NET first; later, we cover some issues related to ASP.NET.

C# and Visual Basic .NET

Listing 7-1 provides a demonstration program that implements a tree-view COM object. For the developer, this is the simplest form of interoperation. When adding a COM object to a WinForm application in this manner, .NET to COM interoperation is almost transparent. The component is added to the form and Visual Studio .NET adds the supporting code.

Listing 7-1: Implementing COM in .NET

```
using System;
using System.Drawing;
using System.Collections;
using System.ComponentModel;
using System.Windows.Forms;
using System.Data;

namespace COMDemo1
{
    /// <summary>
    /// Summary description for Form1.
    /// </summary>
    public class Form1 : System.Windows.Forms.Form
    {
        private AxMSComctlLib.AxTreeView axTreeView1;
        /// <summary>
        /// Required designer variable.
        /// </summary>
        private System.ComponentModel.Container components = null;

        public Form1()
        {
            // Required for Windows Form Designer support
            InitializeComponent();
            // TODO: Add any constructor code after
            // InitializeComponent call
        }

        /// <summary>
        /// Clean up any resources being used.
        /// </summary>
        protected override void Dispose( bool disposing )
        {
            if( disposing )
            {
                if (components != null)
                {
                    components.Dispose();
                }
            }
            base.Dispose( disposing );
        }

        #region Windows Form Designer generated code
```

```csharp
/// <summary>
/// Required method for Designer support - do not modify
/// the contents of this method with the code editor.
/// </summary>
private void InitializeComponent()
{
    System.Resources.ResourceManager resources = new
      System.Resources.ResourceManager(typeof(Form1));
    this.axTreeView1 = new AxMSComctlLib.AxTreeView();
    ((System.ComponentModel.ISupportInitialize)
      (this.axTreeView1)).BeginInit();
    this.SuspendLayout();
    //
    // axTreeView1
    //
    this.axTreeView1.Location =
      new System.Drawing.Point(22, 21);
    this.axTreeView1.Name = "axTreeView1";
    this.axTreeView1.OcxState =
      ((System.Windows.Forms.AxHost.State)
      (resources.GetObject("axTreeView1.OcxState")));
    this.axTreeView1.Size =
      new System.Drawing.Size(132, 154);
    this.axTreeView1.TabIndex = 0;
    //
    // Form1
    //
    this.AutoScaleBaseSize = new System.Drawing.Size(5, 13);
    this.ClientSize = new System.Drawing.Size(314, 273);
    this.Controls.AddRange( new
      System.Windows.Forms.Control[] {
      this.axTreeView1});
    this.Name = "Form1";
    this.Text = "Form1";
    ((System.ComponentModel.ISupportInitialize)
      (this.axTreeView1)).EndInit();
    this.ResumeLayout(false);
}
#endregion

/// <summary>
/// The main entry point for the application.
/// </summary>
[STAThread]
```

Continued

Listing 7-1 *(Continued)*

```
static void Main()
{
    Application.Run(new Form1());
}
}
}
```

In this example, the tree-view COM object is added via the Customize Toolbox dialog shown in Figure 7-1. When a COM object is added through Visual Studio, the type information in the COM type library is automatically converted to metadata in an assembly for reference. This assembly is then automatically added to the list of references for the project.

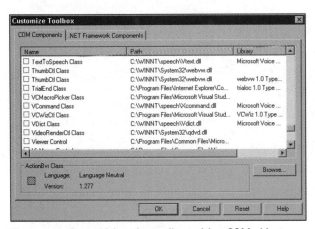

Figure 7-1: Customizing the toolbox with a COM object

In the event that only a reference is needed to the COM object, the developer can access the Add Reference dialog shown in Figure 7-2 by right-clicking the References item under the project listing. When the Add Reference dialog is used, the type library will be imported automatically and the reference established, but the initialization code that was added by Visual Studio in Listing 7-1 will not be added. This interface to COM from .NET is called the Runtime Callable Wrapper (RCW).

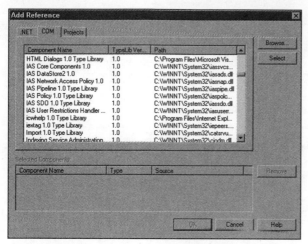

Figure 7-2 Adding a reference to a COM object using
the Add Reference dialog

There are some items of note in Listing 7-1. First the System.ComponentModel is added among the using lines. The System.ComponentModel namespace supplies classes and interfaces that are used by components and controls, including those needed for implementing attributes, binding data sources, and performing type conversion. One of these classes is AxHost, which is used for encapsulating ActiveX controls in .NET. This class is used to retrieve state information in the block of code where the TreeView component is initialized. Another item of note is the use of the ISupportInitialize interface at the start and end of the InitializeComponent function where calls are made to BeginInit() and EndInit(), respectively. The ISupportInitialize interface allows components to optimize multiple Set calls that occur during initialization. The BeginInit() and EndInit() function calls simply indicate the start and end points for this initialization behavior.

As a final note regarding this code, the following line can be seen immediately within the class declaration for Form1:

```
private AxMSComctlLib.AxTreeView axTreeView1;
```

When the TreeView COM object was imported, the namespace AxMSComctlLib was created. Within that namespace, the AxTreeView class was created. AxTreeView1 is simply the declared variable. So, if you happen across Ax in Microsoft-generated code, you can be reasonably sure it relates to ActiveX.

Exposing the COM data type to .NET is half the battle in .NET-to-COM interoperation; the other half is marshalling the data and function calls in .NET. For the developer, there should be no reason to be concerned with the marshalling half of the battle. However, when importing the type information, there are, in fact, a number of ways in which COM type data may be handled in .NET. These are summarized in Table 7-2.

TABLE 7-2 IMPORTING TYPE INFORMATION FROM COM TO .NET

Tool	Description
Visual Studio .NET	Automatically converts COM type information to assembly metadata.
Type Library Importer	A command line process, relying on tlbimp.exe, to convert COM type information that provides several switches, allowing additional control over the process.
TypeConverter Class	Provides methods that perform type conversion and can convert in-memory type library information to metadata.
Custom Wrappers	The developer can write a custom .NET component to wrap the COM object and handle type conversion. This is not a recommended technique, but it is necessary in some circumstances.

TYPE LIBRARY IMPORTER

Although allowing Visual Studio to automatically import the COM type library and establish the required reference is the most efficient manner for referencing a COM object, the developer may need more control over this process. Visual Studio provides the type library importer, tlbimp.exe, as a command line tool to supply the developer with additional control over the process. Tlbimp.exe creates an assembly file and has quite a number of optional parameters, many of which handle digital signatures and key management. Aside from the key management optional parameters, there are several other parameters that are likely to be particularly useful. Following is an example of the tlbimp.exe command line followed by a list of selected parameters:

```
tlbimp typelibraryfile [options]
```

◆ /namespace:{desired namespace name}: Specifies the namespace to be created or used by the import process.

- ◆ `/reference:{filename}`: Specifies an assembly file to use to resolve references to types not defined in the current library. If `/reference` is not used, tlbimp.exe recursively imports any external type library that the current type library references. But if `/reference` is used, the tool will attempt to resolve external types in the referenced assemblies before it imports additional type libraries.

- ◆ `/strictref`: Specifies that the import process should fail if the import process cannot succeed using only assemblies itemized with the `/reference` parameter.

- ◆ `/out:{filename}`: Specifies the output filename for the import process. By default, the output filename will use the same base name as the type library input file and then append .DLL, but if the input file is a DLL the import will fail to prevent an overwrite of the original file.

- ◆ `/asmversion:{version number}`: Specifies the version number to be associated with the output assembly.

- ◆ `/unsafe`: Specifies that tlbimp.exe should import the type library without performing .NET security checks.

Once an assembly has been created to provide an interface to the COM object, almost half the problem is solved. The new namespace and class that are created can be used like any other .NET component. The `Marshall` class will handle the passing of parameters and the function calls, and the developer does not need to be involved in that process. What still remains for the developer is to manage the differing error-handling schemes that were highlighted in Table 7-1. The COM object will be returning HRESULTS and the .NET environment works with Exceptions.

Again, .NET and the `Marshall` class provide some assistance to the developer. The `Marshall` class will examine the results from the COM object and throw an exception in the event of a non-zero HRESULT. If the HRESULT is a standard system-defined value, a corresponding Exception will be located by lookup and thrown by the following function:

`Marshal.ThrowExceptionForHR(HRESULT)`

This function will also populate the additional `Exception` fields, such as `Description`, with the error information supplied by `IErrorInfo`, if that interface is supported by the COM object in question. If the additional error information is not available, the `Exception` fields will be populated with default values.

There is still a gap left by the `Marshall` class, however. If the exception is not defined, then only the generic `ComException` will be thrown. This case will probably not be uncommon when interacting with custom COM objects that supply custom HRESULTs. So, when a developer is working with a COM object that may supply a non-system HRESULT, the developer should catch any generic ComExceptions and re-throw an appropriate custom exception. Listing 7-2 shows a custom exception class and the re-throwing of the ComException in Visual Basic .NET. Listing 7-3 shows the same procedure in C#.

Listing 7-2: Implementing Custom Exception Class in Visual Basic .NET

```
Public Class UserDefinedCOMExceptionClass
    Inherits Exception
    'The value of 129 would be replaced with your hresult
    Dim iUserDefinedHResult As Integer = 129

    Public Function UserDefinedCOMExceptionClass()
        HResult = iUserDefinedHResult
    End Function

    Public Overrides ReadOnly Property Message() As String
        Get
            Message = "UserDefinedCOMException occured."
        End Get

    End Property
End Class
```

Listing 7-3: Implementing Custom Exception Class in C#

```
using System;

namespace ExceptionClassLib
{
    /// <summary>
    /// UserDefinedCOMExceptionClass defines an exception to be
    /// rethrown when a generic COMException is caught with an
    /// equivalent HResult value.
    /// </summary>
    public class UserDefinedCOMExceptionClass : Exception
    {
        // The value of 129 would be replaced with your hresult
        int iUserDefinedHResult = 129;

        public UserDefinedCOMExceptionClass()
        {
            HResult = iUserDefinedHResult;
        }

        override public string Message
        {
```

```
        get
        {
            return "UserDefinedCOMException occured.";
        }
    }
  }
}
```

Using these examples, the developer code would examine the value of the Hresult field in the ComException and re-throw the desired custom exception with the user defined HResult. It's important to note that the Hresult field in the custom exception class is set in the constructor. Otherwise, the field will receive a default value.

CUSTOM WRAPPERS

Although the RCW provided automatically is almost always sufficient, there are still occasions when a custom RCW may be needed. These occasions generally result from one of two issues:

◆ The COM types that need to be employed are not recognized by the marshaller or require additional marshalling information.

◆ A type library contains many more types than are needed and the developer does not want to deploy extra, unneeded types.

So, although we do not cover the details here, if you encounter one of these situations, pursuing the creation of a custom RCW may be worthwhile.

ASP.NET

Accessing COM objects from ASP.NET is really no different than accessing COM objects from WinForms applications. But there are some additional considerations, particularly with regard to early- and late-binding objects. *Binding,* in this case, is the process of linking a function call in code with an address for actual execution. If this process happens at runtime, the function is late-bound, and if this happens at compile-time, the function is said to be early-bound.

LATE BINDING

Late binding always occurs when a generic object reference is used, as in the following line of VB code:

```
Dim myObject as Object
```

When myObject is declared in this manner, there is no associated type information; this includes information as to what properties and functions are available to myObject. So, when a method of myObject is executed, the interface of myObject must be queried for a listing of available methods; if the method exists, its numeric identifier must be retrieved, and then the method may be executed. All this activity is, generally, unnecessary overhead. In the case of ASP.NET, ASP.NET still allows objects to be instantiated through a call to `Server.CreateObject`, but this really should be avoided because any subsequent function calls or property settings will be late-bound.

EARLY BINDING
Early binding occurs at compile-time and, therefore, does not introduce any of the runtime overhead of late binding. Early binding will occur with any type-specific declaration like the declaration in the following line of code:

```
Dim myRecordset as Recordset
```

In this case, all the available methods and properties will be known at compile-time and the desired function call addresses can be inserted into the compiled result. This available information shows up in the form of IntelliSense within Visual Studio .NET. So, back to ASP.NET: If imported type libraries are used with ASP.NET, then early binding can occur and the overhead of late binding will be avoided.

Performance considerations

In general, there is not too much to worry about in terms of performance when calling COM from .NET. The overhead introduced by interoperation is very low, and if the object method being called is performing any substantial work, then the overhead of interoperation will be a minimal percentage of the execution time. If, however, you have an object where a very large number of method calls are to trivial methods, like sets or gets, then the percentage of runtime spent on interoperation can increase. In this case, it may become worthwhile to create a custom wrapper with method calls that support these operations but do not incur interoperation penalties. Or, if the object is a simple object for maintaining state information, then it may well be worthwhile to rewrite it in .NET.

Calling .NET Components from COM

Calling .NET components from COM is certainly a different process than the other way around. When the developer needs to use a COM object in .NET, the information about the COM object can be found in the registry, but this registry information is not automatically available to a COM object for a .NET component. So, when developing .NET components that will be called by COM objects the goal will be to write .NET components that will be conducive to interoperation and then to register them. This interface between COM and .NET objects is referred to as the COM Callable Wrapper (CCW).

Writing .NET components for interoperation

Writing .NET components so that they are conducive to interoperation with COM is somewhat problematic. This may seem odd at first. After all, COM components were not written with interoperation in mind, and interoperation with them is easy, bordering on trivial. However, upon closer inspection, COM can be seen to implement a subset of the functionality available in .NET, so .NET can represent anything that COM can represent. This means that building an assembly that wraps the behavior of a COM object is straightforward.

However, when trying to generate a COM type to represent a .NET component, COM may not possess the ability to represent some of the behaviors of the .NET component. This means that when a .NET component is going to be used for interoperation, consideration must be given to how it will be represented as a COM type.

GENERAL DESIGN GUIDELINES

When writing .NET components that are intended for interoperation with COM, there are several guidelines to follow:

- Managed classes must be public to be accessed from COM. As previously mentioned, a managed assembly must be registered before it can be used by COM. In order to register the assembly, its type information must be exported to a type library, and during this process public classes will be exported. Therefore, only public classes will be available to COM. The next item in the list is a logical extension of the first requirement, so only those members of the class that are themselves declared public will be exported and available to COM. Also, static functions and constant fields will not be available to COM.

- The methods, properties, fields, and events of the managed class must also be declared public for use by COM. Even though methods that are not public will never be available to COM, it is not true that public methods must always be available to COM. Within the managed code, a number of attributes can be set that will affect how a managed class will be exported. One of these attributes is the ComVisible attribute, which can be used to limit the visibility of public fields and methods, leaving some items available to other managed code that will not be available to COM.

- Managed classes must have a public default constructor to be activated from COM. This means a public constructor that requires no parameters. The need for there to be a public constructor follows from the previous discussion, but additionally, when COM creates an object, there is no opportunity to pass parameters to the constructor — thus, the need to provide a default constructor.

◆ **Abstract managed classes cannot be accessed from COM.** This may seem obvious, but given that an abstract class cannot be instantiated without a subclass that defines some undefined methods, it follows that an abstract class will not be able to be instantiated for consumption by COM.

◆ **Managed classes should implement interfaces explicitly.** COM objects work by providing fixed interfaces, which can be interrogated by client for use. When the type exporter runs against a managed class, it will create an interface definition for that class if one does not exist. However, if the class definition changes, the interface may also change. Because COM objects do not expect interfaces to change, objects that implement the managed component may fail when trying to use future versions of the same component. Explicit interfaces help resolve this problem. When a managed interface is exported, it will have the same properties as a COM interface. So, if the developer explicitly defines an interface and implements the interface in the managed class, subsequent changes to the managed class will not directly impact the interface. Thus, the COM objects that consume the managed class via interoperation will not be adversely impacted by changes to the managed class.

THE CLASS INTERFACE

When a managed class is exported for COM interoperation, the interface that is generated by the type library exporter is called the *class interface*. This interface will, by default contain all public methods, properties, events, and fields found in the exported class. The name of the interface will be the class name preceded by an underscore. Furthermore, the type exporter will iterate through the class hierarchy of the managed class, generating a class interface for each super-class based on the public features of each super-class and naming the interfaces in the same manner. As an example, Listing 7-4 shows the initial shell for a data-access class, called myDataAccessClass, and Listing 7-5 shows the results of exporting this class to a type library using tlbexp.exe.

Listing 7-4: Class to Be Exported to a Type Library

```
using System;
using System.Runtime.InteropServices;

namespace myDataAccessLib
{
    /// <summary>
    /// Summary description for myDataAccessClass.
    /// </summary>
    [ClassInterface(ClassInterfaceType.AutoDual)]
    public class myDataAccessClass
    {
```

```
public char[] strConnect = new char[64];

public myDataAccessClass()
{
    //
    // TODO: Add constructor logic here
    //
}

public int Connect()
{
    return 0;
}

public int Disconnect()
{
    return 0;
}
}
}
```

The following line is of particular note:

```
[ClassInterface(ClassInterfaceType.AutoDual)]
```

According to the documentation, this `ClassInterface` attribute line does not seem to be required. However, when the line was not included, the available public data members and functions were not included in the resulting type library. So, the line stayed, and the attribute `ClassInterface` is declared in the `System.Runtime.InteropServices` namespace, which is why that namespace is found among the using lines. In any event, this code was used to produce myDataAccessLib.dll, which was then processed using the type library exporter as follows:

```
tlbexp myDataAccessLib.dll
```

The result was myDataAccessLib.tlb, and this file can be examined using the COM inspector, which is located on the Tools menu in Visual Studio. Upon examination, the type definition in Listing 7-5 can be seen.

Listing 7-5: The Result of Exporting myDataAccessClass to a Type Library

```
[
    uuid(B97ABA41-F6B6-3590-812E-22A9583D8131),
    hidden,
```

Continued

Listing 7-5 *(Continued)*

```
    dual,
    nonextensible,
    custom(0F21F359-AB84-41E8-9A78-36D110E6D2F9,
myDataAccessLib.myDataAccessClass)


]
dispinterface _myDataAccessClass {
    properties:
    methods:
        [id(00000000), propget,
          custom(54FC8F55-38DE-4703-9C4E-250351302B1C, 1)]
        BSTR ToString();
        [id(0x60020001)]
        VARIANT_BOOL Equals([in] VARIANT obj);
        [id(0x60020002)]
        long GetHashCode();
        [id(0x60020003)]
        _Type* GetType();
        [id(0x60020004)]
        long Connect();
        [id(0x60020005)]
        long Disconnect();
        [id(0x60020006), propget]
        SAFEARRAY(unsigned short) strConnect();
        [id(0x60020006), propput]
        void strConnect([in] SAFEARRAY(unsigned short) rhs);
};
```

Looking at this listing, three items are apparent. First, the `ProgID` was autogenerated and given the value of `myDataAccessLib.myDataAccessClass`. Second, the class interface, `_myDataAccessClass`, was generated as expected. Finally, the methods belonging to `_myDataAccessClass` were added to the interface in order of appearance (including those functions that were inherited from the implicit base class, Object) and the DispIDs were assigned incrementally with the methods. This interface, whose form is dependent on the order of the class members, can then become problematic. So although the above methodology is quick and easy, it should probably be restricted to development environments or reserved for classes where it is very unlikely that the managed code will be undergoing future changes.

To avoid these problems and provide a more generic solution, consider the code in Listing 7-6.

Listing 7-6: MyDataAccessClass Using an Explicitly Declared Interface

```
using System;
using System.Runtime.InteropServices;
```

```csharp
namespace myDataAccessLib
{
    public interface ImyDataAccess
    {
        string Connection
        {
            get;
            set;
        }
        int Connect();
        int Disconnect();
    }

    /// <summary>
    /// Summary description for myDataAccessClass.
    /// </summary>
    public class myDataAccessClass : Object, ImyDataAccess
    {
        string strConnect;

        public myDataAccessClass()
        {
            //
            // TODO: Add constructor logic here
            //
        }

        public string Connection
        {
            get
            {
                return strConnect;
            }
            set
            {
                if (value != strConnect)
                {
                    strConnect = value;
                }
            }
        }

        public int Connect()
```

Continued

Listing 7-6 *(Continued)*
```
{
        return 0;
    }

    public int Disconnect()
    {
        return 0;
    }
  }
}
```

This code then results in the type library shown in Listing 7-7.

Listing 7-7: Portions of the Type Library Generated with myDataAccessClass Using an Explicitly Declared Interface

```
[
  uuid(F09E6470-2B0C-306A-A5D9-75EFD5B8BFD4),
  version(1.0),
  custom(0F21F359-AB84-41E8-9A78-36D110E6D2F9,
myDataAccessLib.myDataAccessClass)
]
coclass myDataAccessClass {
    [default] interface _myDataAccessClass;
    interface _Object;
    interface ImyDataAccess;
};

[
  odl,
  uuid(8729AD07-D5D6-3B6F-93F0-2800576C60D5),
  version(1.0),
  dual,
  oleautomation,
  custom(0F21F359-AB84-41E8-9A78-36D110E6D2F9,
myDataAccessLib.ImyDataAccess)

]
interface ImyDataAccess : IDispatch {
    [id(0x60020000), propget]
    HRESULT Connection([out, retval] BSTR* pRetVal);
    [id(0x60020000), propput]
    HRESULT Connection([in] BSTR pRetVal);
    [id(0x60020002)]
    HRESULT Connect([out, retval] long* pRetVal);
```

```
    [id(0x60020003)]
    HRESULT Disconnect([out, retval] long* pRetVal);
};
```

Now the dispatch IDs are associated with the interface ImyDataAccess. So as long as the interface is not modified the dispatch IDs will not change. This allows the developer to modify the class myDataAccessClass in any manner desired without impacting the behavior of objects that consume the ImyDataAccess interface.

GARBAGE COLLECTION

Given that .NET objects are garbage collected, you may wonder what happens to a .NET object enlisted via a COM Callable Wrapper. Well, the CCW behaves like other COM objects and is reference counted. When the reference count for the CCW reaches 0, the wrapper releases the managed object. Then, like any other managed object without anything referencing it, the object will be garbage collected the next time the GC runs.

Deployment and registration

After the class or component has been developed, it must be deployed and registered, and there are several approaches to this process. Whatever methodology is used, the first step in the process will be to generate a type library, and four tools exist for this purpose:

◆ **Type Library Exporter:** The first tool, the type library exporter was generally covered during the earlier discussion about writing managed code for interoperation. However, there are some additional points to be made. Although it was not stated explicitly in the previous discussion, tlbexp.exe works on a whole assembly at once. There is no way to export a subset of the classes in an assembly to a type library. Also, when the type library is generated, it is not registered. So the library will still need to be registered on the client machine. After the library is registered, the component may be created and used just like any other COM object.

◆ **TypeLibConverter Class:** A type library may also be produced via the TypeLibConverter class. This class is located in the System.Runtime.InteropServices namespace and provides all the same functionality as the type library exporter (it implements the ITypeLibConverter interface), just in the form of an API. Therefore, if this tool is used, it will probably be used in conjunction with the RegistrationServices class, which provides an API for registering managed components for interoperation.

◆ **Assembly Registration Tool:** To accomplish both type library generation and registration in one step, the assembly registration tool may be used. The use of regasm.exe is shown below along with some important command line switches:

```
    regasm NameOfAssemblyFile [options]
```

- **/codebase**: This switch is intended only for assemblies not being installed into the GAC. It causes a codebase entry to be created in the registry to allow the Common Language Runtime to locate the assembly. Even though the assembly is not destined for the global assembly cache, it must still be strong named to be used with this switch.

- **/regfile [:registryFile]**: This switch will generate a .reg file with the desired name that will contain all the registry entries, but it will not change the registry. This switch is incompatible with the /u and /tlb switches.

- **/tlb [:typeLibraryFile]**: This switch will generate a type library with the given name and also register the library after it is registered.

- **/u or /unregister**: This switch will unregister the classes found in the assembly file.

From these switches it can be seen that regasm.exe is used both to register and unregister assemblies for interoperation. Also, if the /tlb switch is not used, the tool will register the types in the assembly but not the type library, and without the type library an object cannot be created. Note, too, that the file names that can accompany the /tlb and /regfile switches are output files; that is, a type library generated with tlbexp.exe is not an input for regasm.exe via the /tlb switch.

◆ **.NET Services Installation Tool**: The final method of generating a type library is by using the regsvcs.exe tool. This tool also provides registration services for COM+ applications. The use of regsvcs.exe is shown in the following line and is followed by some important command line switches:

```
regsvcs options assemblyFileName
```

- **/appname:applicationName**: This option specifies the name of the COM+ application to install the assembly under. If the application is not found, then it will be created.

- **/c**: This option specifies that the application should be created.

- **/componly**: This option specifies that only the components should be configured.

- **/exapp**: This option specifies that the application should already exist.

- **/extlb**: This option specifies the use of an existing type library.

- **/fc**: This option specifies to find or create the target application.

- **/noreconfig**: This option specifies that an existing application should not be reconfigured.

- **/parname:applicationName**: This option specifies the name or id of the COM+ application to find or create.

- **/reconfig**: This option specifies that an existing application should be reconfigured (Default).

- **/tlb:typelibraryfile**: This option specifies the existing type library file to install.

- **/u**: Uninstalls the application.

Summary

This chapter covered COM and .NET interoperation. The key to this interoperation is the creation of interfaces that present one technology in the format of the other. In the case of calling COM from .NET, this means using tlbimp.exe to build an assembly from a COM type library. After this intermediate assembly is created, it may be referenced from .NET, allowing .NET code to use the COM object like any other .NET component or class. Flowing in the other direction, from COM to .NET, the goal is to export the types available in an assembly to a type library for use by other COM objects. The basic tool for this is tlbexp.exe, though there are others. Understanding these forms of interoperation will be central to the transition from COM to .NET in the enterprise.

Chapter 8

Threading and Windows Services

IN THIS CHAPTER

◆ Understanding threading

◆ Identifying applications that use threads

◆ Working with thread pools

◆ Making sense of Windows Services

◆ Installing and controlling your services

THIS CHAPTER COVERS THREADING and services development in .NET. Threading is the capability of a process to create and manage sub-activities of work called threads. Services are special programs that are loaded and controlled by the service control manager in the Windows NT/2000/XP kernel. These programs can be loaded at boot-time without a user logging into the system. Many important features of the Windows operating environment are loaded as services. By creating new services, the developer can extend the capabilities of this environment.

You may wonder why threading and services are put into a chapter together and what these two topics have in common? The answer to this question is twofold. Both threading and services are features of the operating system, and many useful services employ threading. So, in this chapter, we explain what threading is and how it can be beneficial to your systems, and then we move on to creating and managing services. Towards the end of the chapter is a demonstration of a rather involved service that listens for events and responds by pulling messages from a queue.

Defining Threading

Put simply, *threading* is the ability of a program to create and manage sub-units of work that may run in parallel while being controlled by the parent process. Great, so what does that mean? Well, we'll start at the underlying application layers and work our way up, looking at what's available from the operating system.

Modern operating systems typically provide support for running multiple applications at the same time. This support for running multiple applications (tasks) at the same time is often referred to as *multitasking*. Multitasking may be further divided into two categories:

◆ **Cooperative multitasking:** In a system with cooperative multitasking, each application voluntarily yields control to the operating system and other applications. Windows 3.x is an example of an operating system that implements cooperative multitasking.

◆ **Preemptive multitasking:** In an operating system with preemptive multitasking, the operating system allows each application to run for a certain time, typically called a *timeslice*. When that time has been completed, the operating system allows another application to run. Windows NT/2000/XP and the Mac OS X are examples of operating systems that support preemptive multitasking.

The key difference between the cooperative and preemptive multitasking operating systems is that of control. By giving control to an application in a cooperative multitasking system, problems in one application can affect the amount of time provided to other applications, or even keep them from getting any timeslice.

Within operating systems like Windows NT/2000/XP or Mac OS X is the capability for each task to further subdivide that task's work into what are called *threads*. Threads are pieces of software code that are used to perform small units of work for an application. Threads are controlled by the task that started the thread. An example of a thread could be the print functionality of a word processor where the word processor will create a thread that formats the output and sends the output to the printer. The thread would handle communication with the printing subsystem of the operating system. Although a thread is handling printing, the thread that is handling the actual input, typing, and screen display could be accepting new input from the user.

Another example is a database product, such as SQL Server. When a request is made against SQL Server, a thread can handle that request. The thread is called, retrieves the data, and makes sure that the data is sent back to the client. After this thread is done, it can be placed back into a pool of threads and made available for additional user requests. By supporting multiple threads, SQL Server is able to support multiple users and support more users than the number of threads that are available at any one moment.

Knowing When to Thread

Now that you know what threading is, you may think that implementing threading everywhere would make an application run much faster. If you could put threading into every nook and cranny of your applications, your users would love you and your applications would be so much faster. Unfortunately, this isn't always true. Threading is a feature that is hard to master. In the following sections, we take a somewhat basic look at computer algorithms, the impact of these algorithms on threading, and some of the dangers associated with threading.

Algorithms and business rules

Algorithms are the processes used to solve problems. In terms of business applications, algorithms are implemented to enforce business rules. Both the algorithms and business rules are made up of different sections. Some sections may be performed in parallel with each other; other sections may only be performed one after the other. Take a look at a manufacturing process where raw material comes in one end and finished telephone/communications wire comes out another. The production steps are as follows:

1. Raw material is formed into a long piece of copper.

2. The long piece is formed into the appropriate length and radius.

3. The copper wire is covered with the appropriate insulation.

4. Two or more insulated wires are twisted together.

5. Items from Step 4 are combined to make the appropriate type of communications wire.

6. The final product is packaged and shipped.

 Testing is performed throughout Steps 4 and 5.

In this production system, there are processes that may be performed in parallel and others that must be serialized. For example, multiple orders of product may be processed at any time. Within a single product order, multiple sets of raw materials may be processed at any one time, multiple pieces may be formed at the same time, multiple wires may be covered with insulation at the same time, and multiple sets of wires may be twisted together at the same time. These operations are *parallel operations* in that the progress of each operation is independent of the progress of the other operations.

At the same time, some operations within this manufacturing process are *serial*. Each individual set of steps represents a serial process. Each manufacturing step must be completed before the next step begins. The business would not be successful if there were an attempt to twist the wires before insulation was placed on those wires.

Threading benefits and limitations

So, now that you see how algorithms can be divided up, how does this relate to the performance benefits that you can get with threads? Computer algorithms, and the business rules that they implement, can be divided up into operations that may be processed in parallel and operations that must be processed in a serial manner.

Applying threading to an application where 90 percent of the operations are serial operations and 10 percent of the operations are parallel will not provide much performance improvement. Creating a second thread to perform processing will only help in processing the 10 percent of the operations that happen to be parallel operations. The end result is that you're going to ideally pick up a 5 percent $(10 \div 2)$ performance improvement.

What about an application that is the exact opposite in its performance characteristics? The second application has 10 percent of its operations running serially and 90 percent of its operations running in parallel. Implementing a second thread within the application will result in a performance improvement of ideally 45 percent $(90 \div 2)$.

When it comes to parallel operations, there is one more item to be aware of. Continually adding threads will not necessarily provide improved performance. Why? Well, even an algorithm that is highly parallel has limits on the number of threads that will improve its performance.

Most business algorithms can be broken down into serial and parallel operations. There are other parts of standard custom-written applications that are outside of running the business rules of the application. Outside of the business rules are other areas within a line of business application that can be excellent candidates for implementing threads. Some of these include printing, network operations, report generation, and other operations that operate without a lot of user input. These are operations that may be handled by starting a thread to process the work and then having that thread go off, complete the work, and return the appropriate result to the appropriate place.

Creating Threads

As mentioned earlier, threads provide a means of allocating processor time to separate activities within a process. On single-processor systems, threading is done to give the user a more responsive environment, while on multi-processor systems, threading can be used to improve runtime by providing units of work that the OS can dispatch to separate processors.

That is, on a single-processor system, any time spent on one thread is not spent on any other threads. However, multiple threads can still enhance the user experience, because by separating work into threads, each of which are progressing by timeslices too short to be perceived by the user, the system can appear to respond to a user's request, on one thread, while appearing to simultaneously perform another operation, like performing a background save on another thread.

On a multiprocessor system, the situation is different. Operating systems send work to different processors on a process-by-process basis or, when available, a thread-by-thread basis. So, a single process cannot take advantage of any additional processors; it will live and die on an individual processor. But if the process employs multiple threads, the OS can send the threads to their own processor. This means that, in a four-way system, a process that splits its work among four threads can theoretically finish in one-fourth the time.

Although threads provide benefits, they can also incur some penalties. Multithreaded applications are subject to bugs that cannot occur in single-process applications. Each thread requires some memory, and since the OS must switch from one thread to another, each thread requires some non-productive processor time. So threads cannot be allowed to increase without consideration, or the system memory and processor can become strapped by thread-management tasks alone. With that said, however, responsibly used threads deliver great advantages.

System.Threading

Within Microsoft .NET, all threading-related classes, components, and enumerations can be found in the System.Threading hierarchy. This hierarchy of threading and thread behavior provides great consolidation and ease of use, especially compared to the veritable threading chaos that exists in Win32 and COM. Managed threads do away with threading apartments, which COM used to manage thread context and synchronization. In place, the System.Threading hierarchy provides a robust set of thread-control mechanisms, which should be employed to ensure proper behavior for multi-threaded components and applications.

From Win32 to .NET

Before covering more of .NET threading, let's compare the common threading functions from the Win32 API with their counterparts in .NET. Table 8-1 provides a summary view of how these functions line up. Because these calls do not have a true one-to-one correspondence, a more detailed discussion follows.

TABLE 8-1 THREAD-MANAGEMENT ROUTINES AVAILABLE
            IN THE WIN32 API AND .NET MANAGED CODE

Win32 API	Managed Code
CreateThread	Thread and ThreadStart
TerminateThread	Thread.Abort
SuspendThread	Thread.Suspend

Continued

TABLE 8-1 THREAD–MANAGEMENT ROUTINES AVAILABLE IN THE
         WIN32 API AND .NET MANAGED CODE *(Continued)*

Win32 API	Managed Code
ResumeThread	Thread.Resume
Sleep	Thread.Sleep
WaitForSingleObject	Thread.Join
ExitThread	**Nothing**
GetCurrentThread	Thread.CurrentThread
SetThreadPriority	Thread.Priority
Nothing	Thread.Name
Nothing	Thread.IsBackground
Similar to CoInitializeEx	Thread.ApartmentState

To provide a quick reminder, in Win32 a thread is created through a two-step process. First, a function that will be called at the start of the thread, a `ThreadProc`, must be defined as follows:

```
DWORD WINAPI ThreadProc(LPVOID lpParameterData);
```

After this function is defined, it is included as a parameter to the `CreateThread` function:

```
HANDLE CreateThread(LPSECURITY_ATTRIBUTES lpThreadAttributes,
              SIZE_T dwStackSize,
              LPTHREAD_START_ROUTINE lpStartAddress,
              // lpStartAddress points to ThreadProc
              LPVOID lpParameter,
              DWORD dwCreationFlags,
              LPDWORD lpThreadId);
```

Within .NET, the process is somewhat different with three pieces involved. A procedure to be called by the thread must still be created, however in .NET this procedure must then be tied to a `ThreadStart` delegate. Finally, this `ThreadStart` delegate is used to create a thread object, which is then set running by a call to the `Start` method of the `Thread` object. Listing 8-1 illustrates this process.

Listing 8-1: Thread Creation in .NET

```csharp
using System;
using System.Threading;

namespace myConsoleThreadDemo
{
    /// <summary>
    /// Create ThreadProcClass to contain the method to run in the
    /// thread.
    /// </summary>
    class ThreadProcClass
    {
        public void myThreadProc()
        {
            int i = 0;
            while(true)
            {
                i++;
                Console.WriteLine("myThreadProc loop has executed "
                                + i + " times.");

            }
        }
    }


    class ThreadProcMain
    {
        /// <summary>
        /// The main entry point for the application.
        /// </summary>
        [STAThread]
        static void Main(string[] args)
        {
            /// Create new ThreadProcClass.
            ThreadProcClass tProc = new ThreadProcClass();
            /// Create a new ThreadStart delegate using myThreadProc
            ThreadStart tsDelegate = new
              ThreadStart(tProc.myThreadProc);
            /// Create a new Thread object using the ThreadStart
            /// delgate
            Thread myThread = new Thread(tsDelegate);
            /// Start the thread
            myThread.Start();
        }
    }
}
```

After creating and starting a thread, many of the thread operations do closely correspond, though they are not shown in this listing. However, if the code in Listing 8-1 is run, it will demonstrate another difference between Win32 and .NET threading: .NET threads can have foreground or background status. This status is controlled by the `Thread.IsBackground` attribute, and if `IsBackground` is set to true, the thread will be a background thread. By default, managed threads are foreground threads, while threads created through the COM Callable Wrapper are background threads. The special property of foreground threads is that, if one is running, the managed application will not close. So, returning to the code in Listing 8-1, `myConsoleThreadDemo` will not stop running on its own. In contrast, a similarly structured Win32 application that didn't have any code waiting for the thread to complete would reach the end of the main function, terminating the process and the thread with it.

Another interesting attribute of managed threads is `Thread.ApartmentState`, which can have values of single-threaded apartment (STA) or multi-threaded apartment (MTA). At first, this attribute may seem odd or out of place since managed code does not use apartments. However, managed code may call unmanaged COM, which, of course, does use apartments. So, this attribute exists for the benefit of interoperation. Given that threads hosted in one apartment type must be proxied by COM to interact with threads in another apartment type, there is a performance penalty for doing this. To avoid this penalty, a managed thread's apartment state may be set to correspond to the apartment type that is hosting the COM object with which the managed code is interoperating. This is why the attribute is roughly lined up with `CoInitializeEx` from the Ole32 API, since `CoInitializeEx` can be used to control the apartment type into which a COM object is initialized.

Multi-Threaded Algorithms

Now that we've covered thread creation, we'll examine multi-threaded algorithms and more-advanced aspects of thread control. When implementing multi-threaded applications, there are some challenges to address, most of which center around execution order. *Remember:* When a thread has been created and activated, it is guaranteed to get a slice of processor time. But there are no guarantees about the order of the time slice with respect to other running threads or about how many operations will be completed before the thread is suspended. These two unknowns cause many of the bugs related to multi-threaded algorithms.

So, in response, there are a number of objects within .NET that allow the developer to manage the behavior of concurrent threads. Several of the most important are listed here:

◆ `WaitHandle`: This class encapsulates the Win32 thread synchronization objects. Objects derived from `WaitHandle` are `Mutex`, `AutoResetEvent`, and `ManualResetEvent`. Because it encapsulates Win32 behavior,

WaitHandle objects are useful for synchronizing between managed and unmanaged code.

◆ **Mutex:** A Mutex is a synchronization object that provides the same functionality as the Win32 CreatMutex call. Using a Mutex, code is synchronized by having threads wait to take ownership of the Mutex before continuing execution and then releasing the Mutex so that other threads waiting for the Mutex may execute.

◆ **ManualResetEvent:** This object is equivalent to the Win32 CreateEvent function with the bManualReset parameter set to true. So, after the event is signaled by a call to Set(), the event will remain signaled until a call to the Reset() method, allowing any number of waiting threads to be released.

◆ **AutoResetEvent:** This object is equivalent to the Win32 CreateEvent function with the bManualReset parameter set to false. So, once the event is signaled by a call to Set(), the event will automatically reset after, but not until, one waiting thread has been released.

◆ **Monitor:** A Monitor object is similar to a Mutex in that it works on a hold and release basis, but a Monitor provides additional functionality in the form of Pulse and PulseAll events that can signal waiting threads to execute. Also, Monitor is fully managed and thus more portable, and Monitor may be more efficient in some circumstances.

◆ **Interlocked:** The Interlocked object provides a high-performance synchronization mechanism for operating on individual variables in shared memory.

◆ **ReaderWriterLock:** This object provides multiple readers with single writer locking. It also supports upgrading and downgrading to and from writer status as well as timeouts.

◆ **Timer:** This is a basic but invaluable object that provides timer events at regular intervals. This Timer also has a higher resolution than the 55ms provided by the earlier Win32 timer event.

◆ **Asynchronous I/O:** This is not an individual object, but an important capacity to allow processing to continue while waiting for some I/O to finish. In .NET, this functionality is implemented using completion ports.

◆ **ThreadPool:** This is a useful object that provides some readymade multi-thread management routines. ThreadPool is covered individually at the end of the Threading section.

Listings 8-2 and 8-3 provide some demonstration code for the Monitor and Interlocked thread-management tools.

Listing 8-2: Thread Synchronization Using a Monitor Object

```
using System;
using System.Threading;
namespace myThreadMonitorDemo
{
    class ThreadActivityClass
    {
        static int i=0;

        public void PerformActivity()
        {
            Monitor.Enter(this);
            while (i<100)
            {
                i++;
                Console.WriteLine("Activity performed " +
                                    i + " times.");
            }
            Monitor.Exit(this);
        }
    }

    /// <summary>
    /// Summary description for ThreadMonitorClass.
    /// </summary>
    class ThreadMonitorClass
    {
        static internal Thread[] threads = new Thread[4];

        /// <summary>
        /// The main entry point for the application.
        /// </summary>
        static void Main(string[] args)
        {
            //
            // TODO: Add code to start application here
            //
            int i = 0;

            ThreadActivityClass ta = new ThreadActivityClass();
            for (i=0;i<4;i++)
            {
                Thread t =
                  new Thread(new ThreadStart(ta.PerformActivity));
                threads[i] = t;
```

```
        }
        for (i=0;i<4;i++)
        {
            threads[i].Start();
        }
      }
    }
}
```

The code in Listing 8-2 shows how synchronization is performed using the Monitor object. Note that the start and end of the critical section is denoted with the Enter() and Exit() methods. This ensures that only one thread at a time may access the variable i and display its value. It is worthwhile to comment out the two method calls around the critical section just to see what happens without thread synchronization.

Listing 8–3: Variable Access Synchronization Using an Interlocked Object

```
using System;
using System.Threading;
namespace myInterlockedDemo
{
    class InterlockedActivityClass
    {
        static long i;

        public void PerformInterlockedActivity()
        {
            while (i<100)
            {
                j = Interlocked.Increment(ref i);
            }
        }
    }
    /// <summary>
    /// Summary description for InterlockedDemoClass.
    /// </summary>
    class InterlockedDemoClass
    {
        static internal Thread[] threads = new Thread[4];

        /// <summary>
        /// The main entry point for the application.
        /// </summary>
```

Continued

Listing 8-3 *(Continued)*

```
static void Main(string[] args)
{
    //
    // TODO: Add code to start application here
    //
    int m = 0;

    InterlockedActivityClass ta =
      new InterlockedActivityClass();
    for (m=0;m<4;m++)
    {
        Thread t = new Thread(new
          ThreadStart(ta.PerformInterlockedActivity));
        threads[m] = t;
    }
    for (m=0;m<4;m++)
    {
        threads[m].Start();
    }
}
```

Listing 8-3 shows the syntax efficiency of the Interlocked component. Often, a critical section is needed to synchronize access to one or two related variables and the Interlocked object does this and provides a number of useful methods including Increment() (which is shown), Decrement(), and additional comparison with operation methods.

Listing 8-4 provides some demonstration code for the ThreadPool object.

Listing 8-4: Using a ThreadPool

```
using System;
using System.Threading;

namespace myThreadPool
{
    public class Sensor
    {
        static int iValue = 0;
        static String strStatus = "Working.";
        static DateTime dtNow;

        [STAThread]
        public static int Main()
```

```
    {
        Console.WriteLine("Processing start.");
        Console.WriteLine("{0}: {1}", iValue, strStatus);

        AutoResetEvent ev = new AutoResetEvent(false);
        ThreadPool.RegisterWaitForSingleObject(
            ev,
            new WaitOrTimerCallback(WaitThreadFunc),
            null,
            20000,
            false);

        for (int i=0;i<5;i++)
        {
            Console.WriteLine("Loop: {0}", i);
            Console.WriteLine("ev.Set() {0}",
              (DateTime.Now).Ticks);
            ev.Set();
            Thread.Sleep(200);
            ThreadPool.QueueUserWorkItem(
              new WaitCallback(ThreadFunc1), 1);
            ThreadPool.QueueUserWorkItem(
              new WaitCallback(ThreadFunc2), 2);
        }
        return 0;
    }

    public static void ThreadFunc1(Object O)
    {
        Console.WriteLine("ThreadFunc1 Called. {0}",
          (DateTime.Now).Ticks);
    }

    public static void ThreadFunc2(Object O)
    {
        Console.WriteLine("ThreadFunc2 Called. {0}",
          (DateTime.Now).Ticks);
    }

    public static void WaitThreadFunc(object O, bool signaled)
    {
        Console.WriteLine("WaitThreadFunc Called. {0} {1}",
          signaled, (DateTime.Now).Ticks);
    }
  }
}
```

Working with Windows Services

Windows Services are executable applications with no user interface that run within their own context within the Windows NT/2000/XP environment. These programs may be stopped, started, paused, and restarted without affecting any of the other running Windows Services or the currently logged-on user. Windows Services can be set to run without a user actually being logged into the console of the system. Because a Windows Service may run within its own security context, it may run as a specific user account. The Windows Service will then have all the rights and privileges of that user while the Windows Service is running. Windows Services are ideal for programs that must run on a server, for a large amount of time, or while the system is up and running, as opposed to while a user is merely logged on to the system.

Before the .NET Framework, creating Windows Services was the domain of Visual C++ programmers. Although there are third-party add-ins for Visual Basic that allow programmers to create Windows Services, programmers working with the Visual Basic out-of-the-box package were not able to create Windows Services. With the .NET Framework, this has changed. Windows Services may be created with any language that supports the .NET Framework. This allows programmers developing in Visual Basic .NET, C#, JScript .NET, Visual C++, or any other language that targets the .NET Framework to develop Windows Services.

Service background

Windows Services are different from other types of applications that are developed within the .NET Framework and Visual Studio .NET. Some of these differences include the following:

◆ **A service may not be debugged like a standard Visual Studio .NET application.** A service must be installed and started, and then a debugger must attach to the service's process to perform the actual debugging. This requires that the service be free of any language errors, that the service must be able to successfully start, and that the service must be able to run without crashing until the debugger is able to attach and set a breakpoint before any offending lines of code.

◆ **Installation components must be created for a service.**

◆ **Windows Service applications usually run within a different security context than the logged-in user.** Most services run within the local system account, which typically has more permissions than a basic user.

◆ **Windows Service applications do not have a user interface.** Errors should be logged to some location, preferably the Event log.

Within the Windows environment, the Services Control Manager (SCM) is the utility used to manage Windows Services. When a service is installed, the service installers are executed and the service is loaded into the SCM. After a service has been installed, it may exist in one of four main states:

◆ **Starting:** Starting a service loads the service and begins processing by calling the `OnStart` method.

◆ **Running:** A running service is one that is processing requests and executing commands in response to something.

◆ **Paused:** A paused service is similar to a stop command, except that all resources allocated by the service are not released. This state requires that `CanPauseAndContinue` is set to true and the `OnPause` and `OnContinue` method are overridden.

◆ **Stopped:** The `OnStop` method has been called and execution has ended. The SCM must check and verify that the service may be stopped by verifying the value of the `CanStop` property.

It is possible to determine the state of a service by getting the `ServiceController.Status` property. The possible values are contained within the `System.ServiceProcess.ServiceControllerStatus` enumeration. The possible values are:

◆ `ContinuePending`: The service continue event is pending.

◆ `Paused`: The service is paused.

◆ `PausePending`: The service is pausing.

◆ `Running`: The service is running.

◆ `StartPending`: The service is starting.

◆ `Stopped`: The service is not running.

◆ `StopPending`: The service is stopping.

Visual Studio .NET supports the creation of two types of services in regards to their process space. A service may run in its own memory space, or it may share its memory space. A complete list of available service types is available through the `System.ServiceProcess.ServiceType` Enumeration. To determine the service type(s), it will be necessary to perform a bitwise *and* operation to test for a specific situation. The service types are:

◆ **Win32OwnProcess:** A Windows process that runs in a process by itself.

◆ **Win32ShareProcess:** A Windows process that shares its process space with other Windows Services.

◆ **Adapter:** A service for a hardware device, requiring its own driver.

◆ **FileSystemDriver:** A kernel level and file system driver.

◆ **InteractiveProcess:** A Windows service that may communicate with the desktop.

◆ **KernelDriver:** A low-level hardware device driver.

◆ **RecognizerDriver:** A file system driver that determines the file systems installed on the system at startup.

Creating a Windows Service

Now that we have talked about the Windows Services in general, let's walk through the creation of a Windows service. The example service that we are going to create is going to process received messages within a Microsoft Message Queue. This example application will be built from an empty project as opposed to the prebuilt Windows Service template included with Visual Studio .NET. The System.ServiceProcess is the namespace that provides support within .NET for creating Windows Services. Here are the steps in creating your service:

1. Within your empty project, add references to the System.dll and System.ServiceProcess.dll assemblies. Add the using or import statements for System and System.ServiceProcess as needed. (*Note:* This is done automatically when the Windows Service project template is used.)

2. Create a class and inherit from System.ServiceProcess.ServiceBase. (*Note:* This, too, is done automatically when the Windows Service project template is used.)

3. Configure the service class by adding code to initialize the class.

   Following is an example in Visual Basic:

```
Public Sub New()
    'Name the service.
    Me.ServiceName = "MSMQProcessing"
    'Allow the service to be stopped.
    Me.CanStop = True
    'Allow the service to be paused and continued.
    Me.CanPauseAndContinue = True
    Me.AutoLog = True
End Sub


//C# Code
public void MSMQProcessingService(){
    //Name the service for the Service Control Manager.
    this.ServiceName = "MSMQProcessing";
    //Allow the service to be stopped.
    this.CanStop = true;
    //Allow the service to be paused and continued.
```

```
    this.CanPauseAndContinue = true;
    this.AutoLog = true;
}
```

4. Create a Main subroutine/void function.

```
'Visual Basic
Public Sub Main()
    ServiceBase.Run(New MSMQProcessingClass())
End Sub
```

```
//C#
public static void Main(){
    ServiceBase.Run(New MSMQProcessingClass());
}
```

In this example, the MSMQProcessingClass is the name of the class within our example code.

5. Override the OnStart method to provide the appropriate processing.

```
'Visual Basic
Protected Overrides Sub OnStart(ByVal pstrArgs() as String)
    'Insert processing code here.
End Sub
```

```
//C#
protected override void OnStart(string[] pstrArgs){
    //Insert processing code here.
}
```

Now that you have overridden the OnStart method, there may be other methods that need to be overridden. For a complete discussion of the service event methods, review the next section on service methods.

6. Add the appropriate installers to the project. First, select the design view of the service needing installation. Then go to the design tab, right-click, and choose the Add Installer option from the context menu. Click within the designer's surface, and then within the description area of the properties window, select the link to add an installer. A new class is added to the project, called ProjectInstaller with the components ServiceProcessInstaller and ServiceInstaller added. Verify that the ServiceInstaller has the correct name for the ServiceName property. Set the StartType of the property to the appropriate type. The possible types are:

- **Manual:** A service set to a StartType of Manual will be started when the service is manually started.

- **Automatic:** A service with a `StartType` of Automatic will start when the system reboots.

- **Disabled:** A service with the `StartType` of Disabled can't be started.

7. The security context of the service is set through the properties of the `ProjectInstaller` component. The `Account` property may be set to one of four different values regarding the context that the service runs within. The `Account` property may be set to:

- **User:** During installation, a user name and password are requested. The service will run within the context of specified account.

- **LocalService:** The service will run within the context of a local account with extensive rights. When communicating over the network, the service will present the local computer's credentials.

- **LocalSystem:** The service will run within the context of a local account with minimal rights. When communicating over a network, the service will present anonymous credentials.

- **NetworkService:** The service runs in within the context of a local account with minimal rights. When communicating over a network, the service will present the local computer's credentials.

8. Build your service by compiling your solution.

9. Install the service for processing. The command line utility `installutil` can be used to install the resulting executable containing our service or a custom installer from Visual Studio .NET may be used to install the service. The installutil command can be employed from the Visual Studio.NET command line as follows:

```
installutil /i servicename.exe
```

This would install the service, servicename.exe, and a `/u` parameter can be used with the command to uninstall the service.

10. The service may be started through the control panel or by using the "net start" command.

Events and services

Services respond to events. The events can be the start command, the stop command, the pause command, or a number of other commands as well as custom application-defined events. When one of these events occurs, the appropriate overridden method within the service is called by the SCM, if the method exists and the service is allowed to call the method. Let's look at this in some more detail.

Within each service is a list of events that may be handled by the service:

◆ **Start/OnStart:** The `OnStart` method handles the start event when a service is started. This method is called when the SCM sends the service the start event. The `OnStart` method accepts an array of type string. This array is the parameters that are passed to the service at startup. These parameters are the ones that are passed to the service through the command line or are set in the control panel. Figure 8-1 shows where the startup parameters may be set in the services applet within the control panel.

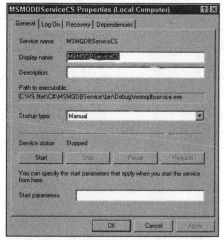

Figure 8-1: Setting the startup parameters in the MSMQDBServiceCS Properties dialog box

◆ **Stop/OnStop:** The `OnStop` method handles the stop event when a service is stopped when the SCM sends the stop event to the service.

◆ **Pause/OnPause:** The `OnPause` method handles the pause event when a pause event is sent to the service from the SCM.

◆ **Continue/OnContinue:** The `OnContinue` method handles the continue event when the SCM sends the service the continue event. This method is called after a service is paused.

◆ **Shutdown/OnShutdown:** The `OnShutdown` method is called when the system is undergoing a shutdown.

◆ **CustomCommand/OnCustomCommand:** The `OnCustomCommand` is called when the SCM passes a custom command to the service.

◆ **PowerEvent/OnPowerEvent:** The `OnPowerEvent` function is called when the computer's power status has changed. For example, this method will be called when a laptop computer goes into suspend mode. The `OnPowerEvent` method accepts a parameter of type `PowerBroadcastStatus`. The

`OnPowerEvent` returns a Boolean. True represents accepting a `QuerySuspend` broadcast. False represents rejecting the query `QuerySuspend` broadcast. This parameter contains the type of power event that occurred. The type of power event that occurs may be determined through comparing with the `PowerBroadcastStatuts` enumeration. This enumeration contains several defined member values. These member values are:

- **BatteryLow:** A message stating that the battery is low has been sent to the service.

- **OemEvent:** An advanced power management (APM) BIOS message stating that an APM OEM event has occurred and has been sent to the service.

- **PowerStatusChange:** Some change in the power status of the system has been detected and the event has been sent to the service.

- **QuerySuspend:** The OS has requested permission to suspend the system. An application has the choice of granting permission to allow a suspend to occur.

- **QuerySuspendFailed:** The OS has denied permission to suspend the system. If any piece of code is running, the previous `QuerySuspend` request will be denied.

- **ResumeAutomatic:** The system has woken up to handle an event. If the OS detects user interaction after a `ResumeAutomatic` message broadcast, the OS will broadcast the `ResumeSuspend` event. This tells applications that may continue with full interaction with the user.

- **ResumeCritical:** The OS and system have resumed operations after some critical suspension of the system. This has probably been caused by a battery failure.

- **ResumeSuspend:** The OS has resumed operations after a suspend event.

- **Suspend:** The OS and system are going to enter a suspended state. Typically, this event occurs when all pieces of code running on the system have returned true to a previous `QuerySuspend` broadcast.

For each of the mentioned events to be called, the service must be set up and allowed to process that event. This is accomplished by setting a series of properties on the service to allow the SCM to pass these events to the service. Let's look at these properties:

- ◆ `CanStop`: If the property is set to true, the stop event is passed to the service and the `OnStop` method is called, if it is defined.

- ◆ `CanPauseAndContinue`: If the property is set to true, the pause and continue events are passed to the service, and the `OnPause` and the `OnContinue` methods are called, if they are defined.

♦ `CanShutdown`: If the property is set to true, the shutdown event is passed to the service, and the `OnShutdown` method is called, if it is defined.

♦ `CanHandlePowerEvent`: If the property is set to true, any power events on the system are sent to the service by the SCM.

These properties may be set programmatically or through properties of the service within the Visual Studio .NET IDE.

Events to monitor

There are two types of computer communications: synchronous and asynchronous. *Synchronous communications* are those that occur at specified intervals with a pre-defined format. Synchronous communications are generally blocking (that is, nothing else within a thread may proceed until the communication is complete). For example, if a function makes a synchronous call to a database that takes two seconds to complete, during those two seconds, nothing else will run in that thread. *Asynchronous communications* are those that can occur at irregular and undefined intervals. Unlike synchronous communications, asynchronous communications are generally non-blocking. So, if a program makes an asynchronous call to a database, it could continue with other processing while waiting for notification of a result.

One of the most important aspects of developing a service is making sure that the service does not use too much of the processor during the time that it doesn't need to be using the processor. The best way to do that is for a service to handle an event that fires asynchronously. The service should not continually monitor and use CPU resources that would better be put to use processing other requests. In other words, when it waits for something to occur, such as a message to appear in a message queue, a network packet to arrive at the system, or a file to arrive or change within a directory, the service needs to use as few CPU cycles as possible. For example, creating a loop whereby the service continually checks the message queue will most likely result in too much CPU utilization. So instead of looping through and continually checking for the message queue, the service creates an event handler to process the event where a message appears within a message queue.

How does a service handle requests without tying up the system's CPU? Typically, a service will instruct the system that when a certain events occurs, the service has a method/function that can handle that event. As a result, when the appropriate event is fired by the message queue service, the .NET Framework sends the appropriate event to the service with the appropriate parameters. The `System.Messaging` namespace contains a set of events to process exactly what is needed.

Working with the Microsoft Message Queue is described in much more detail in Chapter 9. To summarize, MSMQ exposes the `PeekCompleted`, `PeekBegin`, `ReceiveCompleted`, and `ReceiveBegin` events. These events are processed by items that are called event handlers. *Event handlers* are methods/functions that are assigned to handle events programmatically. Typically, an event handler will receive an event along with some type of input parameter associated with that event. It is the responsibility of the program code to process the event in the appropriate manner associated with the business logic of the application.

GENERAL EVENT PROCESSING

We'll cover how to handle events in general, and then we can move on to some more-specific situations.

When a service is started, the `OnStart` event is called. Within the `OnStart` event, the service needs to handle the necessary events within the service by assigning an event to an event handler. Although we have talked about events, we haven't really discussed the process of actually assigning object events to the methods that will actually handle them. The syntax to handle this in Visual Basic is somewhat different than with C#. The VB syntax uses the `AddHandler` method to associate an object's event with the local subroutine that handles that event. The syntax is:

```
AddHandler ObjectName.Event, AddressOf LocalEventHandlingRoutine
```

This method tells the application to send the Event produced by the object `ObjectName` to the `LocalEventHandlingRoutine()` subroutine. The C# syntax is somewhat different but produces the same type of results. The C# syntax is:

```
ObjectName.Event += new (this.LocalEventHandlingRoutine);
```

The following Visual Basic .NET code adds an event to the event handler:

```
OnStart
Protected Overrides Sub OnStart(ByVal args() As String)
'...code to start.
AddHandler ObjectName.Event, AddressOf LocalEventHandler
'...code to end.
End Sub
'Additional code
Public Sub LocalEventHandler(appropriate parameters that vary)
'the params accepted by this sub will vary depending upon the
'specific event that must be handled.
End Sub
```

The C# code is as follows:

```
protected void OnStart(string args[]){
//...code to start.
ObjectName.Event += new (this.LocalEventHandler);
//...code to end.
}
```

```
public void LocalEventHandler(appropriate parameters that vary){
/*the params accepted by this void routine will vary depending upon
the specific event that must be handled.
*/
}
```

Listings 8-5 and 8-6 are code samples that use the .NET Framework and the
System.Messaging namespace to process messages within a message queue.
Listing 8-5 is the code listing for a service written in VB. Listing 8-6 is the code list-
ing for a service in C#.

Listing 8-5: A VB Windows Service Using a Message Queue

```
Option Explicit On
Option Strict On
Imports System
Imports System.Diagnostics
Imports System.Messaging
Imports System.Configuration
Imports System.Threading
Imports System.Reflection.EventInfo
Imports System.Data
Imports System.Data.SqlClient
Imports System.Data.OleDb
Imports System.ServiceProcess
Imports Microsoft.VisualBasic
Public Class MSMQDBService
    Inherits ServiceBase
    ' Event Log information
Private gstrServiceName As String = "MSMQDBService"
Private gstrServiceStarted As String = gstrServiceName & " started."
Private gstrServiceStopped As String = gstrServiceName & " stopped."
Private gstrServiceShutdown As String = gstrServiceName & "
shutdown."
Private gstrServicePaused As String = gstrServiceName & " paused."
Private gstrServiceContinued As String = gstrServiceName & " service
continued."
Private gstrPowerEvent As String = gstrServiceName & " power event
occurred."
' MQ config information
Private gstrMSMQServerName As String
Private gstrMSMQQueueName As String
Private gstrMSMQFullName As String
Private WithEvents pmqQueue As MessageQueue
' Use SQLClient or OleDb.
```

Continued

Listing 8-5 *(Continued)*

```
' True = SqlClient
' False = OleDb
Private pblDBClient As Boolean = True
Private gstrConnectString As String
Public Sub New()
    Me.ServiceName = "MSMQDBService"
    Me.CanStop = True
    Me.AutoLog = True
    Me.CanShutdown = True
    Me.CanPauseAndContinue = True
    Me.CanHandlePowerEvent = True
End Sub
Shared Sub Main()
    System.ServiceProcess.ServiceBase.Run(New MSMQDBService())
End Sub
Protected Overrides Sub OnStart(ByVal args() As String)
Dim ConfigurationAppSettings As
System.Collections.Specialized.NameValueCollection =
System.Configuration.ConfigurationSettings.AppSettings
' Instantiate the private message queue object
pmqQueue = New MessageQueue()
' Write to the event log and state that the OnStart Event has been
called.
EventLog.WriteEntry(gstrServiceName, gstrServiceStarted)
' Get config information for the application config file.
gstrMSMQServerName =
Convert.ToString(ConfigurationAppSettings.Get("MSMQServerName"))
gstrMSMQQueueName =
Convert.ToString(ConfigurationAppSettings.Get("MSMQQueueName"))
gstrMSMQFullName = gstrMSMQServerName & "\" & gstrMSMQQueueName
pblDBClient =
Convert.ToBoolean(ConfigurationAppSettings.Get("UseSQLClient"))
If pblDBClient = True Then
    gstrConnectString =
Convert.ToString(ConfigurationAppSettings.Get("SQLClientString"))
Else
    gstrConnectString =
Convert.ToString(ConfigurationAppSettings.Get("OleDbClientString"))
End If
'  See if the necessary message queue exists.
If Not (MessageQueue.Exists(gstrMSMQFullName)) Then
MessageQueue.Create(gstrMSMQFullName)
End If
pmqQueue.Path = gstrMSMQFullName
```

```vb
pmqQueue.Formatter = New XmlMessageFormatter(New String()
{"System.String, mscorlib"})
' handle the RecieveCompleted event of the pmqQueue object.
AddHandler pmqQueue.ReceiveCompleted, New
ReceiveCompletedEventHandler(AddressOf OnReceiveCompleted)
' Begin an async receive of the information.
pmqQueue.BeginReceive()
End Sub
Protected Overrides Sub OnStop()
   EventLog.WriteEntry(gstrServiceName, gstrServiceStopped)
End Sub
Protected Overrides Sub OnShutdown()
   EventLog.WriteEntry(gstrServiceName, gstrServiceShutdown)
End Sub
Protected Overrides Sub OnPause()
   EventLog.WriteEntry(gstrServiceName, gstrServicePaused)
End Sub
Protected Overrides Sub OnContinue()
   EventLog.WriteEntry(gstrServiceName, gstrServiceContinued)
End Sub
Protected Overloads Function OnPowerEvent(ByVal ppbsStatus As
PowerBroadcastStatus) As Boolean
   EventLog.WriteEntry(gstrServiceName, gstrPowerEvent & vbCrLf &
"EventPassed: " & ppbsStatus.ToString())
   Return True
End Function
Public Sub OnReceiveCompleted(ByVal sender As Object, ByVal e As
ReceiveCompletedEventArgs)
      'place code here to process a completed message.
      Dim mqMsg As Message = pmqQueue.EndReceive(e.AsyncResult)
      Dim strValue As String
      Dim strSql As String
      mqMsg.Formatter = New XmlMessageFormatter(New String()
{"System.String, mscorlib"})
      strValue = Convert.ToString(mqMsg.Body)
      Try
      'Process the value in some way.
      'Generic error processing.
      Catch exc As Exception
          EventLog.WriteEntry(gstrServiceName, "Error Message: " &
exc.Message)
      Finally
          'run another asynchronous recieve
          pmqQueue.BeginReceive()
```

Continued

Listing 8-5 *(Continued)*

```
        End Try
    End Sub
Private Sub InitializeComponent()
Dim configurationAppSettings As
System.Collections.Specialized.NameValueCollection =
System.Configuration.ConfigurationSettings.AppSettings
Me.AutoLog =
Boolean.Parse(configurationAppSettings.Get("MSMQDBService.AutoLog"))
Me.CanHandlePowerEvent =
Boolean.Parse(configurationAppSettings.Get("ManualService.CanHandleP
owerEvent"))
Me.CanPauseAndContinue =
Boolean.Parse(configurationAppSettings.Get("ManualService.CanPauseAn
dContinue"))
Me.CanShutdown =
Boolean.Parse(configurationAppSettings.Get("ManualService.CanShutdow
n"))
Me.CanStop =
Boolean.Parse(configurationAppSettings.Get("MSMQDBService.CanStop"))
Me.ServiceName =
configurationAppSettings.Get("ManualService.ServiceName")
    End Sub
End Class
```

Listing 8-6: A C# Windows Service

```
//   Namespaces that are imported for use by the service.
//    Some are needed by the service.
//    Others are needed by the logic of the service.
using System;
using System.Data;
using System.Data.OleDb;
using System.Data.SqlClient;
using System.ServiceProcess;
using System.Configuration;
using System.Messaging;
using System.Diagnostics;
using System.Reflection;

namespace MSMQDBService
{
// The first step is to create a class and inherit from
System.ServiceProcess.ServiceBase.
//    This provides us with the necessary infrastructure to create a
```

```
service within the
//        .NET Framework.
public class MSMQDBServiceClass : ServiceBase
{
//variables that are used through out the service.
//they are setup as global within the class and to the service.
public static readonly string gstrMSMQDBServiceName =
"MSMQDBServiceCS";
public static readonly string gstrMSMQDBServiceDesc =
"MSMQDBServiceCS";
private string pServiceName = gstrMSMQDBServiceName;
private string gstrServerName;
private string gstrQueueName;
private string gstrQueue;
private bool gblSqlClient;
private string gstrSqlCn;
private string gstrOleDbCn;
private MessageQueue gMQ;
private string gstrServiceStarted = gstrMSMQDBServiceName + "
service started.";
private string gstrServiceStopped = gstrMSMQDBServiceName + "
service stopped.";
private string gstrServicePaused = gstrMSMQDBServiceName + " service
paused.";
private string gstrServiceContinue = gstrMSMQDBServiceName + "
service continue.";
private string gstrServicePowerEvent = gstrMSMQDBServiceName + "
service power event detected.";

private void InitializeComponent()
{
}

public static void Main()
{
ServiceBase.Run(new MSMQDBServiceClass());
}

// Constructor logic goes here.
public MSMQDBServiceClass()
{
ServiceName = pServiceName;
CanStop = true;
AutoLog = true;
```

Continued

Listing 8-6 *(Continued)*

```csharp
CanShutdown = true;
CanPauseAndContinue = true;
CanHandlePowerEvent = true;
}
protected override void OnStart(string[] strArgs)
{
gstrServerName =
ConfigurationSettings.AppSettings["MSMQServerName"];
gstrQueueName = ConfigurationSettings.AppSettings["MSMQQueueName"];
gstrQueue = gstrServerName + "\\" + gstrQueueName;
gblSqlClient =
Convert.ToBoolean(ConfigurationSettings.AppSettings["UseSQLClient"])
;
gstrSqlCn = ConfigurationSettings.AppSettings["SQLClientString"];
gstrOleDbCn =
ConfigurationSettings.AppSettings["OleDbClientString"];
EventLog.WriteEntry(gstrMSMQDBServiceName,gstrServiceStarted);
gMQ = new MessageQueue();
gMQ.Path = gstrQueue;
gMQ.Formatter = new XmlMessageFormatter(new string[]{"System.String,
mscorlib"});
gMQ.ReceiveCompleted += new
ReceiveCompletedEventHandler(this.MQ_ReceiveCompleted );
gMQ.BeginReceive();
}

private void MQ_ReceiveCompleted(object sender,
ReceiveCompletedEventArgs e)
{
// Add code here to respond to a message.
//   The code below is example code to retrieve a message.
Message msg = gMQ.EndReceive(e.AsyncResult);
msg.Formatter = new XmlMessageFormatter(new String[]{"System.String,
mscorlib"});
string strBody = (string)msg.Body;
//   This code example only uses a generic exception handler.
//   More appropriate error handling is suggested.
catch (Exception exc )
{
EventLog.WriteEntry(gstrMSMQDBServiceName, "Exception Message: " +
exc.Message);
}
finally
{
```

```
gMQ.BeginReceive();
}
}
protected override void OnCustomCommand( int pintCustomCommand )
{
EventLog.WriteEntry(gstrMSMQDBServiceName, "A custom command was
sent to the service.  The value sent is " +
pintCustomCommand.ToString() );
}
protected override void OnStop()
{
//Add code to process the Stop Event.
}
protected override void OnPause()
{
//Add code to process the Pause Event.
}
protected override void OnContinue()
{
//Add code to process the Continue Event.
//  This is merely example code.
//  It pulls in data from the application config file.
gstrServerName =
ConfigurationSettings.AppSettings["MSMQServerName"];
gstrQueueName = ConfigurationSettings.AppSettings["MSMQQueueName"];
gstrQueue = gstrServerName + "\\" + gstrQueueName;
gblSqlClient =
Convert.ToBoolean(ConfigurationSettings.AppSettings["UseSQLClient"])
;
gstrSqlCn = ConfigurationSettings.AppSettings["SQLClientString"];
gstrOleDbCn =
ConfigurationSettings.AppSettings["OleDbClientString"];
gMQ.Path = gstrQueue;
gMQ.Formatter = new XmlMessageFormatter(new string[]{"System.String,
mscorlib"});
gMQ.BeginReceive();
}
protected override bool OnPowerEvent(PowerBroadcastStatus pbsStatus)
{
EventLog.WriteEntry(pServiceName, "Power Event handled: " +
pbsStatus.ToString() );
return true;
}
}
}
```

Sending custom commands to a Windows Service

Previously, we noted that a service may accept commands from the SCM while it is running. The CustomCommand event and OnCustomCommand method are used to provide additional functionality beyond the OnStart, OnStop, OnPause, OnPowerEvent, and the other defined commands. The OnCustomCommand method is called when the SCM sends a custom command to the service. The OnCustomCommand accepts an integer value between 128 and 256. Values under 128 are reserved by the system.

How does a programmer develop an application that can send a custom command to a service? Custom commands are raised by the SCM when an ExecuteCommand is called in a ServiceController component. When an instance of a ServiceController is created, two properties need to be set: the name of computer system (MachineName) and the name of the Windows Service (ServiceName). By default, the MachineName is the local system and is set to an empty string. Take a look at some Visual Basic .NET code that creates a service controller object:

```
'Create an instance of the Service Controller object.
Dim scObj as New ServiceController()
'Communicate with the MSMQDBServiceCS.
scObj.ServiceName = "MSMQDBServiceCS";
'Send the custom command 200 to the service.
scObj.ExecuteCommand(200)
'Close the connection to the SCM / Service.
scObj.Close()
```

The following code creates a service controller object in C#:

```
//Create a Service Controller object.
ServiceController scObj = new ServiceController();
//Communicate with the MSMQDBServiceCS Service.
scObj.ServiceName = "MSMQDBServiceCS";
//Send the custom command 200 to the service.
scObj.ExecuteCommand(200);
//Close the connection to the SCM / Service.
scObj.Close();
```

Now that we've covered some of the basics of communicating with a Windows Service, let's look at a list of some of the more advanced methods:

◆ Close(): The Close() method disconnects the ServiceController instance from the associated service and frees all resources that the ServiceController instance allocated.

◆ Continue(): The Continue() method continues a service that has been paused.

◆ **ExecuteCommand():** The ExecuteCommand() method sends a custom command to the associated service.

◆ **GetDevices():** The method GetDevices() returns an array of ServiceController objects with each element associated with a device driver. The GetDevices method does not return any services.

◆ **GetServices():** The method GetServices() returns an array of ServiceController objects with each element associated with a service. The GetServices method does not return any device drivers.

◆ **Pause():** The Pause() method sends the pause event to a service and causes it to pause.

◆ **Refresh():** The Refresh() method sets the properties of the associated ServiceController instance to their default values. The method sets the ServicesDependedOn and DependentServices properties to null (C#) or Nothing (VB).

◆ **Start():** The Start() method starts the service associated with the ServiceController instance. A string array may be passed to the method to pass to the OnStart method of the Windows Service.

◆ **Stop():** The Stop() method stops the service associated with the ServiceController instance.

◆ **WaitForStatus():** The WaitForStatus() method waits for a service to reach a specified state. The method takes one or two arguments. The first is the ServiceControllerStatus that the ServiceController object is waiting for. The second argument is an optional timespan object to specify the amount of time to wait.

Properties of the ServiceController object include the following:

◆ **CanPauseAndContinue:** A read-only value that states whether the service may pause and resume.

◆ **CanShutdown:** A read-only value that states whether a service is to be notified when the system shuts down.

◆ **CanStop:** A read-only value indicated whether the service may be stopped after it has been started.

◆ **DependentServices:** This property returns an array of ServiceController objects that depend on the service associated with the ServiceController array.

◆ **DisplayName:** The friendly name of a service.

◆ **MachineName:** The name of the system associated with the ServiceController instance. By default, the instance will refer to the local machine.

- ◆ ServiceName: The name of the service associated with the ServiceController instance.

- ◆ ServiceDependedOn: An array of ServiceController instances that are each associated with a service that must be running for the specified service to run.

- ◆ ServiceType: The type of service that the ServiceController instance is associated with. The return value is one of the ServiceType values specified previously.

- ◆ Status: The status of the service that the ServiceController instance is associated with. The return value is in the form of a ServiceControllerStatus value.

Identifying Other Namespaces

Within .NET, there are other namespaces that provide the ability to create events and allow these events to be handled programmatically.

FileSystemWatcher

The file system may be monitored for changes by the FileSystemWatcher component. The FileSystemWatcher component is used to watch the assigned areas of the file system for changes. The FileSystemWatcher has four events that it may raise:

- ◆ Created: This event is raised when a directory or file is created within the watched area of the file system.

- ◆ Deleted: This event is raised when a directory or file is deleted within the watched area of the file system.

- ◆ Renamed: This event is raised with a directory or file within the watched area of the file system is renamed.

- ◆ Changed: This event is raised when a directory or file within the watched area of the file system is changed. These changes include size, attributes, last access time, or NTFS security permissions. The .Notify property of the FileSystemWatcher may be used to limit the number of events that the Changed event raises.

The .NotifyFiler property of the FileSystemWatcher event may be used to specify the type of changes that the Changed event will raise. Within the System.IO namespace is an enumeration that contains the filter settings that may be used. These values within the enumeration are:

◆ Attributes: The value that represents the attributes of the file and the folder.

◆ CreationTime: The value that represents the time that the file or folder were created.

◆ DirectoryName: The value that represents the name of the directory.

◆ FileName: The value that represents the name of the file.

◆ LastAccess: The value that represents the date and time that the file/folder was last opened.

◆ LastWrite: The value that represents the date and time that the file/folder was last written to.

◆ Security: The value that represents the security settings on the file/folder.

◆ Size: The value that represents the size of the file/folder.

These values may be combined using a bitwise OR to watch for multiple changes at the same time. For example, the VB syntax would be:

```
Dim fsWatcher as New FileSystemWatcher()
'specify the directory to watch .
fsWatcher.Path = "c:\fsExample"
'Watch for changes on the size and filename.
fsWatcher.NotifyFiler = NotifyFilers.Size or NotifyFilters.FileName
'Watch for changes on .doc files.
fsWatcher.Filter = "*.doc"
'watch for the Changed event.
AddHandler fsWatcher.Changed, AddressOf OnChanged
fsWatcher.EnableRaisingEvents = True
'.....In another section of code.......
Public Shared Sub OnChanged( source as object, fsea as
FileSystemEventArgs)
'Do something with the filename (fsea.FullPath).
'Do something with the changed type (fsea.ChangeType).
End Sub
```

The C# syntax is:

```
FileSystemWatcher fsWatcher = new FileSystemWatcher();
'specify the directory to watch .
fsWatcher.Path = "c:\fsExample";
//Watch for changes on the size and filename.
```

```
fsWatcher.NotifyFiler = NotifyFilers.Size | NotifyFilters.FileName;
//Watch for changes on .doc files.
fsWatcher.Filter = "*.doc";
//watch for the Changed event.
fsWatcher.Changed += new FileSystemEventHandler(OnChanged);
fsWatcher.EnableRaisingEvents = true;
//.....In another section of code.......
public static void OnChanged( object source, FileSystemEventArgs
fsea ) {
/*Do something with the filename (fsea.FullPath).
Do something with the changed type (fsea.ChangeType).
*/
}
```

The currently allowed change types for the file system watcher object are contained within the `WatcherChangeTypes` enumeration. These values are:

♦ `WatcherChangeTypes.All`: A change type has occurred.

♦ `WatcherChangeTypes.Changed`: A change has occurred on a file. The types of changes include size, attributes, security settings, last write, and last access time.

♦ `WatcherChangeTypes.Created`: A file or folder has been created.

♦ `WatcherChangeTypes.Deleted`: A file or folder has been deleted.

♦ `WatcherChangeTypes.Renamed`: A file or folder has been renamed.

The `WatcherChangeTypes` allow a program to detect the appropriate change type within the file system.

Network requests

Another useful set of routines are those that handle network requests. The .NET Framework contains the namespaces `System.Network` and `System.Network.Sockets`. These namespaces provide support for processing network requests and network communication with TCP/IP. Within the `System.Network.Socket` object, the `BeginAccept` method call accepts two parameters. These parameters are an Asynchronous `CallBack` object and a state object:

```
Dim listObj as New System.Network.Socket()
listObj.BeginAccept( new AsynchCallBack(AddressOf
ProcessListenRequest ), listObj )
'......More code
Public Shared Sub ProcessListenRequest(arobj as IAsyncResult)
```

```
'Call EndRequest(arobj) to get the data sent.
'Call BeginRequest to start processing with another socket.
End Sub
```

Summary

Threading is a very important part of the .NET Framework. By implementing threading, a front-end application is able to provide a better user experience by being more responsive to the user. A thread pool allows an application, such as a service, to have a set of prebuilt threads that can respond to events, such as a user's request for a resource. A service allows an application to respond to requests and events without the need to be logged in. The requests may occur on the local system or be from a remote system. Using these features from the .NET Framework together, will assist developers in creating an application that can scale to a larger number of users than without the use of these features.

Chapter 9

Message Queuing Integration

MESSAGE QUEUING IS A service provided by the NT4 Option Pak in Windows NT 4.0 and by COM+ Services in Windows 2000 and later. Message queuing allows for an application to send data from one location to another without a dedicated connection between the two locations. By providing this underlying transport mechanism, Microsoft Message Queue (MSMQ) is a tool that programmers can use to create a high performance application.

Message Queuing Basics

Before we look at the Microsoft Message Queue, let's take a look at some background material that is important to this discussion. You need to think about how applications operate and how commands are sent and received between applications.

Synchronous operations

What is a *synchronous operation?* What does it mean to be synchronous? Typically, when an application (sender) sends data to a service (receiver), the application must wait for processing to occur on the receiver before execution in the application can continue with the next line. This requirement to wait on execution is known as being synchronous, or a synchronous operation. This is typical programming style with ASP and VB. Waiting on operations is not necessarily bad. It's very easy to understand, very easy to program, and very easy to debug. But it does have its limitations. It can have problems when scaling to large numbers of users, if the operations take too long to be processed on the back-end service.

Asynchronous operations

Now that you now what *synchronous* means, what does *asynchronous* or the term *asynchronous operation* mean? Simple. *Asynchronous* means the opposite of *synchronous*. When an application (sender) sends data to a service (receiver) in an asynchronous manner, the application executes the command to send the data to the service and begins processing the next instruction. If and when data is returned from the service back to the client, there is an event that occurs within the client application that processes any returning results. VB applications can use asynchronous operations by defining variables that are global to a class with the WithEvents syntax.

Let's look at an example Web-based application that we wrote with MySQL as the back-end database. We were using IIS4 running on NT4. In this application, we needed to log data regarding certain pieces of information from a Web site. We did not want to save the data in a text file for fear of losing that data through corruption. Unfortunately, MySQL was the only database that we could use at the location the web server was at. We began to log the data to three tables within the MySQL database. The problem we had was that the version of MySQL we were using only supports table locking when inserting data. Combine this problem with the fact that an ASP page cannot support asynchronous operations, and we quickly had delays within our IIS Server. These delays could be seen on the performance monitor in the form of queued requests. After we reached a certain traffic level, the IIS server would begin to place requests on hold (queued requests).

Why? Well, the IIS server was limited to ten threads per CPU by default. Once those ten threads were all used to send data to the database, requests to the IIS Server were placed into a queue for processing. These queued requests would build up until the web server could not handle any more requests and IIS would stop responding completely. To get around this problem, we used a unique feature of the MySQL database. When used to insert records one after the other, MySQL has an enhancement to the classic SQL insert command called a *delayed insert*. A delayed insert allowed ADO to send the insert command to the database without having to wait for a response. By using the delayed insert command, ADO responded as if the command had been processed. The result was that the ASP page continued processing and the database engine handled the insert when it could lock the table for that command. This delayed insert feature is an asynchronous type of feature that is built into MySQL. It allows us to sidestep the synchronous feature of ADO running in ASP. By using an asynchronous feature of MySQL, we were able to achieve the scalability necessary to process database operations faster than the rate of new requests coming into the server. We could not achieve this rate with the standard asynchronous operation of ADO running within ASP.

What are messages and queues?

Quite simply, a *message* is some type of data that is sent between two processes. This data can be simple information, such as text, or it could be complex information containing embedded data and objects. You can think of a message as the same kind of concept as an e-mail sent from one person to another. E-mails can contain simple information, such as text, and more complex information, such as Word documents, pictures, and embedded instructions. The concepts are basically the same. An e-mail is a container of information used to communicate with other people in an asynchronous manner, just as a message queue message is a container of information used to communicate between applications in an asynchronous manner.

A *queue* is the location into which messages are placed to send them between one process and another. An application will place data into a queue and can get data out of a queue. This is very similar to the U.S. Postal Service. You place letters into a mailbox. After the letters are in these locations, the U.S. Postal Service processes the pickup and delivery of these messages. Our applications will place information into and pickup from a queue location.

What is the Microsoft Message Queue?

First, let's think about an existing application. Typically, applications are built with the belief that the all back-end services must be available. This is commonly referred to as a *tightly coupled application.* If any back-end service necessary for processing is not available, then the application will fail when it attempts to access that back-end service. The reason for the failure of the back-end system could be that the physical machine the service is on could be down, the service may not be started, or the connection between the two locations may not be functioning. Any of these issues can cause a failure when attempting to access the remote service.

Imagine that you're running an e-commerce toy company. When a user of your system purchases a product, you need to send a message to the product-delivery company that actually ships the products from your warehouse to the customer. This message contains information about the number of products purchased and the weight of those products. In a classical, tightly coupled application, if your application can't communicate at that moment with your shipping partner's service to tell them about these products to be shipped, then you would have a problem. Either your application would fail with no information sent to your shipping partner or the purchase transaction would fail and you would not allow the customer to actually purchase the product. In either case, you have a problem.

What you would like is for the purchasing transaction to occur and for your shipping partner to receive notification of this shipping product at the earliest possible moment before the shipping company sends their trucks to pick up the shipments. The important element to note in your scenario is that the communication with your shipping partner is not required to be immediate. You would like the communication to be immediate, but that isn't absolutely required. As long as the information is sent to your shipping partner as soon as they can process it, then you're okay. What kind of a tool can be used to communicate between your e-commerce application and your shipping partner? A message queue will provide the mechanism to communicate between two locations without requiring the two locations to talk with each other at any particular moment.

Now that you know what message queuing is, what is the Microsoft Message Queue (MSMQ)? MSMQ is Microsoft's product that provides message queuing services. It was first widely distributed with Windows NT 4.0 Option Pak. It is included with COM+ Services in Windows 2000 and later. It provides several features beyond just message queuing, including the following:

◆ **Transactional services:** By using COM+ Services, if a message is placed in a queue, and within that same transaction, the transaction is aborted, the message is pulled from the queue and not sent, or, in the case of a receive, the message is placed back into the queue on an aborted transaction.

◆ **Fault-tolerance:** If for some reason the system running MSMQ or the MSMQ service fails, there is a chance for the loss of messages. MSMQ can be set to store messages on the file system, thereby saving them in the event of a service or system shutdown.

◆ **Integration with other message queuing systems, such as IBM's MQSeries**

MSMQ provides an excellent architectural feature for building highly scalable applications. It provides the infrastructure for asynchronous message passing between applications and services. Let's take a look at MSMQ in more detail. Figure 9-1 shows a high-level view of the MSMQ architecture.

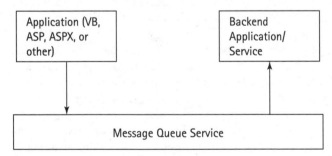

Figure 9-1: High-level message queue architecture

The Microsoft Message Queue Service contains two main types of queues: user-created queues, and system queues. User queues can be one of four types:

◆ **Public queues:** Public queues are replicated throughout the MSMQ network. These queues may be access by all the sites connected by a network.

◆ **Private queues:** Private queues are queues that are not published across an MSMQ network. These queues are only the local computer that contains the queue and may only be read by applications that know the full path name or label that fully identifies the queue.

- ◆ **Administration queues:** Administration queues contain messages that acknowledge that a message was received within a MSMQ network. A program can specify the administration to use, if that is needed.

- ◆ **Response queues:** Response queues contain response messages that are returned to a sending application when a message is received by a destination application.

System-generated queues can be one of four types:

- ◆ **Journal queues:** Journal queues optionally store copies of messages that an application sends and copies of messages removed from a queue. A separate journal queue exists for each individual queue.

- ◆ **Dead-letter queues:** Dead-letter queues store copies of undeliverable or expired messages. Dead letters are stored on the computer where the message has expired. If a message that is to be placed in a dead letter queue is transactional, the message is actually placed into transaction dead-letter queue. This is a special type of dead-letter queue.

- ◆ **Report queues:** Report queues contain message that indicate the route a message took to get to its endpoint. There is only one report queue per computer system.

- ◆ **Private system queues:** Private system queues are a set of private queues that store admin and notification messages that the system needs to process messaging actions.

There are three parts to creating an application that uses MSMQ:

- ◆ **Send data:** The client application must be able to send data to a message queue. The application must be able send it to the appropriate queue in the correct location.

- ◆ **Move the data from one location to another:** Technically, this is the job of the message queue, not the application developer. However, the application developer must know and understand how the message queue is set up in order for the application to work appropriately.

- ◆ **Process the data:** The back-end service must be able to process and receive the data on the other side of the message queue.

Sending data

For an application to communicate to a message queue, it must use some type of external library, much like the System.Data.SqlClient library for communicating to SQL server. The .NET Framework provides an assembly for communicating to the MSMQ product. It is System.Messaging.dll. Within the System.Message.dll file is a namespace that needs to be included in an application to allow it to communicate with MSMQ. Let's take a look at some sample code to send a test message to a queue.

Following is a sample Visual Basic .NET code listing that sends a test message to a queue:

```
'Import the System.Messaging namespace so that we can use methods
'and objects inside of it.  This line is at the top of whatever
'file we are working on in our VB.NET project.
Imports System.Messaging
'Create a MessageQueue object.
Dim mq As New MessageQueue()
'Define the path to the appropriate queue.  In this case, we are
'going to send a message to a private queue on the local machine.
mq.Path = ".\private$\ManualServiceQueue"
'We then send a message.  In this case, we have sent a string
'message to the queue.
mq.Send("string message.........")
```

The following is sample C# code listing that sends a test message to a queue:

```
//Import the System.Messaging namespace so that we can use methods
//and objects inside of it.  This line is at the top of whatever
//file we are working on in our C# project.
using System.Messaging;
//Create a MessageQueue object.
MessageQueue mq = new MessageQueue();
//Define the path to the appropriate queue.  In this case, we are
//going to send a message to a private queue on the local machine.
mq.Path = ".\private$\ManualServiceQueue";
//We then send a message.  In this case, we have sent a string
//message to the queue.
mq.Send("string message.........");
```

The .Send() method is overloaded and can accept four different combinations of input parameters. These are:

- .Send(object): This will serialize an object and places it into the defined message queue. The queue can be either transactional or nontransactional.

- .Send(object, MessageQueueTransaction): Serializes an object and sends it into the defined message queue. The queue must be transactional. The MessageQueueTransaction is the messaging transaction object used to commit or roll back the operation of sending data to queue.

◆ `.Send( object, string )`: Serializes an object, sends it to the defined message queue and gives the message the label of string. The queue can be either transactional or nontransactional.

◆ `.Send( object, string, MessageQueueTransaction )`: Serializes an object, sends it to the defined message queue, and gives the message the label of string. The queue must be transactional. The `MessageQueueTransaction` is the messaging transaction object used to commit or roll back the operation of sending data to queue.

Receiving data

For an application to receive data from a message queue, it must include the System.Message.dll assembly and namespace, just like the sending data application. We can use the methods within this namespace to add message-receiving and message-processing capabilities to our application. Within the System.Message.dll namespace are several mechanisms to receive and process messages.

Let's take a look a look at how to receive messages. This specific example begins an asynchronous receive of a message. When a message comes into the queue defined in the path statement, after the message is completely received, the event `OnReceiveCompleted` is raised.

Following is an example of Visual Basic .NET code that receives messages:

```
'Instantiate the message queue object.
Dim gmqQueue as MessageQueue
gmqQueue = New MessageQueue()
'Set the path and formatting option of the private
'message queue object.
gmqQueue.Path = ".\private$\dotnetqueue"
gmqQueue.Formatter = New XmlMessageFormatter(New String()
{"System.String, mscorlib"})
AddHandler gmqQueue.ReceiveCompleted, New _
ReceiveCompletedEventHandler(AddressOf _
OnReceiveCompleted)
 'Begin an asynchronous receive of a message.
gmqQueue.BeginReceive()
'...........
'The OnReceiveCompletedSub is called when the ReceiveCompletedEvent
occurs.
Public Sub OnReceiveCompleted(ByVal sender As Object, ByVal e As
ReceiveCompletedEventArgs)
   'Process the value received.
Dim mqMsg As Message = pmqQueue.EndReceive(e.AsyncResult)
Dim strValue As String
mqMsg.Formatter = New XmlMessageFormatter(New String()
{"System.String, mscorlib"})
```

```
strValue = CStr(mqMsg.Body)
'Wait on a message from the queue.
gmqQueue.BeginReceive()
End Sub
```

Here is an example of C# code that receives messages:

```
//Instantiate the message queue object.
MessageQueue gmqQueue;
gmqQueue = new MessageQueue();
//Set the path and formatting option of the private
//message queue object.
gmqQueue.Path = ".\private$\dotnetqueue";
gmqQueue.Formatter = new XmlMessageFormatter(new string[]
{"System.String, mscorlib"});
gMQ.ReceiveCompleted += new
ReceiveCompletedEventHandler(this.MQ_ReceiveCompleted );
//Begin a synchronous receive of a message.
gMQ.BeginReceive();
//.........
//Handle the ReceiveCompletedEvent.
private void MQ_ReceiveCompleted(object sender,
ReceiveCompletedEventArgs e)
{
// Add code here to respond to message.
Message msg = pMQ.EndReceive(e.AsyncResult);
msg.Formatter = new XmlMessageFormatter(new String[]{"System.String,
mscorlib"});
string strBody = (string)msg.Body;
//Wait on a message from the queue.
pMQ.BeginReceive();
}
```

This code gets data from a queue and performs some type of processing on that date contained within the message. Let's look at a couple of the functions within the `ReceiveCompleted` event handler code.

FORMATTING OF THE MESSAGE

Within the two preceding code examples , there is a message object. The message object identifies the specific message that the event handler is looking at during that particular event. Associated with that message object is a formatting object. This formatting object is used to determine the formatting value. There are three types of formatting objects available within the message object. These formatting objects are:

◆ `XmlMessageFormatter`: The `XmlMessageFormatter` is the default formatting option within the `MessageQueue` object. In the example, the `XmlMessageFormatter` merely returns the data within the body of the message as a string.

◆ `ActiveXMessageFormatter`: The `ActiveXMessageFormatter` is the formatting object that allows you to serialize and deserialize objects into and out of MSMQ.

◆ `BinaryMessageFormatter`: The `BinaryMessageFormatter` is the formatting object that allows MSMQ to serialize and deserialize object into and out of MSMQ in a binary format.

MESSAGE BODY

Now that you have a message and its format, you need to get its contents. One of the properties of a message is the message body. You can get the contents of the message body by using the property `msg.Body`. The most interesting part of the message body is that the data within the message body is stored with the .NET data type embedded with the body in an XML format, assuming that the `XmlMessageFormatter` is used. This can be verified by looking at the message as it is stored in a queue, which can be seen in Message Queue administrator.

The queue

You've seen that Microsoft Message Queue allows you to effectively design and develop physically distributed applications that can communicate with each other as that communication is possible. Let's take a little deeper look at the architecture of MSMQ. We will look at the programming APIs available for messaging and the administration APIs available to manage this underlying infrastructure.

Using the MSMQ API in .NET

The .NET API that supports MSMQ is feature rich. It contains method calls to both administer MSMQ and to communicate through MSMQ queues. Let's take a look at the APIs.

Programming API for messages

Messages within the MSMQ architecture can be processed several different ways. They can be sent, received synchronous, received asynchronous, peeked synchronous, and peeked asynchronous:

◆ **Send:** The `Send` method enables a client application to place a message object in a queue.

◆ **Receive Synchronous:** `Receive`, `ReceiveById`, and `ReceiveByCorrelationId` provide methods necessary for reading messages from a queue. When a message is received, it is removed from the queue. These methods support overloads. These overloads support transaction queue processing and timeout parameters. The Receive family of methods support synchronous processing. They interrupt until a message is available in the queue or a timeout occurs.

◆ **Peek Synchronous:** Peek functions along the same lines as Receive, with one difference. When a Peek method is called, the message that the Peek method receives is not removed from the queue. Peek contains no support for transactions because it does not remove any messages from the queue or alter the contents of the queue. Peek operates synchronously. The only overload it supports is for specifying a timeout. This prevents the thread from waiting forever.

◆ **Receive Asynchronous:** The Receive Asynchronous methods are very similar to the Receive Synchronous methods, with the exception that the Asynchronous methods are Asynchronous. There are several Begin/End methods that provide a mechanism to reads messages in asynchronous manner. `BeginReceive` and `EndReceive` do not interrupt the current thread while they wait on a message from a queue. These methods handle processing through events that creation of handlers (VB) and delegates (C#).

◆ **Peek Asynchronous:** The Peek Asynchronous methods are very similar to the Peek Synchronous methods, with the exceptions that the Asynchronous methods are just that Asynchronous.

Because we have already looked at the Send, Receive Synchronous, and Send Asynchronous, let's take a quick look at the Peek Synchronous and the Peek Asynchronous methods.

The Peek functions merely go into a queue and look for a message. The Peek methods do not remove a message from the queue, otherwise they operate the same as the nontransactional Receive methods.

Let's take a look at some simple code to use the synchronous peek operation. There two possible overloaded ways to call the `.Peek()` method:

◆ `.Peek()`: Return a message from the queue when one appears. This call will wait indefinitely.

◆ `.Peek( TimeSpan )`: Return a message from the queue when one appears and only wait a certain amount of time as specified by the TimeSpan that is passed to the Peek method. If there is no message within the queue within the given amount of time, a MessageQueueException will be raised. The error code that is returned is MessageQueueErrorCode.IOTimeout.

The following is code written in Visual Basic .NET to get a message from a MSMQ Queue:

```
Dim msmqObj as new MessageQueue("string path")
Dim msmqMsg as Message
msmqMsg = msmqObj.Peek()
```

The following is code written in C# to get a message from a MSMQ Queue:

```
MessageQueue msmqObj = new MessageQueue("string path");
Message msmqMsg;
msmqMsg = msmqObj.Peek();
```

The asynchronous peek is very similar to the asynchronous receive. With the asynchronous peek, a method is called to begin looking the message queue for a message. When a message is returned, an event is fired. This event is called PeekCompleted. Our code will need to process that event through the creation of an event handler, as in the asynchronous receive. Inside the asynchronous receive event handler, the event is processed and then our code can look for another message to peek into.

The following code written in Visual Basic .NET will create an event handler and will allow messages within a MSMQ queue to be processed asynchronously:

```
'Instantiate the message queue object.
Dim gmqQueue as MessageQueue
gmqQueue = New MessageQueue()
'Set the path and formatting option of the private
'message queue object.
gmqQueue.Path = ".\private$\dotnetqueue"
gmqQueue.Formatter = New XmlMessageFormatter(New String()
{"System.String, mscorlib"})
AddHandler gmqQueue.PeekCompleted, New _
PeekCompletedEventHandler(AddressOf _
OnPeekCompleted)
 'Begin an asynchronous receive of a message.
gmqQueue.BeginPeek()
'............
'The OnPeekCompletedSub is called when the PeekCompletedEvent
occurs.
Public Sub OnPeekCompleted(ByVal sender As Object, ByVal e As
PeekCompletedEventArgs)
   'Process the value received.
Dim mqMsg As Message = pmqQueue.EndPeek(e.AsyncResult)
Dim strValue As String
mqMsg.Formatter = New XmlMessageFormatter(New String()
{"System.String, mscorlib"})
strValue = CStr(mqMsg.Body)
```

```
'Wait on a message from the queue.
gmqQueue.BeginPeek()
End Sub
```

The following code written in C# will create an event handler and will allow messages within a MSMQ queue to be processed asynchronously:

```
//Instantiate the message queue object.
MessageQueue gmqQueue;
gmqQueue = new MessageQueue();
//Set the path and formatting option of the private
//message queue object.
gmqQueue.Path = ".\private$\dotnetqueue";
gmqQueue.Formatter = new XmlMessageFormatter(new string[]
{"System.String, mscorlib"});
gMQ.PeekCompleted += new
PeekCompletedEventHandler(this.MQ_PeekCompleted );
//Begin a synchronous receive of a message.
gMQ.BeginPeek();
//..........
//Handle the PeekCompletedEvent.
private void MQ_PeekCompleted(object sender, PeekCompletedEventArgs
e)
{
// Add code here to respond to message.
Message msg = pMQ.EndPeek(e.AsyncResult);
msg.Formatter = new XmlMessageFormatter(new String[]{"System.String,
mscorlib"});
string strBody = (string)msg.Body;
//Wait on a message from the queue.
pMQ.BeginPeek();
}
```

The BeginPeek method supports three other overloaded calling mechanisms for a total of four. These four calling conventions are:

- ◆ BeginPeek(): This is the simplest overload to call because it contains no additional parameters.

- ◆ BeginPeek(TimeSpan): This overload looks in the message queue for the amount of time specified by the TimeSpan that is passed in.

- ◆ BeginPeek(TimeSpan, Object): This overload looks in the message queue for the amount of time specified by the TimeSpan that is passed in and matches the Object that is passed in. For example, BeginPeek(new TimeSpan(0), 5) would look for the sixth (remember, we are zero based) message in the queue.

♦ BeginPeek(TimeSpan, Object, AsynchCallBack): This overload is similar to the BeginPeek(Timespan, Object) overload with the AsynchCallBack function defined directly within the BeginPeek() method call.

ADMINISTRATION

.NET contains a number of methods to assist in the administration of queues within the Microsoft Message Queue Service. The System.Messaging namespace contains methods and properties to create, delete, and test MSMQ queues.

The first step in managing MSMQ is to create a message queue object. From this object, .NET code can then manage the queue. Let's create an MSMQ object.

The following Visual Basic .NET code tests for a Queue's existence:

```
Dim msmqObj as New MessageQueue()
Dim blResult = msmqObj.Exists(".\private$\dotnetqueue")
```

The following C# code tests for the existence of a Queue.

```
MessageQueue msmqObj = new MessageQueue();
boolean blResult = msmqObj.Exists(".\\private$\\dotnetqueue");
```

The preceding code creates a message queue object and then it tests for the existence of the path. If the queue exists, a true is returned. If the queue does not exist, a false is returned.

Creating a queue is very similar to testing for queue existence in the previous code. The process is fairly simple, much like the process of checking for a queue's existence.

The following Visual Basic .NET code will create a queue.

```
Dim msmqObj as New MessageQueue()
try
msmqObj.Create(".\private$\dotnetqueue")
catch exc as MessageQueueException
    messagebox.Show("Error occurred.  Message:" & exc.Message)
finally
end try
```

The following C# code will create a queue.

```
MessageQueue msmqObj = new MessageQueue();
try()
{
msmqObj.Create(".\\private$\\dotnetqueue");
}
```

```
catch(MessageQueueException exc )
{
    MessageBox.Show("Error occurred. Message:" + exc.Message);
}
finally(){}
```

This code creates a message queue object. Wrapped within a try...catch **block** is the method call to attempt to create a message queue. If the message queue is successfully created, the code continues on into the finally block. If there is any type of problem resulting in an error, the catch block is executed and a message is displayed onscreen. What could cause an error? Typically, if the logged in user does not have the appropriate security rights to create a queue or the queue that the code is attempting to create is a system queue, which cannot be performed.

Now you know how to create a message queue. What do you do if you want to create a message queue that is transactional? .NET provides an overload to the Create() method to create a transaction queue. The Create() method can accept two parameters. The first is a string representing the path. The second parameter is a Boolean. If that parameter is set to true, the queue is transactional. If the parameter is set to false, a non-transactional queue is created.

Deleting a queue is almost exactly the same as creating a queue. The following Visual Basic .NET code shows how to delete a queue:

```
Dim msmqObj as New MessageQueue()
try
msmqObj.Delete(".\private$\dotnetqueue")
catch exc as MessageQueueException
    messagebox.Show("Error occurred.  Message:" & exc.Message)
finally
end try
```

The following C# code shows how to delete a queue:

```
MessageQueue msmqObj = new MessageQueue();
try()
{
msmqObj.Delete(".\\private$\\dotnetqueue");
}
catch( MessageQueueException exc )
{
    MessageBox.Show("Error occurred. Message:" + exc.Message);
}
finally(){}
```

If either the message queue delete or create generates an error, your program can check for more specific failure information. The MessageQueueErrorCode enumerator contains over 100 error codes for greater information. Testing against these error codes allows a program to provide more detailed information regarding the error(s) that have occurred. The following Visual Basic .NET code shows how to use the `MessageQueueErrorCode` enumeration:

```
Try
'do something related to a message queue
Catch exc as MessageQueueException
If exc.ErrorCode = MessageQueueErrorCode.AccessDenied then
    MessageBox.Show("Error accessing the message queue.  Mostly
likely a security access problem." & vbcrlf & "Error Message: " &
exc.Message )
End if
Finally
End Try
```

The following C# code shows how to use the `MesageQueueErrorCode` enumeration object:

```
Try{
//do something related to a message queue
}
catch( MessageQueueException exc){
if ( exc.ErrorCode == MessageQueueErrorCode.AccessDenied ) {
    MessageBox.Show("Error accessing the message queue.  Most likely
a security access problem.\r\nError Message: " + exc.Message );
}
}
finally{}
```

Now you know how to send messages and receive messages, along with how to create and delete message queues. The last thing that you need to do with a message queue is how to programmatically set permissions on a message queue.

One of the methods exposed by the `MessageQueue` object is the `SetPermissions` method. The `SetPermissions` method is overloaded, so it can take four possible sets of parameters. The four possible sets of parameters are:

◆ `SetPermissions( AccessControlList )`: `SetPermissions` assigns access rights to a queue defined by the `MessageQueue` object based on the contents of the access control list (acl) passed in.

◆ `SetPermissions( MessageQueueAccessControlEntry )`: `SetPermissions` assigns access rights to the queue defined by the `MessageQueue` object based on the contents of the `MessageQueueAccessControlEntry` passed in.

◆ SetPermissions(String, MessageQueueAccessRights):
  SetPermissions assigns access rights to the queue defined by the
  MessageQueue object based on the user defined by the first parameter
  (String) and the message queue access rights defined by the second
  parameter (MessageQueueAccessRights).

◆ SetPermissions(String, MessageQueueAccessRights,
  AccessControlEntryType): SetPermissions assigns access rights to
  the queue defined by the MessageQueue object based on the user defined
  by the first parameter (String), the message queue access rights defined
  by the second parameter (MessageQueueAccessRights) and the access
  right defined by the last parameter (AccessControlEntryType).

The following Visual Basic .NET code is a complete example showing how to set
permissions on a message queue.

```vb
Dim msmqObj As New MessageQueue()
Dim aclObj As New AccessControlList()
Dim aceObj As MessageQueueAccessControlEntry
Dim objT As New Trustee()
Dim strPath As String = ".\private$\MSMQQueue"
Try
If msmqObj.Exists(strPath) Then
    msmqObj.Delete(strPath)
End If
msmqObj.Create(strPath)
objT.Name = "Administrator"
aceObj = New MessageQueueAccessControlEntry(objT,
MessageQueueAccessRights.FullControl)
aclObj.Add(aceObj)
'Add a second user to this access control list
objT = New Trustee("SYSTEM")
aceObj = New MessageQueueAccessControlEntry(objT,
MessageQueueAccessRights.FullControl)
aclObj.Add(aceObj)
msmqObj.Path = strPath
msmqObj.SetPermissions(aclObj)
Catch exc As MessageQueueException
    MessageBox.Show(exc.Message & "Error Code: " & exc.ErrorCode)
End Try
End Sub
```

The following C# example is a complete example that showing how to set permissions on a message queue:

```csharp
MessageQueue msmqObj = new MessageQueue();
```

```
AccessControlList aclObj = new AccessControlList;
Trustee objT = new Trustee();
MessageQueueAccessControlEntry aceObj;
String strPath = ".\private$\MSMQQueue";
Try{
If (msmqObj.Exists(strPath)){
    msmqObj.Delete(strPath);
}
msmqObj.Create(strPath);
objT.Name = "Administrator";
aceObj = New MessageQueueAccessControlEntry(objT,
MessageQueueAccessRights.FullControl);
aclObj.Add(aceObj);
objT = new Trustee("SYSTEM");
aceObj = new MessageQueueAccessControlEntry(objT,
MessageQueueAccessRights.FullControl);
aclObj.Add(aceObj);
msmqObj.Path = strPath;
msmqObj.SetPermissions(aclObj);
}
Catch{MessageQueueException exc ){
MessageBox.Show(exc.Message & "Error Code: " & exc.ErrorCode);
}
```

Take a look at the preceding code. The first thing it does is to check for the existence of a queue defined by the path `.\private$\DotNetTestQueue`. If the queue exists, it is deleted. Why do you delete it? Your application needs to define a queue with a set of features, so for this application, your application goes ahead and deletes the queue. The next thing that your program does is define an element called a Trustee and populate properties. In your application, you will define a Trustee on the local machine and define that Trustee to the be Administrator and the System account on the local system. Your next step is to define a `MessageQueueAccessControlEntry` object. This object is made of the Trustee defined previously and a set of rights. These rights are defined as a bit-wise *or* of a set of integers that represent the access rights to be applied to the queue. The two access control entries are then placed into an object called an `AccessControlList`. An `AccessControlList` is just a collection of access control entries that define a user/trustee and the permissions that the user has. Notice that through this, you have not defined an actual path of the `MessageQueue` object — that is the next step of your program. Note that even though your code has referenced a path within your `if` statement, there is still a need to define an actual path for the `MessageQueue` object. With an object defined, your program can then call the method `SetPermissions()` to actually set the permissions of the queue. Figures 9-2 and 9-3 show the queues created by the preceding code.

Figure 9-2 shows possible security properties for a message queue, and Figure 9-3 shows general properties for a message queue.

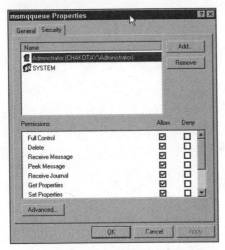

Figure 9-2: Security properties for a queue

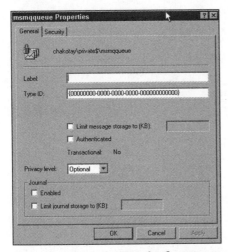

Figure 9-3: General properties for a queue

MessageQueueAccessRights

A number of access rights are accepted by a message queue. These rights are listed in Table 9-1 along with the descriptions. These access rights are defined within the MessageQueueAccessRights enumeration. To select multiple values from the enumeration, a program needs to perform a bitwise *or* among all the necessary security levels that are needed. Table 9-1 shows all the entries within the MessageQueueAccessRights enumeration.

TABLE 9-1 MESSAGEQUEUEACCESSRIGHTS ENUMERATION ENTRIES

Member Name	Description
ChangeQueuePermissions	The right to modify queue permissions.
DeleteJournalMessage	The right to delete messages from the journal queue.
DeleteQueue	The right to delete the queue defined in the messagequeue object of which your program calls setpermissions () method on.
FullControl	Full rights to the queue. This is a union of all the rights defined within the MessageQueueAccessRights enumeration.
GenericRead	A union of the GetQueueProperties, GetQueuePermissions, ReceiveMessage, and ReceiveJorunalMessage rights within the enumeration.
GenericWrite	A union of the GetQueueProperties, GetQueuePermissions, and WriteMessage rights within the enumeration.
GetQueuePermissions	The right to read queue permissions.
GetQueueProperties	The right to read properties of the queue.
PeekMessage	The right to peek messages from the queue.
ReceiveJournalMessage	The right to receive messages from the journal queue. This includes a union of the DeleteMessage and PeekMessage rights within the enumeration.
ReceiveMessage	The right to receive messages.
SetQueueProperties	The right to modify properties of the queue.
TakeQueueOwnership	The right to take ownership of the queue.

MSMQ transactions

Transactions are an important component of an enterprise application. The ability to perform work and roll that work back based on all the work completing or none of the work completing is a very important and powerful concept. Incorporating the capability to perform transactions with message queuing is nearly a requirement with regards to building a database-oriented application that effectively uses messaging. Think about this issue: You're an online distributor of physical music, such as CDs. You have just sold 1,000 copies of a CD to a local music chain store. You have sent a message to your shipping partner that you need to have these CDs shipped to your customer. What happens if, later on down the purchasing pipeline, your application decides to invalidate the work performed? Your application needs to be able to rollback any work performed, including the sending of the message.

The .NET Framework and MSMQ provide a class within the System.Messaging namespace for just this purpose. The MessageQueueTransaction class provides the capabilities to perform operations with a message queue that are transactional and are manually controlled by the application calling the message queue. The MessageQueueTransaction class may be passed to either the Send or Receive method. In addition to support for manual transactions, the .NET Framework supports the use of automatic transactions against MSMQ in COM+. When a rollback occurs in a Send() that is transactional, the message is removed from the message queue and not sent. When a commit occurs in a Send() that is transactional, the message is sent through the message queue. When a rollback occurs in a Receive() that is transactional, the message is returned to the message queue and not removed. When a commit occurs in a Receive() that is transactional, the message is removed from the message queue. From a design perspective, a message queue transaction is used with a try...catch...finally block.

The following Visual Basic .NET code is an example of sending a message to a queue that is transactional:

```
Dim mqObj as new MessageQueue()
Dim mqtObj as new MessageQueueTransaction()
Try
mqtObj.Begin
mqObj.Send(strMessage, mqtObj )
mqtObj.Commit
Catch exc as MessageQueueException
mqtObj.Rollback
Finally
'perform any necessary cleanup.
End Try
```

The following C# code is an example of sending a message to a queue that is transactional:

```
MessageQueue mqObj = new MessageQueue();
MessageQueueTransaction mqtObj = new MessageQueueTransaction();
Try{
mqtObj.Begin;
```

```
mqObj.Send(strMessage, mqtObj );
mqtObj.Commit;
}
Catch ( MessageQueueException exc ) {
mqtObj.Rollback;
}
Finally{
//perform any necessary cleanup.
}
```

Summary

Message queuing is an important feature of building enterprise applications. Proper usage of message queuing will allow application architects and developers to implement applications that are scalable, available, and more responsive to users while running within an environment that cannot guarantee a connection between two locations.

Part III

Specific Database Scaling Issues

Chapter 10

SQL Server

IN THIS CHAPTER

◆ Knowing SQL Server Architecture

◆ Understanding SQL Server Connectivity

◆ Connecting to SQL Server using SQLClient, OLE-DB, ODBC, and SqlXml

◆ Generating primary keys

◆ Integrating COM+ Services

SQL SERVER IS MICROSOFT'S enterprise database. SQL Server 2000, the latest version, currently runs on Windows NT 4.0, Windows 2000, and Windows XP. It is available in several separate versions:

◆ **Personal Edition, also known as Microsoft Data Engine (MSDE):** MSDE is a scaled-down version of SQL Server. MSDE contains the functionality of SQL Server with several limits, including the amount of data, the number of concurrent connections, and the number of concurrent operations it could perform. In most other ways, MSDE is SQL Server.

◆ **Standard Edition:** Standard Edition of SQL Server supports up to four CPUs and 2 GB of memory. Standard Edition does not contain a few of the high-end OLAP features of the Enterprise Edition, but otherwise it's the same product.

◆ **Enterprise Edition:** Enterprise Edition is the high-end edition of SQL Server. It supports up to 64 GB of memory and 32 CPUs. Enterprise Edition is designed for installation on Windows systems running a clustering solution.

◆ **Developer Edition:** Developer Edition is the version of SQL Server designed for developers. Within its license, developers may distribute solutions based on MSDE and SQL Server for CE.

◆ **SQL Server for CE Edition:** SQL Server for CE is a scaled-down version of SQL Server that runs on Windows CE 2.11 and later. SQL Server for CE is not part of the discussion in this chapter.

Connecting to SQL Server

Connecting to a database is one of the most important, and at the same time one of the most overlooked, parts of an application. If an application can't connect to a datasource, it doesn't matter how well that application is written, how cute the programming tricks are, or how much effort was put into implementing the business rules of the application. If the connection is working, it's often overlooked. The problem is that there are several types of connection possibilities. Each connection possibility has its own advantages and disadvantages. Following are the options for connecting to a SQL Server database:

◆ **Open Database Connectivity (ODBC):** The ODBC standard is the original Windows standard to communicate with a database. ODBC is designed to connect to relational databases. There is an ODBC driver for communicating with SQL Server. The .NET Framework provides an ODBC Data Provider that allows a .NET program to use an ODBC driver. This driver is available as a download from Microsoft's Developer site at `msdn.microsoft.com`. The SQL Server ODBC driver is available as part of the Microsoft Data Access Components (MDAC).

◆ **Object Linking and Embedding Database Connectivity (OLE-DB):** The OLE-DB standard is an updated standard to communicate with a database. The main design point difference between ODBC and OLE-DB is that OLE-DB is designed to communicate with any type of datasource, such as searching a directory of Word documents with Index Server, whereas ODBC is designed with relational databases in mind. The .NET Framework provides an OLE-DB Data Provider. This Data Provider allows a .NET program to communicate with a datasource over OLE-DB.

◆ **Data Providers:** Data Providers are the preferred mechanism within the .NET Framework to communicate with SQL Server. The SQL Server Data Provider is optimized for data access and contains few capabilities for managing SQL Server objects beyond SQL statements. The SQL Server Data Provider will work with SQL Server 7.0 and later along with the Microsoft Data Engine, SQL Server Standard Edition, and SQL Server Enterprise Edition.

SQL Data Provider

The SQL Server Data Provider, also known as the SqlClient, is a high-performance data-access layer within .NET designed to communicate with Microsoft SQL Server 7.0 and later. The SQL Server Data Provider is contained within the `System.Data.SqlClient` namespace and is housed within the System.Data.dll assembly. It provides a mechanism for an application to communicate with a SQL Server datasource. The Data Provider retrieves and updates changes between the application and the datasource.

The SQL Data Provider supports the four core objects of .NET Data Provider:

◆ **Command:** Executes a command against a datasource.

◆ **Connection:** Establishes a connection to a datasource.

◆ **DataReader:** Obtains a forward-only, read-only stream of data.

◆ **DataAdapter:** Communicates between a dataset and a datasource.

For a complete discussion of these four objects, refer to Chapter 5.

There are two main differences between the SQL Data Provider and the ODBC/OLE-DB drivers:

◆ **When a program uses ODBC or OLE-DB, there is a need to communicate through a series of layers before the messages are sent to the database or data is returned back to the client application.** Passing through these layers takes time. This type of design provides maximum flexibility when it comes to providing a database independent layer to an application. This is in direct conflict with the way that most applications are designed. Database independence is typically not a requirement during the design, development, and lifecycle of an application. Instead of going through a number of layers, the SQL Data Provider communicates directly with the SQL Server Tabular Data Stream (TDS) protocol. By bypassing the layers associated with ODBC and OLE-DB, the SQL Data Provider will make fewer calls between object methods. The result is an increase in performance as the number of users and calls per second increase.

◆ **The SQL Data Provider is designed for data access.** It is not designed to provide a way to easily make data schema and administration operations, such as the COM-based ADOX. To get ADOX-style functionality, a program will either need to use COM-based ADOX or send the SQL statements to perform these data definition language (DDL) operations, such as `CREATE TABLE`.

Microsoft has developed a COM-based interface to managed database tables, views, users, and other objects. This standard is called the Microsoft ADO eXtensions for DDL and Security (ADOX).

Because the SQL Data Provider is optimized for communicating with SQL Server, it can also expose certain features within SQL Server that have not been extensively used when accessing COM-based ADO, such as Transaction Save Points.

The Data Provider for SQL Server has one limitation relative to previous data-access technologies. The SQL Server Data Provider does not support server-side cursors. In other words, a program cannot open a resultset and lock the underlying rows in the table for changes without pulling the data back to the calling application layer. Rows of a table can be locked as needed, but the resultset is going to be returned to the client application. The result may be that memory, CPU, and network utilization can be much higher than expected.

COM+ and the SQL Data Provider

The SQL Data Provider has support for Microsoft COM+ 1.0 Services and later. It supports the full suite of services in COM+ including Distributed Transactions and Object Pooling.

Connection pooling with the SQL Data Provider

Pooling of connections to a database can provide significant benefit to the performance of an application. *Connection pooling* is the storing of multiple database connections so that, when a database connection is needed, the connection can quickly and easily be handed to the requesting application with no need to go through steps of creating a database connection. This connection is already available for use. So why is connection pooling a big deal? The amount of time needed to create a database connection is not small. A connection across a network can take longer to create. By having a connection in the pool, there is no need to create a new connection. Reusing an existing connection saves your program time and CPU cycles that can be used for something else.

With ODBC, connection pooling can be configured through the Connection Pooling Tab in the ODBC Data Source Administrator. With OLE-DB, session pooling may be configured through settings within the registry or through the connection string.

 For a complete discussion of ODBC and OLE-DB pooling, check out the Microsoft White Paper on Connection Pooling located at `http://msdn.microsoft.com/library/default.asp?url=/library/en-us/dnmdac/html/pooling2.asp`.

The SQL Data Provider supports connection pooling automatically for an ADO.NET client application. When the first connection to a database is made, a connection pool is created. This connection pool is associated with the connection string of the first connection. When a second connection to a database is made, a comparison is made between the first and second connections' connection strings. If both connections' parameters are the same, the second connection is pulled from the connection pool (assuming that the first connection is available). If the connection parameters of the two connections are different, then two separate connection pools are created. Figure 10-1 shows the Windows Performance Monitor utility displaying connection pooling from the SQL Data Provider. The connection pool has approximately 35 connections in it this time.

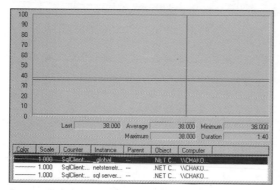

Figure 10-1: Connection pooling as shown in the Windows Performance Monitor

CONNECTION POOL RULES

Connection pools follow rules. These rules govern when connections are added and removed from the pool. Here are the rules that govern the addition of connections to the pool:

◆ If two connection objects differ in any connection string attributes, each connection object is placed within a different connection pool. If two connection objects use the same string attributes, the two objects will be placed within the same connection pool when the connection objects are closed.

◆ When a connection pool is created, multiple connection objects are created until the minimum number of connections is reached.

◆ Multiple connection objects may be added to the pool, until the maximum number of connection objects are reached in the pool.

◆ For a connection object to be added to the pool, it must be explicitly closed. This may be done by calling either the Dispose or Close methods. Connection objects that aren't explicitly closed aren't returned or added to the connection pool.

Connection pools also have rules regarding removing connections from the pool. These rules are:

◆ When a connection's lifetime has been reached, it is removed from the pool.

◆ If the connection between a server and the connection pool is severed, the connection is removed from the pool. This can only be detected when there is an attempt to communicate with the server.

Take a look at a SqlClient connection pooling example in Visual Basic .NET:

```
Dim cnDB1 as SqlConnection = new SqlConnection()
Dim cnDB2 as SqlConnection = new SqlConnection()
Dim cnDB3 as SqlConnection = new SqlConnection()
cnDB1.ConnectionString = "Initial Catalog=northwind;Data
Source=(local);User Id=sa;PassWord=. . . . . ."
cnDB1.Open()
'If this application has not run before, a connection is created
'along with a connection pool.
cnDB1.Close()
'On closing, the connection is passed to the pool.
cnDB2.ConnectionString = "Initial Catalog=northwind;Data
Source=(local);User Id=user;PassWord=. . . . . ."
cnDB2.Open()
'Because this connection string is different, a separate connection
'and connection pool is created
cnDB2.Close()
'The connection is returned to the pool.
cnDB3.ConnectionString = "Initial Catalog=northwind;Data
Source=(local);User Id=. . . . . .;PassWord=. . . . . ."
cnDB3.Open()
'This connection is created from the same connection pool as the
'first, and is the connection that was cnDB1, assuming that the
'minimum number of connections in the pool is 1.  If the
'minimum number of connections in the pool is more than 1,
'there is no guarantee which connection is obtained.
cnDB3.Close()
```

TRANSACTION SUPPORT

Connections are created from the connection pool and assigned based on transaction contexts. The context of the associated thread and the assigned connection must be the same. Each connection pool is further subdivided into connections with no transaction context and into N subpools that contain connections with a particular transaction context. When a connection is closed and returned to the pool, it is released not only into the pool but into the appropriate subpool.

CONNECTION STRING KEYWORDS

The `SqlConnection` object supports several string settings that are used to adjust the behavior of connection pools. These settings are passed into the `ConnectionString` property. Table 10-1 describes these settings.

TABLE 10-1 CONNECTIONSTRING PAIR VALUES

Name	Default Value	Description of the Setting
Connection Lifetime	0	The amount of time, in seconds, that a connection stays alive. This value is calculated from the time the connection is created.
Connection Reset	True	Determines whether the database connection is reset when being removed from the pool.
Enlist	True	When set to true, the pool automatically enlists the connection in the current transaction context, if a transaction context is used.
Max Pool Size	100	The maximum number of connections allowed in the pool.
Min Pool Size	0	The minimum number of connections that are kept in the pool.
Pooling	True	When set to true, a connection is drawn from the appropriate pool or created and added to the appropriate pool.

VERIFYING CONNECTION POOLING WITH COUNTERS

The SQL Server Data Provider contains several performance counters that enable a programmer to fine-tune the connection pooling characteristics and to determine some information as to how the connection pool is operating. Refer to Figure 10-1 to view connection pooling information in the Windows 2000 performance monitor. Table 10-2 details the counters that may be monitored through the performance monitor. These items are available from the Performance Object ".NET CLR Data."

TABLE 10-2 CONNECTION POOLING INFORMATION AVAILABLE
FROM THE PERFORMANCE MONITOR

Counter in Performance Monitor	Description
SqlClient: Current number of pooled and non-pooled connections	Current number of pooled and nonpooled connections.
SqlClient: Current number of pooled connections	Current number of connections in all pools associated with a process.
SqlClient: Current number of connection pools	Current number of pools associated with a process.
SqlClient: Peak number of pooled connections	The highest number of connections in all the pools since process start. (This counter is not available with a process. It is not available with the _global_ instance. The +global process will always return 0.)
SqlClient: Total number of failed connects	Total number of connection open attempts that have failed for any reason.
SqlClient: Total number of failed commands	Total number of command executes that have failed for any reason.

SQL Client transactions

The SQL Data Provider exposes the ability to manage transactions within a program and allows programs to manually commit and rollback transactions based on certain conditions. (Most of these manual transaction features are discussed in Chapters 4 and 5.) There are several features of SQL Server that are exposed by the SQL Data Provider that are available in SQL Server but have not been easily used under OLE-DB and classic ADO and, therefore, may not be familiar to most programmers.

SQL Server exposes the concept of a point within a transaction that can be regarded as complete—a *SavePoint*. When a transaction is created, you normally think of either committing or rolling back the complete transaction. SQL Server allows you to mark certain operations within a transaction as complete, so if an error occurs and a rollback is necessary, a program can rollback to the last SavePoint. When a transaction is rolled back to a SavePoint, the transaction is still open. On a rollback to a SavePoint, it is still the responsibility of a program to close the transaction by either committing or rolling back the transaction. For a SavePoint to work properly, a SavePoint must be named uniquely and then uniquely referenced in a rollback call.

In the following sections, we take a look at some of these features available through the SqlClient.

BEGINTRANSACTION

The `BeginTransaction` method of the connection object creates a transaction based on a connection object. The resulting object is typically assigned to an explicit SqlTransaction object code. The `BeginTransaction` method provides the following options:

- `.BeginTransaction()` takes not parameters.

- `.BeginTransaction( string )` takes a string parameter that names the transaction.

- `.BeginTransaction( IsolationLevel )` takes an isolation level as a parameter.

- `.BeginTransaction( string, IsolationLevel )` takes a string parameter to name the transaction and an IsolationLevel as the isolation level of the transaction object.

 For more information on isolation levels, turn to the discussion of isolation levels in Chapters 3 and 4.

SAVE

The `Save` method of the `SqlTransaction` object is the method that creates a SavePoint in SQL Server. The `Save` method maps to the Transact SQL Statement "SAVE TRANSACTION." SavePoints are useful when errors are unlikely to occur. Updates and rollbacks are expensive operations in terms of the time they take in a database operation. SavePoints are useful if the likelihood of encountering an error is low and the cost of checking the validity of an operation is relatively high.

The syntax of the `Save` method is very simple: `SqlTransaction.Save("string")` where the `"string"` is the name of the SavePoint.

ROLLBACK

The `Rollback` method of the `SqlTransaction` object is the method that rolls back a transaction to either the beginning of a transaction or to the specified SavePoint. The syntax to roll back a transaction to a SavePoint is fairly simple: `Rollback ("string")` allows a program to manually roll back either the named transaction or to roll back to the named SavePoint specified by the `"string"` parameter.

SQL client code examples

Now that we have taken a more detailed look at the SQL Server Architecture and the System.Data.SqlClient, let's take a look at some examples. These samples will show different ways to perform operations against a SQL Server database.

NO TRANSACTION EXAMPLE

The following code performs a SQL-based insert into a database. This code does not use any type of transaction support beyond the support provided by SQL Server. There is no use of a .NET SqlTransaction object or of COM+ Distributed Transactions. The SQLClient is the data access mechanism.

```
string strCn = "Initial Catalog=TimeSheet;Data Source=chakotay;User
Id=. . . . . .;PassWord=. . . . . .";
string strSql;
SqlConnection sqlCn = new SqlConnection( strCn );
SqlCommand sqlCm = new SqlCommand();
try
{
strSql = "insert into tblProjectEntry (tblProjectId, tblEmployeeId,
HoursEntered, tblCodeId, Rate, EntryState ) values " +
    "('" + GetProjectId() + "','" + GetEmployeeId() + "'," +
GetHours() + ",'" + GetCodeId() + "', 75, 0)";
sqlCn.Open();
sqlCm.CommandText = strSql;
sqlCm.CommandType = CommandType.Text;
sqlCm.Connection = sqlCn;
sqlCm.ExecuteNonQuery();
}
//Process a SQL Exception
catch ( SqlException sqlExc )
{
throw( sqlExc );
}
//Process all other Exceptions
catch ( Exception Exc )
{
throw( Exc );
}
//Clean up.
finally
{
if ( sqlCn.State != ConnectionState.Closed )
{
    sqlCn.Close();
```

```
}
sqlCn = null;
sqlCm = null;
}
```

MANUAL TRANSACTION CODE

The following code performs a SQL-based update of data already in a database. This code does use the transaction support beyond the support provided by the SQLTransaction object. The SQLClient is the data access mechanism.

```
string strCn = gstrSqlCn;
string strSql;
SqlConnection sqlCn = new SqlConnection( strCn );
SqlCommand sqlCm = new SqlCommand();
sqlCn.Open();
SqlTransaction sqlTx =
sqlCn.BeginTransaction(IsolationLevel.RepeatableRead);
try
{
strSql = "Update tblProjectEntry set Rate=" + GetRate() + " where
tblEmployeeId='" + GetEmployeeId() + "' and tblProjectId='" +
GetProjectId() + "'";
sqlCm.CommandTimeout = gintCommandTimeOut;
sqlCm.CommandText = strSql;
sqlCm.CommandType = CommandType.Text;
sqlCm.Connection = sqlCn;
sqlCm.Transaction = sqlTx;
sqlCm.ExecuteNonQuery();
sqlTx.Commit();
}
catch ( SqlException sqlExc )
{
sqlTx.Rollback();
throw( sqlExc );
}
catch ( Exception Exc )
{
sqlTx.Rollback();
throw( Exc );
}
finally
{
if ( sqlCn.State != ConnectionState.Closed )
{
sqlCn.Close();
```

```
    }
    sqlCn = null;
    sqlCm = null;
    sqlTx = null;
    }
    }
```

COM+ TRANSACTION CODE

The following code performs a SQL-based insert of data into a database. This code does uses COM+ Services transaction. The SQLClient is the data access mechanism.

```
string strCn = "Initial Catalog=TimeSheet;Data Source=(local);User
Id=sa;PassWord=bradley";
string strSql;
SqlConnection sqlCn = new SqlConnection( strCn );
SqlCommand sqlCm = new SqlCommand();
try
{
    sqlCn.Open();
    strSql = "insert into tblProjectEntry (tblProjectId,
tblEmployeeId, HoursEntered, tblCodeId, Rate, EntryState )
values " + "('" + pstrProjectId + "','" + pstrEmployeeId +
"'," + pstrHours + ",'" + pstrCodeId + "', 75, 0)";
    sqlCm.CommandTimeout = gintCommandTimeOut;
    sqlCm.CommandText = strSql;
    sqlCm.CommandType = CommandType.Text;
    sqlCm.Connection = sqlCn;
    sqlCm.ExecuteNonQuery();
    ContextUtil.SetComplete();
}
catch ( SqlException sqlExc )
{
    if ( sqlCn.State == ConnectionState.Open )
    {
        ContextUtil.SetAbort();
    }
    throw( sqlExc );
}
catch ( Exception Exc )
{
    if ( sqlCn.State == ConnectionState.Open )
    {
        ContextUtil.SetAbort();
    }
    throw( Exc );
```

```
}
finally
{
    if ( sqlCn.State != ConnectionState.Closed )
    {
        sqlCn.Close();
    }
    sqlCn = null;
    sqlCm = null;
}
```

OLE–DB Data Provider

The OLE-DB Data Provider is a data-access layer within .NET that is designed for .NET applications that need to communicate with datasources through OLE-DB. The OLE-DB Data Provider is contained within the `System.Data.OleDb` namespace and is within the System.Data.dll assembly. OLE-DB is a set of Component Object Model (COM) interfaces that allow programs to access datasources. By supporting OLE-DB in .NET, Microsoft is able to bring forward nearly all datasources that are accessible through OLE-DB.

What is OLE-DB? Technically, OLE-DB is a set of COM components that enable the transfer of data from a datasource to a consumer of that data. OLE-DB can be broken down into two general sets of applications:

◆ **OLE-DB Data Providers:** These are the components that provide access to data. Typically, OLE-DB Data Providers are written by programmers and companies that control access to data, such as Microsoft with SQL Server, Oracle with its database, and so on.

◆ **OLE-DB Data Consumers:** These use data that is provide by the OLE-DB Providers. Typically, OLE-DB Consumers are programs that are authored by those programmers who are trying to access data, such as a company attempting to get at data in its SQL Server database. The OLE-DB Provider takes data from a datasource and formats it into a tabular format as needed by the OLE-DB Consumer application.

The OLE-DB Managed Provider allows an application to communicate with SQL Server through the OLE-DB layer. Why would an application want to do this instead of using the SQL Managed Provider? The problem with the SQL Managed Provider for applications that must run over multiple databases is that the SQL Data Provider only communicates with SQL Server. The SQL Managed Provider currently has no way of communicating with Oracle, DB/2, and other databases. Because Microsoft does not want .NET only tied to SQL Server, the OLE-DB Data Provider allows programs to communicate with these other platforms, and even with SQL Server.

The biggest advantage to using the SQL Server OLE-DB provider instead of the SQL Server Data Provider is perceived stability. The problem with using the OLE-DB provider for Sql Server within the .NET Framework is that each call to the database will result in a call through the interop layer and a slight performance hit. The slight performance hit will be caused by the call(s) through the interop layer and the fact that the SqlClient Data Provider is optimized for data operations and does not need to include support for other items, such as ADOX. Native OLE-DB providers have been with us for several years. They have been debugged and tested extensively. By using the OLE-DB provider for SQL Server, programmers can benefit from several years' worth of bug fixes of the OLE-DB Driver for SQL Server.

The OLE-DB Managed Provider does not support the MSDASQL driver. This driver is designed to provide an OLE-DB interface on top of ODBC drivers. For support for ODBC drivers, .NET applications should use the ODBC Data Provider. Other drivers not supported include the Microsoft Exchange, Internet Publishing Drivers, and those drivers supporting the OLE-DB version 2.5 interface. To use those drivers, programs should continue to use Classic ADO through COM interop.

One of the concerns with using the OLE-DB driver for SQL Server within the .NET Framework is that OLE-DB is a COM interface. To communicate with COM, it is necessary for a .NET application to go through the COM interop layer. This communication route will not only go through the usual OLE-DB layers but must also go through the COM interop layer. This layer will add a small amount of time to your processing, though in comparison with the amount of time database processing takes, this time to go through COM interop is probably insignificant.

There are two ways to use OLE-DB to connect to a datasource:

◆ OLE-DB contains a Windows API that allows a C++ programmer to communicate with a datasource. Due to the complexity of writing directly to the OLE-DB API, most programs are not written using the OLE-DB API. These programs are typically written to a higher-level API, such as ADO.

◆ Active Data Objects (ADO) provides a high-level API to communicate with OLE-DB datasource. Visual Basic and Active Server Pages (ASP) programmers should be very well aware of it. ADO is the primary interface into OLE-DB and is the primary API for using OLE-DB. ADO supports a disconnected mechanism to access data in relational, ISAM, and nonstandard database formats, such as Word files.

OLE-DB transactions

The OLE-DB Data Provider exposes the ability to manage transactions within a program and allows programs to manually commit and roll back transactions based on certain conditions along with supported COM+ Distributed Transactions. Most of these manual transaction features are discussed in Chapters 4 and 5.

OLE-DB client code examples

The following sections contain examples on using the OleDb Data Provider with SQL Server. These examples are broken down into the type of transaction support each sample has. Properly supporting transactions is very important when you're building an application.

NO TRANSACTION EXAMPLE

The following code performs a SQL-based insert into a database. This code does not use any type of transaction support beyond the support provided by SQL Server. There is no use of a .NET SqlTransaction object or of COM+ Distributed Transactions. The OleDb client is the data access mechanism.

```
string strCn = "Provider=SQLOleDb;Initial Catalog=TimeSheet;Data
Source=(local);User Id=. . . . . .;PassWord=. . . . . . ";
string strSql;
OleDbConnection oledbCn = new OleDbConnection( strCn );
OleDbCommand oledbCm = new OleDbCommand();
try
{
    oledbCn.Open();
    strSql = "insert into tblProjectEntry (tblProjectId, " +
     "tblEmployeeId, HoursEntered, tblCodeId, Rate, EntryState ) " +
     "values " + "('" + pstrProjectId + "','" + pstrEmployeeId +
     "'," + pstrHours + ",'" + pstrCodeId + "', 75, 0)";
    oledbCm.CommandTimeout = gintCommandTimeOut;
    oledbCm.CommandText = strSql;
    oledbCm.CommandType = CommandType.Text;
    oledbCm.Connection = oledbCn;
    oledbCm.ExecuteNonQuery();
}
catch ( OleDbException oledbExc )
{
    throw( oledbExc );
}
catch ( Exception Exc )
{
    throw( Exc );
}
```

```
finally
{
    if ( oledbCn.State != ConnectionState.Closed )
    {
        oledbCn.Close();
    }
    oledbCn = null;
    oledbCm = null;
}
```

TRANSACTION EXAMPLE

The following code performs a SQL-based insert into a database. This code uses a .NET OleDbTransaction object. The OleDb client is the data access mechanism.

```
string strCn = gstrOleDbCn;
string strSql;
OleDbConnection oledbCn = new OleDbConnection( strCn );
OleDbCommand oledbCm = new OleDbCommand();
oledbCn.Open();
OleDbTransaction oledbTx = oledbCn.BeginTransaction(
IsolationLevel.RepeatableRead );
try
{
    strSql = "insert into tblProjectEntry (tblProjectId, " +
     tblEmployeeId, HoursEntered, tblCodeId, Rate, EntryState ) " +
     "values " + "('" + GetProjectId() + "','" +
     "GetEmployeeId() + "'," + GetHours() + ",'" + GetCodeId() +
     "', 75, 0)";
    oledbCm.CommandText = strSql;
    oledbCm.CommandType = CommandType.Text;
    oledbCm.Connection = oledbCn;
    oledbCm.Transaction = oledbTx;
    oledbCm.ExecuteNonQuery();
    oledbTx.Commit();
}
catch ( OleDbException oledbExc )
{
    if ( oledbCn.State == ConnectionState.Open )
    {
        oledbTx.Rollback();
    }
    throw( oledbExc );
}
catch ( Exception Exc )
{
```

```
    if ( oledbCn.State == ConnectionState.Open )
    {
        oledbTx.Rollback();
    }
    throw( Exc );
}
finally
{
    if ( oledbCn.State != ConnectionState.Closed )
    {
        oledbCn.Close();
    }
    oledbCn = null;
    oledbTx = null;
    oledbCm = null;
}
```

COM+ TRANSACTION EXAMPLE

The following code performs a SQL-based insert into a database. This code uses COM+ Distributed Transaction support beyond the support provided by SQL Server. The OleDb client is the data access mechanism.

```
string strCn = "Provider=SQLOleDb;Initial Catalog=TimeSheet;Data
Source=(local);User Id=...;PassWord=...";
string strSql;
OleDbConnection oledbCn = new OleDbConnection( strCn );
OleDbCommand oledbCm = new OleDbCommand();
try
{
    oledbCn.Open();
    strSql = "Update tblProjectEntry set Rate=" + pstrRate +
     " where tblEmployeeId='" + pstrEmployeeId +
     "' and tblProjectId='" + pstrProjectId + "'";
    oledbCm.CommandTimeout = gintCommandTimeOut;
    oledbCm.CommandText = strSql;
    oledbCm.CommandType = CommandType.Text;
    oledbCm.Connection = oledbCn;
    oledbCm.ExecuteNonQuery();
    ContextUtil.SetComplete();
}
catch ( OdbcException odbcExc )
{
    if ( oledbCn.State == ConnectionState.Open )
    {
        ContextUtil.SetAbort();
```

```
        }
        throw( odbcExc );
}
catch ( Exception Exc )
{
    if ( oledbCn.State == ConnectionState.Open )
    {
        ContextUtil.SetAbort();
    }
    throw( Exc );
}
finally
{
    if ( oledbCn.State != ConnectionState.Closed )
    {
        oledbCn.Close();
    }
    oledbCn = null;
    oledbCm = null;
}
```

ODBC Data Provider

The ODBC (Open DataBase Connectivity) Data Provider is a data-access layer with .NET that is designed for .NET applications that need to communicate with data-sources through ODBC. SQL Server, Oracle, DB/2, and many other client/server databases have ODBC drivers. Although most databases have an OLE-DB driver at this time, there are still several that do not, including MySQL. In addition to the issue of availability of OLE-DB drivers, a secondary issue is stability. ODBC was the first well-accepted database interface standard. From the very beginning, ODBC was designed for accessing relational and indexed sequential access method (ISAM) databases. This includes SQL Server, Oracle, DB/2, MySQL, Access, Foxpro, and other databases. Programs that were written to use ODBC could fairly easily be used to run against multiple databases, assuming that relatively standard SQL statements were used. ODBC has been around in some form for the last ten years. A lot of time, effort, and money have been spent over the years to improve performance and resolve issues within each vendor's drivers.

 At one time (pre-.NET), the fastest way to communicate with SQL Server was through a Visual C++ program that used the SQL Server ODBC driver.

Currently, the ODBC Data Provider is not included within the .NET Framework. It is slated to be available as a download from Microsoft's developer Web site after the official shipment of the .NET Framework.

> At the time of this writing, the ODBC .NET Data Provider is available from http://msdn.microsoft.com/downloads.

ODBC is a standard application programming interface. It has been available in some form since the early 1990s, back in the days of Windows 3.x. SQL Server supports ODBC as one of several APIs that may be used for accessing data through C, C++, Visual Basic, and other applications. SQL Server setup installs an ODBC driver when the SQL Server client utilities are installed. In addition, updates to the Microsoft Data Access Components (MDAC) contain an ODBC driver for SQL Server that is installed when an updated version of MDAC is installed.

Previous APIs

C, C++, Visual Basic, and other RAD-development tools may be used to call ODBC directly. Although programmers may call directly into the ODBC API, there are several higher-level APIs that sit on top of ODBC and provide a simpler and easier interface to use. These APIs include:

◆ **Data Access Objects (DAO):** DAO was the first API designed for accessing data. DAO resolved a number of problems in that it provided a common high-level API to access data. Its problem was that it was heavily tied to the Microsoft Jet database engine. Being tied to DAO presented a number of problems that could not be easily resolved with the Jet engine.

◆ **Remote Data Objects (RDO):** RDO was the first client/server API for accessing data. Designed for client/server applications, it provides a mechanism to connect to a database and retrieve those results. Unfortunately, RDO has two issues with the current world. RDO is designed with the idea that data will remain on the server until it is needed at the application. RDO is not designed with the idea of data residing at the client in a disconnected manner where a connection is made, results are returned, connections are dropped, and processing on that data continues along with the ability to reconnect that data back to the datasource. RDO is tightly coupled with the backend datasource.

The .NET Framework does not support data binding with either RDO or DAO.

◆ **Active Data Objects (ADO):** ADO provides a data-access API to allow applications to interface with relational and indexed sequential access method (ISAM) datasources along with datasources that are not normally considered to be datasources, such as word processing documents within a directory. To communicate with ADO, there is an intermediate layer that allows an ODBC driver to appear to be an OLE-DB driver. This intermediate layer is a special type of OLE-DB driver whose provider name is MSDASQL. ADO allowed programs to process data while the program is both connected and disconnected. In addition, it had basic support for XML.

For Visual Basic programmers and other RAD-style programming environments, RDO, DAO, and ADO are the most popular APIs to use when accessing data, with ADO being used by most pre-.NET developers. For Visual C++ applications, these programs may use any of the high-level APIs along with the ODBC APIs directly. Typically, the choice of whether to use a high-level API, such as ADO, or to use the ODBC API depends on the comfort level of the programmer and the amount of control necessary to meet the application's needs. The amount of time to retrieve data from a database is typically much larger than the amount of time necessary to process API commands.

ODBC Data Provider transactions

The ODBC Data Provider exposes the ability to manage transactions within a program and allows programs to manually commit and roll back transactions based on certain conditions along with support COM+ Distributed Transactions. Most of these manual transaction features are discussed in Chapters 4 and 5.

NO TRANSACTION

The following code performs a SQL-based insert into a database. This code uses transaction features beyond the support provided by SQL Server. The ODBC client is the data-access mechanism.

```
string strCn = gstrOdbcCn;
string strSql;
OdbcConnection odbcCn = new OdbcConnection( strCn );
OdbcCommand odbcCm = new OdbcCommand();
try
{
    strSql = "insert into tblProjectEntry (tblProjectId, " +
```

```
        "tblEmployeeId, HoursEntered, tblCodeId, Rate, EntryState ) " +
        "values " + "('" + GetProjectId() + "','" + GetEmployeeId() +
        "'," + GetHours() + ",'" + GetCodeId() + "', 75, 0)";
    odbcCn.Open();
    odbcCm.CommandText = strSql;
    odbcCm.CommandType = CommandType.Text;
    odbcCm.Connection = odbcCn;
    odbcCm.ExecuteNonQuery();
}
catch ( OdbcException oledbExc )
{
    throw( oledbExc );
}
catch ( Exception Exc )
{
    throw( Exc );
}
finally
{
    if ( odbcCn.State != ConnectionState.Closed )
    {
        odbcCn.Close();
    }
    odbcCn = null;
    odbcCm = null;
}
```

MANUAL TRANSACTION
The following code performs a SQL-based insert into a database. This code use the
OdbcTransaction object for transaction support. The OleDbClient is the data-
access mechanism.

```
string strCn = gstrOdbcCn;
string strSql;
OdbcConnection odbcCn = new OdbcConnection( strCn );
OdbcCommand odbcCm = new OdbcCommand();
odbcCn.Open();
OdbcTransaction odbcTx =
odbcCn.BeginTransaction(IsolationLevel.RepeatableRead);
try
{
    strSql = "Update tblProjectEntry set Rate=" + GetRate() +
      " where tblEmployeeId='" + GetEmployeeId() +
      "' and tblProjectId='" + GetProjectId() + "'";
    odbcCm.CommandText = strSql;
```

```
        odbcCm.CommandType = CommandType.Text;
        odbcCm.CommandTimeout = gintCommandTimeOut;
        odbcCm.Connection = odbcCn;
        odbcCm.Transaction = odbcTx;
        odbcCm.ExecuteNonQuery();
        odbcTx.Commit();
    }
    catch ( OdbcException odbcExc )
    {
        odbcTx.Rollback();
        throw( odbcExc );
    }
    catch ( Exception Exc )
    {
        odbcTx.Rollback();
        throw( Exc );
    }
    finally
    {
        if ( odbcCn.State != ConnectionState.Closed )
        {
            odbcCn.Close();
        }
        odbcCn = null;
        odbcCm = null;
    }
```

COM+ DISTRIBUTED TRANSACTION

The following code performs a SQL-based insert into a database. This code uses COM+ Distributed Transaction support beyond the support provided by SQL Server. The ODBC client is the data-access mechanism.

```
string strCn = "DSN=TimeSheet;UId=sa;PWD=bradley";
string strSql;
OdbcConnection odbcCn = new OdbcConnection( strCn );
OdbcCommand odbcCm = new OdbcCommand();
try
{
    odbcCn.Open();
    strSql = "insert into tblProjectEntry (tblProjectId, " +
    "tblEmployeeId, HoursEntered, tblCodeId, Rate, " +
    "EntryState ) values ('" + pstrProjectId + "','" +
    pstrEmployeeId + "'," + pstrHours + ",'" + pstrCodeId +
    "', 75, 0)";
    odbcCm.CommandTimeout = gintCommandTimeOut;
```

```
    odbcCm.CommandText = strSql;
    odbcCm.CommandType = CommandType.Text;
    odbcCm.Connection = odbcCn;
    odbcCm.ExecuteNonQuery();
    ContextUtil.SetComplete();
}
catch ( OdbcException odbcExc )
{
    if ( odbcCn.State == ConnectionState.Open )
    {
        ContextUtil.SetAbort();
    }
    throw( odbcExc );
}
catch ( Exception Exc )
{
    if ( odbcCn.State == ConnectionState.Open )
    {
        ContextUtil.SetAbort();
    }
    throw( Exc );
}
finally
{
    if ( odbcCn.State != ConnectionState.Closed )
    {
        odbcCn.Close();
    }
    odbcCn = null;
    odbcCm = null;
}
```

Classic ADO 2.x in .NET

Yes, that's right. You can continue to use the Classic ADO 2.x COM interface within a .NET-managed program. Why would anyone want to do such a thing? Well, there are several reasons:

◆ **Stability:** Classic ADO 2.x has been around for several years. It has been debugged extensively.

◆ **Familiarity:** Many programmers are already familiar with the Classic ADO 2.x Object Model. It may not make sense to suddenly move a set of programmers to ADO.NET.

◆ **Featureset:** If your application needs to use a specific feature that is not in ADO.NET, you'll need to continue to use ADO. For example, server-side cursors are not available in ADO.NET, but they are available in Classic ADO 2.x.

When Classic ADO 2.x is used, a conversion between the managed world of .NET and the unmanaged world is needed. The term for this is using an interop layer. How does a managed program perform a call into an unmanaged object? Sitting between the managed objects and the unmanaged objects is a layer called the *runtime callable wrapper (RCW).* This layer allows a managed program to call into unmanaged code.

How do you create the appropriate runtime callable wrapper? There are several options:

◆ **Visual Studio .NET:** Visual Studio .NET automates the process of creating an RCW. All that is required of a programmer is to add a reference, except select a COM object instead of a .NET-managed object.

◆ **TypExp.exe:** TypExp is a command-line utility used to generate an RCW.

◆ **Late Binding:** Visual Basic .NET supports late binding to objects. As a result, it's possible to use the CreateObject syntax to instantiate an instance of a COM object, just as in previous versions of Visual Basic. C# does not support late binding.

One of the things that is important to remember if you are moving from VB6/Visual Basic .NET to C# is the fact that C# does not provide support for optional parameters. As a result, there will be a need to specify parameters that most Visual Basic programmers are not familiar with.

No transactions

The following code performs a SQL-based insert into a database. This code uses no transaction support beyond the support provided by SQL Server. OLE-DB is the data-access mechanism within ADO.

```
string strCn = gstrOleDbCn;
string strSql;
ADODB.Connection adodbCn = new ADODB.ConnectionClass();
System.Object intRecordsAffected = new System.Object();
try
{
    adodbCn.Open( strCn, ". . . .", ". . . .", 0);
    strSql = "insert into tblProjectEntry (tblProjectId, " +
      "tblEmployeeId, HoursEntered, tblCodeId, Rate, EntryState ) " +
      "values " + "('" + GetProjectId() + "','" + GetEmployeeId() +
```

```
            "'," + GetHours() + ",'" + GetCodeId() + "', 75, 0)";
        adodbCn.Execute( strSql, out intRecordsAffected, (int)
         ADODB.CommandTypeEnum.adCmdText);
}
catch ( Exception Exc )
{
    throw( Exc );
}
finally
{
    adodbCn.Close();
    adodbCn = null;
}
```

Manual transaction

The following code performs a SQL-based update into a database. This code uses an Classic ADO 2.x Connection for transaction support beyond the support provided by SQL Server. The OLE-DB Data Provider for SQL Server is the data-access mechanism.

```
string strCn = gstrOleDbCn;
string strSql;
ADODB.Connection adodbCn = new ADODB.ConnectionClass();
System.Object intRecordsAffected = new System.Object();
try
{
    adodbCn.Open( strCn, "sa", "bradley", 0);
    adodbCn.BeginTrans();
    adodbCn.IsolationLevel =
     ADODB.IsolationLevelEnum.adXactRepeatableRead;
    strSql = "Update tblProjectEntry set Rate=" + GetRate() +
     " where tblEmployeeId='" + GetEmployeeId() +
     "' and tblProjectId='" + GetProjectId() + "'";
    adodbCn.Execute( strSql, out intRecordsAffected, (int)
     ADODB.CommandTypeEnum.adCmdText);
    adodbCn.CommitTrans();
}
catch ( Exception Exc )
{
    adodbCn.RollbackTrans();
    throw( Exc );
}
finally
{
    if ( adodbCn.State !=
```

```
          Convert.ToInt32(ADODB.ObjectStateEnum.adStateClosed ) )
     {
          adodbCn.Close();
     }
     adodbCn = null;
}
```

COM+ Distributed Transaction

The following code performs a SQL-based update into a database. This code uses
COM+ Distributed Transaction support beyond the support provided by SQL Server.
The OLE-DB Data Provider for SQL Server is the data-access mechanism.

```
string strCn = "Provider=SQLOleDb;Initial Catalog=TimeSheet;Data
Source=(local);User Id=sa;PassWord=bradley";
string strSql = "";
System.Object objOut;
ADODB.Connection adodbCn = new ADODB.ConnectionClass();
try
{
     strSql = "insert into tblProjectEntry (tblProjectId, " +
     "tblEmployeeId, HoursEntered, tblCodeId, Rate, " +
     "EntryState ) values " + "('" + pstrProjectId + "','" +
     pstrEmployeeId + "'," + pstrHours + ",'" + pstrCodeId +
     "', 75, 0)";
     adodbCn.Open( strCn, String.Empty, String.Empty, -1 );
     adodbCn.Execute( strSql, out objOut, -1 );
     ContextUtil.SetComplete();
}
catch ( Exception exc )
{
     ContextUtil.SetAbort();
     throw( exc );
}
finally
{
     if ( adodbCn.State !=
      Convert.ToInt32(ADODB.ObjectStateEnum.adStateClosed ) )
     {
          adodbCn.Close();
     }
     adodbCn = null;
     objOut = null;
}
```

Other Ways to Communicate

There are other ways to communicate with SQL Server besides using the SQL Data Provider, OLE-DB, and ODBC. Before the idea of a common interface to access data, applications could be code to directly access a database. For example, rapid application development (RAD) environments, such as Sybase's Powerbuilder, will many times include database-specific support. By providing this database-specific support, these environments have the ability to sidestep any problems with using the "least common denominator" of having a layer, such as OLE-DB and ODBC to communicate through. This allows these applications to communicate directly with the database with little to no overhead. Typically, this database-specific support will be in addition to support for ODBC and OLE-DB.

If these were the only ways to communicate with SQL Server, they would solve almost all your issues, except for the ability to perform administrative functions. To that end, you can use ADOX, which provides Data Definition Language support through a standard COM style of interface. In addition to ADOX, there are some COM interfaces that SQL Server supports. These COM interfaces are known as Distributed Management Objects (DMO or SQL-DMO) and Name Space (NS or SQL-NS). SQL DMO provides a programmatic mechanism to perform administrative-level functions within a SQL Server. SQL NS provides an object model that allows a programmer to mimic the functionality of the SQL Enterprise Manager snap-in for the MMC.

Accessing SQL with XML for SQL Server

The SqlClient contained within Microsoft.Data.SqlClient is not able to use the XML support within SQL Server. As a result, Microsoft has released a set of managed classes called SqlXml. SqlXml is a set of .NET-managed classes that expose the functionality of XML for SQL Server inside of the managed .NET Framework. SqlXml is stored within the `Microsoft.Data.SqlXml` namespace. SqlXml is designed to access the XML features of SQL Server, access data within an XML format in a .NET application, process the data, and send changes back to SQL Server. The changes to the processed data is termed a *diffgram*.

 The `Microsoft.Data.SqlXml` object is available as a separate download from Microsoft. It's currently available at the Microsoft SQL Server Web site at `www.microsoft.com/sql`.

`SqlXmlCommand` is the object used to connect to a SQL Server instance and send commands back and forth between the client and the server. The object accepts one construction parameter, which is the ADO/OLE-DB connection string, which identifies the server and other appropriate logon information. To instantiate the object perform, use the following code in VB:

```
Dim SqlXmlObj as New
SqlXmlCommand( "Provider=SqlOleDb;Server=servername;Initial
Catalog=TimeSheet;user id=. . . . . .;PassWord=. . . . . .;")
```

Use the following code to instantiate the code in C#:

```
SqlXmlCommand SqlXmlObj = new
SqlXmlCommand"Provider=SqlOleDb;Server=servername;Initial
Catalog=TimeSheet;user id=. . . . . .;PassWord=. . . . . .;");
```

The `SqlXmlCommand` object supports a number of methods and properties, as described in the following section.

SqlXmlCommand Methods

`SqlXmlCommand` supports a number of methods designed to directly integrate the XML support with SQL Server and the .NET Framework, as shown in Table 10-3.

TABLE 10-3 SQLXMLCOMMAND METHODS

Method	Description
`void ClearParameters()`	The `ClearParameters()` method clears the parameters associated with a `SqlXmlCommand` object and should be used for the execution of multiple queries on the same command object.
`SqlXmlParameter CreateParameter()`	The `CreateParameter()` method creates a `SqlXmlParameter` object. The name/value pairs may be set as parameters on the command. This allows a prepared SQL statement to be created for processing.
`void ExecuteNonQuery()`	The `ExecuteNonQuery()` method executes the supplied command, but much like the `ExecuteNonQuery()` method of `Command()` object, it does not return anything. This method is designed to execute a nonquery command, such as process the operations associated with the insert, update, and delete set of operations (DiffGram).

Method	Description
Stream ExecuteStream()	The Stream ExecuteStream() method returns a new Stream object. This method should be used when a query result needs to be placed into a new stream.
void ExecuteToStream (Stream xmlStream)	The void ExecuteToStream(Stream xmlStream) method executes a query and returns the results to an existing stream that is passed as the xmlStream stream object in the method definition.
void ExecuteXmlReader()	The void ExecuteXmlReader() method returns an XmlReader object.

SqlXmlCommand properties

The SqlXmlCommand object provides a number of properties to be used with the above methods, as shown in Table 10-4.

TABLE 10-4 SQLCOMMAND PROPERTIES

Property	Description
BasePath	The BasePath property is the base directory path used to resolve relative paths for the XslPath and SchemaPath properties.
ClientSideXml	The ClientSideXml property is a Boolean property. When set to True, processing of the rowset to XML is performed on the client and not on the server. This moves that processing off of the database server.
CommandText	The CommandText property is the text that the SqlXmlCommand property will execute.
CommandType	The CommandType property identifies the type of command being executed. The allowed values are SqlXmlCommandType.Sql, SqlCmlCommandType.XPath, SqlXmlCommandType.Template, SqlXmlCommandType.UpdateGram, SqlXmlCommandtype. Diffgram, and SqlXmlCommandType.TemplaceFile. The CommandStream property is the command stream to execute. The only types supported are Template, UpdateGram, and DffGram values.

Continued

TABLE 10-4 SQLCOMMAND PROPERTIES *(Continued)*

Property	Description
Namespaces	The Namespaces property enables the execution of XPath queries that use namespaces.
OutputEncoding	The OutputEncoding property is the encoding for the stream returned by SqlXmlCommand method. UTF-8 is the default setting. Other common settings are ANSI and Unicode.
RootTag	The RootTag property provides the single root element for the XML generated by the SqlXmlCommand object.
SchemaPath	The SchemaPath property is the directory path to an XPath query mapping schema file. If the path specified is relative, the BasePath property is used in conjunction to assist in resolving the location of the file.
XslPath	The XslPath property is the directory path to an Xsl file used for transforms. If the path specified is relative, the Basepath property is used in conjunction to assist in resolving the location of the file.

SqlXmlParameter

The SqlXmlParameter object is the SqlXml equivalent of a Parameter in a prepared statement, such as stored procedure, in our other major database access technologies (SQL/OLE-DB/ODBC). A SqlXmlParameter is created by calling the CreateParameter method of the SqlXmlCommand object. The SqlXmlParameter object exposes two properties: The Name property is the name of the parameter; the Value property is the value of the parameter.

SqlXmlAdapter

The SqlXmlAdapter object is an object that allows SQLXML to interact with a dataset object within the .NET Framework.

The SqlXmlAdapter supports three constructors and two methods. The three forms of the SqlCmlAdapter constructor are:

◆ SqlXmlAdapter(SqlXmlCommand SqlXmlCmd)

◆ SqlXmlAdapter(string strCm, SqlXmlCommandType SqlXmlCmdType, string strCn)

◆ SqlXmlAdapter(Stream strmCmd, SqlXmlCommandType SqlXmlCmdType, string strCn)

Whichever data-access technology your development team chooses to use, make sure that your team properly implements a Data Access Layer (DAL). A DAL is a layer of code that sites between your presentation and user interface code and the database. For additional discussion of the Data Access Layer concept, see Appendix B.

SQL Server Architecture

The architecture of SQL Server is designed for high performance and tight integration with the Microsoft Windows platform and specifically with MS Windows Server platforms (NT 4.0 Server, Windows 2000 Server, Windows.NET Server, and future versions of the server platform). SQL Server 7.0 and later will run on Windows9x, however, this is meant more for development, testing, and use in small workgroups, not in enterprise applications.

In the following sections, we take a look at the network/communication layer, the Enterprise Manager, and the SQL Server engine.

Net/Communications Library

Net-Library is an abstraction layer that SQL Server uses to read from and write to different network protocols. Each protocol has a specific driver that plugs into the Net-Library. This feature allows network protocol support to be added easily to SQL Server. SQL Server supports the TCP/IP, IPX/SPX (also called NWLink), NetBEUI, Banyan Vines SPP, Named Pipes, and Appletalk network protocols for communication. The Named Pipes and Multiprotocol network protocols are layers on top of the basic network communications. However, for our discussion, we will assume that they are part of the basic network protocols. SQL Server supports Net-Library on both client and server systems. This allows SQL Server to support different clients communicating with different protocols simultaneously with the same server system. For example, if a server is listening on IPX/SPX, the client may use IPX/SPX to communicate with the server. If that same server is listening on TCP/IP, another client machine may communicate with the server through TCP/IP. That server is able to communicate to both clients at the same time even though both clients are using different network protocols. Neither client needs to know that there is another client using a different network protocol.

SQL Server Engine

The SQL Server Engine is the item that programmers are concerned about the most. SQL Server implements a version of the Structured Query Language (SQL) that is called Transact-SQL (TSQL). The SQL Server 2000 implementation of TSQL is compliant with the Entry Level implementation of the SQL-92 Standard. TSQL supports additional features from the Intermediate and Full implementations of the SQL-92 standard.

It's your responsibility, as a programmer, to understand how the SQL Server Engine works. Knowing how to get your programs to work efficiently with it is very important in moving toward your goal of having your applications work as efficiently as possible.

The SQL Server Engine is made up of two basic parts: the Relational Engine, which is the part of SQL Server that parses and optimizes queries, and the Storage Engine, which is in charge of data on disk.

RELATIONAL ENGINE

The Relational Engine is made up of several subparts. These parts include the Command Parser, the Optimizer, the Expression Manager, and the Query Executor. As programmers, we are going to concern ourselves with the Command Parser and Optimizer and how they work.

COMMAND PARSER   The Command Parser handles events that are brought to it by users running queries within SQL Server. The command parser takes the textual input (`"select * from tblProjectEntries"`) and converts that into an internal format that can be used. This internal format is called a *query tree*.

THE OPTIMIZER   The Optimizer takes the output from the command parser (query tree) and prepares the command for execution. The Optimizer takes the query tree, compiles the entire patch operation, optimizes the commands, and verifies that there are no security problems. To perform these actions, the Optimizer performs the following steps:

1. The query is normalized. If the query can be broken down into additional smaller queries, that occurs at this point.

2. The query is optimized. There are multiple ways (plans) to execute a query, and each query has multiple operations to perform. Each operation has a cost associated with it. The cost of each query is the sum of the cost of each individual operation within that query. These costs are compared to those of the other plans; the plan with the lowest cost is chosen as the plan to execute.

3. The chosen plan is compiled into an execution plan.

At this point, the optimizer hands the execution plan down the line to the pieces of the Relational Engine that will communicate with the Storage Engine, perform the execution plan, and return the results, if any, to the requesting application.

One interesting thought about the Optimizer and the execution plan that it generates. Consider the following statement: `'update tblProjectEntry set tblCodeId='........', tblProjectId='.........' where tblProjectEntryId='.........'"`. This command appears to be very simple. Because we have limited the inputs on both the columns tblCodeId and tblProjectId, it appears that this should be an easy command to execute. Unfortunately, there are a number of foreign key constraints on that table within our Timesheet database. These constraints will result in other tables being accessed to verify the data that is being placed into the system. In addition, the existence of a trigger may cause additional tables to be accessed and additional steps to be added to the generated execution plan, though a trigger's execution plan is not directly added to that of an operation. The end result is that a relatively simple statement may result in a relatively long execution plan.

 What is *cost?* What does it mean to be cost based? First off, every thing that you do has a cost associated with it. If you go out for steak, there is a cost of going to the restaurant, ordering the steak, paying for it, and going home. If you decide to go about something in different ways, each way has a cost associated with it. If your primary goal is to save money, you would like to choose the way that has the lowest cost associated, when all factors are taken into account. The same is true in regards to processing instructions in a database. You want to do the least amount of processing based on the cost of processing. For example, performing a table lookup using a row that is not indexed could result in a cost of 100. Performing a table lookup after that same row has been indexed could result in a cost of 10. You would much rather perform the operation that costs 10 as opposed to the one that costs 100.

Another feature of the Optimizer is that it attempts to not overoptimize an operation. For example, it may choose to use a relatively simple plan, if the generation of a more complex plan would require more time than a less-than-thoroughly optimized execution of the query, SQL Server will try to use the less-than-thoroughly optimized plan. Within the SQL Server Optimizer, this is called *pruning heuristics.*

As with many products, the SQL Server Optimizer has become better with each release. However, the Optimizer is not able to be perfect every time. If it produces the best plan possible 75 percent of the time, that means that the Optimizer does not produce the best plan 25 percent of the time. Because this will sometimes be the case, if you know that there is a problem with the query plan that is generated, you can use the ability to add query hints to your queries to use certain indexes. The use of query hints forces the optimizer to generate a query plan using features of the database structure that the programmer has defined as being better than what is used by default. Here is an example:

```
select * from tblProjectEntry A ( serializable ,
Index(idx_tblProjectEntry_tblProjectId)) JOIN tblProject B ON
A.tblProjectId=B.tblProjectId where EntryState=0
```

The preceding code provides a hint to the optimizer to use a specific index within the table tblProjectEntry. In addition to that, the optimizer has been told to hold the records returned from the operation within the tblProjectEntry table with the transaction level of serializable. These hints are sent to the optimizer and the optimizer uses these to generate a query plan that could be different from the default query plan.

The planning and execution of statements is one area where prepared statements, such as Stored Procedures and Prepared Statements, can provide a performance improvement. Why? When a stored procedure is created, its execution plan is created when the stored procedure is compiled. Therefore, the execution of stored procedures does not require that an execution plan be created each time the stored procedure is executed. The only downside is that if indexes and other database objects change significantly, and these changes result in an execution plan that is not optimal, the stored procedure's execution plan is not automatically updated to reflect the changes in the system. When a prepared statement is sent to the database, an execution plan is created the first time the call is made over that connection. Subsequent calls use the same execution plan.

STORAGE ENGINE

The Storage Engine is the part of SQL Server that handles the storage of data on the file systems. Communications between the Relational Engine and the Storage Engine is handled mostly over OLE-DB. Here's what happens when a query is passed to the Storage Engine:

1. The Relational Engine makes a request of from the Storage Engine over OLE-DB: `select * from tblProjectEntry`. This request is made through the OLE-DB API.

2. The Storage Engine transfers the matching rowsets to the Relational Engine.

3. The Relational Engine combines the Storage Engine results into a resultset that is transmitted back to the user.

Locking hints

The Storage Engine within Microsoft SQL Server has the ability to finetune the locking of tables specified within the SELECT, INSERT, UPDATE, and DELETE operations. These finetuning commands are called *locking hints*. These locking hints can be used to override the current transaction isolation level for the session. These hints should only be used when a change is required to the default locking behavior. Table 10-5 contains the table locking hints.

TABLE 10-5 LOCKING TYPES

Locking Types	Description
HOLDLOCK	HOLDLOCK holds a shared lock until the complete of the current transaction. HOLDLOCK is equivalent to SERIALIZABLE.
NOLOCK	Shared locks are not issued and exclusive locks are not honored. NOLOCK only applies to the SELECT statement.
PAGLOCK	Use page locks where a single table lock would usually be used. This option is useful if there is a need to try to keep locks from escalating to something higher, such as a table lock.
READCOMMITTED	The default isolation level of SQL Server 2000. It performs a scan with the same locking semantics as a transaction running at the READ Committed isolation level.
READPAST	Skips rows that are locked by other transactions that would normally appear within the results that are returned. READPAST applies only to transactions running under the READ COMMITTED isolation level and will only read through row-level locks. In addition, READPAST only applies to the SELECT statement.
READUNCOMMITTED	Equivalent to NOLOCK.
REPEATABLEREAD	Performs a lookup with the same locking characteristics as a transaction with the isolation level REPEATABLE READ.
ROWLOCK	Uses row-level locks instead of locking at the page or table level. This hint is useful if there is a need to keep locks from escalating to a set of page locks or a table lock.
SERIALIZABLE	Performs a lookup with the same locking characteristics as a transaction with the isolation level SERIALIZABLE. With a SERIALIZABLE transaction, the underlying rows are not available for any operation. Access to those underlying rows is not allowed until the transaction running with a SERIALIZABLE locking hint is completed.
TABLOCK	Uses a table lock instead of locking at the page or row level. This option is useful if there is a need to go ahead and lock the entire table without going through the process of locking rows, escalating to a set of page locks, and then escalating to a table lock.
TABLOCKX	Uses an exclusive table lock.

Continued

TABLE 10-5 LOCKING TYPES *(Continued)*

Locking Types	Description
UPDLOCK	Uses update locks instead of shared locks while reading a table. It holds locks until the end of the transaction. An application can read data (without blocking other readers), that data can be updated later, and the data has not changed since the last read.
XLOCK	Use an exclusive lock on all data processed by the transaction and is held until the end of the transaction.

Lock timeout options and deadlocks

There are times during the course of any running application that SQL Server will not be able to provide a lock for a resource because another transaction already owns a lock on that resource. As a result, the first transaction must wait on that resource. The common term used is that the application asking for this lock is blocked until the transaction holding the lock releases it. Unfortunately, there is no way to test to see if a resource is locked before attempting to obtain a lock. The only way to test for a lock is to actually access the data that is locked.

Within SQL Server, there is a LOCK_TIMEOUT setting that allows an application to set a maximum time that a statement waits on a resource that is locked by another transaction. The command SET LOCK_TIMEOUT X sets the lock timeout to X milliseconds. The command SELECT @@LOCK_TIMEOUT returns the current setting of the lock_timeout setting of the system. The default setting is –1. When a connection runs beyond the LOCK_TIMEOUT time, the statement that is blocked is automatically canceled and an error message is returned to the calling application.

Deadlock priority can be set for each connection to control how a session reacts when it encounters a deadlock situation. The syntax is

```
SET DEADLOCK_PRIORITY {LOW | NORMAL | @DEADLOCK_VAR }
```

Setting the DEADLOCK_PRIORITY to LOW sets the current session to be the preferred deadlock victim. Setting the DEADLOCK_PRIORITY to NORMAL sets the current session to return to the default deadlock-handling method.

Primary key information

One of the most important things in dealing with a database application is handling, creating, and dealing with primary key information. One of the most important questions regarding primary key information is, "What is the primary key of the record that was just inserted into a table?"

UNIQUEIDENTIFIERS

A uniqueidentifier is a column type within SQL Server 7.0 and later that is designed specifically for providing primary keys. A uniqueidentifier is a 128-bit identifier. It is the SQL Server equivalent of a Windows globally unique identifier (GUID) or universally unique identifier (UUID). So how do you get the GUID back for a row? There are several ways:

◆ **Let application code do the hard work to get your primary key.** There are two commands that need to be executed. The first command is `"select newid()"`. When this command is executed, the value is stored and then used in the accompanying insert command.

> If you're familiar with Oracle, this is very similar to the concept of a sequence.

◆ **Similar to the first option, instead of asking SQL Server to generate the uniqueidentifier, a program may use .NET to create a GUID to be used in the insert statement.** The advantage in using this approach that only one command is sent to the database for processing.

◆ **Use a stored procedure to insert a row.** The stored procedure can return the uniqueidentifier of the inserted row.

◆ **Use a stored procedure to insert a row and return the uniqueidentifier in the form of an out parameter of the stored procedure.**

◆ **Use Classic ADO 2.x to perform a recordset-based insert and then re-read the generated uniqueidentifier.**

IDENTITY COLUMNS

An Identity Column is an integer column type. In SQL Server 2000, an identity column type may be either an `integer` (32-bit) or a `bigint` (64-bit) column type.

> It's possible to use the 16– and 8-bit integer data types (`smallint` and `tinyint`). If only a few records must be stored within the table, then this will work. If the number of records within the table is expected to outgrow `smallint` or `tinyint` datatypes, which is often the case, then using a `smallint` or `tinyint` datatype is not the way to go. This is why these datatypes are rarely used as identity fields.

SQL Server can be configured to autogenerate the identity column and to return that value to the calling program. Several of the ways are similar to getting a uniqueidentifier back from the table in the previous section. Here are several ways to accomplish this:

◆ Use a stored procedure to insert a row. The stored procedure can return the identity column value as a returned value to program code.

◆ Use a stored procedure to insert a row and return the identity column value as an out parameter. With .NET, it's fairly easy to obtain this value through a dataset.

◆ Use Classic ADO 2.x to perform a recordset-based insert and then re-read the automatically generated identity field.

As you can see from looking at the options, they're very similar to each other. The only one that is particularly different is the third option where a program creates the GUID/UniqueIdentifier on its own and hands that to the SQL command to insert the data into the database.

Take a look at the database schema for this. In this example, we deviate from the database schema of our example app.

To familiarize yourself with the coding standards that are in use for these code examples, check out Appendix B.

The identity value table definition is shown here. This table has an integer-defined identity field named tblIdentityId. The field tblIdentityId is defined as the primary key.

```
CREATE TABLE [dbo].[tblIdentity] (
    [tblIdentityId] [int] IDENTITY (1, 1) NOT NULL ,
    [ValueField] [varchar] (50) COLLATE SQL_Latin1_General_CP1_CI_AS
NULL
) ON [PRIMARY]
GO
ALTER TABLE [dbo].[tblIdentity] WITH NOCHECK ADD
    CONSTRAINT [PK_tblidentity] PRIMARY KEY  CLUSTERED
    (
        [tblIdentityId]
    )  ON [PRIMARY]
GO
```

The GUID/uniqueidentifier table definition is shown here. This table has a uniqueidentifier defined primary key field name tblUniqueIdentifierId:

```
CREATE TABLE [dbo].[tblUniqueIdentifier] (
    [tblUniqueIdentifierId] [uniqueidentifier] NOT NULL ,
    [ValueField] [varchar] (50) COLLATE SQL_Latin1_General_CP1_CI_AS
NULL
) ON [PRIMARY]
GO
ALTER TABLE [dbo].[tblUniqueIdentifier] WITH NOCHECK ADD
    CONSTRAINT [PK_tblUniqueIdentifier] PRIMARY KEY  CLUSTERED
    (
        [tblUniqueIdentifierId]
    )  ON [PRIMARY]
GO
ALTER TABLE [dbo].[tblUniqueIdentifier] WITH NOCHECK ADD
    CONSTRAINT [DF_tblUniqueIdentifier_tblUniqueIdentifierId]
DEFAULT (newid()) FOR [tblUniqueIdentifierId]
```

The stored procedure sp_tblIdentityDS is a stored procedure used to insert a record into the table tblIdentity. It takes one input parameter and uses the second parameter to pass a parameter back that is the value of the tblIdentityId value from the inserted record.

```
CREATE PROCEDURE dbo.sp_tblIdentityDS
    @ValueIn varchar(20),
    @IdentityValue int OUT
AS
Insert into tblIdentity (ValueField) values (@ValueIn)
set @IdentityValue = SCOPE_IDENTITY()
RETURN
```

The stored procedure sp_tblIdentityReturn is a stored procedure used to insert a record into the table tblIdentity. It takes one input parameter and a resultset consisting of the value identity field value used to insert into the field tblIdentityId.

```
CREATE PROCEDURE dbo.sp_tblIdentityReturn
    @ValueIn varchar(20)
AS
begin
DECLARE @ValOut int
insert into tblIdentity (ValueField) values (@ValueIn)
select ( Scope_Identity() )
end
```

The stored procedure sp_tblUniqueIdentifierDS is a stored procedure used to insert a record into the table tblUniqueIdentifier. It takes one input parameter and uses the second parameter to pass a parameter back that is the value of the tblUniqueIdentifierId value that has just been inserted.

```
CREATE PROCEDURE [dbo].[sp_tblUniqueIdentifierDS]
    @ValueIn varchar(20),
    @Id uniqueidentifier out
AS
begin
declare @TempId uniqueidentifier
select @tempId = ( select newid() )
insert into tblUniqueIdentifier (ValueField, tblUniqueIdentifierId)
values (@ValueIn, @tempId)
set @Id = @tempId
end
```

The stored procedure sp_tblUniqueIdentifierInsert is a stored procedure used to insert a record into the table tblUniqueIdentifier. It inputs data into the ValueField column and returns the tblUniqueIdentiefierId as a resultset.

```
CREATE PROCEDURE dbo.sp_tblUniqueIdentifierInsert
AS
begin
    declare @pkid as uniqueidentifier
    select @pkid = (select newid())
    insert into tblUniqueIdentifier ( ValueField,
        tblUniqueIdentifierId ) values (getdate(), @pkid)
    select @pkid
end
```

Now that you have the underlying database schema and stored procedures, take a look at the options for getting the primary key for the row that was just inserted into a table. Because the code for the Uniqueidentifier and the Identity columns are similar, we won't show both sets of code, though we did include the tables and stored procedures for both sets of applications (with notations where appropriate).

◆ **SQL Server generates the key with a separate call.**

```
//setup the first call to SqlServer.
string strSql = "select newid()";
SqlConnection sqlCn = new SqlConnection( gstrCn );
SqlDataReader sqlDr;
SqlCommand sqlCm = new SqlCommand( strSql, sqlCn );
sqlCn.Open();
//Execute the command to return the datareader to our code.
sqlDr = sqlCm.ExecuteReader();
//Since a datareader is not on the first row, call .Read()
//to go to the first row.
sqlDr.Read();
//Get the value and put it in our label.
```

```
lblValue.Text = Convert.ToString(sqlDr.GetValue(0));
sqlDr.Close();
//Go ahead and test the connection state.  If it is not
//closed, the go ahead and close it.
if ( sqlCn.State != ConnectionState.Closed )
{
    sqlCn.Close();
}
```

In this code, the data is returned to the SQL data reader and is contained within the `sqlDr(0)` structure.

◆ A slightly different take on the first option is to generate the uniqueidentifier by making a call into the .NET Framework and using the resulting return value as the primary key for the row that is to be inserted. Here is a code sample:

```
Guid guidObj;
guidObj = System.Guid.NewGuid();
lblValue.Text = guidObj.ToString();
```

In this example, a `Guid` object is created, a new value is placed within it by the call to `System.Guid.NewGuid()`, and the resulting value is displayed on the screen. The advantage of this over the first option is that only one call would need to be placed to the database. The only disadvantage to using this procedure is that, embedded within the GUID, is an identifier for the program that created the GUID and the network (MAC) address of the network card in the system. If for some reason, that information was needed, it would be possible to get the wrong information. This method will not work for an identity column.

◆ Return the primary key through a stored procedure's returned value. The advantage of performing the operation this way is that this technique is very much like a functional call and will make a lot of sense to those with a programming background. The disadvantage is that a return structure must be created on the client to hold a one-row and one-column resultset.

```
//The stored procedure takes no inputs and merely returns
//the unique identifier value of the insert record is
//returned.
string strSql = "sp_tblUniqueIdentifierInsert";
string strCn = gstrCn;
SqlConnection sqlCn = new SqlConnection( strCn );
SqlDataAdapter sqlDa = new SqlDataAdapter( strSql, sqlCn );
//This example uses a dataset, but could use a datareader
//with little additional coding.
DataSet dsData = new DataSet();
```

```
sqlDa.SelectCommand.CommandType =
CommandType.StoredProcedure;
sqlDa.Fill( dsData );
lblValue.Text = dsData.Tables[0].Rows[0][0].ToString();
//Always check the state of the connection.
//if the state is not closed, then go ahead and
//close it.
if ( sqlCn.State != ConnectionState.Closed )
{
    sqlCn.Close();
}
```

◆ **Similar to the third option, a stored procedure can be created that performs the insert and returns the uniqueidentifier in the form of an out
parameter on the stored procedure.**

```
    SqlConnection sqlCn;
SqlDataAdapter sqlDa;
//We need to know what the structure of the database
//table is.  Since we don't have the structure, we
//retrieve one record from the table and use that to
//base our inserted rows on.
string strSql = "select top 1 ValueField,
tblUniqueIdentifierId from tblUniqueIdentifier";
string strCn = gstrCn;
DataSet dsData;
sqlCn = new SqlConnection( strCn );
sqlDa = new SqlDataAdapter( strSql, sqlCn );
dsData = new DataSet();
//Define an insert command to call and set the command
//type to a stored procedure.
sqlDa.InsertCommand = new
SqlCommand("sp_tblUniqueIdentifierDS", sqlCn );
sqlDa.InsertCommand.CommandType =
CommandType.StoredProcedure;
sqlDa.InsertCommand.Parameters.Add("@ValueIn",
SqlDbType.VarChar, 20, "ValueField" );
SqlParameter sqlParm =
sqlDa.InsertCommand.Parameters.Add("@Id",
SqlDbType.UniqueIdentifier, 0, "tblUniqueIdentifierId" );
sqlParm.Direction = ParameterDirection.Output;
sqlCn.Open();
sqlDa.Fill(dsData, "tblUniqueIdentifier");
DataRow drData =
dsData.Tables["tblUniqueIdentifier"].NewRow();
drData["ValueField"] = Convert.ToString(DateTime.Now);
```

```
dsData.Tables["tblUniqueIdentifier"].Rows.Add(drData);
sqlDa.Update(dsData, "tblUniqueIdentifier");
lblValue.Text = drData["tblUniqueIdentifierId"].ToString();
//Test the connection state and close it if it is not open.
//Rememeber that this allows us to
if ( sqlCn.State != ConnectionState.Closed )
{
    sqlCn.Close();
}
```

◆ For situations where there is a need to use Classic ADO 2.x to perform this operation, it is still possible to use ADO 2.x style code for this operation.

```
string strCn = gstrOleDbCn;
string strSql = "tblUniqueIdentifier";
string strValue;
//Create an ADO Connection and Recordset.
//The managed objects have already been created and the
//namespace added to the .cs file.
ADODB.Connection adodbCn = new ADODB.Connection();
ADODB.Recordset adodbRs = new ADODB.Recordset();
//In C#, parameters are not optional.  All values must
//be specified.
adodbCn.Open(strCn, ". . . .", ". . . .", 0 );
adodbRs.Open( strSql, adodbCn,
ADODB.CursorTypeEnum.adOpenKeyset,
ADODB.LockTypeEnum.adLockOptimistic, -1 );
adodbRs.AddNew("ValueField", DateTime.Now.ToString() );
strValue =
adodbRs.Fields["tblUniqueIdentifierId"].Value.ToString();
lblValue.Text = strValue.ToLower();
adodbRs.Close();
adodbRs = null;
adodbCn.Close();
adodbCn = null;
```

PERFORMANCE OF UNIQUEIDENTIFIERS AND IDENTITY COLUMNS
We've looked at the options for using primary keys for database tables. What are the performance issues associated with using identity fields and unique identifiers for these primary keys? As with many things, it depends on the application that they are going to be used in. Remember that your options for a primary key are a 32-bit integer, a 64-bit integer (bigInt), and a 128-bit unique identifier/GUID. A 32-bit integer is going to be good until $2^{31} - 1$ integer values, which is roughly 2 billion rows of data. A 64-bit integer is going to be good for $2^{63} - 1$ integer values, which is roughly 9 quintillion rows of data. A 128-bit GUID provides roughly 2^{128} rows of data, which is more than we are able to comprehend.

From a speed standpoint, it makes sense to use the field type that provides all the necessary rows, but no more. There is a performance difference between using a bigint column type and a uniqueidentifier. This performance difference was tested using the primary key database schema from earlier. Table 10-6 shows a comparison of identity fields and unique identifier fields. Numbers listed are relative to the time to add 10,000 records to a table that already has the stated number of records. These tests were performed on a 1 GHz Pentium III system with 512 megabytes of RAM. The client and database server were running on the same system.

TABLE 10-6 COMPARISON OF IDENTITY FIELDS AND UNIQUE IDENTIFIER FIELDS

	10,000 Existing Rows at the Start	100,000 Existing Rows at the Start	1,000,000 Existing Rows at the Start
BigInt Primary Key Column	1.0	1.02	1.02
Unique Identifier Primary Key Column	1.0	1.31	2.35 to 16.47

Adding records to a table that has a uniqueidentifier as the primary key does not appear to scale well in the specific configuration we used. We investigated but could not come up with a resolution to this issue before this book's publication. Check out www.scalabilitywith.net for additional information on this issue.

General Comparisons

In this section, we look at a general comparison between our different ways to communicate and get data back from SQL Server. We compare how to communicate how each driver works within the distributed transactional environment of COM+, with manual transactions controlled by the application, and with no transactional support.

About our test application

Our base application is a timesheet application. From that application, we created a WinForms client application that modeled some of the operations of the timesheet application. We decided to take two operations and model them within our test harness application to see how well the different connection options worked when communicating with SQL Server. The connection options that were used were the SQL Data Provider (SqlClient), OLE-DB, ODBC, and Classic ADO 2.x. Due to the fact that transactions are an integral part of a database-oriented application, we further divided each connection option with support COM+ Transactions, also called Automatic Transactions, Manual Transactions, and No Transactions.

So, what are we testing within this application? There are four basic operations that all database-oriented applications perform: SELECT, INSERT, UPDATE, and DELETE. Typically, the SELECT operation is used to return data back to the calling application. Although it clearly depends on the exact situation, there are very few reasons to make a SELECT statement transactional. The INSERT, UPDATE, and DELETE operations are good candidates for encapsulating within a transaction, under the correct circumstance. What is the correct circumstance? With SQL Server, a single INSERT, UPDATE, or DELETE command is by itself transactional. As a result, the best candidates for operations to be wrapped within a transaction are those operations that use multiple commands to perform a business rule. Because an INSERT command typically inserts one row of data at a time, INSERT commands do not lock rows besides the one that they are inserting. In the case of multiple INSERT commands bundled together, there is the ability to lock multiple rows or to escalate to a higher lock, but these are rare instances. Because an UPDATE or DELETE more easily operates on multiple rows at a time, the operations tend to cause more locking and more processing to provide for the possibility of rolling back the operations. As a result, our application contains INSERT and UPDATE operations.

The classic example of a transaction is the movement of $200 from one bank account to another. This operation requires that the complete movement either succeeds or fails. We don't want the $200 to be removed from one account and not placed into the other, and neither do we want no money removed from the first account and $200 added to the second account. We want the money to either be transferred and deducted from the first account or for no activity to occur at all.

Having said that, what is the best way to test our database access methodologies and include transactions? The best way to test is to use some type of database operations that mimic our application. Using these operations, we built a test application, also called a *harness* or *saddle,* that mimics our application and applies these commands against our database.

The test application only contains one command within each transaction. Because we're just trying to see and understand the benefits and implications of each option, only one database command is used per method call. As a result, you'll probably want to tweak our commands to fit your application. Otherwise, the premise and foundation of our application should fit the needs of your application pretty well.

General performance analysis

"Figures don't lie, but liars sure can figure." As we've worked through setting up the testing for this chapter, we were often reminded of this statement. The goal here is to show the relative amount of time to perform specific operations. These operations will be performed using the .NET Data Provider, the OLE-DB driver, and the ODBC driver. The goal is to create a general framework for performing a set of operations while merely varying the underlying connectivity layer. Our harness application is downloadable from `http://www.scalabilitywith.net`.

It isn't fair to Microsoft, Oracle, IBM, DB/2, MySQL, or any product to use specific performance numbers, given the amount of resources available. The goal of showing general performance numbers is to create a baseline and to show how certain features and options affect performance. Any performance numbers specifically generated are only valid for the specific application running and the specific configuration. Because of limited resources, different configurations will be used with each database, and a direct comparison is not possible. As a result, no specific times will be listed. Each time will be relative to a base time within each test. Therefore, the numbers generated as a comparison between Oracle, SQL Server, IBM DB/2, and MySQL will not be comparable and will not be listed.

Indexing Optimization

Creating a fast-performing application with a database requires intelligent front-end programming in the .NET environment. It also requires intelligent setup and use of the backend database. Because programmers must many times double as database administrators, it's necessary for us to look at the features in SQL Server for creating a set of indexes. One of the features of SQL Server is the ability to assist in the creation of a set of indexes. There are two tools included as utilities to SQL Server that allow for the monitoring operations sent to the database and the creation of these indexes. SQL Profiler monitors all commands sent to a SQL Server database and can store those commands into a file on the hard drive called a *trace file*. The Index Tuning wizard is the utility that will analyze a set of commands, such as the commands stored by a SQL Trace, or single queries, such as those generated by a query to a data warehouse.

SQL Profiler

The SQL Profiler, as shown in Figure 10-2, included with Microsoft SQL Server, is a utility that allows an administrator to monitor SQL commands sent to a SQL Server database server along with the events that occur on that server. These events and the data associated with the events may be saved in a trace file or SQL Server table for analysis.

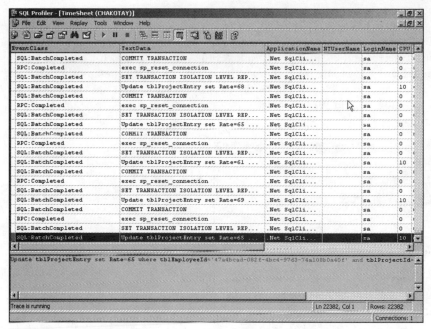

Figure 10-2: The SQL Profiler

When attempting to optimize database performance, the ability of the SQL Profiler to save these events and commands becomes very important. By saving the commands into a file, these commands may be monitored and analyzed by other utility programs, such as the Index Tuning Wizard utility included with SQL Server.

How do you create a trace file? Here are the steps to create a trace file that we'll use to improve the performance of an application:

1. Start the SQL Profiler.

2. Attach to the appropriate instance of SQL Server.

3. Create a name for your trace and filename to save the trace file to.

4. Begin running your trace.

5. Begin running a set of commands against your database that mimics the operation of your application. This will involve running your production application or a simulated set of the most common commands against your Sql Server database.

6. When a significant number of database operations have been performed through the application, stop the trace and save the file. At this point, you're done using the SQL Profiler, and you will move onto using the Index Tuning Wizard.

Index Tuning Wizard (ITW)

The Index Tuning Wizard is a utility included with MS SQL Server that allows a developer to select and create a set of indexes that are optimized for a given workload. The wizard will create these indexes based on the table schema of a database and the commands (workload) sent to the database. Figure 10-3 shows the startup of the SQL Index Tuning Wizard.

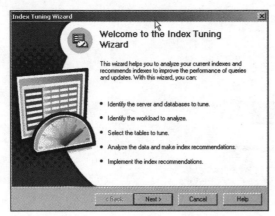

Figure 10-3: The Index Tuning Wizard startup screen

Here's an example of using the Index Tuning Wizard:

1. Open the ITW. Typically, this will be done through the SQL Profiler because, in most cases, there will be a SQL Trace File. The ITW is available from the Tools menu on the SQL Profiler. The ITW is also available from Management option within the SQL Enterprise Manager.

2. Connect to the appropriate system.

3. Select the appropriate server and database. Figure 10-4 shows the screen to select the server and database. At this point, it's very important to select the Keep All Existing Indexes checkbox. By selecting this option, it becomes easier to tune pieces of the application at one time. If this option is not selected, any existing indexes may be dropped as those indexes may not be. Although it takes longer to run in the Thorough mode, the ITW will produce a better set of indexes if the Thorough mode is used.

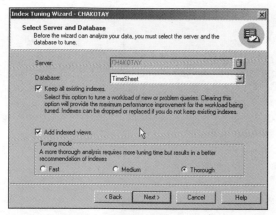

Figure 10-4: Select the server, database, and other options.

4. Select the appropriate workload file. Figure 10-5 shows the screen for selecting the workload file along with other options. Within the Advanced Options, the appropriate Index Tuning Parameters should be selected for your application and database. For example, we did not select to use a sample set of queries and we allowed the system to use a very large amount of index space.

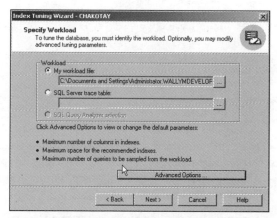

Figure 10-5: Select the appropriate workload file for analysis.

5. Select the appropriate tables to analyze. Figure 10-6 shows the tables that may be used in the analysis.

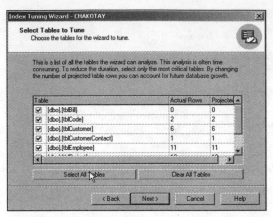

Figure 10-6: Select the appropriate tables to analyze.

6. After the ITW produces a set of indexes, a result is returned showing the predicted performance increase from applying these suggested queries. It's recommended that these changes be saved to a file and that the resulting file be examined and have the names of indexes and other structures modified to match the appropriate standards within your organization. The resulting file can be applied through the SQL Query Analyzer, included with SQL Server.

There are a couple of possible problems associated with the ITW that programmers should be aware of:

◆ Tables outside of the current database will not be analyzed.

◆ System tables are not analyzed.

◆ Primary keys and unique column suggestions are not made.

◆ By not selecting to keep existing indexes, it's very possible that indexes that are already created could be removed. This is important to keep in mind if your team is breaking apart different sections of your application and optimizing the different sections one at a time.

◆ The upper limit on commands that may be analyzed at one time is 32,767.

These are just several of the utilities associated with SQL Server.

Summary

There are issues with designing and developing an application in .NET based on SQL Server. By knowing how to access SQL Server with the SqlClient, OLE-DB,

ODBC, and legacy ADO data providers, there are a number of operations that can be performed that can meet nearly every need of every application available. By looking at the SQL Profiler and the Internet Tuning Wizard, it becomes much easier to develop these high-end applications.

Chapter 11

Oracle

IN THIS CHAPTER

◆ Understanding Oracle Database architecture

◆ Connecting to Oracle with OLE-DB and ODBC

◆ Using primary keys with Oracle

◆ Tuning an Oracle database for high performance.

THIS CHAPTER LOOKS AT the Oracle database platform and how to integrate applications written with .NET Framework with our database platform. Oracle's database product is a very popular product. Oracle's database currently has a little over 30 percent of the database marketplace.

Oracle Database Platform

Typically, when developers think high-end scalable database, they think Oracle. The Oracle Database platform is available on more hardware — from handheld PDAs to big iron mainframes — than practically any other database platform. It has a reputation for being the highest performance and most tunable database platform of them all. The Oracle Database platform is available in several editions.

Oracle Database Enterprise Edition

The Enterprise Edition of the Oracle Database is the high-end version of Oracle's database platform. It's geared toward enterprise applications, such as online transaction processing and data warehousing, while providing high availability of those features through Oracle's clustering technologies. Included within the Oracle Enterprise Edition are Real Application Clusters, Partitioning, Online Analytical Processing (OLAP), Data Mining, Spatial Services, and Security Services. Real Application Clusters is Oracle's technology for what is termed *scaling out* or *scale-out* technology. Real Application Clusters allows hardware systems to be added, which allows more processing power to be added to the system.

With Oracle Enterprise Edition, OLAP is a set of functions included with the product that provides features such as prediction and planning for complex multidimensional queries, support for a large number of concurrent users, a large number

315

of OLAP dimensions, and terabyte-size datasets. Data Mining support provides an interface to search data from patterns that allow companies to predict likely customer reactions. Spatial Services is used in the online/e-business area to allow online service providers to provide information relevant to users based on their location in the physical world. Oracle has advanced security services to allow users authenticated and encrypted access to data through either digital certificates. Beyond just the security measures placed on accessing the database, Oracle has implemented a row-level security feature called Label Security. Label Security allows users to have access only to specific rows within a table.

Oracle Database Standard Edition

The Standard Edition of Oracle provides the basic Oracle Database features and functions. It supports from one to four processors and provides the features that most businesses need in a database, such as:

- ◆ SQL Language support
- ◆ Data type support
- ◆ Java and XML support

Oracle Database Personal Edition

The Personal Edition of Oracle provides a version of Oracle targeted at individuals, yet it provides full compatibility with the Oracle Database family. It provides advanced replication and distribution features to allow applications to be easily deployed into an enterprise environment based on Oracle.

Oracle Database Lite

Oracle Lite is the version of Oracle designed to allow applications to be deployed on mobile devices and synchronized with an enterprise environment based on Oracle. These mobile devices included Windows CE, Palm Systems, Symbian EPOC, and 32-bit Windows systems.

Features and Terms in the Oracle Database

Oracle has several features and terms that may not be familiar to programmers. Before getting too far into Oracle, you need to know what these items are and what they mean:

♦ **Instance:** All of the memory and processes necessary to have a functioning database product.

♦ **Schema:** A set of database tables, views, and other database objects. A schema is named after the user that owns it.

♦ **Tablespace:** A database storage unit that groups together logical structures.

♦ **Net Services:** To connect to an Oracle instance, a client system connects to a listener service. To find that listener, the client system must have several pieces of information including the host system name, port, and identifier on the host system. This information is stored within a piece of the client called Net Services. Net Services stores connection (alias) information to connect to an Oracle database.

♦ **TNSName:** A fairly common way to store Net Services information at the client. It requires configuration at the client without the use of any of the server-based mechanisms to communicate, such as the Lightweight Directory Access Protocol (LDAP) or Oracle Name Services.

♦ **Enterprise Manager:** A Java-based application that provides a configuration and management interface into instances of Oracle. It is functionally very similar to the SQL Server Enterprise Manager snap-in for the Microsoft Management Console (MMC).

Oracle 9i Database Architecture

The Oracle database platform is widely considered to be the most rugged and scalable database platform in existence. The client/server version of Oracle will run on multiple platforms consisting of WindowsNT/2000/XP, several distributions of Linux, IBM AIX, Sun Sparc Solaris, HP 9000 Series Unix, and Compaq Tru64 Unix. In this section, we look at the Oracle Architecture and how processes are managed on the database server.

All users who connect to an Oracle database have two pieces of code that are performing some type of action for that user. There is the application/code that the user sees on their system. It could be a piece of custom written code or an Oracle tool, such as SQL*Plus. This application passes statements from the front-end user to the back-end Oracle database. On the Oracle Database, a piece of code is spun up from the Oracle Database server and executes on behalf of the user who has made the connection. This piece of code is referred to in the Oracle documentation as a *process, thread, task,* or *job,* depending on the operating system. This *thread* assists in performing operations on the server for that user.

The Oracle Database server further supports two types of processes on the server: dedicated-server process and shared-server process. With a dedicated-server process, each user process creates a process on the server to handle that request.

With a shared-server process, each server process may service multiple user requests. In general, a shared-server process is more efficient for most activities, because these activities tend to connect, run a set of commands, and disconnect. Activities that run on the server for a long period of time, such as a large amount of batch processing, will probably run better with a dedicated process.

When a user makes a request of an Oracle resource, the Oracle database creates a server process to handle the request. Server processes perform the functions to parse and execute SQL statements received from the user, read the necessary data on disk into the shared database buffers of the System Global Area (SGA), if that data does not exist within the SGA already, and returns the results back to the calling application.

Oracle instances

A running Oracle database is always associated with an Oracle instance. When an Oracle database is started, the database server allocates memory for an area called the System Global Area (SGA) and starts the appropriate Oracle processes. The combination of SGA and the appropriate Oracle processes is termed an Oracle instance.

After an instance is started, Oracle associates the specified database and instance with each other. The instance is termed mounting the database at this point. The next step is to open the database and make it accessible to the appropriate users. Startup and shutdown of Oracle instances are controlled by the database administrator.

System Global Area

A System Global Area (SGA) is a set of memory structures within one Oracle database instance. Multiple users connected to the same instance share the SGA with each other. The SGA is read/write and contains the Database buffer cache, Redo log buffer, Shared pool, Java pool, large pool (which is optional), Data dictionary cache, and other information. Starting with Oracle 9i, an Oracle instance may change its SGA configuration without being shut down.

Several initialization parameters directly affect the amount of memory dedicated to the SGA. These parameters are stored within the INIT.ORA file. The parameters that have the most effect on the SGA size are:

- ◆ **DB_CACHE_SIZE:** The size of the cache of standard blocks.

- ◆ **LOG_BUFFER:** The number of bytes assigned to the redo log buffer.

- ◆ **SHARED_POOL_SIZE:** The size in bytes of the area devoted to shared SQL and PL/SQL statements.

- ◆ **LARGE_POOL_SIZE:** The size of the large pool. The default value is zero.

For optimal performance, the SGA should fit in real memory. If the SGA_MAX_SIZE is less than the amount of memory necessary at startup, then the setting is ignored.

Background processes

A multiprocessor Oracle system runs additional Oracle processes that are called *background processes*. These background processes are designed to maximize performance and accommodate a large number of users. A running Oracle instance will have some combination of Database Writer (DBWn), Log Writer (LGWR), Checkpoint(CKPT), System Monitor (SMON), Process Monitor (PMON), Archiver (ARCn), Recoverer (RECO), Lock Manager Server (LMS) for Real Application Clusters only, Queue Monitor (QMNn), Dispatcher (Dnnn), and Server (Snnn).

DATABASE WRITER PROCESS

The Database Writer (DBWn) process is responsible for writing the contents of buffers to data on disk and making sure that any modified database buffers in the database buffer are written to disk. For most systems, one DWB process is fine. If additional write performance is needed, DBW1 through DBW9 may be added to the system. This is useful if the application significantly modifies data. In order for additional DBW processes to be appropriate, the hardware system must be a multi-processor system.

LOG WRITER PROCESS

The Log Writer (LGWR) process handles writing the redo log buffer to a redo log file on disk. LGWR writers all redo entries that are in the buffer since the last time the LGWR wrote to the buffer. The redo log buffer is a circular buffer.

CHECKPOINT PROCESS

The Checkpoint (CKPT) process handles updating the headers of all datafiles to record the details of a checkpoint when a checkpoint occurs. The CKPT process handles communicating with the DBWn process to actually write data to the headers.

SYSTEM MONITOR PROCESS

The System Monitor (SMON) process handles process recovery when an Oracle instance starts. It is responsible for cleaning up the tablespaces. Periodically, the SMON process starts up and checks whether it is needed. Other processes may call the SMON process if needed.

PROCESS MONITOR PROCESS

When a user process fails, the Process Monitor (PMON) performs process recovery. The Process Monitor is responsible for cleanup of resources that a user process was using on the server. If a user process fails, PMON will reset the status of items, such as the active transaction table, locks, and the process IDs associated with the user process. PMON will periodically check the status of server processes and restart any that died unintentionally. PMON may also be called by another process that has a need for cleanup.

RECOVERER PROCESS

The Recoverer (RECO) process runs as a background process that is used in a distributed database configuration to automatically resolve failures with distributed transactions. The RECO process automatically works with other databases working in an in-doubt transaction. The RECO process only runs if the instance allows distributed transactions and the DISTRIBUTED_TRANSACTIONS parameter is greater than zero. If that DISTRIBUTED_TRANSACTIONS parameter is zero, the RECO process is not started during instance initialization.

JOB QUEUE PROCESS

The Job Queue process is used for batch processing. The Job Queue process executes user jobs. It can be viewed as a scheduling service that can be used to schedule statements and procedures within an Oracle database instance. With Oracle 9i, the Job Queue processes are managed dynamically. The initialization parameter JOB_QUEUEPROCESSES, within the INIT.ORA file, sets the maximum number of Job Queue processes that may run at any one time in an instance.

ARCHIVER PROCESS

The Archiver (ARCn) process copies online redo log files to a specified storage device when a log switch occurs. ARCn processes are available only when a database is in ARCHIVELOG mode and automatic archiving is enabled. An Oracle instance may have up to ten archiver processes. If a large amount of archiving workload is expected, such as bulk loading of data, multiple archive processes may be specified with the initialization parameter LOG_ARCHIVE_MAX_PROCESSES in the INIT.ORA file. The default value for this parameter is 1, however, the system will determine how many archiver processes are needed and will automatically start up more processes as required.

OTHER PROCESSES

Within Oracle9i Real Application Clusters, the Lock Manager Server (LMS) provides resource management between instances. Oracle provides a message queuing service that is monitored by the Queue Monitor Processes (QMNn).

Shared server architecture

Within an Oracle shared server architecture, the need for a dedicated-server process for each connection is eliminated. A dispatcher sends incoming network requests to a group of shared-server processes. A small number of shared servers can perform the same amount of processing as more dedicated servers because an idle shared-server process from this group of shared processes picks up a request from a common queue of incoming network requests.

When an Oracle instance starts up, the network listener process starts up and begins allowing users to connect. Each dispatcher process then gives the listener process an address where the dispatcher will listen for requests for connections. Each network protocol that database clients may use requires at least one of the dispatcher processes. When a user process makes a request for a connection, the listener examines the request to see if the user process is capable of using shared memory. If the answer is yes, the listener returns the address of the dispatcher process that currently has the lightest load so that the user process may connect to the dispatcher directly. If a user process cannot talk with the dispatcher directly or if a user process requests a dedicated server, the listener creates a dedicate server and creates the appropriate connection.

Oracle is able to dynamically adjust the number of shared-server processes based on the number of items in the request queue. The initialization parameters SHARED_SERVERS and MAX_SHARED_SERVERS allows the system to create a range of shared-server processes.

Dedicated server configuration

When a separate server process is created for each user process, this process is called a dedicated server process. This dedicated server process responds to the requests only for the associated user process. Depending on the type of activity that the application is performing, a dedicated server process may not be the best configuration.

Consider a shopping cart application on a Web site. A customer searches and selects the product that they want to purchase. During most of the time the user is browsing, shopping, selecting products, and entering additional data, the user is actually looking at the results on his web browser, not actually doing database processing on the database server. As a result, the dedicated process on the server is not needed during most of the operation. For an application such as this, a shared server architecture may provide better performance, due to the shared server architecture being able to handle more than one incoming request per shared process.

Accessing Oracle Databases

How do you programmatically access an Oracle database? There are a number of different ways to access Oracle. Some involve using different access mechanisms underneath ADO and ADO.NET, such as the Microsoft and Oracle OLE-DB and ODBC drivers. Another access mechanism is Oracle Objects for OLE, which is a product from Oracle that provides data access in a COM-based environment.

Basics of Oracle communications

The basic underpinnings of communication with an Oracle database involve using a product that is called SQL*Net. SQL*Net is the general term used to describe the software to talk from the client to the Oracle database server. SQL*Net provides a common interface that allows a client to communicate with Oracle over various network protocols, such as TCP/IP, Named Pipes, InterProcess Communications (IPC), and IPX/SPX.

On top of the Oracle SQL*Net layer is a layer of software code called the Oracle Call Interface (OCI) layer. The OCI layer provides an Oracle-specific interface to programs above it in the call stack. API layers above the OCI convert their code from standard code (ODBC, OLE-DB, and other calls) into the OCI layer that is needed to communicate with Oracle.

In addition to knowing the layers of the communications, it's also important to know how to connect to a specific Oracle database. Somewhere, somehow, the OCI layer must understand how to find a specific server. With other databases, such as SQL Server, all connection information is handled in the connection string. With Oracle, there is a tool that incorporates the information containing the Oracle server and the database instance to communicate with. This tool is called the Oracle DBA Studio. DBA Studio allows an admin user to add entries to communicate with Oracle and to manage Oracle instances. DBA Studio stores its information in a file called TNSNAMES.ORA, shown in Figure 11-1. The file contains information that looks like the following entries:

```
TSHEET_PAVEL =
  (DESCRIPTION =
    (ADDRESS_LIST =
      (ADDRESS = (PROTOCOL = TCP)(HOST = pavel)(PORT = 1521))
    )
    (CONNECT_DATA = (SID = tsheet)(SERVER = DEDICATED))
  )
```

After this information is entered into DBA Studio, DBA Studio can be used to manage the database instance.

Now that you have entries in the system, your programs can connect to a database. Instead of using the database server name, instance name, and specific database information, the name of the connection, as stored in the TNSNAMES.ORA file, is typically used as the database connection. This value is used as the Data Source parameter in an ADO/OLE-DB connection statement. The initial catalog value is not used.

Microsoft OLE-DB Provider for Oracle

The Microsoft OLE-DB Provider for Oracle (MSDAOra) is Microsoft's driver to communicate with the Oracle Database platform using the OLE-DB specification. Figure 11-2 has a view of the OleDb stack when calling into an Oracle database.

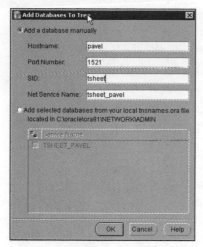

Figure 11-1: Adding an instance in DBA Studio

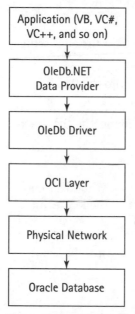

Figure 11-2: OleDb stack when calling into an Oracle database

The MSDAOra Provider is written to communicate through the API provider by the Oracle 7.x OCI. As a result, the MSDAOra Provider only supports the feature set of Oracle 7.x, no matter whether it's communicating with an Oracle 7.x, 8.x, or 9.x database server using the Oracle 7.x, 8.x, or 9.x versions of SQL*Net. As a result, the MSDAOra Provider cannot support features provided by the latest versions of the Oracle Database. Some of these features not supported are all large objects (LOB, CLOB, BLOB) data types, Oracle 8.x–specific and later datatypes, multiple Oracle home directories, and other features.

 Check out Chapter 5 for a discussion of datatype support.

CONNECTION STRING ATTRIBUTES

The MSDAOra Provider supports the standard connection string attributes that you will see with the other ODBC and OLE-DB options. The standard options are:

♦ **Provider:** The Provider value for the Microsoft OLE-DB Provider for Oracle is MSDAOra.

♦ **Data Source:** The value of the Data Source is the name of the alias setup in the TNSNAMES.ORA file.

♦ **User Id:** This is the user id that will be used to connect to the Oracle database.

♦ **PassWord:** This is the password that will be used to connect to the Oracle database.

TRANSACTIONS

The MSDAOra Provider provides support for manual and COM+ distributed transactions through the Microsoft Distributed Transaction Coordinator. The MSDAOra driver communicates by default in auto-commit mode. In auto-commit mode, each discrete transaction is treated as a complete transaction by the Oracle database. The driver does not natively support nested transactions, though they may be simulated within the use of the Oracle SAVEPOINT keyword.

Microsoft ODBC Driver for Oracle

The Microsoft ODBC Driver for Oracle is Microsoft's driver to communicate with the Oracle Database platform using the ODBC standard. Figure 11-3 contains a view of the ODBC stack when talking to Oracle. The Microsoft ODBC Driver for Oracle provides a program access to the Oracle environment including the PL/SQL language, stored procedures, packages, and other features of the Oracle database platform. The Microsoft ODBC Driver for Oracle supports communications over NetBIOS, IPX/SPX, TCP/IP, VINES, and DECnet. The Microsoft ODBC Driver for Oracle can be used from any programming environment that supports ODBC, including Visual Basic, ADO, and other development environments that support ODBC.

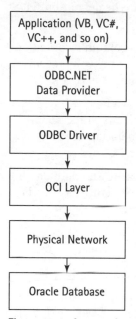

Figure 11-3: An overview of the ODBC stack when calling into an Oracle database

Just like the Microsoft OLE-DB Provider for Oracle, the Microsoft ODBC Driver for Oracle is written to communicate through the API provided by the Oracle 7.x OCI. This is still true if the Oracle Server is version 8.x or 9.x. As a result, the Microsoft ODBC Driver for Oracle can only support the featureset provided by the Oracle 7.x client software, even when the Oracle 8.x or later client software is used. This means that certain features — such as all large object support (LOBs, CLOBs, BLOBs, and such), direct connection timeouts, Unicode from the server, multiple Oracle home directories, multiple resultsets from stored procedures, and other items — are not supported.

CONNECTION STRING ATTRIBUTES

Just like the other drivers to connect to the various databases, the Microsoft ODBC Driver for Oracle supports a number of connection string attributes. Take a look at these options:

◆ **DSN:** The data source name used to create the connection.

◆ **PWD:** The password used to connect to the database.

◆ **UID:** The user id used to connect to the database.

◆ **BufferSize:** The amount of space set aside to store data that is returned from the database. The driver will retrieve enough rows to fill the amount of space. Larger values result in fewer roundtrips between the client and server at the expense of longer times to retrieve data. The default buffer size setting is 65535.

◆ **Synonymcolumns:** When this value is set to true (1), column information is returned. If the value of this attribute is set to false, only columns are returned for tables and views, and no column information is returned. The default value is true (1).

◆ **Remarks:** Setting the value of this attribute to true results in the remark information being returned with a resultset. Faster operation is achieved when this attribute is set to false, the default value.

◆ **StdDayOfWeek:** The attribute is used to enable the ODBC standard day of the week. If there is a need to use the value that Oracle returns as the day of the week scalar value, this attribute should be turned off.

◆ **GuessTheColDef:** Specifies whether the driver should return a non-zero value for the cbColDef argument of the SQLDescribeCol. This attribute only applies to columns that have no Oracle-defined scale.

TRANSACTION SUPPORT

The Microsoft ODBC Driver for Oracle provides support for manual and automatic transactions. The manual transaction support is provided by the local running application. The automatic transaction support is provided by COM+ Services.

Oracle OLE-DB Driver

The Oracle Provider for OLE-DB is Oracle's OLE-DB interface into the Oracle database. Oracle's driver exposes the COM-based interfaces necessary to act as an OLE-DB Provider. The Oracle Provider supports being called from Visual Basic, Visual C++, Active Data Objects, other COM-based development environments, and the OLE-DB .NET Provider.

 This discussion in this chapter is based on the Oracle 9i SQL*Net. In this section, the OleDb Provider will be the one provided with Oracle 9i.

Take a look at the connection string settings that are needed to connect to an Oracle Database. The Oracle OLE-DB Provider requires:

◆ **Provider:** OLE-DB requires the name of the OLE-DB Provider to communicate through. The value for the Oracle Provider is OraOleDb.Oracle.

◆ **Data Source:** The Data Source specified is the name of the alias as specified within the tnsnames.ora file.

◆ **User Id:** The User Id is the user id that will be used to connect to the Oracle Database.

◆ **Password:** The Password is the password for the specified user id that will be used to connect to the Oracle Database.

In addition to these specified parameters, The OraOleDb has several provider-specific connection string attributes that may be set along with the required connection string attributes. The provider-specific attributes are:

◆ **CacheType:** CacheType specifies the type of cache used to store the data that is returned on the client. There are currently two types of caching provided by OraOleDb:

■ **Memory:** The default setting for the CacheType is Memory. The provider will store all data in memory. The result is better performance and higher memory requirements at the client.

■ **File:** Setting the CacheType to File results in the provider storing all the returned data in a temporary file on the system. The result is decreased performance and fewer memory requirements at the client.

◆ **ChunkSize:** ChunkSize specifies the size, in bytes, of the data in LONG and LONG Raw columns that are fetched and stored in the provider cache. The default value for this setting is 100. The valid settings are 1 to 65,535. A higher value results in improved performance at the expense of increased memory utilization.

◆ **DistribTX:** DistribTX enables or disables support for distributed transactions enlistment. The default value is 0 (disabled). Setting the value to 1 enables the sessions for distributed transactions. DistribTX must be set to 1 to use the distributed transaction capabilities of the Microsoft Transaction Server/COM+ Environment.

◆ **FetchSize:** FetchSize specifies the number of rows that the provider will fetch at one time. The default value for this setting is 100. This value depends heavily on the amount of data to be returned and the response time of the network connection between the client and server. Setting the value to low may result in too many roundtrips to the server. Setting the value to high may result in a longer wait time to return data to the client.

◆ OSAuthent: OSAuthent specifies whether OS Authentication will be used when a connection is made to an Oracle database. The valid values are 1 (enabled) and 0 (disabled). The default value is 0, which results in OS Authentication being turned off.

◆ PLSQLRSet: PLSQLRSet specifies whether the provider *must* return a rowset for a PL/SQL stored procedure to the client system. By default, this value is set to false (disabled). This value may also be set at call time in the connection string that is passed to the OleDb driver.

◆ PwdChgDlg: PwdChgDlg attribute specifies whether the Password Change dialog box will be displayed when an attempted logon fails because of an expired password. The default value is 1 (enabled). The other possible value is 0 (disabled).

TRANSACTIONS

The Oracle OLE-DB driver supports both manual and automatic transactions within the .NET Framework. This transaction support supplies support for commit and abort. The Oracle OLE-DB provider doesn't support nested transactions. For example, a local transaction can't start a local transaction and a distributed transaction can't start a distributed transaction. In addition, a local transaction can't start a distributed transaction nor can a distributed transaction start a local transaction.

MANUAL TRANSACTIONS   OraOleDb supports defined manual transactions. By default, OraOleDb performs autocommitted, meaning that each command processed by the database is automatically committed. Through the use of manual transactions, .NET applications may define their own units of work that are to be committed or aborted by the application. By default, OraOleDb support the Read Committed isolation level.

AUTOMATIC TRANSACTIONS   Applications that use OraOleDb will work with the Distributed Transaction support within COM+ Services. For OraOleDb to work with the Distributed Transaction support in COM+ Services/Microsoft Transaction Server, Oracle has a product called Oracle Services for MTS that must be used. Oracle Services for MTS manages the distributed transaction communication between the Microsoft Distributed Transaction Coordinator and any Oracle database involved in the transaction.

POSSIBLE PROVIDER ISSUES

A programmer using Oracle.OraOleDb should be aware of several interesting behavioral issues involving OraOleDb:

◆ **The LockPessimistic LockType setting is not supported.** Be mindful of this if the application you're involved with uses Classic ADO 2.x.

◆ **OraOleDb doesn't actually lock the underlying rows.** If the resultset is changed between the time of the query and when the update is sent to the database, the update is disallowed, thereby nullifying an attempted dirty read.

◆ The ADO CursorTypes of adOpenKeySet and adOpenDynamic are not supported. Be mindful of this if the application you're working on uses Classic ADO 2.x.

Oracle ODBC Driver

The Oracle ODBC Driver enables ODBC-based applications to communicate between the Windows platform and an Oracle database. The Oracle ODBC driver supports network transports such as Netbios, IPX/SPX, and TCP/IP. The Oracle8 Driver communicates through the Oracle Call Interface (OCI). The Oracle8 Driver translates ODBC SQL into the necessary Oracle syntax and results are translated back into the necessary ODBC results.

CONNECTION STRING OPTIONS

The connection string for the Oracle ODBC driver supports several options. The connection string for the Oracle ODBC Driver supports the following attributes:

◆ DSN: The name of the ODBC Data Source.

◆ DRIVER: The name of the Oracle ODBC Driver when used with a DSN-less connection. The valid entry is {Oracle ODBC Driver}.

◆ DBQ: TNS Service Name as stored in the tnsnames.ora file.

◆ UID: The UserId used to connect to the Oracle Database.

◆ PWD: The Password used to connect to the Oracle Database.

◆ DBA: Database Attribute. The two valid settings are W (write access, which is the default) and R (read-only access).

◆ APA: Application Attribute. The two valid settings are T (Thread Safety Enabled, which is the default) and F (Thread Safety Disabled).

◆ RST: Results sets enabled. The two valid settings are T (Result Sets Enabled, which is the default) and F (Result Sets Disabled).

◆ QTO: Query Timeout Options. The two valid settings are T (Query Timeout Enabled, which is the default) and F (Query Timeout Disabled).

◆ CSR: Close Cursor Enabled. The two valid settings are T (Close Cursor Enabled) and F (Close Cursor Disabled, which is the default).

◆ BAM: Batch Autocommit Mode. The valid settings are IfAllSuccessful (commit only if all statements are successful, default), UpToFirstFailure (commit up to the first failing statement), and AllSuccessful (commit all successful statements, only available when connected to an Oracle8 database).

- ◆ **PFC:** Prefetch Count. This is a user-supplied numeric value. The default value is 10.

- ◆ **FEN:** Failover Enabled. The two valid entries are T (Failover Enabled, the default) and F (Failover Disabled).

- ◆ **FRC:** Failover Retry Count. The default value is 10.

- ◆ **FDL:** Failover Delay. The default value is 10.

- ◆ **LOB:** LOB (Large Object) Writes Enabled. The two valid entries are T (LOBs Enabled, the default) and F (LOBs Disabled).

- ◆ **FRL:** Force Retrieval of Oracle Long Column. The two valid entries are T (Forced Long Reads Enabled) and F (Forced Long Reads Disabled, the default).

- ◆ **MTS:** Microsoft Transaction Server Support. The two valid entries are T (Disabled) and F (Enabled, the default).

- ◆ **FWC:** Force SQL_WCHAR Support. The two valid entries are T (Force SQL_WCHAR Enabled) and F (Force SQL_WCHAR Disabled, the default).

- ◆ **EXC:** EXEC Syntax Enabled. The two valid entries are T (EXEC Syntax Enabled) and F (EXEC Syntax Disabled, the default).

- ◆ **XSM:** Schema Field. The valid entries are Default (default), Database, and Owner.

- ◆ **TLC:** Translation Option. This is a numeric value. The default value is 0.

- ◆ **TLL:** Translation Library Name. This is the user-supplied name.

When using the Oracle ODBC driver with a data source name (DSN), the DSN, user id (UID), and password (PWD) are the only required values. When using a connectionless ODBC connection, the driver name (DRIVER), TNS name (DBQ), user id (UID), and password (PWD) are the only required values.

PERFORMANCE SETTINGS
The Oracle ODBC driver has several settings that directly affect performance. The following is a listing of those settings and some discussion concerning them:

- ◆ **Lock TimeOut:** By default, the Oracle ODBC driver waits indefinitely for lock conflicts between transactions to be resolved. This default setting (LockTimeOut=0) can be overwritten by modifying the oraodbc.ini file. By setting this value to a non-zero number, the application will return after the number of seconds specified in the LockTimeOut section.

- ◆ **Thread support:** If an application accesses the Oracle Database through multiple threads, such as with a multi-threaded client/server application, a service, or IIS, this option is needed. If an application does not use multiple threads, disabling threading support over the connection will provide a small amount of performance improvement.

◆ **Prefetching Rows:** The Oracle ODBC driver by default only returns one row to the client at a time. In the Oracle ODBC Driver configuration in the ODBC Data Source Manager, this value may be changed to return as many rows per request as necessary.

◆ **LOB Support:** If there is no need for Large Objects within the application, there is a small performance improvement by disabling them within the Oracle ODBC Driver.

◆ **Returning Results:** If there is no need to return rows of data within the application, the Enable Result Sets for Application Option controls whether the Oracle ODBC driver creates a result set.

◆ **Closing Cursors for Applications:** By default, the Enabling Closing Cursors for Application option is not checked. This means that the database server does not automatically close any open cursors. Enabling this option forces the database server to immediately close any open database cursors, which will result in a small performance penalty.

◆ **Read Only:** If the application only performs reads against the database, set the Oracle ODBC driver to connect in a read-only mode.

OLE-DB CODE SAMPLES

This section shows several examples of using the OLE-DB drivers for Oracle to perform operations with different transaction options. There are several items of note:

◆ The function `GetOleDbConnectionString()` will check the front-end WinForms application to determine the appropriate connection string to use. There are two radio buttons on the WinForms application for OLE-DB. One is for selecting the Microsoft OLE-DB Provider for Oracle; the other is for selecting the Oracle OLE-DB Provider.

◆ The functions `GetCodeId()`, `GetEmployeeId()`, `GetHours()`, and `GetProjectId()` return a random selected codeid, employeeid, number of hours, and projected, respectively. These functions are the same as the ones used with the ODBC code samples.

◆ On any type of error, an attempt will be made to roll back a transaction (either manual or COM+).

NO TRANSACTIONS   The following is code to perform a SQL-based insert of data already in a database. This code does not use any transaction support beyond the support provided by the OleDbTransaction object or COM+. The OleDb .NET Data Provider is the data-access mechanism.

```
string strSql;
string strCn = GetOleDbConnectionString();
OleDbConnection oledbCn = new OleDbConnection( strCn );
OleDbCommand oledbCm = new OleDbCommand();
try
{
    strSql = "select SQ_TIMESHEET.NEXTVAL from DUAL";
    oledbCm.CommandText = strSql;
    oledbCm.CommandType = CommandType.Text;
    oledbCm.Connection = oledbCn;
    oledbCn.Open();
    oledbDr = oledbCm.ExecuteReader();
    oledbDr.Read();
    strSql = "insert into TBLPROJECTENTRY (TBLPROJECTENTRYID,
     TBLPROJECTID, TBLEMPLOYEEID, HOURSENTERED, TBLCODEID, RATE,
     ENTRYSTATE ) values " +
     "('" + Convert.ToString(oledbCm.ExecuteScalar()) + "','" +
     GetProjectId() + "','" + GetEmployeeId() + "'," + GetHours() +
     ",'" + GetCodeId() + "', 75, 0)";
    oledbCm.CommandText = strSql;
    oledbCm.ExecuteNonQuery();
}
catch ( OleDbException oledbExc )
{
    throw( oledbExc );
}
catch ( Exception Exc )
{
    throw( Exc );
}
finally
{
    if ( oledbCn.State != ConnectionState.Closed )
    {
        oledbCn.Close();
    }
    oledbCn = null;
    oledbCm = null;
}
```

MANUAL TRANSACTIONS   The following is code to perform a SQL-based update of data already in a database. This code uses the transaction support beyond the support provided by the `OleDbTransaction` object. The OLE-DB .NET Data Provider is the data-access mechanism.

```
string strSql;
string strCn = GetOleDbConnectionString();
OleDbConnection oledbCn = new OleDbConnection( strCn );
OleDbCommand oledbCm = new OleDbCommand();
OleDbTransaction oledbTx;
oledbCn.Open();
oledbTx = oledbCn.BeginTransaction( IsolationLevel.RepeatableRead );
try
{
    strSql = "Update tblProjectEntry set Rate=" + GetRate() + "
     where tblEmployeeId='" + GetEmployeeId() + "' and
     tblProjectId='" +
     GetProjectId() + "'";
    oledbCm.CommandText = strSql;
    oledbCm.CommandType = CommandType.Text;
    oledbCm.Connection = oledbCn;
    oledbCm.Transaction = oledbTx;
    oledbCm.ExecuteNonQuery();
    oledbTx.Rollback();
}
catch ( OleDbException oledbExc )
{
    oledbTx.Rollback();
    throw( oledbExc );
}
catch ( Exception Exc )
{
    oledbTx.Rollback();
    throw( Exc );
}
finally
{
    if ( oledbCn.State != ConnectionState.Closed )
    {
        oledbCn.Close();
    }
    oledbCn = null;
    oledbCm = null;
}
```

COM+ DISTRIBUTED TRANSACTIONS The following is code to perform a SQL-based insert of data already in a database. This code uses the transaction support beyond the support provided by COM+. The OLE-DB .NET Data Provider is the data-access mechanism. On an error, the SetAbort() method of the ContextUtil object is called. On successful completion of the business logic, the `SetComplete()` method of the `ContextUtil` object is called. Oracle Services for MTS is running on the system.

```
public void OracleOleDbInsert( string pstrCn ,  string
pstrProjectId, string pstrEmployeeId, string pstrHours, string
pstrCodeId )
{
string strSql;
string strCn = pstrCn;
OleDbConnection oledbCn = new OleDbConnection( strCn );
OleDbCommand oledbCm = new OleDbCommand();
try
{
    strSql = "select SQ_TIMESHEET.NEXTVAL from DUAL";
    oledbCm.CommandText = strSql;
    oledbCm.CommandType = CommandType.Text;
    oledbCm.Connection = oledbCn;
    oledbCn.Open();
    strSql = "insert into TBLPROJECTENTRY (TBLPROJECTENTRYID, " +
      "TBLPROJECTID, TBLEMPLOYEEID, HOURSENTERED, TBLCODEID, RATE, "
      + "ENTRYSTATE ) values " +
      "(" + oledbCm.ExecuteScalar() + ",'" + pstrProjectId + "','" +
      pstrEmployeeId + "'," + pstrHours + ",'" + pstrCodeId + "', " +
      "75, 0)";
    oledbCm.CommandText = strSql;
    oledbCm.ExecuteNonQuery();
    ContextUtil.SetComplete();
}
catch ( OleDbException oledbExc )
{
    ContextUtil.SetAbort();
    throw( oledbExc );
}
catch ( Exception Exc )
{
    ContextUtil.SetAbort();
    throw( Exc );
}
finally
{
    if ( oledbCn.State != ConnectionState.Closed )
    {
        oledbCn.Close();
    }
```

```
        oledbCn = null;
        oledbCm = null;
    }


    }
```

ODBC CODE SAMPLES

This section shows several examples of using the OLE-DB drivers for Oracle to perform operations with different transaction options. There are several items of note:

◆ The function GetOdbcConnectionString() will check the front-end WinForms application to determine the appropriate connection string to use. There are two radio buttons on the WinForms application for ODBC. One is for selecting the Microsoft ODBC Driver for Oracle; the other is for selecting the Oracle ODBC driver.

◆ The functions GetCodeId(), GetEmployeeId(), GetHours(), and GetProjectId() return a random selected codeid, employeeid, number of hours, and projectid, respectively. These functions are the same as the ones used with the OLE-DB code samples.

◆ On any type of error, an attempt will be made to roll back a transaction (either manual or COM+).

NO TRANSACTIONS   The following is code to perform a SQL-based insert of data already in a database. This code does not use any transaction support beyond the support provided by the OdbcTransaction object or COM+. The ODBC .NET Data Provider is the data-access mechanism.

```
string strSql;
string strCn = GetOdbcDbConnectionString();
OdbcConnection odbcCn = new OdbcConnection( strCn );
OdbcCommand odbcCm = new OdbcCommand();
try
{
    strSql = "select SQ_TIMESHEET.NEXTVAL from DUAL";
    odbcCm.CommandText = strSql;
    odbcCm.CommandType = CommandType.Text;
    odbcCm.Connection = odbcCn;
    odbcCn.Open();
    strSql = "insert into TBLPROJECTENTRY (TBLPROJECTENTRYID, " +
     "TBLPROJECTID, TBLEMPLOYEEID, HOURSENTERED, TBLCODEID, " +
     "RATE, ENTRYSTATE, DATEENTERED ) values " +
     "('" + Convert.ToString(odbcCm.ExecuteScalar()) + "','" +
     GetProjectId() + "','" + GetEmployeeId() + "'," + GetHours() +
     ",'" + GetCodeId() + "', 75, 0, TO_DATE('" +
```

```
        DateTime.Now.ToShortDateString() + "','MM/DD/YYYY'))";
    odbcCm.CommandText = strSql;
    odbcCm.ExecuteNonQuery();
}
catch ( OdbcException odbcExc )
{
    throw( odbcExc );
}
catch ( Exception Exc )
{
    throw( Exc );
}
finally
{
    if ( odbcCn.State != ConnectionState.Closed )
    {
        odbcCn.Close();
    }
    odbcCn = null;
    odbcCm = null;
}
```

MANUAL TRANSACTIONS   The following is code to perform a SQL-based insert of data already in a database. This code uses the transaction support provided by the OdbcTransaction object or COM+. The Odbc .NET Data Provider is the data-access mechanism.

```
string strSql;
string strCn = GetOdbcDbConnectionString();
OdbcConnection odbcCn = new OdbcConnection( strCn );
OdbcCommand odbcCm = new OdbcCommand();
OdbcTransaction odbcTx;
odbcCn.Open();
odbcTx = odbcCn.BeginTransaction();
try
{
    strSql = "Update tblProjectEntry set Rate=" + GetRate() + "
     where tblEmployeeId='" + GetEmployeeId() + "' and
     tblProjectId='" + GetProjectId() + "'";
    odbcCm.CommandText = strSql;
    odbcCm.CommandType = CommandType.Text;
    odbcCm.Connection = odbcCn;
    odbcCm.Transaction = odbcTx;
    odbcCm.ExecuteNonQuery();
```

```
    odbcTx.Commit();
}
catch ( OleDbException odbcExc )
{
    odbcTx.Rollback();
    throw( odbcExc );
}
catch ( Exception Exc )
{
    odbcTx.Rollback();
    throw( Exc );
}
finally
{
    if ( odbcCn.State != ConnectionState.Closed )
    {
        odbcCn.Close();
    }
    odbcCn = null;
    odbcCm = null;
}
```

COM+ DISTRIBUTED TRANSACTIONS The following is code to perform a SQL-based insert of data already in a database. This code uses transaction support provided by COM+. The ODBC .NET Data Provider is the data-access mechanism. On an error, the SetAbort() method of the ContextUtil object is called. On successful completion of the business logic, the SetComplete() method of the ContextUtil object is called. Oracle Services for MTS is running on the system.

```
public void OracleOdbcUpdate( string pstrCn, string pstrProjectId,
string pstrEmployeeId, string pstrRate)
{
string strSql;
string strCn = pstrCn;
OdbcConnection odbcCn = new OdbcConnection( strCn );
OdbcCommand odbcCm = new OdbcCommand();
odbcCn.Open();
try
{
    strSql = "Update tblProjectEntry set Rate=" + pstrRate +
    " where tblEmployeeId='" + pstrEmployeeId +
    "' and tblProjectId='" + pstrProjectId + "'";
    odbcCm.CommandText = strSql;
    odbcCm.CommandType = CommandType.Text;
```

```
    odbcCm.Connection = odbcCn;
    odbcCm.ExecuteNonQuery();
    ContextUtil.SetComplete();
}
catch ( OdbcException odbcExc )
{
    ContextUtil.SetAbort();
    throw( odbcExc );
}
catch ( Exception Exc )
{
    ContextUtil.SetAbort();
    throw( Exc );
}
finally
{
    if ( odbcCn.State != ConnectionState.Closed )
    {
        odbcCn.Close();
    }
    odbcCn = null;
    odbcCm = null;
}
}
```

ORACLE SERVICES FOR MTS

If there is a need to use the Oracle ODBC Driver or the Oracle OLE-DB Provider with COM+/MTS-style distributed transactions, an additional Oracle application must be enabled. This application is called Oracle Services for Microsoft Transaction Server (MTS). Oracle Services for MTS provides a distributed transaction environment that the Oracle database platform needs. Oracle Services for MTS may be utilized from any language that runs on the Windows platform that accesses Oracle through an Oracle-supplied driver. These drivers include ODBC, OLE-DB, Oracle Objects for OLE, and directly through the OCI layer. Although Oracle Services for MTS runs as a service on a Windows platform, the database platform may run on Windows, Unix, or any platform that is supported by the Oracle database platform.

Why do we need an Oracle Services for MTS? After all, the Microsoft ODBC and OLE-DB drivers for Oracle don't require Oracle Services for MTS. The problem revolves around the architectures of Oracle and MTS. Oracle uses a transaction technology called XA Transactions. Microsoft's MTS service is coordinated through a product called the Distributed Transaction Coordinator (DTC or MSDTC). The DTC requires the use of COM and a Microsoft-supported transaction standard called OLE Transactions. Oracle databases run on operating systems that do not support COM, such as Sun Unix and Linux. Oracle has implemented a service that is external to the DTC to managed transaction support with Oracle databases. This service is called the Oracle Services for MTS. Oracle Services for MTS supports distributed transactions with the Oracle Call Interface, Oracle Objects for OLE, Oracle's ODBC Driver, and Oracle Provider for OLE-DB.

Oracle MTS Recovery Service is installed after the Oracle Services for MTS. The Oracle MTS Recovery Service assists in handling the distributed transactions from that computer to any Oracle database.

Initial versions of the Oracle Services for MTS required a good amount of configuration. Fortunately, with the version that ships with Oracle 9i, the configuration of the Oracle Services for MTS has been greatly simplified. For the 9i version of Oracle Services for MTS, the only requirement for the Oracle ODBC and OLE-DB drivers to work with MSDTC is for the Oracle Services for MTS to be installed and running.

CLASSIC ADO 2.X WITH ORACLE

Yes, that's right. You can continue to use the Classic ADO 2.x COM interface within a .NET-managed program. Why would anyone want to do such a thing? Well, there are several reasons that may occur within your development group:

◆ **Stability:** Classic ADO 2.x has been around for several years. It has been debugged extensively.

◆ **Familiarity:** Many programmers are already familiar with the Classic ADO 2.x Object Model. It may not make sense to move a set of programmers to ADO.NET suddenly.

◆ **Featureset:** If your application needs to use a specific feature that is not in ADO.NET, you'll need to continue to use ADO.

◆ **Maturity:** Support for .NET data access is incompatible with some feature of the database. Obviously, Microsoft will be working with third parties, such as Oracle, to make sure that .NET data access works very well with their databases. Initially, there may be some feature within the Oracle database that for some reason will not work correctly with ADO.NET. With the backward compatibility of Classic ADO 2.x within .NET, a development group may choose to implement a data-access layer based on Classic ADO 2.x and update it at a future time to ADO.NET.

When Classic ADO 2.x is used, a conversion between the managed world of .NET and the unmanaged world is needed. The term for this conversion is using an *interop layer.* How does a managed program perform a call into an unmanaged object? Sitting between the managed objects and the unmanaged objects is a layer called the *runtime callable wrapper* (RCW). This layer allows a managed program to call into unmanaged code.

How do you call the appropriate COM component? You have several options:

♦ **Visual Studio .NET.** Visual Studio .NET automates the process of creating an RCW. All that is required of a programmer is to add a reference, except select a COM object instead of a .NET-managed object.

♦ **TypExp.exe:** TypExp is a command-line utility used to generate an RCW.

♦ **Late Binding:** Visual Basic .NET supports late binding to objects. As a result, it's possible to use the `CreateObject` syntax to instantiate an instance of a COM object, just as in previous versions of Visual Basic. C# does not support late binding.

One of the things that is important to remember when moving from VB6/Visual Basic .NET to C# is the fact that C# does not provide support for optional parameters. As a result, there will be a need to specify parameters that most programmers are not familiar with. For example, most VB programmers are not familiar with the five parameters necessary to open an ADO recordset within C#.

ORACLE OBJECTS FOR OLE

Oracle provides a set of objects that are optimized for communication with an Oracle database. These objects are called the Oracle Objects for OLE and are commonly referred to as *OO4O*. OO4O is callable from just about any Windows-based development environment that can use COM. This includes Visual C++, Visual Basic, ASP, and other COM-based development environments. Because the .NET runtime and Visual Studio .NET support COM, the .NET environment also supports the Oracle Objects for OLE.

 To communicate with a COM object in .NET, it's necessary to use the COM interop layer to communicate. It's possible to communicate with OO4O by using the COM interop layer.

OO4O consists of the Oracle In-Process Server, Oracle Data Control, and Oracle Objects for OLE C++ Class Libraries. The Oracle In-Process Server is a set of COM objects that are used to connect to an Oracle database, executing PL/SQL statements, and managing the results. The biggest difference between OO4O and the generic COM-based APIs, such as ADO, OLE-DB, and ODBC is that the OO4O product is optimized for working with the Oracle database. The Oracle Data Control is a visual control used to design and develop visual displays of information with controls such as text, list, and grid controls. The Oracle Objects for OLE C++ Class Libraries is designed to provide C++ developers with the necessary interfaces to communicate through OO4O. We'll take a look at the Oracle In-Process Server for communicating with an Oracle database.

CONNECT TO AN ORACLE DATABASE AND RUN A QUERY To connect to an Oracle Database, the first thing that is done is to create a session of the OO4O objects. The following examples show this being done by Visual Basic .NET:

```
Dim oo4oObj as New OracleInProceServer.OraSessionClass()
```

And this example shows it being done with C#:

```
OracleInProcServer.OraSession oo4oObj = new
OracleInProceServer.OraSessionClass();
```

Now that you have an instance of the OO4O Session, you need to create an object that points at a database. The OpenDatabase method takes three parameters. The first parameter is the TNS name of the system to connect to. The second parameter is the userid and password to logon to the database. The third parameter is a set of optional parameters that are specified by a bit flag word. The default value for this parameter is 0.

Here is the Visual Basoc .NET example:

```
Dim oo4oDb as OracleInProcServer.OraDatabase
oo4oDb = oo4oObj.OpenDatabase("tsheet_pavel", "scott/tiger")
```

And here is the C# example:

```
OracleInProcServer.OraDatabase oo4oDb;
oo4oDb = oo4oObj.OpenDatabase("tsheet_pavel","scott/tiger", 0);
```

OTHER CONNECTIVITY OPTIONS

There are a couple of other connectivity options for communicating with an Oracle database. When you look at how communications occur through the ODBC and OLE-DB drivers down to the OCI layer and then out to the network card, you may wonder how much of a slowdown the OCI layer causes when all you need is to perform a standard SQL operation. As a result, there are third-party drivers for communicating to the Oracle Database.

One of the more popular third-party providers is the Oracle OLE-DB Provider by Merant/DataDirect.

 The following information has been picked up in comments from people on newsgroups, online lists, and a beta 1 copy of the Oracle .NET Data Provider from DataDirect. Between the time that the book is published and the products are shipped, there will likely be changes. This part is meant to be more of a general idea as to what to expect from an Oracle .NET Data Provider.

A second option, and one that is more desirable, is the option to use a native Oracle .NET Data Provider. By being able to bypass unmanaged code, a native Oracle .NET Data Provider would be able to communicate exclusively within the .NET environment and not have to go outside of the managed world of .NET until the actual bits are sent across the network to communicate with the Oracle database platform. At the time of this writing, there has been no availability of any prerelease code from MS or Oracle related to a .NET Data Provider. Even though there has not been any statement along those lines, that won't stop us from making a few guesses about what form it will take and how to program against it. A .NET Data Provider for Oracle might live within a namespace such as System.Data.Oracle. A connection to a database will probably look like this in Visual Basic .NET:

```
Dim oraCn as OraConnection( strCn ) =  new OraConnection()
```

And like this in C#:

```
OraConnection oraCn = new OraConnection();
```

The DataReader object will probably be called something like OraDataReader. The DataAdapter will be called something like OraDataAdapter. In addition, we're guessing that there will be some type of support for the Oracle data types and that they will likely be stored in a System.Data.Oracle.OraTypes namespace.

The interesting part of Oracle connectivity within the .NET Framework will be what the connection string looks like. A pure .NET ADO.NET provider will not have any knowledge of the OCI layer within SQL*Net. As a result, it will not be able to read the aliases within the NetServices provided by Oracle, unless the provider reads the TNSNames.ora file to retrieve the aliases directly and then processes the connectivity information internally. A .NET ADO.NET provider may integrate with the OCI layer to provide direct support for the aliases within the TNSNames.ora file along with other features within the SQL*Net client. An alternative will be to require that information typically stored within the TNSNames.ora file be specifically specified within the connection string. If an Oracle Data Provider is a managed provider that makes calls out to the OCI layer provided by SQL*Net, the provider could use the aliases fairly easily.

Having said that, we were able to take a look at a beta copy of the Oracle .NET Data Provider from DataDirect Technologies. This provider will be apart of the DataDirect Technologies Connect line of products. This provider is contained within the DDTek.Oracle.dll assembly. The name of the namespace is DDTek.Oracle. Let's take a quick look at this provider.

The Oracle .NET Data Provider from DataDirect Technologies is completely written in C#. Some of the objects that it exposes are a connection object (OracleConnection()), command object (OracleCommand()), dataadapter object (OracleDataAdapter()), datareader object (OracleDataReader()), exception object (OracleException()), along with other objects.

The connection string attributes used by this provider are different than those used by the OLE-DB and ODBC providers used in the COM/Classic ADO 2.x environment.

An example connection string looks like `"Host=Martok;Port=1521; SID=ORCL;User Id=sys;Password=change_on_install;"`. Table 11-1 lists the connection string attributes used by the DataDirect Data Provider.

TABLE 11-1 CONNECTION STRING ATTRIBUTES FOR THE DATADIRECT TECHNOLOGIES.NET DATE

Attribute	Description
Connection Lifetime.	The number of seconds to keep a connection in the connection pool. The valid entries are 0 to 65,335. The default value is 0 resulting in a connection not being removed from the pool.
Connection Reset.	A Boolean value specifying whether a connection object is reset when it is removed from the pool to be used by an application. Resetting the connection causes additional processing in the database. The default value is false which results in the connection not being reset.
Fetch Array Size.	The number of bytes of data — between 1 byte and 2 gigabytes — that the connection may use to fetch multiple rows of data.
Host	The IP address or name of the server running the Oracle database.
Max Number of Pools	The maximum number of connection pools at any one time during the life of the process. The allowed values are between 1 and 65,535. The default value is 100.
Max Pool Size	The maximum number of connections within a pool at any one time. The allowed values are between 1 and 65,535. The default value is 100.
Min Pool Size	The minimum number of connections within a pool at any one time. The allowed values are between 0 and 65,535. The default value is 0.
Password	The password that will be used to connect to the Oracle database.
Pooling	A Boolean value specifying whether connections are pooled. The default value is true.
Port	The TCP port that the Oracle Listener is running. On the default value is 1521, which is the default port for the Oracle Database.
SID	The System Identifier that identifies the specific instance of the database.
User Id	The user id that will be used to connect to the Oracle database.

Primary keys

A *primary key* is a column or group of columns that is used to uniquely identify a row contained within a database table. Primary keys automatically cause an index to be created on the columns associated with the primary key. By creating the index, access to rows when the primary key is specified can be as fast as is possible.

As a result, primary keys are a very important part of a database application. Although it's always possible to use nearly any combination of values within a database table to uniquely identify the rows within a database table, Oracle provides two mechanisms to manage primary keys within a table. These two items are sequences and rowids. In the following sections, we take a look at them in detail.

SEQUENCE

A *sequence* is a database object within an Oracle database that generates integer values. These integer values are a series (sequence) of integers that are unique (1, 2, 3, and so on). Because a sequence can be made to generate unique integers on each request, sequences are great ways to create primary keys that have nothing to do with your application (for example, an item's SKU number, which management will want to change next week).

So what does a sequence look like? To a programmer, a sequence looks exactly like a column within a table. How do you create a sequence? A sequence may be created through the CREATE SEQUENCE command.

CREATE SEQUENCE SYNTAX   This is the complete syntax for creating a sequence

```
CREATE SEQUENCE [SCHEMA]."[SEQUENCE NAME]"
INCREMENT BY X START WITH Y
MAXVALUE MaxValue MINVALUE MinValue [CYCLE|NOCYCLE]
CACHE CACHENUMBEROFRECORDS [ORDER|NOORDER]
```

Table 11-2 contains a listing of the options provided within the Create Sequence statement.

Following are some examples of using the Create Sequence statement:

```
CREATE SEQUENCE SQ_TBLIDENTITY INCREMENT BY 1;
```

The preceding code will create a sequence named SQ_TBLIDENTITY. The first call into the sequence will result in the value 1 being returned, the second call into the sequence will result in the value 2 being returned, the third call into the sequence will result in the value 3 being returned, and so on.

```
CREATE SEQUENCE "SYS"."SQ_TBLIDENTITY" INCREMENT BY 1 START WITH
    1 MAXVALUE 99999999 MINVALUE 1 NOCYCLE
    CACHE 20 NOORDER
```

TABLE 11-2 CREATE SEQUENCE STATEMENT OPTIONS

Attribute	Description
SCHEMA	The name of the schema containing the sequence. The default value is the schema that you're logged onto.
SEQUENCE NAME	The name of the sequence that is to be created.
INCREMENT BY	The interval between the generated sequence numbers. This value may be any non-zero positive or negative number. A positive number results in a sequence that increases with each call. A negative number results in a sequence that decreases with each call.
START WITH	The first number of the sequence.
MAXVALUE	The maximum number that may be generated by the sequence. MAXVALUE must be greater than MINVALUE.
NOMAXVALUE	The maximum value of 2,147,483,647 for an ascending sequence and −1 for a descending sequence are used.
MINVALUE	The minimum number that may be generated by the sequence. MINVALUE must be less than MAXVALUE.
NOMINVALUE	The minimum value of −2,147,483,647 for a descending sequence and 1 for an ascending sequence are used.
CACHE	The number of values that are pre-allocated and stored within the database.
CYCLE/NOCYCLE	Specifies whether the sequence should continue to generate values after reaching the appropriate maximum/minimum value.
ORDER/NOORDER	Specifies that the sequences are to be generated in the order of the request.

The preceding code will create a sequence named SQ_TBLIDENTITY within the SYS schema. The first number generated is a 1. Because the sequence is set to increment by 1, the next number will be 2, with the next number being 3, and so on. The maximum value is 9,999,999. Ordering and cycling are set to off. Twenty values will be cached for quick response when there is a request. After the number of cached values is assigned, 20 additional values are placed within the cache.

RETURNING VALUES FROM A SEQUENCE   How do you get your values out of the sequence? The SQL Command SELECT SQ_TBLIDENTITY.NEXTVAL FROM DUAL; will result in the returning of a unique value from the sequence and incrementing

the currently value stored within the sequence. The SQL Command SELECT
SQ_TBLIDENTITY.CURRVAL FROM DUAL; will result in returning the current value
from the sequence without incrementing the current value stored within the
sequence.

What is this thing that is called DUAL? For a programmer, DUAL is merely a
dummy table within the Oracle database. It does have a usage deep within the
Oracle database, but programmers building business-oriented applications don't
have to worry about DUAL.

So now that you're thinking that sequences are these great things, what's wrong
with them? There are two issues that occur with a sequence. The first is the use of a
sequence within a transaction. If a call to a sequence is made within a transaction
and that transaction is rolled back, the value within the sequence is *not* rolled back.
This does not occur with Oracle Lite, just the client/server versions of Oracle. The
second issue is more of a management and architectural issue. How should the
application you're involved with associate sequences? Should each table have its
own sequence, or should the application have one sequence associate with it so that
all the tables pull their primary key information from a common sequence? This is
a management issue that your development team will need to decide.

Now that you know what a sequence is, you can use the data from the sequence
as a primary key for your database tables. Because our example application is
designed to use primary keys that are not a part of the user data of our application,
and our example application uses a Data Access Layer (DAL), it's fairly easy to
modify our database schema to use a numeric data type to provide the support for
our primary key. If there is a need to return the primary key of the just inserted row,
our program already has the key and therefore, it's very easy to return that key to
the calling application layer of the program.

ROWIDS

Oracle has a second mechanism to uniquely identify rows within a table. Within
each table of a database is a column called a ROWID. The column value of each
ROWID identifies each row of data by its location or address within a table.
Technically, Oracle refers to a ROWID as a pseudocolumn, because it is a column
that is a part of the table, yet a user did not definite the column explicitly and a
command "select * from table" does not display the ROWID column. ROWIDs are
constant for a given row during the life of that row. So as long as a row is not
deleted, the value of the rowid column is constant. The two types of ROWID
columns are Physical ROWIDs and Logical ROWIDs:

◆ Physical ROWIDs store the actual address of rows in a tables (those not
being index-organized), clustered tables, table partitions and subpartitions, indexes, index partitions, and index subpartitions.

◆ Logical ROWIDs store the addresses of rows in tables that are index
organized.

Oracle provides a single datatype called a Universal ROWID, which supports both the physical ROWIDs and logical ROWIDs, and the ROWIDs contained within a foreign table.

As mentioned above a ROWID is a pseudocolumn. Its existence is not shown by called "select * from table" or when calling the DESCRIBE statement. It is still possible to determine a ROWID value by explicitly requesting the value from the table within a select statement.

```
SELECT ROWID, A.* FROM TBLPROJECTENTRY A
```

Figure 11-4 displays the results of the preceding query. The query returns the ROWID of each row.

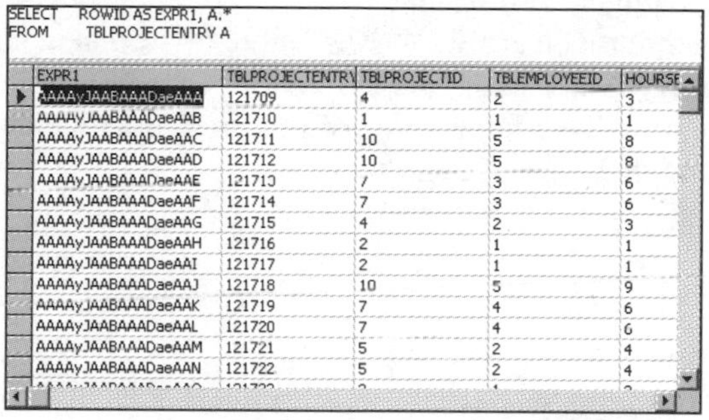

EXPR1	TBLPROJECTENTRY	TBLPROJECTID	TBLEMPLOYEEID	HOURSE
AAAAyJAABAAADaeAAA	121709	4	2	3
AAAAyJAABAAADaeAAB	121710	1	1	1
AAAAyJAABAAADaeAAC	121711	10	5	8
AAAAyJAABAAADaeAAD	121712	10	5	8
AAAAyJAABAAADaeAAE	121713	7	3	6
AAAAyJAABAAADaeAAF	121714	7	3	6
AAAAyJAABAAADaeAAG	121715	4	2	3
AAAAyJAABAAADaeAAH	121716	2	1	1
AAAAyJAABAAADaeAAI	121717	2	1	1
AAAAyJAABAAADaeAAJ	121718	10	5	9
AAAAyJAABAAADaeAAK	121719	7	4	6
AAAAyJAABAAADaeAAL	121720	7	4	6
AAAAyJAABAAADaeAAM	121721	5	2	4
AAAAyJAABAAADaeAAN	121722	5	2	4

Figure 11-4: A database query using ROWIDs

Anything that provides a way to uniquely identity a row within a table would seem to be a good thing. But there are a couple of issues with ROWIDs. First, there is no easy way to get the ROWID back for an inserted row. As a result, you have no easy way to get the ROWID back for the record that has just been inserted. Because there are many situations where you need to return a primary key for a newly inserted record, this limits the ROWID column right off the bat. A second issue with a ROWID is that a ROWID value does not travel with a table. As a result, if a table is moved from one database to another or to another machine, the ROWID may change, and as a result, many foreign key relationships would be broken. For these reasons, the ROWID column is probably not a good way to track primary keys.

Now that you've taken a quick look at a ROWID, ask yourself what good they are and how best you can use them. ROWIDs are the fastest way to access rows within a table. Due to the fact that a ROWID is specific to a given database instance on a specific server, the ROWID column has minimal value as a primary or foreign key column within a table. If the application you're involved with already has access to the ROWID column of your database, then use the ROWID column as a mechanism for fast database queries. If the application does not already have access to the

ROWID column, do not query the table for the ROWID and then query the table for the specific column information. Go ahead and use the existing primary key values that the application has access to.

ROWNUM

Oracle exposes another pseudocolumn called a ROWNUM. Although it's not a good idea to use a ROWNUM as a primary key column, it is a good idea to know that it exists and why it isn't a good idea to use it as a primary key. A ROWNUM is an integer representing the order that that row exists within a query. For example, `Select * from tblProject` will result in all the rows within the table tblProject being returned. The first row that is returned has a ROWNUM value of 1, the second row that is returned has a ROWNUM value of 2, the third row that is returned has a ROWNUM value of 3, and so on. The biggest issue associated with a ROWNUM is that the ROWNUM value of a query changes with respect to the results in a query. For example, for a given query, a specific row has a ROWNUM value of 12. There is no guarantee that rerunning that query will result in a ROWNUM value for that specific row to be 12, 11, or 572. Figure 11-5 shows the results of a query that returns the ROWNUM associated with reach row of the query.

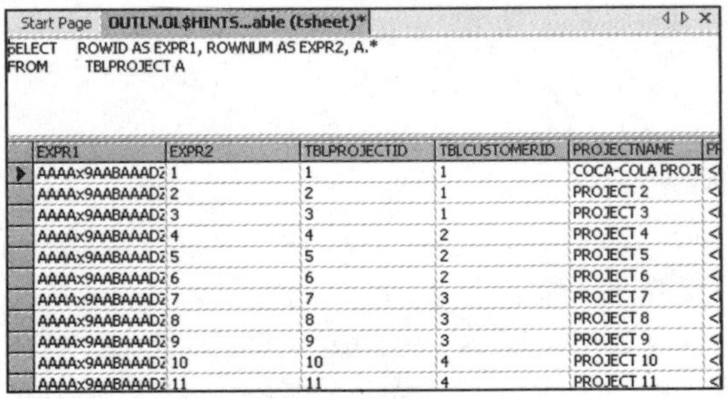

Figure 11-5: ROWNUM results

CREATING A PRIMARY KEY

We've shown that using a sequence as the basis for a primary key is a good thing. There are several ways to use a sequence to generate a primary key.

MAKING MULTIPLE CALLS INTO THE DATABASE   In this scenario, two calls are made into the database. The first call is made to a sequence to get a value and to increment the value within the sequence.

The following is some example code written in Visual Basic .NET:

```
Dim oledbCn As OleDbConnection
Dim oledbCm As OleDbCommand
Dim strCn As String = "Provider=OraOleDb.Oracle;Data
Source=dotnet_localhost.wallymdevelopment.com;User
```

```
Id=usruser;PassWord=usruser;"
Dim strSql As String
Dim oledbDr As OleDbDataReader
Dim lngVal As Int64
Try
    oledbCn = New OleDbConnection(strCn)
    strSql = "select sq_tblIdentity.nextval from dual"
    oledbCm = New OleDbCommand(strSql, oledbCn)
    oledbCm.CommandType = CommandType.Text
    oledbCn.Open()
    lngVal = Convert.ToInt64(oledbCm.ExecuteScalar())
    strSql = "insert into tblIdentity ( tblIdentityId," & _
      "FieldValue ) values (" & lngVal & ", '" & _
      DateTime.Now & "')"
    oledbCm.CommandText = strSql
    oledbCm.ExecuteNonQuery()
    MessageBox.Show(lngVal)
Catch exc As System.Exception
    MessageBox.Show(exc.Message)
Finally
    If oledbCn.State <> ConnectionState.Closed Then
        oledbCn.Close()
    End If
    oledbCn = Nothing
    oledbCm = Nothing
End Try
```

The following is a stored procedure (written in PL/SQL) that performs an insert into a table and returns the sequence value that is used as the primary key. This specific stored procedure retrieves a value from the sequence, uses that value within the insert, and then returns that value from the stored procedure to the calling routine. By returning the value to the calling routine, the calling routine may immediately act on that specific row.

```
CREATE OR REPLACE PROCEDURE "USRUSER"."SP_TBLIDENTITY_INSERT"
         (myvalin IN VARCHAR2, OutVal out NUMBER) AS
nSeqVal NUMBER;
BEGIN
  /*  Get out sequence value */
  SELECT sq_tblIdentity.nextval
    INTO nSeqVal
    FROM dual;
  /*  Put the value in the  table */
  INSERT INTO tblidentity( tblIdentityId, fieldvalue )
    VALUES(nSeqVal, myvalin);
```

```
COMMIT;
/* Return the sequence value to the input parameter.  */
OutVal:= nSeqVal;
END;
```

The following sequence (written in PL/SQL) is the sequence used to retrieve unique values for creating a primary key for the insert:

```
CREATE SEQUENCE "USRUSER"."SQ_TBLIDENTITY" INCREMENT BY 1 START
    WITH 41 MAXVALUE 1.0E28 MINVALUE 1 NOCYCLE
    CACHE 20 NOORDER
```

USING A STORED PROCEDURE TO HANDLE THE INSERT   A stored procedure may be used to handle the communications regarding getting the value from the sequence, handling the insert, and then returning the sequence value from the stored procedure. In this example, the stored procedure returns the value as an out parameter of the procedure. The sequence and table definitions are listed in the following code. It may be somewhat inaccurate to state that this method does not make multiple calls to the database. Our routine needs the table and column structure. The easiest way to get this information is to query the database and get that information. In this example, the query for table information is performed on each insert. This problem makes this solution inefficient for situations where a small number of inserts is performed at one time.

The following is some example Visual Basic .NET code to call into a stored procedure to insert a record and return the primary key of the inserted row.

```
Dim oledbCn As OleDbConnection
Dim oledbCm As OleDbCommand
Dim strCn As String = "Provider=OraOleDb.Oracle;Data Source=. . . .
;User Id=. . . . . .;PassWord=. . . . . .;"
Dim strSql As String
Dim oledbDa As OleDbDataAdapter
Dim dsData As DataSet = New DataSet()
Dim drRow as DataRow
Try
    oledbCn = New OleDbConnection(strCn)
    strSql = "select * from tblIdentity where RowNum=1"
    oledbDa = New OleDbDataAdapter(strSql, oledbCn)
    'setup the insert command. This is our stored procedure.
    oledbDa.InsertCommand = New OleDbCommand("sp_tblIdentity_Insert",
oledbCn)
    oledbDa.InsertCommand.CommandType = CommandType.StoredProcedure
    'Create the first insert parameter.
```

```
    'Associate the myvalin parameter with the FieldValue column
    'of the table and define the lengths of the myvalin parameter.
    oledbDa.InsertCommand.Parameters.Add("myvalin",
OleDbType.VarChar, 50, "FieldValue")
    'Set the direction of our myvalin parameter.
    oledbDa.InsertCommand.Parameters("myvalin").Direction =
ParameterDirection.Input
    'Associate the OutVal parameter with the tblIdentityId table
    'column of our table and define the size of the tblIdentityId
    ' column of our table and define the data type and lengths.
    oledbDa.InsertCommand.Parameters.Add("OutVal", OleDbType.Integer,
0, "tblIdentityId")
    'set the direction of the OutVal parameter
    oledbDa.InsertCommand.Parameters("OutVal").Direction =
ParameterDirection.Output
    'go ahead and get some data from our data source so that we can
    'setup our datasource to put data back into our table.
    oledbDa.Fill(dsData, "tblIdentity")
    strSql = "sp_tblidentity_Insert"
    'create a new row
    drRow = dsData.Tables("tblIdentity").NewRow()
    'Fill a column with data.
    drRow("FieldValue") = Convert.ToString(DateTime.Now)
    'Add our row to our dataset.
    dsData.Tables("tblIdentity").Rows.Add(dsRow)
    'Update our datasource.
    oledbDa.Update(dsData, "tblIdentity")
    'Show our returned value to our user.
MessageBox.Show(dsData.Tables("tblIdentity").Rows(dsData.Tables("tbl
Identity").Rows.Count - 1)("tblIdentityId"))
    'Handle errors
Catch exc As System.Exception
    MessageBox.Show(exc.Message)
Finally
    'Clean up the objects in our routine.
    If oledbCn.State <> ConnectionState.Closed Then
        oledbCn.Close()
    End If
    oledbCn = Nothing
    oledbDa = Nothing
    dsData = Nothing
    drRow = Nothing
End Try
```

IDENTIFYING VARIATIONS ON THE PREVIOUS SOLUTIONS There are several variations on the preceding two solutions. If the primary key for a row does not need to be returned to the calling routine, there is no need to perform the select operation on the sequence as a separate step. The select operation on the sequence may be placed within the insert command. The insert operation would look something like `INSERT INTO TBLIDENTITY (TBLIDENTITYID, TBLFIELDVALUE ) VALUES ( SELECT SQTBLIDENTITY.NEXTVAL, 'VALUE TO BE INSERTED' )`. Using this type of insert routine will result in your application only making one call into the database. If there is no need to use the primary key immediately after the insert operation, this is a good alternative to the options that return the primary key to the calling routine.

USING OTHER MECHANISMS TO CREATE AND MANAGE THE VALUES PLACED INTO A PRIMARY KEY Although it is possible to use a GUID that is generated from the .NET Framework and then used in a varchar2 column, it would result in a primary key on a column defined as a varchar2 and the resulting index being placed on a varchar2 column would result in a less than optimal index.

Table 11-3 shows a comparison of generating primary keys using two database commands and a stored procedure to create a primary key and perform an insert into a database table and return that primary key back to the calling routine. The test performed 1,000 insert operations. The database server is Oracle 9i for Windows 2000 and is running on a 1 GHz system with 512 megabytes of RAM. Both the database server and the client application are running on the same system.

TABLE 11–3 COMPARISON OF PRIMARY KEY CREATION

Number of Rows	0 Rows	100,000 Rows	1,000,000 Rows
Two database commands	1.0	1.04	1.02
Stored procedure	1.15	1.20	1.18

There are a couple of interesting ideas from the preceding testing. We had assumed that the stored procedure would result in the fastest time. Strangely, it did not. Remember that the client code needs to get some data from the table before the stored procedure is run. This data is used to hold the primary key that is inserted into the table. This communication back requires time and slowed down the stored procedure test.

There are other strategies for inserting data into a table using a sequence. Instead of returning the sequence value back to the calling routine through an out parameter, an alternative is to select the sequence value directly into the insert statement using the SQL statement `INSERT INTO tblidentity( tblIdentityId, fieldvalue ) VALUES(select sq_tblIdentity.nextval, myvalin);`. If there is no need to use the sequence value immediately, this technique removes the need to send two commands from the client to the database server. Another way to perform this operation is to create a trigger that fires when an insert occurs on that table. The trigger will get a value from the sequence and use it along with the insert statement. Like the saying, "There is more than one way to skin a cat," we're sure that there are other ways to insert records while using Oracle's sequence facility.

Performance Optimizations

Tuning of an application can be a very large operation. Many parts of an application must be developed, tested, and optimized in order for an application to run successfully. The typical pattern for tuning an application involves an inside-out approach. With an inside-out approach, tuning begins at the inside of an application and typically moves outward as the performance-based needs of the application are determined. As a result, tuning typically occurs in the following sequence:

1. Monitor the business rules of an application for efficiency. This typically involves verifying that the rules are correct for a business process.

2. Verify that the database design is properly designed to provide the highest possible performance and still provide proper database normalization.

3. Verify that the SQL used to access the data stored within the database is as efficient as possible. This may involve the testing of SQL statements and stored procedures for performance testing.

4. Verify that the application design is appropriate for the business logic, database interaction is minimized, and that additional operations are appropriate for the application.

5. Verify that the application connects with the database through the fastest method possible for the environment given any type of data-access requirements, such as must use ODBC or must use OLE-DB.

6. The physical database platform must be tuned to properly support a database services running on it. This includes the amount of memory available to the operating system as well as the operating system that is hosting the database platform.

7. The network must be able to supply the bandwidth and reliability to meet the application's needs.

8. The client system must be able to properly host the application and provide enough available resources for the application to properly run.

The tools that we look at in this section focus on performance issues just outside of the business-rules area.

Oracle has a great reputation for being the most tunable database platform available. It has a large number of parameters that can be changed to improve the performance of a database server. Unfortunately, in the past, the large number of parameters available for tuning usually meant that a company had to either understand the underlying architecture of the Oracle database platform and understanding how the Oracle database product works, or they were required to go out and hire database administrator (DBA) expertise.

Many times, programmers must take on the roll of DBA. For a person who doesn't deal with Oracle administration on a day-to-day basis, attempting to tune an Oracle database may be a rather large task. Versions of Oracle before 9i did not include many utilities to automatically tune the Oracle database. With the introduction of Oracle9i, the Oracle database now includes utilities and wizards to improve the performance of a database running on Oracle. These utilities are bundled together into a piece of the Oracle Enterprise Manager called the Oracle Tuning Pack. With the Tuning Pack, development teams are able to proactively identify and resolve performance problems, test whether certain indexes will provide performance improvements, and provide management of the space requirements of an Oracle instance.

Within this section, we look at the utilities of the Oracle Tuning Pack that are included within the Oracle9i database.

Tuning SQL

SQL is a math-based language based on set theory. Because most developers are familiar with a looping style of development, where application logic will loop through a given set of data to find the ones that match certain criteria, the idea of a language based on set theory may cause them some performance problems during development, because programmers may not grasp how to effectively use the SQL language to return their results while using the least amount of resources on the server, network, and client systems. SQL statements that don't efficiently use the SQL language are a problem for many applications. Generating efficient SQL statements requires an awareness of the local database environment, knowledge of the other database objects within the schema, an understanding of how the Oracle Optimizer runs, and in-depth knowledge of the SQL language as implemented by Oracle. Without efficient SQL statements, an application will not be able to operate at 100-percent efficiency.

Oracle includes a utility within the Oracle Tuning Pack called SQL Analyze. This utility is designed to analyze the SQL statements that are input and will attempt to provide suggestions for improvement to the SQL based on knowledge of the database. Oracle includes a feature within the Tuning Pack called TopSQL. TopSQL allows an administrator to search the Oracle SQL cache for some type of predefined criteria. The criteria may be the user that is running the query, tables that are accessed, or SQL commands that meet certain performance criteria. The performance criteria may include "Buffer Cache Hit Ratio," "Disk Reads," "Executions," "Rows Processed," "Sorts," and other criteria. SQL Analyze also provides access to SQL History. SQL History is a listing of all the commands that have been sent to the database.

The SQL Analyzer provides several features that may be used to analyze the SQL that is sent to database server. These are the analysis of an explain plan, optimizer modes, hints, general rules, and object factors.

The explain plan allows developers to evaluate the execution path for a SQL statement without requiring that the statement be executed.

The explain plan provides the relative cost of executing a statement (for cost-based optimization), the optimizer's chosen execution path, the indexes used, the methods used to join any tables, and the order of the joins performed. SQL Analyze may be used to generate explain plans for each mode available from the optimizer. SQL Analyze may generate a graphical view of the explain plan along with detail on how the joins are performed.

The Oracle optimizer's function is to find the most efficient method to execute a SQL statement based on one of four primary modes:

◆ **Rule:** Rule-based optimization rates possible execution paths based on a set of rules.

◆ **Cost first:** Cost first optimization executes the statement in a way that will most efficiently return the first row of data.

◆ **Cost all:** Cost all optimization executes the statement in a way that will impact overall database performance the least.

◆ **Choose:** Choose invokes the appropriate optimizer mode. If the tables have not been analyzed, the system uses rule-based optimization. If the tables have been analyzed, a cost all analysis is performed.

The default optimizer mode may be set within the init.ora file for the database by setting the OPTIMIZER_MODE property.

The optimizer may be influenced in its choices when using a cost-based optimization by the specifying of hints within the query. Table 11-4 shows a list of optimizer hints available.

TABLE 11-4 OPTIMIZER HINTS

Hint	Area	Description	Syntax
ALL_ROWS	Optimizer	Instructs the Optimizer to use an all rows cost-based optimization.	`SELECT /* ALL_ROWS */ * FROM TBLPROJECT`
FIRST_ROWS	Optimizer	Instructs the Optimizer to use a cost-based optimization that returns based on returning the first X number of rows.	`SELECT /* FIRST_ROWS(10) FROM TBLPROJECTENTRYID`
CHOOSE	Optimizer	Instructs the optimizer to choose between a rule-based and cost-based optimization for a SQL statement.	`SELECT /*+ CHOOSE */ * FROM TBLPROJECTENTRY WHERE TBLPROJECTENTRYID=2889`
RULE	Optimizer	Instructs the optimizer to use a rule-based optimization for a SQL Statement.	`SELECT /*+ RULE */ * FROM TBLPROJECTENTRY WHERE TBLPROJECTENTRYID=3214`
FULL	Access Path	Performs a full table scan on the specified table, even if there is an index on the column TBLPROJECTID.	`SELECT /*+ FULL(TBLPROJECT) */ * FROM TBLPROJECT WHERE TBLPROJECTID=25`
ROWID	Access Path	Chooses a table scan by rowid for the specified table.	`SELECT /*+ROWID(TBLPROJECT) */ * FROM TBLPROJECT WHERE TBLPROJECTID=12345 AND ROWID > 'AAAATKAABBAAFNTAAA'`

Hint	Area	Description	Syntax
CLUSTER	Access Path	Chooses a cluster scan to access the specified table. This hint applies only to clustered objects.	`SELECT /*+ CLUSTER */ * FROM TBLPROJECT A JOIN TBLPROJECTENTRY B ON A.TBLPROJECTID= B.TBLPROJECTID AND A.TBLPROJECTID=3476`
HASH	Access Path	Chooses a has scan to access the specified table. This hint applies only to tables stored in a cluster.	`SELECT /*+ HASH(TBLPROJECT) FROM TBLPROJECT WHERE TBLPROJECTID=3456`
INDEX	Access Path	Explicitly chooses an index scan for the specified table. Oracle recommends using INDEX_COMBINE rather than INDEX for bitmap indexes.	`SELECT /*+ INDEX(TBLPROJECTENTRY IDX_TBLPROJECTENTRY_PROJ) */ * FROM TBLPROJECTENTRY WHERE TBLPROJECT=234`
INDEX_ASC	Access Path	Explicitly chooses an index scan for the specified table. This hint differs from the INDEX in that INDEX_ASC may be used to specify an ascending range scan, should the default behavior of the table(s) change.	`SELECT /*+ INDEX_ASC( TBLPROJECTENTRY, DX_TBLPROJECT_PROJ) */ FROM TBLPROJECTENTER WHERE TBLPROJECT=321`
INDEX_ COMBINE	Access Path	Chooses a bitmap access path for the table. If no indexes are specified, then the optimizer used the Boolean combination of bitmapped indexes that provides the best cost estimate for the table.	`SELECT /*+ INDEX_COMBINE (TBLPROJECTENTRY IDX_TBLPROJECTENTRY_PROJ) */ WHERE TBLPROJECT=324`

Continued

TABLE 11–4 OPTIMIZER HINTS *(Continued)*

Hint	Area	Description	Syntax
INDEX_JOIN	Access Path	Uses an index join.	SELECT /*+ INDEX_JOIN(TBLPROJECT IDX_TBLPROJECT_CUST) */ * FROM TBLPROJECT WHERE TBLCUSTOMERID=432
INDEX_DESC	Access Path	Chooses an index scan for the specified table. If the statement uses an index range scan, Oracle scans the index entries in descending order of their indexed values.	SELECT /* + INDEX_DESC(TBLPROJECT IDX_TBLPROJECT_CUST) */ * FROM TBLPROJECT WHERE TBLCUSTOMERID=432
INDEX_FFS	Access Path	Uses a fast full index scan as opposed to a full table scan.	SELECT /* + INDEX_FFS(TBLPROJECT IDX _TBLPROJECT_CUST) */ * FROM TBLPROJECT WHERE TBLCUSTOMERID=432
NO_INDEX	Access Path	Disallows a set of indexes for the table specified.	SELECT /* +NO_INDEX(TBLPROJECTENTRY IDX_TBLPROJECTENTRY_PROJ) * FROM TBLPROJECTENTRY WHERE TBLPROJECT=321
AND_EQUAL	Access Path	Chooses an execution plan that uses an access path that merges scans on single-column indexes.	SELECT /* +AND_EQUAL(TBLPROJECTENTRY IDX_TBLPROJECTENTRY_PROJ IDX_TBLPROJECTENTRY_EMP) */ * FROM TBLPROJECTENTRY WHERE TBLPROJECTID=456 AND TBLEMPLOYEEID=543

Hint	Area	Description	Syntax

USE_CONCAT	Query Transformations	Forces the combined OR conditions in the WHERE clause of a query to be transformed in a query using the UNION ALL. This transformation occurs only if the cost of the query using the concatenations is cheaper than the cost without them.	`SELECT /* + USE_CONCAT */`
			`* FROM TBLPROJECTENTRY`
			`WHERE TBLPROJECT=23 OR`
			`DATEENTERED>TO_DATE(`
			`'2002-01-25',`
			`'YYYY-MM-DD')`

NO_EXPAND	Query Transformations	Prevents the cost-based optimizer from considering OR-expansion for queries with OR conditions or IN conditions within the WHERE clause.	`SELECT /* + NO_EXPAND */`
			`FROM TBLPROJECTENTRY WHERE`
			`TBLPROJECTID=4 OR`
			`TBLEMPLOYEEID=2`

REWRITE	Query Transformations	Rewrites a query in terms of materialized views, as possible, without cost consideration.	`SELECT /* + REWRITE(View`
			`List) */ FROM`
			`TBLPROJECTENTRY A,`
			`TBLPROJECT B WHERE`
			`A.TBLPROJECTID=`
			`B.TBLPROJECTID AND`
			`A.TBLEMPLOYEEID=4`
			(*Note:* Our application does not have views, so this query will not functionally provide any value. View List is a list of views separated by commas.)

NOREWRITE	Query Transformations	Disables query rewrite for that query block. This setting overrides the parameter QUERY_REWRITE_ ENABLED.	`SELECT /* +NOREWRITE */`
			`FROM TBLPROJECT A,`
			`TBLPROJECTENTRY B WHERE`
			`A.TBLPROJECTID=`
			`B.TBLPROJECTID AND`
			`B.IBLEMPLOYEEID=456`

Continued

TABLE **11-4** OPTIMIZER HINTS *(Continued)*

Hint	Area	Description	Syntax
MERGE	Query Trans-formations	Allows the merging of views on a per-query basis.	SELECT /* + MERGE(VIEW LIST) */ * FROM TBLPROJECTENTRY A, TBLPROJECT B WHERE A.TBLPROJECTID= B.TBLPROJECTID AND A.PROJECTENTRYID=4
NO_MERGE	Query Trans-formations	Prevents the use of mergeable views.	SELECT /* + NOMERGE */ * FROM TBLPROJECTENTRY A, TBLPROJECT B WHERE A.TBLPROJECTID= B.TBLPROJECTID AND A.PROJECTENTRYID=4
STAR_TRANS-FORMATION	Query Trans-formations	Uses the best plan in which a trans-formation is used.	SELECT /* +STAR_TRANSFORMATION */ * FROM TBLPROJECT WHERE TBLPROJECTID=4
FACT	Query Trans-formation	Indicates the trans-formation that the hinted table should be considered as a fact table.	SELECT /* + FACT */ * FROM TBLCODE
NO_FACT	Query Trans-formation	Indicates the trans-formation that the hinted table should not be considered as a fact table.	SELECT /* + NO_FACT */ * FROM TBLCODE

Hint	Area	Description	Syntax
ORDERED	Join Orders	Tables are joined in the order in which they appear in the FROM clause. This hint may be used if there is knowledge of the number of rows selected from each table that the optimizer does not know. This would allow the developer to choose an inner and outer table better than the optimizer.	SELECT /* + ORDERED */ * FROM TBLPROJECT A, TBLPROJECTENTRY B WHERE A.TBLPROJECTID= B.TBLPROJECTID
STAR	Join Orders	The largest table in the query is last in the join order. This table is joined with a nester set of loop joins on a concatenating index.	SELECT /* + STAR */ * FROM TBLPROJECT A, TBLPROJECTENTRY B WHERE A.TBLPROJECTID= B.TBLPROJECTID
USE_NL	Join Operations	Join each specified table to a row source with a nested loop join using the specified table as the inner table. In many cases, a nested loop join will return the first row of a join faster than a sort merge join.	SELECT /* + USE_NL(TBLPROJECTENTRY) */ * FROM TBLPROJECT A, TBLPROJECTENTRY B WHERE A.TBLPROJECTID= B.TBLPROJECTID
USE_MERGE	Join Operations	Join each specified table with another row source using a sort-merge join.	SELECT /* + USE_MERGE(TBLPROJECT) */ * FROM TBLPROJECT A, TBLPROJECTENTRY B WHERE A.TBLPROJECTID= B.TBLPROJECTID

Continued

TABLE 11-4 OPTIMIZER HINTS *(Continued)*

Hint	Area	Description	Syntax
USE_HASH	Join Operations	Use a hash join to join each specified table.	SELECT /* + USE_HASH(TBLPROJECTENTRY) */ * FROM TBLPROJECT A, TBLPROJECTENTRY B WHERE A.TBLPROJECTID= B.TBLPROJECTID
DRIVING_SITE	Join Operations	Each query execution is performed at a different site than the one selected by Oracle.	SELECT /* + DRIVING_SITE (TBLPROJECTENTRY) */ * FROM TBLPROJECT A, TBLPROJECTENTRY B WHERE A.TBLPROJECTID= B.TBLPROJECTID
LEADING	Join Operations	The specified table is used as the first table in the join order.	SELECT /* + ORDERED */ * FROM TBLPROJECT A, TBLPROJECTENTRY B WHERE A.TBLPROJECTID= B.TBLPROJECTID
HASH_AJ, MERGE_AJ, and NL_AJ	Join Operations	Causes the NOT IN PL/SQL to use the appropriate join operation. HASH_AJ specifies a hash NOT IN join. MERGE_AJ specifies a sort-merge NOT IN join. NL_AJ specifies a nested loop NOT IN join.	SELECT /* + LEADING(TBLPROJECT) */ * FROM TBLPROJECT A, TBLPROJECTENTRY B WHERE A.TBLPROJECTID= B.TBLPROJECTID
HASH_SJ, MERGE_SJ, and NL_SJ	Join Operations	Causes the EXISTS PL/SQL to use the appropriate join operation. HASH_SJ uses a hash join. MERGE_SJ uses a sort merge join. NL_SJ uses a nested loop join.	

Hint	Area	Description	Syntax
PARALLEL	Parallel Execution	Specifies the desired number of servers that may be used concurrently for a parallel operation. If a sorting or grouping hint is used, the number of servers may be twice the value specified.	`SELECT /* + PARALLEL(TBLPROJECT) */ * FROM TBLPROJECT`
NOPARALLEL	Parallel Execution	Overrides a PARALLEL specification in the table clause.	`SELECT /* + NOPARRALLEL(TBLPROJECT) */ * FROM TBLPROJECT`

PQ_DISTRIBUTE	Parallel Execution	Specifies how rows of joined table should be distributed amongst query servers.	`SELECT * /*+ORDERED PQ_DISTRIBUTE (TBLPROJECTENTRY HASH, HASH) USE_HASH (TBLPROJECTENTRY)*/`
			
			`FROM TBLPROJECT A, TBLPROJECTENTRY B`
			
			`WHERE A.TBLPROJECTID= B.TBLPROJECTID;`

PARALLEL_ INDEX	Parallel Execution	Specifies the desired number of servers that may be used to parallelize index range scans for partitioned indexes.	`SELECT /* + NOPARRALLEL_INDEX (IDX_TBLPROJECT_TBLCOMP) */ * FROM TBLPROJECT`
NOPARALLEL_ INDEX	Parallel Execution	Overrides a PARALLEL attribute setting on an index to avoid a parallel index scan.	`SELECT /* + NOPARRALLEL_INDEX (IDX_TBLPROJECT_TBLCOMP) */ * FROM TBLPROJECT`

Continued

TABLE **11–4** OPTIMIZER HINTS *(Continued)*

Hint	Area	Description	Syntax
APPEND	Other hints	Enables a direct-path INSERT if the database is running in serial mode. A direct-path INSERT bypasses the buffer cache and ignores constraints, and data is added to the end of the table.	INSERT INTO TBLPROJECTENTRY / * + APPEND */ (.........
NOAPPEND	Other hints	Enables conventional INSERT. Disables parallel mode for the duration of the INSERT statement.	INSERT INTO TBLPROJECTENTRY / * + NOAPPEND */ (.........
CACHE	Other hints	Blocks retrieved for the table are placed at the most recently used end of the least recently used list in the buffer scan during a full table scan. This option is useful for small lookup tables.	SELECT /* + CACHE */ * FROM TBLPROJECT WHERE TBLPROJECTID=2
NOCACHE	Other hints	Blocks retrieved for the table are placed at the least recently used end of the LRU list in the buffer cache during a full table scan. This is the default behavior of blocks within the buffer cache.	SELECT /* + NOCACHE */ * FROM TBLPROJECT WHERE TBLPROJECTID=2

Hint	Area	Description	Syntax
UNNEST	Other hints	This hint works with the UNNEST_SUBQUERY session parameter. If the parameter is true, UNNEST checks the subquery block for validity only.	SELECT /* + CACHE */ * FROM TBLPROJECT WHERE TBLPROJECTID=2
NO_UNNEST	Other hints	Turns off the UNNEST_SUBQUERY session parameter for subsequent subquery blocks.	SELECT /* + NO_UNNEST */ * FROM TBLPROJECT WHERE TBLPROJECTID=2
PUSH_PRED	Other hints	Forces pushing of a join predicate into the view.	SELECT /* + PUSH_PRED(VIEW) */ * FROM TBLPROJECT A, TBLPROJECTENTRY B WHERE A.TBLPROJECTID= B.TBLPROJECTID AND TBLPROJECTID=2
NO_PUSH_ PRED	Other hints	Prevents the pushing of a join predicate into a view.	SELECT /* + NO_PUSH_PRED(VIEW) */ * FROM TBLPROJECT A, TBLPROJECTENTRY B WHERE A.TBLPROJECTID= B.TBLPROJECTID AND TBLPROJECTID=2
PUSH_SUBQ	Other hints	Non-merged subqueries are evaluated at the earliest possible place in the execution plan.	SELECT /* + PUSH_SUBQ */ * FROM TBLPROJECT WHERE TBLPROJECTID=2
ORDERED_ PREDICATES	Other hints	Preserves the order of predicate evaluations, except for predicates used as index keys.	SELECT /* + ORDERED_PREDICATES */ * FROM TBLPROJECT WHERE TBLPROJECTID=2

Continued

TABLE **11-4** OPTIMIZER HINTS *(Continued)*

Hint	Area	Description	Syntax
CURSOR_ SHARING_ EXACT	Other hints	No attempt to replace literals with bind variables occurs.	SELECT /* + CURSOR_SHARING_EXACT */ * FROM TBLPROJECT A, TBLPROJECTENTRY B WHERE A.TBLPROJECTID= B.TBLPROJECTID AND TBLPROJECTID=2

Now that we've looked at the features of the SQL Analyzer and some of the Oracle Optimizer hints, we'll walk through an example of using the SQL Analyzer to verify that our SQL statements are as efficient as possible:

1. Open up the SQL Analyze program and connect to the appropriate Oracle Instance.

2. Within the selected instance, right-click on the instance and select Create New SQL. In the open area on the right, insert the appropriate select statement or select a statement from the TopSQL or History sections.

3. On the SQL Statement in the left window, select the SQL Tuning Wizard for a wizard to walk through an analysis of the statement.

Figure 11-6 shows the SQL Analyze product.

Indexes and indexing strategies

Indexes are a set of database objects that provide fast access to data within tables without the overhead of searching through every row within a table. Indexing a set of database tables to match the SQL operations that are being sent to the database is one of the simplest things that may be done to improve performance.

Which columns should be indexed? Several types of columns and expressions are very good candidates for indexing, including the following:

◆ Columns that are used frequently in the WHERE section of a SQL statement.

◆ Columns that are used to join tables.

◆ Columns that are used as foreign keys.

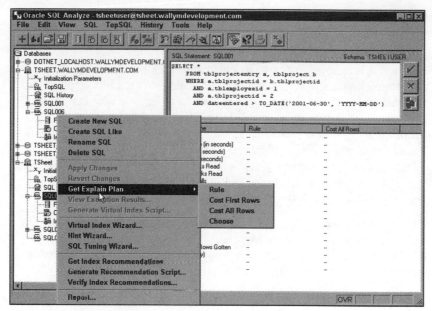

Figure 11-6: SQL Analyzer

Some columns are *not* good candidates for indexes. These columns are:

◆ Columns with a small number of distinct, such as less than 4 or 5.

◆ Columns that are updated frequently. Updates to indexed columns take longer than updates to non-indexed columns.

◆ Columns that only appear in the WHERE clause within functions and operators, besides MIN and MAX.

Oracle supports several types of indexes. These index types may be used in several situations, depending on the exact need. Here is a list of different types of indexes in Oracle:

◆ **Unique:** Unique indexes will keep two rows within a table from having duplicate values in the column(s) used. Nonunique indexes do not force this restriction on their column values.

◆ **Composite:** A composite index is an index in which multiple columns are used within the index.

◆ **Function-based:** A function-based index contains columns that are transformed by a function or are included in an expression. A function-based index can be beneficial when SQL statements include transformed columns. For a function-based index to work properly, the function must be deterministic, meaning that calling a function with the same input at two different times will result in the same output on each call.

◆ **Bitmap:** A bitmapped index is an index that may be used with other bitmapped indexes to evaluate a WHERE clause. With a bitmapped index, a bitmap for each indexed column is used to determine whether a specific row matches the specific search criteria. Bitmapped indexes are only useful in a comparison with a specific value. Columns that are queried with less-than or greater-than comparison will not work effectively with bitmap indexes. Bitmapped indexes are not suitable for Online Transaction Processing Systems with a large amount of updates. Bitmapped indexes are only available with Oracle Enterprise Edition.

◆ **B-Tree:** Oracle indexes are stored in B Trees to speed up data access. The upper blocks of a B-tree index contain index data that points to lower-level index blocks. The lowest level index blocks contain the indexed data value and the corresponding rowed of the actual row.

Now that you know a little bit about the indexes and structure of indexes, we'll take a look at how you go about using the tools included with the Oracle Tuning Pack and walk through the steps to create these indexes, using our previous example:

1. Using the SQL Analyze, enter a query as the statement as before.

2. Right-click in the left window on the name of the SQL statement to generate a rule-based explain plan.

3. Generate the appropriate cost-based explain plan as in Step 2.

4. At this point, it is possible to generate a set of indexes that will be optimized for the query that has been tested. This index recommendation may be saved to a text file for visual analysis and application at a later date.

At this point, you've seen how to use the Oracle SQL Analyze product included with Oracle to help programmers generate indexes that are optimized for the running application. With the SQL Analyze product, we can test the index before it is put into use through a feature called the Verify Index Recommendation. Verify Index Recommendation will calculate the performance improvement that may be gained by running the selected query or queries through the selected index. The wizard will report the expected performance improvement of the queries with the index applied.

Another wizard included within SQL Analyze is the Virtual Index Wizard. The Virtual Index Wizard allows indexes to be tested based on user input to the wizard. The user may select the schema, table, and columns within an index. When the wizard has collected the data and finished the analysis, a graphical report is provided that details the expected performance improvement. The Virtual Index Wizard is closely related to the Verify Index Recommendation discussed earlier.

Instance and space management

Although not typically thought of as ways to improve performance in an Oracle database, tuning the Oracle instance and the space used by that instance can provide a boost in performance. Effectively tuning the Oracle instance and the space used by that instance will improve performance by optimizing memory used, minimizing I/O on the server, and reducing performance problems involving space utilization.

Oracle Expert is a tool included with the Oracle Tuning Pack that provides instance and space management. Oracle Expert (shown in Figure 11-7) evaluates many of the underlying settings regarding instance and space management of a running Oracle Instance and will make recommendations to improve performance and reliability.

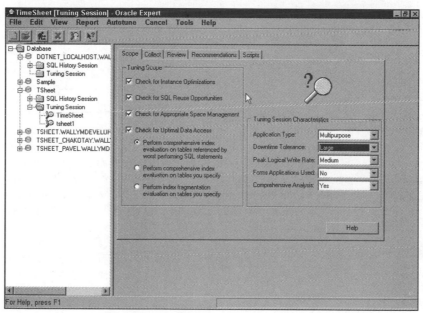

Figure 11-7: Oracle Expert

With Oracle Expert, it's possible to tune and verify the following types of items:

◆ **Space:** By checking the Appropriate Space Management checkbox, the structure of tablespaces and schema objects will be checked for appropriate placement and sizing. Recommendations will be made if guidelines are not being followed.

◆ **Application Type:** The instance may be tuned for different types of workloads, including OLTP, data warehouse, and multipurpose workloads.

◆ **Downtime:** The instance may be modified for performance or recovery. The lower the tolerance for downtime, the more the Oracle Expert will be optimized for recover time. There are four tolerances provided within the Oracle Expert: none, small, medium, and large.

◆ **Peak Logical Write Rate:** This provides an indication of the maximum number of transaction volume. The values are low (up to 5 operations per second), medium (up to 50 operations per second), large (up to 500 operations per second), and huge (more than 500 operations per second).

◆ **Forms Applications Used:** This tells Oracle Expert whether a forms-based application is used to connect to the environment. The possible values are Yes and No.

◆ **Comprehensive Analysis:** Tells Oracle Expert that there is a complete workload in the selected database. A comprehensive analysis analyzes the workload for the most efficient tuning recommendations.

Summary

There are a large number of items that can be taken into account to build a high-performance .NET application with Oracle. Oracle is a very tuneable database. Unfortunately, the sheer number of options for tuning Oracle can result in an overwhelming number of items to possibly modify. The choice of data provider, the indexing of the database tables, how primary keys are selected, and the setup of the Oracle database instance all contribute to providing a high-performance application or an application that performs poorly and does not meet the performance expectations of the application's users.

Chapter 12

DB/2 Universal Database

IN THIS CHAPTER

- ◆ Exploring the DB/2 environment
- ◆ Examining DB/2 on the iSeries (AS/400)
- ◆ Connecting to DB/2 from .NET
- ◆ Demonstrating ADO.NET and ADO with DB/2
- ◆ Studying the impact of connection choice
- ◆ Considering performance bottlenecks

DB/2 IS THE FLAGSHIP database product from IBM and is available on a wide range of both operating systems and hardware platforms. The history of DB/2 dates back to the early 1980s, when it grew out of IBM research on the relational database model. Today, along with Oracle, Microsoft's SQL Server, and a few others, DB/2 is one of the most powerful third-generation, object-relational database systems. In terms of scalability, DB/2 has a long track record. DB/2 is currently available in the Satellite edition, which is a lightweight version for laptops with built-in synchronization capabilities, and it also runs on mainframes with OS/390. In addition, it runs in single processor, SMP, and parallel, shared-nothing configurations. Although it is not as prevalent on the average server as either Oracle or Microsoft, the amount of data held by DB/2 systems of all types is vast.

In this chapter, we examine DB/2 with respect to Microsoft .NET. We look at the ODBC and OLE-DB drivers available for connecting to DB/2 and see what, if any, impact results from choosing one over the other. Then the focus turns to a variety of application types and how DB/2 is utilized from each of the application types. In addition, examples illustrate using both ADO and ADO.NET with DB/2 connectivity. Finally, consideration is given to any bottlenecks that are uncovered.

DB/2 Platforms

DB/2 is available on a wide variety of platforms, from Windows 2000 and OS/2 to the AS/400 and OS/390, not to mention a number of Unix platforms and their hardware. Also the current version of DB/2, Universal Database Version 7.X, is available in several distributions: Personal Edition, Workgroup Edition, Enterprise

Edition, Enterprise Extended Edition, Personal Developer's Edition, and Universal Developer's Edition. To paraphrase a common advertisement, DB/2 is anywhere you want to be. However, the code for this chapter was primarily developed and run against the Personal Developer's Edition.

Despite this broad array of choices, in this chapter the focus is on just two platforms DB/2 for Windows NT (2000) and DB/2 for the iSeries (AS/400). We selected the NT platform because we expect that many users developing .NET solutions will be targeting NT servers. We also chose to look at DB/2 for the AS/400 because it is widespread among medium and large businesses, and a large amount of important corporate information is held on that platform. So, even though AS/400s are not everywhere the way NT servers are, it will definitely be important for some development communities to access AS/400 data from .NET.

DB/2 for Windows NT

To establish the lay of the land, this section briefly covers DB/2 on the NT platform and highlights the key tools for managing data, monitoring performance, and writing procedures. DB/2 has many more tools than those covered here, but the goal here is to provide an overview of the five tools you could not live without and to give some context to the development environment.

DATA MANAGEMENT

The two key tools for managing databases and data in DB/2 are the Control Center, shown in Figure 12-1, and the Command Center, shown in Figure 12-2. The Control Center provides all the basics that a developer would expect to find. This is the tool used to log into the local or remote servers. The Control Center then allows the developer or DBA to connect to and manage the databases found on the server. The Selected menu provides the same menu that right-clicking on an object provides; for a database, this includes such items as backup, restore, drop, alter, and restart, just to name a few. The Tools menu, also represented by the first block of icons on the toolbar, provides access to other tools available for DB/2 database administration, including Command Center and Stored Procedure Builder, which are covered next.

The Command Center, shown in Figure 12-2, provides a query and scripting environment for the developer. The tool provides four tabs: one tab for interactive SQL execution; a second tab for authoring, saving, and executing scripts; a third tab for displaying query results; and a fourth and final tab for showing the access plan the server used to execute the query. Again, the common toolbar is present, allowing the developer to access the other tools easily. As a final note, the Script menu contains a Schedule item that allows the developer or administrator to schedule the execution of a script, saved in the Script Center, for any given time.

The Script Center serves to centralize scripts that need to be run on a given system. It allows a DBA point-and-click execution of jobs and allows you to see pending and running jobs as well as the job history. After a script has been added to the script center, it may be scheduled to run automatically using a robust set of scheduling options.

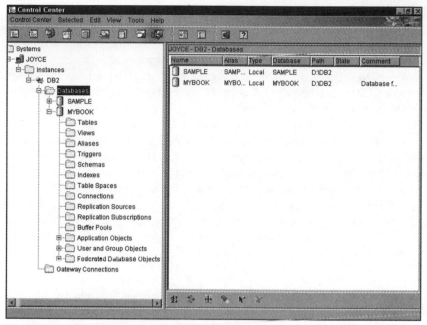

Figure 12-1: The DB/2 Control Center

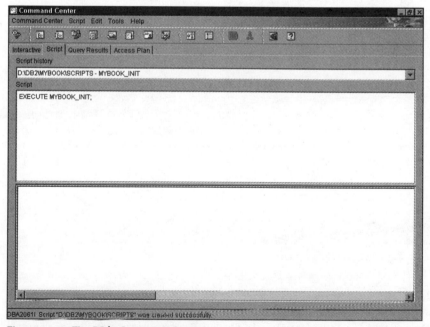

Figure 12-2: The DB/2 Command Center

STORED PROCEDURES

Stored procedures are central to many database designs, enabling the developer to remove code and business logic from the client software. Although most databases provide an environment for creating stored procedures, those environments are frequently lacking even the simplest of debugging facilities. The Stored Procedure Builder found in DB/2, and shown in Figure 12-3, represents a great improvement over the common text editor environment.

The procedure builder provides easy access to stored procedures on the local or a remote server. In addition, the coding window has row and column indicators and color-coded text like all modern programming editors. Most important, however, is the ability to set breakpoints and to perform meaningful debugging. When debugging is underway, the debug window shows a list of breakpoints, the call stack, and the values of local variables. Also, the debugger contains full tracing capabilities allowing the developer to step into, step over, step return, and step to cursor. Given the amount of time that has been spent developing stored procedures, it's good to see that some tools are finally evolving to provide adequate levels of usability.

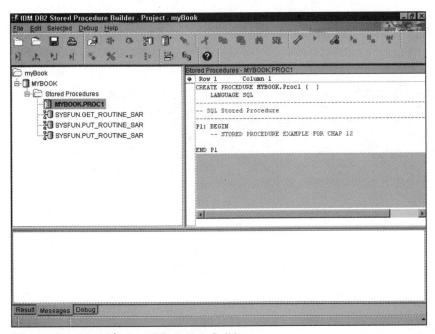

Figure 12-3: The DB/2 Stored Procedure Builder

PERFORMANCE MANAGEMENT

Along with managing data and writing procedures, monitoring the performance of the database server is an essential task. The tools that are central to performance management with DB/2 are the Event Monitor and the Show Monitor. The Event

Monitor (shown in Figure 12-4) allows a DBA or developer to create sets of monitored events on the server. These monitored events can be tailored to match almost any event that can occur on the system. As these events occur, they are logged to a file for reference, allowing the data to be reviewed offline. The event monitoring activity can be turned on and off to track usage statistics at given intervals and not simply accumulate data for the complete runtime of the server. This data is robust and useful, but it is not graphical. If you want to see what is happening on the server now, the next application, Show Monitor, is the tool for the job.

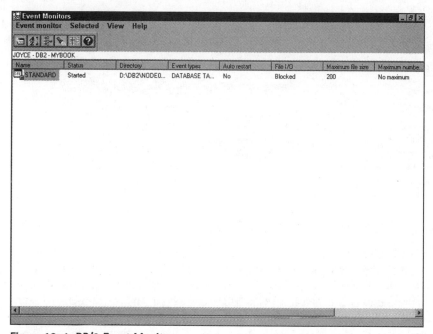

Figure 12–4: DB/2 Event Monitor

Show Monitor (shown in Figure 12-5) provides a running graphical display of system activity. This tool can be accessed from the Selected menu item in the Control Center when a database instance has been selected or, alternately, from the menu that pops up when right-clicking on a database instance. The items tracked on the Show Monitor graph can be customized along with the sampling rate and the graph settings. This form also provides a Thresholds tab that can be used to link a performance threshold to a system response event, such as activating an alarm, running a command, or sending a user message.

In addition to the Show Monitor form is another, more specialized graphical Query Monitor. The Query Monitor is actually a sub-component of the larger Query Patroller system, which provides job management for queries. If the Query Patroller server is installed and running, the query monitor tool is very useful for examining the performance and behaviors of queries submitted through it.

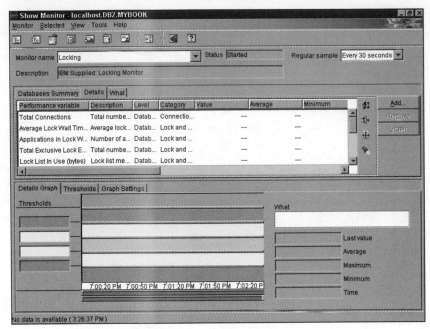

Figure 12-5: DB/2 Show Monitor

DB/2 for the iSeries 400 (AS/400)

DB/2 for the iSeries 400 is the 64-bit relational database management system that is included with the iSeries 400 (also known as, AS/400). It is a member of the DB/2 family of databases. From a development standpoint, DB/2 for the iSeries has been greatly improved over the past few years. DB/2 has added support for SQL, triggers, and referential integrity.

Included with DB2 for the iSeries is Operations Navigator, shown in Figure 12-6. Operations Navigator is a tool that allows an administrator to manage an iSeries 400, including DB/2 for the iSeries.

A large amount of corporate data is contained on DB/2 for the iSeries 400. Being able to access that data is a very important for developers. DB/2 is fully integrated with the iSeries.

SQL AND FILE SYSTEM ACCESS

DB2 for the iSeries has two types of data-access methods for getting at data within data and the underlying database tables:

◆ SQL: Since Version 3 Revision 7 (V3R7) of the iSeries operating system, the iSeries 400 (AS/400) has supported the SQL Language. SQL data access is the preferred direction for database development according to IBM.

◆ **System access:** Prior to the V3R7 of the iSeries operating system, system access was the data-access method used. Many iSeries 400 databases are accessed through the system-access methods.

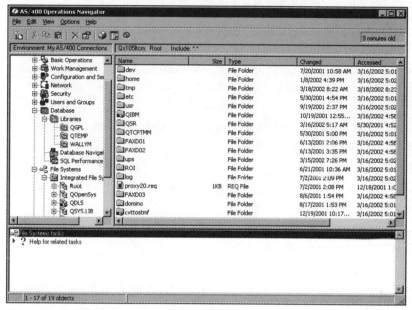

Figure 12-6: AS/400 Operations Navigator

LAYOUT OF A DB/2 DATABASE FOR THE ISERIES 400

The file system layout for DB2 for the iSeries is divided into two types of files:

◆ **Physical files:** A *physical file* is a file that stores data. It contains a description of the data that is stored along with that data. A programmer using SQL to access data will view physical files as the equivalent of a database table.

◆ **Logical files:** A *logical file* is a file that represents one or more physical files. A logical file does not contain data. A logical file contains a description of the data contained within a set of physical files. A programmer using SQL to access data will view logical files as the equivalent of database views and associated indexes.

Operating conceptually on top of the physical and logical files is a library. A *library* is a database structure that contains tables, views, and other object types. A library is used to group related objects.

SQL DATATYPES

DB/2 for the iSeries 400 supports a large number of data types:

◆ **BigInt:** A 64-bit integer. The allowed values range from −9,223,372,036,854,775,808 to 9,223,372,036,854,775,807.

◆ **Binary Large Object (BLOB):** A variable-length field containing binary data.

◆ **Char:** A fixed-length character string column. The length of this column is determined by the definition of the column. This column's maximum length is 32,766.

◆ **Character Large Object (CLOB):** A variable-length character string with a maximum length of 2,147,483,647.

◆ **Datalink:** A link to external data, such as data on another iSeries 400.

◆ **Date:** A three-part value consisting of year, month, and day that designates a time within the Gregorian calendar.

◆ **Decimal:** A packed decimal with an implicit decimal point. The allowed range is $-10^{31} + 1$ to $10^{31} - 1$.

◆ **Double-Byte Character Large Object (DBCLOB):** A variable-length sequence of two-byte characters. The maximum length of this column is 1,073,741,823.

◆ **Double:** A double-precision floating point number as defined by the IEEE.

◆ **Graphic:** A fixed-length graphic string column consisting of two-byte characters. The maximum length of the column is 16383.

◆ **Integer:** A 32-bit integer. The allowed values range is from −2,147,483,648 to 2,147,483,647.

◆ **Numeric:** A zoned-decimal number with an implicit decimal point.

◆ **Real:** A single-precision floating-point number as defined by the IEEE.

◆ **Time:** A three-part value consisting of hour, minute, and second designating the time of day in a 24-hour day.

◆ **Timestamp:** A seven-part value (year, month, day, hour, minute, second, and millisecond) that defines everything down to the millisecond.

◆ **SmallInt:** A 16-bit integer. The allowed values range is from −32,768 to 32,767.

◆ **VarChar:** A variable-length character string column. The maximum length of this column is 32,740.

◆ **VarGraphic:** A variable-length sequence of two-byte characters. The maximum length of this column is 16,370.

There is one type of column that DB/2 for the iSeries 400 does not have. It is missing some type of column that facilitates the creation of a primary key not related to the data stored within the tables. For example, there is no auto-number, sequence, or other mechanism to create a primary key. This capability must be provided by a programmer or database administrator. This may be done by creating a table with a routine that locks the table, reads the data into the application, and then increments the data in the table.

HOW TO CONNECT

There are several options to use to connect to the iSeries 400 system and use the database. Among the connection options are Client Access Express, Host Integration Server, and Hit Software, each of which we examine here.

CLIENT ACCESS EXPRESS   IBM provides a product with the iSeries 400 that is called Client Access Express. Microsoft provides a server gateway product that is called Host Integration Server (IIIS). In addition to these products, there are several third-party products that connect to the iSeries 400 database.

Included within IBM's Client Access Express (CAE) is support for OLE-DB and ODBC. OLE-DB is the data-access mechanism provided within CAE, and support for OLE-DB is provided within the .NET Framework by using the `System.Data.OleDb` namespace. The name of the OLE-DB provider within CAE is IBMDA400. Included within CAE is support for ActiveX. By using ActiveX and the COM Interop in the .NET Framework, a .NET application may access the iSeries data queues, call a number of system APIs and user programs, manage and validate security, and perform a number of other tasks on the iSeries.

By using OLE-DB and `System.Data.OleDb` namespace, a program may interface with iSeries database through SQL or system-level access, call stored procedures and programs, interact with data queues, and utilize other features of the iSeries database.

HOST INTEGRATION SERVER 2000   Microsoft has a gateway product that allows multiple systems to connect to the iSeries 400. This product is called Host Integration Server (HIS). HIS allows programs to integrate with the IBM iSeries 400 and Mainframe systems without having to install the complete set of client connectivity tools and programs such as IBM's Client Access Express (CAE). HIS provides COM access to a number of features of the iSeries 400, including CICS and IMS, MQSeries (IBM's message queuing product), emulator access to the iSeries 400, and access to the database on the iSeries 400 through either OLE-DB or ODBC.

By using the `System.Data.OleDb` namespace, the .NET Framework may use the OLE-DB data providers included with HIS. HIS includes two providers. The first provider is the OLE-DB Provider for the AS/400 and VSAM. This provider provides file system style access to the iSeries 400. This provider handles the complexity of communicating with the iSeries 400.

The other provider included with HIS is the OLE-DB Provider for DB/2. This provider handles access to a remote DB/2 database. This provider is written as an

IBM Distributed Relational Database Architecture (DRDA) application requester. By being a DRDA requester, it may connect to all DRDA-compliant DB/2 systems. This allows it to connect to DRDA systems running DB/2 on MVS, OS/400, various Unix systems, Windows NT/2000, and OS/2. This provider allows programs to connect and use SQL statements and stored procedures.

Along with the OLE-DB drivers, HIS provides an ODBC Driver for DB/2. This driver provides ODBC access to DB/2. By using the `Microsoft.Data.Odbc` namespace, an application written in the .NET Framework may access data in a DB/2 database using this driver.

HIT SOFTWARE   There are certain situations in which IBM's CAE has not been able to scale to meet the demands of a large number of users connecting through a Web application to an iSeries 400 system. In this situation, the CAE product running on middle-tier IIS or COM+ Server is not able to handle the load from a large number of simultaneous users. Some companies are fearful of using gateway types of products. They may believe that this creates some type of security problem. As a result, several third parties have stepped into this area and have created data-access products for communicating with DB/2 on the iSeries400. One of the more popular data-access products, according to discussion in several online lists, is from Hit Software. One of their products is an OLE-DB driver. This OLE-DB driver, called HiT OLE-DB/DB2, allows for an application to connect to DB/2 on the iSeries400. The Hit OLE-DB/DB2 driver connects through Distributed Relational Database Architecture (DRDA) protocol as defined by IBM and may be used to connect to a number of different versions of DB/2 running on different platforms.

Connection Choice

Having covered the AS/400 and connectivity to that platform, we're going to focus again on Windows 2000. Again, the common drivers for connectivity between .NET and DB/2 are ODBC and OLE-DB. IBM supplies both of the drivers used here.

IBM DB/2 OLE-DB driver

In order to use the OLE-DB provider from IBM with DB/2 version 7, you must first install a fix pack from IBM (fix pack 1 or later). When the OLE-DB provider is available, it is important to note the restrictions to which the provider is currently subject, because they may affect your application:

◆ Nested, distributed, and coordinated transactions are not supported.

◆ Large objects (BLOB, CLOB, and DBCLOB data types) are not supported.

◆ Stored procedures called with ADO must explicitly bind their parameters.

◆ Multiple parameter sets are not supported.

If any of these restrictions will impact the application then under development, the IBM ODBC driver can either be employed directly or employed via the OLE-DB provider for ODBC from Microsoft. In addition to these restrictions are two other properties of which you need to be aware:

♦ The provider supports the free threading model.

♦ The OLE-DB provider only supports read-only and forward-only cursors, natively. Cursors that are both scrollable and updateable must be maintained on the client using a client cursor.

When an application gets or sets data, the OLE-DB provider will automatically perform type conversion between the DB/2 data types and the OLE-DB data types. Table 12-1 lists the conversions between the data types available in DB/2 and those available in OLE-DB.

TABLE 12-1 THE TYPE CONVERSIONS BETWEEN DB/2 AND OLE-DB

DB/2 Type	OLE-DB Type
SMALL_INT	DBTYPE_I2
INTEGER	DBTYPE_I4
BIG_INT	DBTYPE_I8
REAL	DBTYPE_R4
FLOAT	DBTYPE_R8
DOUBLE	DBTYPE_R8
DECIMAL	DBTYPE_NUMERIC
NUMERIC	DBTYPE_NUMERIC
DATE	DBTYPE_DBDATE
TIME	DBTYPE_DBTIME
TIMESTAMP	DBTYPE_DBTIMESTAMP
CHAR	DBTYPE_STR
VARCHAR	DBTYPE_STR
LONG VARCHAR	DBTYPE_STR
CLOB	Not supported in current provider

Continued

TABLE 12-1 THE TYPE CONVERSIONS BETWEEN DB/2 AND OLE-DB *(Continued)*

DB/2 Type	OLE-DB Type
GRAPHIC	DBTYPE_WSTR
VARGRAPHIC	DBTYPE_WSTR
LONG VARGRAPHIC	DBTYPE_WSTR
DBCLOB	Not supported in current provider
CHAR FOR BIT DATA	DBTYPE_BYTES
VARCHAR FOR BIT DATA	DBTYPE_BYTES
LONG VARCHAR FOR BIT DATA	DBTYPE_BYTES
BLOB	Not supported in current provider
DATALINK	DBTYPE_STR

When it comes to connecting to the database using the OLE-DB provider, the connection string may contain the following three values:

◆ DSN: Set the value to the desired DB/2 database alias.

◆ UID: Set the value to the user ID.

◆ PWD: Set the value to the user password.

Listing 12-1 demonstrates a simple connection to DB/2 using the OLE-DB provider.

Listing 12-1: A Connection to DB/2 with OLE-DB

```
using system;
using System.Data.OleDb;

namespace myDB2ConnectionDemo
{
    class myDB2ConnectionDemoClass
    {
        [STAThread]
        static void Main(string[] args)
        {
```

```
String strConn = "Provider=IBMDADB2;" +
                 "DSN=MYBOOK;UID=db2admin;PWD=xxxx;";
OleDbConnection myOleDb =
  new OleDbConnection(strConn);
try
{
    myOleDb.Open();
    Console.WriteLine("Connection Open.");
}
catch (Exception e)
{
    Console.WriteLine("Connection Failed.");
    Console.Write(e.Mesage);
}

myOleDb.Close();
        }
    }
}
```

This is a simple program that establishes a connection with the DB/2 database MYBOOK using the specified user ID and password. A simple message is printed on success, and if the connection cannot be opened, a failure message along with the error message is printed.

IBM DB/2 ODBC driver

Typically, ODBC drivers are not the objects of much discussion. The installation process is usually automatic, and the configuration process often involves little more that entering a data source name, a description, and a target database. Normally, no more than a few fairly insignificant customizable options exist. With DB/2 the ODBC driver is installed automatically upon installation of the server or the client software. However, when the Advanced button is selected from the DB/2 driver's Data Source Configuration window, the developer will find a slew of meaningful configuration options.

IBM breaks these configuration options into eight groups, each occupying a separate tab in the Advanced CLI/ODBC Settings dialog. Each of these item groups is detailed in the following sections.

TRANSACTION

Table 12-2 provides a listing of the options under the Transaction tab. These options all affect the behavior of transactions or connections to the database, which can impact the operation of transactions.

TABLE 12-2 THE ODBC TRANSACTION CONFIGURATION OPTIONS

ODBC Parameter	Description
Connect Type — CONNECTYPE/ SYNCPOINT	Indicates whether the connection will be remote or distributed. If the connection will be distributed, the SYNCPOINT parameter indicates whether a 1– or 2-phase commit will be employed.
Cursor Hold — CURSORHOLD	Determines whether the cursor will be destroyed after a transaction commit.
Connection Cache — KEEPCONNECT	Provides connection caching sometimes called pooling by setting the number of connections to cache.
Connection Mode — MODE	Sets the default connection mode to shared or exclusive.
Maximum Number of Connections — MAXCONN	Sets an upper limit on the number of connections a single application may open.
Asynchronous ODBC — ASYNCENABLE	Enables or disables the ability to perform asynchronous queries.
Share Single Physical Connection — MULTICONNECT	Determines whether additional connections will share the same physical connection, or whether they will each have their own connection.
Isolation Level — TXNISOLATION	Sets the default isolation level used for a connection.

Setting Cursor Hold to 0 will benefit performance by allowing the database to immediately discard unneeded resources. However, it is important not to close a cursor that could be reused. KEEPCONNECT can benefit performance through connection caching, or pooling. Share Single Physical Connection can benefit connections in an application in a manner similar to pooling, however, you need to keep in mind that transactions are tied to connections and a COMMIT or ROLLBACK could have unintended consequences for connections in other sections of code.

DATA TYPE
Table 12-3 provides a listing of the options available on this tab. These options affect how the driver will handle some special data types.

TABLE 12-3 THE ODBC DATA TYPE CONFIGURATION OPTIONS

ODBC Parameter	Description
Binary Data Treatment — BITDATA	Determines whether binary fields will be treated strictly as binary or as character data.
IBM GRAPHIC Support — GRAPHIC	Determines how the driver will handle fields defined as GRAPHIC.
Long Object Binary Support	Determines how the driver will handle fields defined as large objects.

ENTERPRISE

Table 12-4 lists the options available on the Enterprise tab. These options can be used to tune performance when connecting to large databases, but some options apply only to certain versions of DB/2. In addition, the options here only affect the performance related to database structure information and not to the database as a whole.

TABLE 12-4 THE ODBC ENTERPRISE CONFIGURATION OPTIONS

ODBC Parameter	Description
MVS Current SQLID — CURRENTSQLID	Allows for more efficient references to SQL objects but applies only to environments were SET CURRENT SQLID is valid, such as MVS.
MVS DBNAME Filter — DBNAME	Allows for more efficient retrieval of table information on MVS systems in some situations.
Schema List — SCHEMALIST	Limits the number of schemas used to gather table information.
System Schema — SYSSCHEMA	Specifies the use of an alternate SCHEMA for querying table information.
Table Types — TABLETYPE	Limits the results of a table information query to the tables of the type specified by this parameter.

Continued

TABLE 12-4 THE ODBC ENTERPRISE CONFIGURATION OPTIONS *(Continued)*

ODBC Parameter	Description
Grantee List	Reduces the table privilege information returned to the tables or columns that have been granted to the listed user IDs.
Grantor List	Reduces the table privilege information returned to the tables or columns that have been granted by the listed user IDs.

The system schema option is worth noting here. By default, system schema information is held in SYSIBM for DB/2 UDB. If you have a large database with many tables, you may define a schema that provides a limited view of the schema tables in SYSIBM. Then using this view will provide better response time when querying information on database structures.

OPTIMIZATION

Table 12-5 lists the options available on the Optimization tab. These settings generally affect the optimizations employed by the server like query optimization, and some settings, once again, only affect specific systems.

TABLE 12-5 THE ODBC OPTIMIZATION CONFIGURATION OPTIONS

ODBC Parameter	Description
DB2 Explain – DB2EXPLAIN	Determines whether explain table or snapshot information will be generating.
Optimization Estimate – DB2ESTIMATE	Sets a threshold value that will trigger a dialog that reports the optimizer estimates following statement preparation.
Optimization Level – DB2OPTIMIZATION	Sets a value for the level of query optimization employed by the server.
Parallelism Level – DB2DEGREE	Sets the degree of parallelism employed by a database cluster.
Statement Handle Cache – KEEPSTATEMENT	Sets the number of statement handles that are cached for used by the next statement.

ODBC Parameter	Description
Optimize for N Rows — OPTIMIZEFORNROWS	Sets the number of rows, the n, to optimize retrieval time.
Wildcard — UNDERSCORE	Determines whether the underscore character (_), is treated as a wildcard or as an underscore.

The most useful setting here is likely to be Optimize for N Rows, particularly for client applications. This setting causes the driver to append the statement OPTIMIZE FOR N ROWS to queries where N will be the value specified by this setting. This statement instructs the server to retrieve the N rows by the fastest means possible and return records in blocks of N. So, when filling a table or list box containing ten rows, this option will optimize response time.

COMPATIBILITY

Table 12-6 shows the parameters underneath the Compatibility tab. These parameters are available for compatibility with earlier versions of DB/2. The last two settings assist with code page conversions to version 1, while the multithreading setting provides serialization compatibility with version 2. The deferred prepare and early close are generally beneficial settings that are set to true by default.

TABLE 12-6 THE ODBC COMPATIBILITY CONFIGURATION OPTIONS

ODBC Parameter	Description
Deferred Prepare — DEFERREDPREPARE	Defers the Prepare statement until the related Execute statement is called reducing network traffic.
Multithreading (Common) — DISABLEMULTITHREAD	Disables multithreading resulting in the serialization of all database calls.
Early Cursor Close — EARLYCLOSE	Determines if the cursor on the server should be closed automatically when the last record has been sent.
Translation DLL	Sets the location of the DB2TRANS.DLL, which contains code page mappings.
Translation Codepage	Sets the code page used by DB/2 version 1.

ENVIRONMENT

The environment parameters are listed in Table 12-7. These parameters allow adjustments to the ODBC environment.

TABLE **12-7** THE ODBC ENVIRONMENT CONFIGURATION OPTIONS

ODBC Parameter	Description
Current Function Path — CURRENTFUNCTIONPATH	Specifies the schemas to search to resolve function and data type references used in dynamic SQL statements.
Default Procedure Library — DEFAULTPROCLIBRARY	Specifies the default library on the server used to resolve stored procedure calls.
Temporary Directory — TEMPDIR	Specifies the directory on the client machine used to store temporary files related to retrieving large objects such as BLOBs or CLOBs from the server.

SERVICE

The Service tab contains a set of options used to modify the behavior of the ODBC service. These are shown in Table 12-8. Known Workarounds provides a list of workaround behaviors for ODBC applications, and there are two lists grouped into Patch 1 and Patch 2. If some odd issue has arisen with your application, check here for a possible solution. Trace turns on ODBC tracing for a particular data source. The Warnings and Error popup options allow you to control what errors and warnings will be propagated back to the application or ignored altogether. The final option, SQLError handling will append the name of the ODBC API function that reported an error, which can be useful for debugging.

STATIC SQL

Table 12-9 lists the options available beneath the Static SQL tab. These options are essentially debugging and logging options that may be useful for development. They enable the developer to capture static SQL statements from dynamic statements issued through the ODBC connection. However, before using these options, the DB2CAP command must be issued on the server to bind the capture file to the server.

TABLE 12-8 THE ODBC SERVICE CONFIGURATION OPTIONS

ODBC Parameter	Description
Known Workarounds — PATCH1/PATCH2	Lists available workaround patches.
Trace (Common) — TRACE	Enables tracing of the ODBC activity.
Warnings — IGNOREWARNINGS	Enables the downgrading of errors and ignoring of warnings.
Error Popup — POPUPMESSAGE	Activates error dialogs outside of the application to the user.
SQLError() Handling — APPENDAPINAME	Appends the API function name that generated an error to the error message.

TABLE 12-9 THE ODBC STATIC SQL CONFIGURATION OPTIONS

ODBC Parameter	Description
Convert ODBC/CLI to Static SQL — STATICMODE	Determines whether dynamic SQL statements will be captured for logging or converted to static SQL statements.
Statement Conversion Log — STATICLOGFILE	Sets the path of the log file to record the captured activity.

The DB/2 ODBC driver is quite robust, as illustrated by all of these settings. Given the issues related to the OLE-DB driver, you may end up working with this driver; so become familiar with these options and review the list of workarounds built into the driver, because one may apply to you. Listing 12-2 provides a code fragment illustrating a connection to DB/2 with ODBC.

Listing 12-2: Connecting to DB/2 with ODBC

```
String strConn = "DSN=MYBOOKDB2;UID=db2admin;" +
                 "PWD=xxxxxx;DATABASE=MYBOOK;";
OdbcConnection myODBC = new OdbcConnection(strConn);
OdbcTransaction myTxn;
String strCommand =
        "INSERT INTO MYSCHEMA.SIMPLE_TBL (SIMPLE_DESC)" +
```

Continued

Listing 12-2 *(Continued)*

```
                    "VALUES ('ODBC INSERT');";
OdbcCommand cmd = new OdbcCommand();

try
{
    myODBC.Open();
}
```

Using ADO.NET and ADO

ADO.NET provides a greater degree of flexibility in managing the flow of data between the client and server. ADO.NET also enables a greater degree of sophistication in managing the relationships among the data at the client. However, ADO.NET is new and advances are rarely problem-free. This section will demonstrate the use of ADO.NET and ADO with DB/2. In addition, we consider some of the advantages of the .NET methodology over ADO, as well as compare the performance of each in some narrow circumstances.

ADO.NET performance

Whether ADO.NET actually runs faster that ADO is probably not as important as its new data model. ADO.NET provides an additional level of abstraction from the database. Although ADO.NET was covered in detail earlier in the book, here we focus on two key components of ADO.NET: the data adapter and the dataset.

DATA ADAPTER

The data adapter now provides a level of indirection between the connection and the data structures that hold the results. The benefit of this indirection is the ability to build data manipulation code above the data adapter level that does not need to know anything about the connection method below the data adapter. Listing 12-3 provides a code fragment using a data adapter.

Listing 12-3: Connecting the Use of a Data Adapter

```
OleDbDataAdapter daDB2 = new OleDbDataAdapter();
OleDbCommand cmdDB2 = new OleDbCommand();
DataSet dsDB2 = new DataSet();
cmdDB2.Connection = connDB2;  // connDB2 is a connection object
cmdDB2.CommandText = strSIMPLE_TBL;
daDB2.SelectCommand = cmdDB2;
daDB2.Fill(dsDB2,"SIMPLE_TBL");
```

As shown here, the data adapter handles the connection and the command and then fills the dataset. So the dataset knows nothing of where the data came from, which is useful when data can now arrive from so many sources. The other feature of this design methodology is that the connection is no longer the focus when working with data. More on this in a minute, but first we'll cover the dataset.

DATASET

The DataSet is a new structure capable of aggregating data on the client. The RecordSet that was the focus of ADO has been supplanted by the DataTable in .NET, though it should be noted that a DataTable is a more advanced structure. A DataSet is capable of holding multiple DataTables and maintaining relationships between them. In Listing 12-3, the DataSet dsDB2 is filled by the DataAdapter daDB2; and the DataSet creates a new table within itself called SIMPLE_TBL, in this case that will hold the data.

Now, picking up from the previous thought, the DataSet knows nothing of the connection. It is filled with data, and if the connection disappears there is no problem, unlike RecordSets that were dependent on the connection to supply the data. The importance of this is that connections are often performance killers for data servers, so the DataSet assists in keeping the focus on using data in a disconnected manner that relieves the server from maintaining a large number of open connections.

The downside to this strategy is that the code becomes somewhat more complicated, and consideration must be given to updating data that is altered while disconnected from the server. Also, care must be taken when filling a DataSet, because accidentally filling a DataSet with a million records will result in resource and performance issues on the client. However, used effectively, ADO.NET should reduce server load, enhance client responsiveness, and simplify some client display operations.

ADO performance

In comparison to ADO.NET, ADO now seems very basic. Establish a connection to data, open a recordset from the connection, and use the data. The only real choice to make is whether the recordset should be client-side or server-side.

CLIENT-SIDE RECORDSET

With a client-side RecordSet, the data in the recordset is transferred to the client. The advantage of such a RecordSet is that after the client has the data, working with the data is fast. Another advantage of the client-side RecordSet is that it does not require an ongoing connection with the server, which can be very harmful to the goal of scalability. The disadvantage of this RecordSet is the initial transfer of data to the client.

SERVER-SIDE RECORDSET

The server-side `RecordSet` avoids the problems of transferring the whole result of a query to the client when the `RecordSet` is opened. With the server-side `RecordSet`, the data is held at the server and transferred on an as-needed basis. This prevents unneeded data from traversing the network, and it improves the response time when opening the `RecordSet`. The problem with server-side `RecordSet` is that they hold an open connection to the server for the duration of the `RecordSet`'s use.

The Effect of Connection Type on Applications

Once again, we want to examine the impact of the connection choice on a range of applications created with .NET. Here, two sets of applications will be examined. The first set is a WinForm and an N-Tier WinForm application, and the second set is an ASP.NET and an N-Tier ASP.NET application. In each case, we compare the pros and cons of different connectivity choices, looking for impacts on either performance or functionality.

WinForm application

The application in Listing 12-4 is a simple WinForm application that implements a table component using an ADO.NET `DataSet`. In addition, this example demonstrates both an ODBC connection and an OLE-DB connection. The program essentially has two parts. The first part uses an ODBC connection to populate the records in a detail table, and the second part uses an OLE-DB connection to fill a dataset. The dataset that is created contains two tables with a one-to-many relationship.

Listing 12-4: A WinForm Application Using DB/2

```
using System;
using System.Timers;
using System.Drawing;
using System.Collections;
using System.ComponentModel;
using System.Windows.Forms;
using System.Data;
using Microsoft.Data.Odbc;
using System.Data.OleDb;

namespace myDB2WinForm
{
```

```csharp
/// <summary>
/// Summary description for frmMain.
/// </summary>
public class frmMain : System.Windows.Forms.Form
{
    private System.Windows.Forms.Button cmdInsert;
    private System.Windows.Forms.TextBox txtIterations;
    private System.Windows.Forms.TextBox txtConnectTime;
    private System.Windows.Forms.TextBox txtInsertTime;
    private System.Windows.Forms.TextBox txtCreateTime;
    private System.Windows.Forms.TextBox txtTotalTime;
    private System.Windows.Forms.Button cmdFill;

    private OleDbConnection connDB2;
    private OleDbDataAdapter daDB2;
    private OleDbCommand cmdDB2;
    private DataSet dsDB2;
    private System.Windows.Forms.DataGrid dgSimple;

    /// <summary>
    /// Required designer variable.
    /// </summary>
    private System.ComponentModel.Container components = null;

    public frmMain()
    {
        //
        // Required for Windows Form Designer support
        //
        InitializeComponent();
}

    /// <summary>
    /// Clean up any resources being used.
    /// </summary>
    protected override void Dispose( bool disposing )
    {
        if( disposing )
        {
            if (components != null)
            {
                components.Dispose();
            }
```

Continued

Listing 12-4 *(Continued)*

```
        }
    base.Dispose( disposing );
}

#region Windows Form Designer generated code
/// <summary>
/// Required method for Designer support - do not modify
/// the contents of this method with the code editor.
/// </summary>
private void InitializeComponent()
{
    this.cmdInsert = new System.Windows.Forms.Button();
    this.txtIterations = new System.Windows.Forms.TextBox();
    this.txtConnectTime = new
      System.Windows.Forms.TextBox();
    this.txtInsertTime = new System.Windows.Forms.TextBox();
    this.txtCreateTime = new System.Windows.Forms.TextBox();
    this.txtTotalTime = new System.Windows.Forms.TextBox();
    this.cmdFill = new System.Windows.Forms.Button();
    this.dgSimple = new System.Windows.Forms.DataGrid();
    ((System.ComponentModel.ISupportInitialize)
      (this.dgSimple)).BeginInit();
    this.SuspendLayout();
    //
    // cmdInsert
    //
    this.cmdInsert.Location =
      new System.Drawing.Point(12, 12);
    this.cmdInsert.Name = "cmdInsert";
    this.cmdInsert.Size = new System.Drawing.Size(84, 28);
    this.cmdInsert.TabIndex = 0;
    this.cmdInsert.Text = "Insert";
    this.cmdInsert.Click +=
      new System.EventHandler(this.cmdInsert_Click);
    //
    // txtIterations
    //
    this.txtIterations.Location =
      new System.Drawing.Point(144, 12);
    this.txtIterations.Name = "txtIterations";
    this.txtIterations.Size =
      new System.Drawing.Size(108, 20);
    this.txtIterations.TabIndex = 1;
```

```
this.txtIterations.Text = "";
//
// txtConnectTime
//
this.txtConnectTime.Location =
  new System.Drawing.Point(144, 36);
this.txtConnectTime.Name = "txtConnectTime";
this.txtConnectTime.Size =
  new System.Drawing.Size(108, 20);
this.txtConnectTime.TabIndex = 2;
this.txtConnectTime.Text = "";
//
// txtInsertTime
//
this.txtInsertTime.Location =
  new System.Drawing.Point(144, 60);
this.txtInsertTime.Name = "txtInsertTime";
this.txtInsertTime.Size =
  new System.Drawing.Size(108, 20);
this.txtInsertTime.TabIndex = 3;
this.txtInsertTime.Text = "";
//
// txtCreateTime
//
this.txtCreateTime.Location =
  new System.Drawing.Point(144, 84);
this.txtCreateTime.Name = "txtCreateTime";
this.txtCreateTime.Size =
  new System.Drawing.Size(108, 20);
this.txtCreateTime.TabIndex = 4;
this.txtCreateTime.Text = "";
//
// txtTotalTime
//
this.txtTotalTime.Location =
  new System.Drawing.Point(144, 108);
this.txtTotalTime.Name = "txtTotalTime";
this.txtTotalTime.Size =
  new System.Drawing.Size(108, 20);
this.txtTotalTime.TabIndex = 5;
this.txtTotalTime.Text = "";
//
// cmdFill
```

Continued

Listing 12-4 *(Continued)*

```
//
this.cmdFill.Location =
  new System.Drawing.Point(12, 136);
this.cmdFill.Name = "cmdFill";
this.cmdFill.Size = new System.Drawing.Size(84, 28);
this.cmdFill.TabIndex = 6;
this.cmdFill.Text = "Fill";
this.cmdFill.Click +=
  new System.EventHandler(this.cmdFill_Click);
//
// dgSimple
//
this.dgSimple.DataMember = "";
this.dgSimple.HeaderForeColor =
  System.Drawing.SystemColors.ControlText;
this.dgSimple.Location =
  new System.Drawing.Point(12, 180);
this.dgSimple.Name = "dgSimple";
this.dgSimple.Size = new System.Drawing.Size(428, 172);
this.dgSimple.TabIndex = 7;
//
// frmMain
//
this.AutoScaleBaseSize = new System.Drawing.Size(5, 13);
this.ClientSize = new System.Drawing.Size(452, 361);
this.Controls.AddRange(
  new System.Windows.Forms.Control[] {
    this.dgSimple,
    this.cmdFill,
    this.txtTotalTime,
    this.txtCreateTime,
    this.txtInsertTime,
    this.txtConnectTime,
    this.txtIterations,
    this.cmdInsert});
this.Name = "frmMain";
this.Text = "WinForm Application";
((System.ComponentModel.ISupportInitialize)
  (this.dgSimple)).EndInit();
this.ResumeLayout(false);

}
```

```
#endregion

/// <summary>
/// The main entry point for the application.
/// </summary>
[STAThread]
static void Main()
{
    Application.Run(new frmMain());
}


private void cmdInsert_Click(object sender,
                            System.EventArgs e)
{
    DateTime dtStart;
    DateTime dtEnd;
    String strConn = "DSN=MYBOOKDB2;UID=db2admin;" +
                    "PWD=xxxxxx;DATABASE=MYBOOK;";
    OdbcConnection myODBC =
        new OdbcConnection(strConn);
    OdbcTransaction myTxn;
    String strCommand =
        "INSERT INTO JCROFT.SIMPLE_TBL (SIMPLE_DESC)" +
        "VALUES ('ODBC INSERT');";
    OdbcCommand cmd = new OdbcCommand();

    try
    {
        dtStart = DateTime.Now;
        myODBC.Open();
        dtEnd = DateTime.Now;
        txtConnectTime.Text = (dtEnd-dtStart).ToString();
        cmd.Connection = myODBC;

        // Profile establishing inserting records
        dtStart = DateTime.Now;
        for (long i=1;i<10001;i++)
        {
            for (long j=0;j<4;j++)
            {
                cmd.CommandText =
                    "INSERT INTO JCROFT.SIMPLE_DETAIL_TBL " +
                    "(SIMPLE_ID,SIMPLE_DET_DESC) " +
```

Continued

Listing 12-4 *(Continued)*

```
                    "VALUES (" + i + ",'ODBC INSERT');";
                cmd.ExecuteNonQuery();
            }
        }

        dtEnd = DateTime.Now;
        txtTotalTime.Text = (dtEnd-dtStart).ToString();
    }
    catch (Exception ex)
    {
        Console.Write(ex.Message);
        Console.Write(ex.StackTrace);
    }

    myODBC.Close();

}

private void cmdFill_Click(object sender,
                           System.EventArgs e)
{
    String strConn = "Provider=IBMDADB2;" +
        "DSN=MYBOOK;UID=db2admin;PWD=0root0r;";
    String strSIMPLE_TBL =
        "SELECT * FROM JCROFT.SIMPLE_TBL WHERE " +
        "SIMPLE_ID < 101;" ;
    String strSIMPLE_DETAIL_TBL =
        "SELECT * FROM JCROFT.SIMPLE_DETAIL_TBL " +
        "WHERE SIMPLE_ID < 101;";
    connDB2 =
        new OleDbConnection(strConn);
    connDB2.Open();
    daDB2 = new OleDbDataAdapter();
    cmdDB2 = new OleDbCommand();
    dsDB2 = new DataSet();
    cmdDB2.Connection = connDB2;
    cmdDB2.CommandText = strSIMPLE_TBL;
    daDB2.SelectCommand = cmdDB2;
    daDB2.Fill(dsDB2,"SIMPLE_TBL");
    cmdDB2.CommandText = strSIMPLE_DETAIL_TBL;
    daDB2.SelectCommand = cmdDB2;
    daDB2.Fill(dsDB2,"SIMPLE_DETAIL_TBL");
```

```
DataColumn simpleCol;
DataColumn simpleDetailCol;
simpleCol =
  dsDB2.Tables["SIMPLE_TBL"].Columns["SIMPLE_ID"];
simpleDetailCol =
  dsDB2.Tables["SIMPLE_DETAIL_TBL"].Columns["SIMPLE_ID"];
// Create DataRelation.
DataRelation simpleRelation;
simpleRelation = new DataRelation("SimpleDetail",
  simpleCol, simpleDetailCol);
// Add the relation to the DataSet.
dsDB2.Relations.Add(simpleRelation);

dgSimple.DataSource = dsDB2;
connDB2.Close();
      }
    }
}
```

There are a couple of additional comments to be made about the components of
this program. In general, the ODBC connection seems to perform better than the
OLE-DB connection in terms of connection time, data updates, and data selects.
Also, although it may seem cumbersome, it is worth setting up the relations
between the data gathered into the dataset. In this example, when the dataset is
assigned to the data grid, the data grid becomes aware of the master-detail relationship and displays the data accordingly. This master-detail relationship also
enables consistent behaviors such as cascading deletes and referential integrity.

N-Tier WinForm application

This example illustrates how a form might employ a remote object in an N-Tier
configuration. Generally, the reason for structuring an application in this manner is
to either abstract business logic from the client application to the server or to
engage in a distributed transaction. The case for using an N-Tier configuration to
abstract business rules from a client application is not always clear cut, given that
the behavior of the client is often affected by the business rules. However, if the
client needs to execute a distributed transaction, the best solution is almost always
to engage COM+ and the DTC.

In Listing 12-5, the code for the COM+ component that is employed by the
application in Listing 12-6 is shown. This is a simple component that inserts
records into the database and tracks the time to connect and the time to insert. Also,
the number of inserts performed may be altered using the CommandIterations
property. The component explicitly declares an interface, which is then implemented by the control.

Listing 12-5: A COM+ Component

```
using System;
using System.Windows.Forms;
using System.Data;
using System.EnterpriseServices;
using System.Runtime.InteropServices;
using System.Reflection;
using System.Data.OleDb;

namespace myDB2COMPlusControl
{
    /// <summary>
    /// Summary description for myDB2COMPlusControl.
    /// </summary>

    [System.Runtime.InteropServices.ComVisible(true)]
    public interface ImyDB2Interface
    {
        int InsertData();
        String ConnectTime
        {
            get;
        }
        String InsertTime
        {
            get;
        }
        int CommandIterations
        {
            get;
            set;
        }
    }

    [ObjectPooling(true)]
    [JustInTimeActivation(true)]
    [EventTrackingEnabled(true)]
    [Transaction(TransactionOption.Supported)]
    [ClassInterface(ClassInterfaceType.None)]
    public class myDB2COMPlusControlClass :
        System.EnterpriseServices.ServicedComponent, ImyDB2Interface
    {
        DateTime dtStart;
        DateTime dtEnd;
```

```
String strConn = "Provider=IBMDADB2;" +
                 "DSN=MYBOOK;UID=db2admin;PWD=0root0r;";
String strCommand =
    "INSERT INTO JCROFT.SIMPLE_TBL (SIMPLE_DESC)" +
    "VALUES ('COM PLUS INSERT');";
OleDbConnection myOleDb;
OleDbTransaction myTxn;
OleDbCommand cmd;
String strConnectTime;
String strInsertTime;
int iCmdIterations;

public myDB2COMPlusControlClass()
{
    strConnectTime = "NA";
    strInsertTime = "NA";
    iCmdIterations = 1000;
}

public void Construct() {   }

protected override void Activate() {   }

protected override void Deactivate() {   }

protected override Boolean CanBePooled()
{
    return true;
}

public int InsertData()
{
    Connect();

    cmd.CommandText = strCommand;
    cmd.CommandType = CommandType.Text;
    cmd.Connection = myOleDb;

    dtStart = DateTime.Now;
    for (long i=0;i<iCmdIterations;i++)
    {
        cmd.ExecuteNonQuery();
    }
```

Continued

Listing 12-5 *(Continued)*

```csharp
        dtEnd = DateTime.Now;
        strInsertTime = (dtEnd - dtStart).ToString();

        Disconnect();

        return 0;
    }

protected void Connect()
{
    // Profile opening connections
    myOleDb = new OleDbConnection(strConn);
    cmd = new OleDbCommand();

    try
    {
        dtStart = DateTime.Now;
        myOleDb.Open();
        dtEnd = DateTime.Now;
        //MessageBox.Show("Connect: " + (dtEnd-dtStart));
        strConnectTime = (dtEnd - dtStart).ToString();
    }
    catch (Exception e)
    {
        MessageBox.Show(e.Message);
        MessageBox.Show(e.StackTrace);
    }
    //finally
    //{
    //    myOleDb.Close();
    //}
}

protected void Disconnect()
{
    myOleDb.Close();
}

public String ConnectTime
{
    get
    {
```

```
                return strConnectTime;
            }
        }

    public String InsertTime
    {
        get
        {
            return strInsertTime;
        }
    }

    public int CommandIterations
    {
        get
        {
            return iCmdIterations;
        }
        set
        {
            iCmdIterations = value;
        }
    }
    }
}
```

After building this component, two additional steps must be taken for the component to be enlisted by COM+ Services. First, the component must be installed into the global assembly cache (GAC) with the following command:

```
gacutil /i myDB2COMPlusControl.dll
```

Then the component must be registered with the system using the next command:

```
regasm /tlb myDB2COMPlusControll.dll
```

After that, the control will be available to COM+ Services, and the component does not need to be manually installed into COM+ Services. If you choose to manually install the component, you will only be importing a registered type; you will not be installing the DLL that was generated by the build process.

The code in Listing 12-6 demonstrates a WinForm application that enlists the prior component, now registered with COM+.

Listing 12-6: An N-Tier WinForm Application

```csharp
using System;
using System.Timers;
using System.Drawing;
using System.Collections;
using System.ComponentModel;
using System.Windows.Forms;
using System.Data;
using System.EnterpriseServices;
using myDB2COMPlusControl;

namespace myDB2WinForm
{
    /// <summary>
    /// Summary description for frmMain.
    /// </summary>
    public class frmMain : System.Windows.Forms.Form
    {
        private System.Windows.Forms.Button cmdInsert;
        private System.Windows.Forms.TextBox txtIterations;
        private System.Windows.Forms.TextBox txtConnectTime;
        private System.Windows.Forms.TextBox txtInsertTime;
        private System.Windows.Forms.TextBox txtCreateTime;
        private System.Windows.Forms.TextBox txtTotalTime;
        /// <summary>
        /// Required designer variable.
        /// </summary>
        private System.ComponentModel.Container components = null;

        public frmMain()
        {
            //
            // Required for Windows Form Designer support
            //
            InitializeComponent();
        }

        /// <summary>
        /// Clean up any resources being used.
        /// </summary>
        protected override void Dispose( bool disposing )
        {
            if( disposing )
            {
```

```
            if (components != null)
            {
                components.Dispose();
            }
        }
        base.Dispose( disposing );
    }

    #region Windows Form Designer generated code
    /// <summary>
    /// Required method for Designer support - do not modify
    /// the contents of this method with the code editor.
    /// </summary>
    private void InitializeComponent()
    {
        this.cmdInsert = new System.Windows.Forms.Button();
        this.txtIterations = new System.Windows.Forms.TextBox();
        this.txtConnectTime =
            new System.Windows.Forms.TextBox();
        this.txtInsertTime = new System.Windows.Forms.TextBox();
        this.txtCreateTime = new System.Windows.Forms.TextBox();
        this.txtTotalTime = new System.Windows.Forms.TextBox();
        this.SuspendLayout();
        //
        // cmdInsert
        //
        this.cmdInsert.Location =
            new System.Drawing.Point(12, 12);
        this.cmdInsert.Name = "cmdInsert";
        this.cmdInsert.Size = new System.Drawing.Size(84, 28);
        this.cmdInsert.TabIndex = 0;
        this.cmdInsert.Text = "Insert";
        this.cmdInsert.Click +=
            new System.EventHandler(this.cmdInsert_Click);
        //
        // txtIterations
        //
        this.txtIterations.Location =
            new System.Drawing.Point(144, 12);
        this.txtIterations.Name = "txtIterations";
        this.txtIterations.Size =
            new System.Drawing.Size(108, 20);
        this.txtIterations.TabIndex = 1;
```

Continued

Listing 12-6 *(Continued)*

```
            this.txtIterations.Text = "";
            //
            // txtConnectTime
            //
            this.txtConnectTime.Location =
                new System.Drawing.Point(144, 36);
            this.txtConnectTime.Name = "txtConnectTime";
            this.txtConnectTime.Size =
                new System.Drawing.Size(108, 20);
            this.txtConnectTime.TabIndex = 2;
            this.txtConnectTime.Text = "";
            //
            // txtInsertTime
            //
            this.txtInsertTime.Location =
                new System.Drawing.Point(144, 60);
            this.txtInsertTime.Name = "txtInsertTime";
            this.txtInsertTime.Size =
                new System.Drawing.Size(108, 20);
            this.txtInsertTime.TabIndex = 3;
            this.txtInsertTime.Text = "";
            //
            // txtCreateTime
            //
            this.txtCreateTime.Location =
                new System.Drawing.Point(144, 84);
            this.txtCreateTime.Name = "txtCreateTime";
            this.txtCreateTime.Size =
                new System.Drawing.Size(108, 20);
            this.txtCreateTime.TabIndex = 4;
            this.txtCreateTime.Text = "";
            //
            // txtTotalTime
            //
            this.txtTotalTime.Location =
                new System.Drawing.Point(144, 108);
            this.txtTotalTime.Name = "txtTotalTime";
            this.txtTotalTime.Size =
                new System.Drawing.Size(108, 20);
            this.txtTotalTime.TabIndex = 5;
            this.txtTotalTime.Text = "";
            //
            // frmMain
```

```
        //
        this.AutoScaleBaseSize = new System.Drawing.Size(5, 13);
        this.ClientSize = new System.Drawing.Size(292, 273);
        this.Controls.AddRange(
          new System.Windows.Forms.Control[] {
             this.txtTotalTime,
             this.txtCreateTime,
             this.txtInsertTime,
             this.txtConnectTime,
             this.txtIterations,
             this.cmdInsert});
        this.Name = "frmMain";
        this.Text = "WinForm Application";
        this.ResumeLayout(false);

    }
#endregion

/// <summary>
/// The main entry point for the application.
/// </summary>
[STAThread]
static void Main()
{
    Application.Run(new frmMain());
}

private void cmdInsert_Click(object sender,
                             System.EventArgs e)
{
    myDB2COMPlusControlClass myDB2Control;
    int i;
    DateTime tStart;
    DateTime tEnd;

    tStart = DateTime.Now;
    myDB2Control = new myDB2COMPlusControlClass();
    tEnd = DateTime.Now;
    txtCreateTime.Text = (tEnd - tStart).ToString();

    myDB2Control.InsertData();
    txtConnectTime.Text = myDB2Control.ConnectTime;
    txtInsertTime.Text = myDB2Control.InsertTime;
    txtIterations.Text =
```

Continued

Listing 12-6 *(Continued)*

```
              myDB2Control.CommandIterations.ToString();
          tEnd = DateTime.Now;
          txtTotalTime.Text = (tEnd - tStart).ToString();
      }
   }
}
```

In this example, some issues come to light. One is that, whether you employ manual or auto registration for the component object, creation time is about the same. Another point relates to object pooling, which has a very significant impact on object creation time. Object pooling reduced the creation time for a COM application by 75 percent and reduced the creation time for the .NET application even more.

Summary

This chapter addresses a number of topics in conjunction with IBM's DB/2 Universal Database. Some shortcomings of the OLE-DB driver were pointed out, and the ODBC driver provides a number of configuration options that should be kept in mind. Overall, the ODBC connections performed marginally better than the OLE-DB connections. Both connection pooling and object pooling showed the benefits expected from those optimizations. Further, no glaring performance issues — that is, no gotchas — came to light. Overall, running .NET code against DB/2 is a satisfying combination.

Chapter 13

MySQL

MYSQL IS A WELL-PROVEN and highly reliable database server. The initial design strategy behind MySQL was to create a data server that was Web-oriented (that is, robust, providing data reliably on a 24/7/365 basis, and retrieval optimized, getting data from the database as fast as possible). The second design goal stemmed from the fact that there is far more data retrieval than data modification performed on the Web, especially at the outset. As a consequence, however, support for transactions was initially left out of MySQL so that the associated overhead could be removed allowing data to be retrieved more quickly. That is, in a transactional system employing isolation beyond read uncommitted, even selected records require locking or versioning, which will necessarily increase retrieval time.

Also in the name of efficiency, only table-level locks were supported. These are the fastest locks to secure on a table, but they do introduce problems. In situations where one table is frequently updated and scanned, performance problems will arise. So, primarily for these two reasons, lack of transactions and table-only locking, many people considered MySQL inappropriate for the enterprise. But in the past couple of years, MySQL has added support for additional table types that resolve these issues by providing row-level locking and transaction support. So with stability, fine-grained locking, and support for transactions, as well as an excellent price-point, no one can doubt that MySQL has a role to play in the enterprise.

Although MySQL was developed and has evolved primarily on the Linux platform, its robustness and reputation have led it to the NT platform among others. Currently pre-packaged downloads exist for 12 platforms at www.mysql.org, ranging from Win32 to NT across several flavors of Unix to the MacOS X. Both ODBC and OLE-DB drivers exist for the NT platform, as well as Windows-based management tools. The management tools are not currently at the same level as the graphical tools for the other database systems discussed in this book; however, with the growing use of MySQL on NT, we should expect that they soon will be. Meanwhile, in this chapter, the focus will remain on the command-line tools, mostly because these tools are available across all platforms.

MySQL is open source, which means the source code is available. That means you can download and build your own version of MySQL that could have a different default behavior and configuration from the versions discussed in this chapter. The discussion here focuses on working with pre-built distributions of MySQL, particularly the latest development version MySQL-Max 4.0.1. So, discussions that are concerned with changing the configuration of MySQL assume that you're starting with a given version, and they likely won't mention compile-time configuration options.

Connection Choice

MySQL supports a number of connection methods from a wide variety of programming languages and environments including C, Java, Python, and, most notably, Perl. MySQL and Perl together supply the *M* and *P* of the LAMP Web development strategy. The acronym LAMP stands for Linux, Apache, MySQL, and Perl, which has been an effective and widespread combination of Web-development tools. It is in the LAMP arena that MySQL has established itself as a solid and robust tool for handling large amounts of data. However, here we of course examine using MySQL in conjunction with Visual Studio .NET, and consider the connection mechanisms available within that context.

As illustrated with the other databases, the connection choice that you make can significantly affect your performance. Here we examine three different connection methods for Windows-based clients. The first is the MyODBC driver, which provides generic connectivity on Windows platforms for custom database clients as well as applications like Excel and Access. Second, we look at the MyOLE-DB driver; though it is currently at the beta level and is missing some features, we look at what it currently provides. Finally, we examine making connections using the MySQL API and making calls from C# and managed C++.

MyODBC driver

The MyODBC drivers were developed by MySQL AB under the GPL. At the time of writing, the MyODBC driver is commonly available at revision 2.50, which is the stable release, and at revision 3.51, which is the development revision. MyODBC 2.50 driver is a 32-bit driver based on the ODBC 2.50 specification, while MyODBC 3.51 is a 32-bit driver based on the ODBC 3.5x specification. You can download both of these drivers from www.mysql.com as part of a Windows setup package that will install the drivers. Listing 13-1 demonstrates connecting to a MySQL database using the ODBC 3.51 driver.

Listing 13-1: Connecting to a MySQL Database Using the MyODBC Driver in .NET

```csharp
using System;
using Microsoft.Data.Odbc;

namespace mySQLODBCConnectDemo
{
    /// <summary>
    /// Summary description for mySQLODBCConnectClass.
    /// </summary>
    class mySQLODBCConnectClass
    {
        /// <summary>
        /// The main entry point for the application.
        /// </summary>
        [STAThread]
        static void Main(string[] args)
        {
            //
            // TODO: Add code to start application here
            //
            String strConn = "DRIVER={MySQL ODBC 3.51 Driver};" +
                            "SERVER=localhost;UID=Administrator;" +
                            "PASSWORD=xxxx;DATABASE=myBook";
            OdbcConnection myConnection =
              new OdbcConnection(strConn);
            try
            {
                myConnection.Open();
                Console.WriteLine("Connection Open.");
                myConnection.Close();
            }
            catch (Exception e)
            {
                Console.WriteLine("Connection Failed.");
                Console.Write(e.StackTrace);
            }
        }
    }
}
```

Listing 13-2 builds on Listing 13-1 to show an update performed using the ODBC driver against a MyISAM table.

Listing 13-2: Performing an Update of a MyISAM Table Using the MyODBC Driver in .NET

```csharp
using System;
using System.Data;
using Microsoft.Data.Odbc;

namespace mySQLODBCConnectDemo
{
    /// <summary>
    /// Summary description for mySQLODBCConnectClass.
    /// </summary>
    class mySQLODBCConnectClass
    {
        /// <summary>
        /// The main entry point for the application.
        /// </summary>
        [STAThread]
        static void Main(string[] args)
        {
            //
            // TODO: Add code to start application here
            //
            String strConn =
                "DSN=myBookDemo;UID=Administrator;PASSWORD=xxxxxx;";
            String strCmd = "INSERT INTO SIMPLE_TBL ( SIMPLE_DESC )
                VALUES ('THIS IS A TEST.');";
            OdbcConnection myConnection = new
                OdbcConnection(strConn);

            try
            {
                myConnection.Open();
                Console.WriteLine("Connection Open.");
                OdbcCommand cmd = new OdbcCommand();
                cmd.CommandText = strCmd;
                cmd.CommandType = CommandType.Text;
                cmd.Connection = myConnection;
                DateTime dtStart = DateTime.Now;
                for (int i=0;i<10000;i++)
                {
                    cmd.ExecuteNonQuery();
                }
                DateTime dtEnd = DateTime.Now;
                Console.WriteLine("Run time: " + (dtEnd-dtStart));
                cmd.Connection.Close();
            }
```

```
            catch (OdbcException odbc_e)
            {
                Console.WriteLine(odbc_e.Message);
            }
            catch (Exception e)
            {
                Console.WriteLine(e.Message);
            }
        }
    }
}
```

The prior program simply inserts 10,000 records into the database and exits. The insert statement is passed to the database using the `ExecuteNonQuery` that is typically used to execute statements that won't return any data rows.

MyOLE-DB driver

The MyOLE-DB provider used here was developed by Swsoft. Version 1.0 is only a base-level provider, implementing only the mandatory interfaces. So, although it may not be a robust OLE-DB implementation, it still provides the associated benefits of working with controls that expect an ADO interface. Listing 13-3 provides an example using the OLE-DB data provider.

Listing 13-3: Connecting to a MySQL Database Using the MyOLE-DB Driver in .NET

```
using System;
using System.Data.OleDb;

namespace mySQLOLEDBConnectDemo
{
    /// <summary>
    /// Summary description for mySQLOLEDBConnectClass.
    /// </summary>
    class mySQLOLEDBConnectClass
    {
        /// <summary>
        /// The main entry point for the application.
        /// </summary>
        [STAThread]
        static void Main(string[] args)
        {
            //
            // TODO: Add code to start application here
```

Continued

Listing 13-3 *(Continued)*

```
                //
                String strConn = "Provider=MySQLProv;" +
                                 "Data Source=myBookDemo;" +
                                 "server=localhost;DB=myBook";
                                 // Alternately replace the prior
                                 // two lines with the following:
                                 // "Data Source=myBook";
                OleDbConnection myOleDb =
                  new OleDbConnection(strConn);
                try
                {
                    myOleDb.Open();
                    Console.WriteLine("Connection Open.");
                    myOleDb.Close();
                }
                catch (Exception e)
                {
                    Console.WriteLine("Connection Failed.");
                    Console.Write(e.StackTrace);
                }
            }
        }
}
```

Once again, the technique for establishing the connection is pretty straightforward; the most important aspect of establishing the connection is getting the correct connection string. The program shown in Listing 13-4 expands on Listing 13-3 and performs a batch of inserts on a MyISAM table.

Listing 13-4: Inserting Records into a MySQL Database Using the MyOLE-DB Driver in .NET

```
using System;
using System.Data.OleDb;

namespace mySQLOLEDBConnectDemo
{
    /// <summary>
    /// Summary description for mySQLOLEDBConnectClass.
    /// </summary>
    class mySQLOLEDBConnectClass
    {
        /// <summary>
        /// The main entry point for the application.
        /// </summary>
```

```
    [STAThread]
    static void Main(string[] args)
    {
        //
        // TODO: Add code to start application here
        //
        String strConn = "Provider=MySQLProv;" +
                         "Data Source=myBook;";

        OleDbConnection myOleDb =
            new OleDbConnection(strConn);
        try
        {
            myOleDb.Open();
            Console.WriteLine("Connection Open.");
            OleDbCommand myOleDbCmd = myOleDb.CreateCommand();
            myOleDbCmd.CommandText =
              "INSERT INTO SIMPLE_TBL (SIMPLE_DESC) VALUES
                ('This is an OleDb test.');";
            DateTime dtStart = DateTime.Now;
            for (int i=0;i<10000;i++)
            {
                myOleDbCmd.ExecuteNonQuery();
            }
            DateTime dtEnd = DateTime.Now;
            Console.WriteLine("Run time: " + (dtEnd-dtStart));
            myOleDb.Close();
        }
        catch (Exception e)
        {
            Console.WriteLine("Connection Failed.");
            Console.Write(e.StackTrace);
        }
    }
}
}
```

The preceding program simply inserts 10,000 records into the table using the MyOLE-DB driver. It should be noted that this program runs substantially slower than the previous ODBC program that inserted the same number of records.

MySQL API

Finally, if you don't want to use an ODBC or OLE-DB driver, or requirements necessitate that you can't use ODBC, you may use the MySQL API directly. The MySQL distribution provides a dynamic link library (DLL) and a statically linked library along with header files to write programs in C or C++, which can connect to and interact with a MySQL server.

Listing 13-5 shows a simple program that uses the libmysql.dll to connect to the MySQL server. The project was created as a C++ application with managed extensions. Two files were included from the MySQL\include directory, and the project was modified to link to the libmysql.lib, the stub for the libmysql.dll. After that, the program simply attempts to connect to the MySQL server and then prints a message to the console indicating success or failure.

Listing 13-5: Connecting to a MySQL Database Using the MySQL API in .NET

```
// This is the main project file for VC++
// application project generated using
// an Application Wizard.

#include "stdafx.h"

#using <mscorlib.dll>
#include <tchar.h>

#include "\mysql\include\config-win.h"
#include "\mysql\include\mysql.h"

using namespace System;

// This is the entry point for this application
int _tmain(void)
{
    // Basic database connection using MySQL API
    MYSQL *myDB = mysql_init(NULL);

    myDB = mysql_real_connect(myDB, NULL, NULL, NULL, NULL,
                              MYSQL_PORT, NULL, 0);
    if (myDB)
    {
        Console::WriteLine(S"Connection Established.");
        mysql_close(myDB);
    }
    else
    {
        Console::WriteLine(S"Connection Failed.");
    }

    return 0;
}
```

Listing 13-6 expands on Listing 13-5 by demonstrating the insertion of records into a MyISAM table.

Listing 13-6: Inserting Records into a MyISAM Database Using the MySQL API in .NET

```cpp
// This is the main project file for VC++
// application project generated using
// an Application Wizard.

#include "stdafx.h"

#using <mscorlib.dll>
#include <tchar.h>

#include "\mysql\include\config-win.h"
#include "\mysql\include\mysql.h"

using namespace System;

// This is the entry point for this application
int _tmain(void)
{
    // Basic database connection using MySQL API
    MYSQL *myDB = mysql_init(NULL);

    myDB = mysql_real_connect(myDB, "localhost", NULL, NULL,
                            "myBook", MYSQL_PORT, NULL, 0);
    if (myDB)
    {
        Console::WriteLine(S"Connection Established.");
        Console::WriteLine(S"Server:   {0}",
          new String(mysql_get_server_info(myDB)));
        Console::WriteLine(S"Host:     {0}",
          new String(mysql_get_host_info(myDB)));
        Console::WriteLine(S"Client:   {0}",
          new String(mysql_get_client_info()));


        DateTime dtStart = DateTime::Now;

        for (int i=0;i<10000;i++)
            mysql_query(myDB,"INSERT INTO SIMPLE_TBL (SIMPLE_DESC)
                            VALUES ('This is a C++ test.')");
```

Continued

Listing 13-6 *(Continued)*

```
        DateTime dtEnd = DateTime::Now;
        Console::WriteLine(S"Run time: {0}",
                            (dtEnd-dtStart).ToString());

        mysql_close(myDB);
    }
    else
    {
        Console::WriteLine(S"Connection Failed.");
    }

    return 0;
}
```

It's worth noting here that this connection method, the C API, provided the best performance for both this and some other test scripts that were written to test the relative performance of the connection methods.

MySQL Table Types

Unlike the other, previously covered, databases in this book, MySQL has a modular design that allows different table types to be used by the server. The type of table that is used can greatly impact the performance of the database and its capabilities. Table 13-1 itemizes the different table types supported by MySQL; a more detailed discussion of the table types follows.

TABLE 13-1 THE MULTIPLE TABLE TYPES SUPPORTED BY MYSQL

Table Type	Description
ISAM	The original table type used by MySQL. It has been deprecated and, therefore, is no longer recommended. It is still available but will probably go away with the release of 4.1.
MyISAM	The new, default table type used by MySQL. Contains some improvements over the ISAM format.
Heap	This is a volatile, in-memory table type that provides very fast access to data but is not durable. That is, the data only exists in memory and if the system fails, the data is not saved.

Table Type	Description
Merge	Provides the ability to use a collection of identical MyISAM tables as a single table.
InnoDB	Table type developed by InnoBase Oy that passes the ACID test (outlined in Chapter 4) and provides row-level locking. It is shipped with MySQL Max and supported by MySQL AB.
BDB	Berkley database tables handler developed by Sleepycat Software that supports transactions and page-level locking.
Gemini	Table type developed by NuSphere to provide transactions that pass the ACID test with row-level locking. It is still in alpha at the time of this writing.

So with seven different table types, MySQL provides the database developer the opportunity to make some additional design decisions. Given that the Gemini handler is not fully functional and the ISAM table type is no longer recommended for use, the focus will be on the other five table types.

MyISAM

The first table type to discuss is the MyISAM table type. This table type represents an enhancement over the original ISAM table type. The table and its index are physically stored as two files with a third file containing the table definition; the data file contains a .myd extension, the index file has a .myi extension, and the data definition file has a .frm extension. Additionally, MyISAM:

◆ Uses OS-independent data storage with all data stored low-byte first.

◆ Supports large files (up to 2^{63} bytes) on an OS that also supports large files.

◆ Internally supports AUTO_INCREMENT on one column per table.

◆ Has a default maximum key length of 500 bytes.

◆ Has a default maximum of 32 keys per table.

◆ Supports concurrent reads and inserts when there are no free blocks in the middle of the table.

MyISAM tables can be

◆ Compressed using the myisampack utility.

◆ Repaired using the myisamchk utility.

It's important to note that MyISAM tables do not support transactions, and they do not support concurrent reads and updates. MyISAM tables can support concurrent reads and inserts, but only if there are no empty blocks in the middle of the table. This situation may occur with logged data being appended to a table but not deleted from it or not updated in a manner that would leave gaps. So, in general, MyISAM tables will be good when there are mostly short reads or mostly short writes but not where there is a mix of reads and writes when some operations may be long-running.

The issues surrounding concurrency in MySQL are important for large databases. The specifics of concurrency and locking with MyISAM and InnoDB tables are found in the "Comparison of InnoDB and MyISAM Table Types" section later in this chapter. This description of the tables is intended to be more general.

Additionally MyISAM tables fall into one of three formats shown in Table 13-2, each of which has its own characteristics. The first two table formats are automatically assigned, while the third is the result of developer modification.

TABLE 13-2 THE MULTIPLE TABLE FORMATS SUPPORTED BY THE MYISAM TABLE TYPE

Table Type	Description
FIXED LENGTH	A table that contains no VARCHAR, TEXT, or BLOB columns.
DYNAMIC	A table that contains a VARCHAR, TEXT, or BLOB column, or a table created with ROW_FORMAT = dynamic option.
COMPRESSED	A table that has been compressed using the myisampack utility.

The fixed-length table format is used by default when creating a table that does not use fields with variable-length data, while the dynamic format is used by default when a table contains a field that can hold variable-length data. The difference between the two is the format of the individual rows; the rows in a dynamically formatted table have headers that indicate the length of the row, while rows in a fixed-length formatted table do not require any such header. So, tables that have a fixed-length format will generally be faster, though they may consume more disk space.

The compressed table format results from passing a table through the myisam-pack utility. This utility will compress the table providing the most efficient use of disk space of any of the formats, but there are two important items to keep in mind when employing the compressed format:

◆ The table will be read-only.

◆ Reading the table will require more time and processing power to decompress the data.

Nevertheless, if storage is very tight, as it may be with an embedded application, the compressed format may be very useful.

Merge

The second table type to address is the Merge table type. To be more specific, a merge table is not actually a table but a definition that allows multiple MyISAM tables to be treated like a single table. The behavior can be compared to what would happen if you created a view that consisted of a union of identically structured tables. Merge can be used to beneficially segment large amounts of data. However, Merge tables do not support replace, they require more open file handles, and AUTO_INCREMENT fields are not automatically updated on insert into the merge table.

Heap

The third table type, Heap, is quite interesting. A heap table exists only in memory, but all clients can see it like any other table. So, a heap table is permanently cached, and that makes a Heap table fast. The downside is that if the server is unexpectedly shut down, all data in the heap table is lost. Nevertheless, a Heap table can be useful for temporary tables or for holding relatively static but frequently referenced data in memory. With respect to the last point, a heap table that is too large could consume all available memory. Also, the performance benefit would be mitigated by the fact that frequently referenced rows in MyISAM tables will end up cached as well. Still, this intriguing table type can be put to good use. There are additional constraints on Heap tables; these are the central ones:

◆ Heap tables must have fixed-length records.

◆ Indexes will only be used with = and <=> (null safe equals).

◆ Heap tables do not support AUTO_INCREMENT.

◆ Heap tables do not support BLOB and TEXT fields.

One final note concerning Heap tables: Deleting records from a Heap table will free memory. Whether records are removed using DELETE, TRUNCATE, or DROP TABLE does not matter.

InnoDB

The most important features of the InnoDB table type are the support for ACID-compliant transactions and a high degree of concurrency. To be clear, InnoDB is not actually a table type but an alternate backend table handler that maintains its own table space and caching mechanisms. So, like the other databases mentioned in this book, and unlike MyISAM tables, the tables stored in InnoDB do not occupy their own files but a common table space. Furthermore, InnoDB provides row-level locking and Oracle-styled non-locking reads. All of this is aimed at improving multi-user concurrency for MySQL beyond its capabilities when MyISAM tables are used.

While MySQL-Max 3.23 and MySQL-Max 4.0.1 support InnoDB, neither is configured to use InnoDB by default with the installations that are provided for download. To activate InnoDB, some changes must be made to the my.cnf file. Table 13-3 lists the configuration parameters for InnoDB found in the my.cnf file, and Table 13-4 lists the set variable parameters.

TABLE 13-3 THE INNODB CONFIGURATION PARAMETERS FOUND
          IN THE MY.CNF FILE

Configuration Parameter	Description
Innodb_data_file_path	Listing of all individual InnoDB data files and their sizes using paths relative to the innodb_data_home_dir location.
Innodb_data_home_dir	Root path for all InnoDB data files. The default value is the MySQL data directory.
Innodb_log_group_home_dir	Path to the InnoDB log files.
Innodb_flush_log_at_trx_commit	Indicates that the log file should be flushed to disk when a transaction commits. The default value is 1, but this could be set to 0 to reduce log file I/O at the expense of transaction safety.
Innodb_log_arch_dir	Path to the archives of the log files if log archiving is used.
Innodb_log_archive	Indicates the use of log archiving. The default value is 0 and should remain 0 because MySQL uses its own log files to recover from backup.

So, activating InnoDB tables for use in the 4.0.1 download under Windows 2000 and using all the default settings was a simple process. First, the my_example.cnf file was copied from the C:\MySQL directory, where MySQL was installed, to the C:\ directory and renamed my.cnf. Then the my.cnf file was edited. Under the [mysqld] heading, the InnoDB configuration lines and set variable lines were uncommented. Also, two directories, C:\IBDATA and C:\IBLOGS, were created because they're specified in the my.cnf file after editing. Finally, the service was restarted. If you use the default settings you need to have more than 290 MB available on the disk drive when the service is restarted, because the table space file and the log files will be created at startup, and the defaults specify a 200 MB data file and 30 MB log files, of which there will be three.

TABLE 13-4 THE INNODB SET VARIABLE PARAMETERS FOUND IN THE MY.CNF FILE

Configuration Parameter	Description
Innodb_mirrored_log_groups	Sets the number of identical log groups for the database. The default value is 1 and should not be modified.
Innodb_log_files_in_group	Sets the number of log files in the group, which InnoDB uses in rotation. The recommended value is 3.
Innodb_log_file_size	Sets the size of the log files in a log group.
Innodb_log_buffer_size	Sets the size of the buffer InnoDB uses for writing to the log files.
Innodb_buffer_pool_size	Sets the size of the memory buffer InnoDB uses to cache table data and indexes.
Innodb_additional_mem_pool_size	Sets the size of the memory buffer InnoDB uses to cache data dictionary information and other internal data structures.
Innodb_file_io_threads	Sets the number of file I/O threads used by InnoDB.
Innodb_lock_wait_timeout	Sets the time in seconds that InnoDB should wait to secure a lock before rolling back the transaction.

So, with that, the MySQL server should be running with InnoDB available. At this point, MyISAM is still the default table type. When creating tables in MySQL, the CREATE TABLE command needs to specify TYPE, as follows, for an InnoDB table to be created:

```
CREATE TABLE EMPLOYEE (ID INT, NAME CHAR(32)) TYPE = InnoDB;
```

This command would result in the creation of the EMPLOYEE table in the InnoDB table space, which in turn allows the developer a greater number of options when managing the EMPLOYEE table resource including row locking and transactional control. Again, if TYPE were omitted from the preceding command when running in the default configuration, a MyISAM table would be created under the C:\ MySQL\data directory and would be subject to the table-locking constraints of the MyISAM table type.

BDB

The Berkeley DB table type is another back-end table handler for MySQL. The Berkeley DB handler was written by SleepyCat Software (www.sleepycat.com) to bring Berkeley DB capabilities to MySQL. That is, unlike InnoDB, Berkeley DB existed before MySQL, but Berkeley DB is a toolkit allowing developers to add database functionality to their systems. So, bringing the Berkeley DB to the MySQL data-management system provided MySQL additional functionality over the native MyISAM format and provided the Berkeley DB tools another very popular interface.

The Berkeley database engine is also supported by the Max versions of the MySQL distributions, but it is not configured by default. Indicated by the BDB table type when creating a table, the Berkeley database handler also provides support for transactions with COMMIT and ROLLBACK, but, unlike the InnoDB engine, BDB only performs fine-grained locking at the page level and not at the row level. There are a number of startup options available when using the BDB engine and several properties of Berkeley tables to consider when using them, but they aren't covered here.

Also, the Berkeley DB engine isn't currently available with MySQL on as many platforms as the InnoDB engine; the Berkeley DB engine is not proven with MySQL on NT, in particular. So, although the Berkeley DB engine is a viable alternative to use with MySQL on the Linux, SCO, or Solaris platforms, the choice to use it will probably be driven by experience with the Berkeley DB format and tools. The discussion in the remainder of the chapter focuses primarily on the InnoDB engine and the MyISAM table types.

Comparison of InnoDB and MyISAM table types

Having reviewed the table types available to MySQL, this section provides a comparison of the advantages and disadvantages of the two main table types: MyISAM and InnoDB. Given that the developer has a choice about what type of tables to use in any given database, it is worth considering when to use a given table type.

LOCKING AND CONCURRENCY

With MySQL, only InnoDB and Berkeley DB table types can implement anything other than table locking. Berkeley DB table types implement page locking by default and InnoDB table types implement row locking by default. As mentioned before in this book, concurrency is affected by lock granularity. So the InnoDB row locking provides higher concurrency than the Berkeley DB page locking, which provides higher concurrency than the table locking used on all the other table types.

MYISAM MySQL provides the following commands to control table locking explicitly:

```
LOCK TABLES table1 options, table2 options, ...
UNLOCK TABLES
```

LOCK TABLES provides the following options, and it should be noted that the READ, READ_LOCAL, and WRITE options are mutually exclusive:

- **AS alias:** This assigns the alias name to the table.

- **READ:** This establishes a read lock on the table that will prevent any other thread from establishing a write lock on the table.

- **READ LOCAL:** This also establishes a read lock on the table but will still allow non-conflicting inserts to run against the table.

- **LOW_PRIORITY:** This modifies the effect of the write option to cause the thread to wait until no other thread needs a read lock before establishing a write lock.

- **WRITE:** This establishes a write lock on a table allowing the thread establishing the lock to read and write to the table while blocking all other threads. This can be modified by the prior LOW_PRIORITY option.

There are some additional points of interest regarding table locking in MySQL, the first of which is that table locking in MySQL will never result in deadlocks. The reason for this is twofold:

- MySQL ensures that all tables will be locked one at a time in the same order, system-wide. This is independent of the order or number of tables used by the lock tables command.

- If the thread issues a second lock tables command, all previously locked tables will be released. So, a thread either gets all the locks it needs at once or it doesn't get any. Therefore, a thread cannot hold a lock on one table while attempting to get a lock on another, which is a precondition for a deadlock scenario.

Another point to be made about the LOCK TABLES command is that it can be used with InnoDB and Berkeley DB tables without any errors. However, this is not recommended, because both table types maintain their own locking mechanisms and LOCK TABLES provides no additional benefits.

Also, if you're securing a set of read locks to provide a consistent read for a query it's important to issue the LOCK TABLES command using the same number of tables and aliases used by the query. That is, imagine you're going to issue a query that selects from three tables using one table twice with aliases, as in the following SQL fragment:

```
FROM T1 AS PARENT,
     T1 AS CHILD,
     T2, T3
```

Then the LOCK TABLES command issued before that select statement should be as follows:

```
LOCK TABLES T1 AS PARENT READ,
            T1 AS CHILD READ, T2 READ, T3 READ;
```

Finally, the last topic to cover with respect to LOCK TABLES is that of command precedence. There are several ways to affect command precedence:

◆ HIGH_PRIORITY command modifier

◆ LOW_PRIORITY command modifier

◆ LIMIT command modifier

◆ DELAYED command modifier

◆ SET SQL_LOW_PRIORITY_UPDATES variable

◆ max_write_lock_count startup option

◆ low-priority-updates startup option

To understand these precedence modifiers, you first need to know that MySQL gives updates a higher priority that selects by default. This is to prevent large numbers of selects from blocking an update indefinitely, given that any random update is likely to be more important than any typical select. Of course, there is always an exception, and these precedence modifiers assist the developer in handling the exceptions.

HIGH_PRIORITY is a command modifier that can be used with SELECT statements to raise their priority above the pending updates, inserts, or deletes. Conversely, LOW_PRIORITY can be used with update statements to set the priority below that of pending selects.

The LIMIT command is used in conjunction with DELETE commands to restrict the number of rows deleted before the command terminates. This doesn't really change execution priority so much as it prevents the DELETE command from stalling everything while 100,000 records are deleted. Also along these lines is the DELAYED command modifier. This is used in conjunction with INSERT and causes the INSERT to be processed by another thread when the table is available and control returns to the client thread immediately. INSERT DELAYED does possess one important caveat: The pending data is held in memory and if the server dies unexpectedly, the unwritten data is lost.

The SQL_LOW_PRIORITY_UPDATES is a variable that, if set to true (=1) for a thread, will result in all updates from that thread being executed with low priority without need of the LOW_PRIORITY modifier. Then you can also set some properties at startup. The max_write_lock_count can be set at the command line or in the my.cnf file. This property will result in the escalation of select statements after the given number of writes has been performed. The low-priority-updates property can also be set at the command line or the my.cnf file. This reverses the default behavior of the server resulting in all updates having a low priority while the server is executing with this configuration.

Listing 13-7 is an example of a program that uses explicit locking against MyISAM tables.

Listing 13-7: Explicit Locking with MyISAM Tables

```
using System;
using System.Data;
using Microsoft.Data.Odbc;

namespace mySQLLockDemo
{
    /// <summary>
    /// Summary description for mySQLLockDemoClass.
    /// </summary>
    class mySQLLockDemoClass
    {
        [STAThread]
        static void Main(string[] args)
        {
            String strConn =
             "DSN=myBookDemo;UID=Administrator;PASSWORD=xxxxxx;";
            String strLockCmd =
             "LOCK TABLES SIMPLE_TBL READ, SIMPLE_DETAIL_TBL READ;";
            String strSelectCmd = "SELECT * FROM SIMPLE_TBL, " +
             "SIMPLE_DETAIL_TBL WHERE SIMPLE_TBL.SIMPLE_ID = " +
             "SIMPLE_DETAIL_TBL.SIMPLE_ID;";
```

Continued

Listing 13-7 *(Continued)*

```
OdbcConnection myConnection =
 new OdbcConnection(strConn);

try
{
    myConnection.Open();
    Console.WriteLine("Connection Open.");
    OdbcCommand cmd = new OdbcCommand();
    cmd.CommandType = CommandType.Text;
    cmd.Connection = myConnection;
    DateTime dtStart = DateTime.Now;

    cmd.CommandText = strLockCmd;
    cmd.ExecuteNonQuery();
    cmd.CommandText = strSelectCmd;
    OdbcDataReader myReader = cmd.ExecuteReader();
    while(myReader.Read())
    { /* insert display code here */ }
    myReader.Close();
    cmd.CommandText = "UNLOCK TABLES;";
    cmd.ExecuteNonQuery();

    DateTime dtEnd = DateTime.Now;
    Console.WriteLine("Select Run time: " + (dtEnd-
dtStart));

    cmd.Connection.Close();
}
catch (OdbcException odbc_e)
{
    Console.WriteLine(odbc_e.Message);
}
catch (Exception e)
{
    Console.WriteLine(e.Message);
}
    }
  }
}
```

INNODB   With InnoDB, locking happens automatically at the row level without the need for any explicit locking by the developer. There are two statements that can affect the locking behavior, but of greater interest with InnoDB is what locking is performed by different operations. To begin, InnoDB has four types of locks that can be placed on a row:

◆ **Shared:** This lock is compatible with other shared locks, and it is limited in effect to the row being locked.

◆ **Shared Next-Key:** This lock is compatible with other shared locks, but the next-key condition prevents records from insertion between the current row and the next row in the sequence.

◆ **Exclusive:** This lock is incompatible with any other lock, resulting in access being limited to the thread that obtains the lock.

◆ **Exclusive Next-Key:** Again, this lock has the properties of an exclusive lock but prevents insertion of records between the current row and the next row in the series.

Typical select statements against InnoDB tables use a versioning mechanism to perform a consistent read without placing any locks. This behavior can be modified by one of two qualifiers of the select statement:

◆ **LOCK IN SHARE MODE:** When this is added to a select statement shared next-key locks will be placed on all relevant records.

◆ **FOR UPDATE:** When this is added to a select statement, an exclusive next-key lock will be placed on all relevant records.

When inserts are performed, exclusive locks are placed on the inserted records. Updates and deletes cause exclusive next-key locks to be placed on all the records affected by the operation. When these statements include sub-selects the sub-selects are performed as consistent reads without any locking. The exception to this rule is that, if logging is on, an insert that is drawing data from a sub-select will place a shared next-key lock on all the records identified by the sub-select.

Unlike the other databases discussed in this book that implement row locking, InnoDB does not employ any form of lock escalation. So, there is no reason to worry about unselected records becoming locked via lock escalation. And as a final note, LOCK TABLES can still be used with InnoDB tables; however, the automatic deadlock detection that is part of InnoDB will not discover deadlocks involving tables locked with this statement. So, as mentioned earlier, it's best not to use this statement with InnoDB tables.

READ AND WRITE PERFORMANCE

Given that the MyISAM table type requires no transactional overhead, you may expect that this table type would perform better in situations where there are large amounts of reading or writing with low concurrency requirements. So it's worth examining the code in Listing 13-8, which performs a large number of inserts and selects on both table types, for comparison.

Listing 13-8: Inserts and Selects with ODBC against MyISAM Tables

```csharp
using System;
using System.Data;
using System.Threading;
using Microsoft.Data.Odbc;

namespace myISAMInsertsAndSelects
{
    /// <summary>
    /// Summary description for myISAMInsertsAndSelectsClass.
    /// </summary>
    class myISAMInsertsAndSelectsClass
    {
        [STAThread]
        static void Main(string[] args)
        {
            myISAMInsertsAndSelectsClass tIProc =
              new myISAMInsertsAndSelectsClass();
            ThreadStart tsInsertDelegate =
              new ThreadStart(tIProc.myInsertThreadProc);
            Thread myInsertThread = new Thread(tsInsertDelegate);

            myISAMInsertsAndSelectsClass tSProc =
              new myISAMInsertsAndSelectsClass();
            ThreadStart tsSelectDelegate =
              new ThreadStart(tSProc.mySelectThreadProc);
            Thread mySelectThread = new Thread(tsSelectDelegate);

            mySelectThread.Start();
            myInsertThread.Start();
        }

        public void mySelectThreadProc()
        {
            String strConn =
              "DSN=myBookDemo;UID=Administrator;PASSWORD=xxxxxx;";
            String strCmd = "INSERT INTO SIMPLE_TBL(SIMPLE_DESC) " +
              "VALUES ('THIS IS A TEST.');";
            OdbcConnection myConnection =
              new OdbcConnection(strConn);

            try
            {
                myConnection.Open();
```

```
            Console.WriteLine("Connection Open.");
            OdbcCommand cmd = new OdbcCommand();
            cmd.CommandText = strCmd;
            cmd.CommandType - CommandType.Text;
            cmd.Connection = myConnection;
            DateTime dtStart = DateTime.Now;
            for (int i=0;i<100000;i++)
            {
                cmd.CommandText =
                  "SELECT * FROM SIMPLE_TBL " +
                  "WHERE SIMPLE_ID = " + i.ToString() + ";";
                OdbcDataReader myReader =
                  cmd.ExecuteReader(CommandBehavior.SingleRow);
                while(myReader.Read()) { }
                myReader.Close();
            }

            DateTime dtEnd = DateTime.Now;
            Console.WriteLine("Select Run time: " +
                              (dtEnd-dtStart));
            cmd.Connection.Close();
        }
        catch (OdbcException odbc_e)
        {
            Console.WriteLine(odbc_e.Message);
        }
        catch (Exception e)
        {
            Console.WriteLine(e.Message);
        }
    }

    public void myInsertThreadProc()
    {
        String strConn =
          "DSN=myBookDemo;UID=Administrator;PASSWORD=xxxxxx;";
        String strCmd = "INSERT INTO SIMPLE_TBL(SIMPLE_DESC) +
                        "VALUES ('THIS IS A TEST.');";
        OdbcConnection myConnection =
          new OdbcConnection(strConn);

        try
        {
```

Continued

Listing 13–8 *(Continued)*

```
            myConnection.Open();
            Console.WriteLine("Connection Open.");
            OdbcCommand cmd = new OdbcCommand();
            cmd.CommandText = strCmd;
            cmd.CommandType = CommandType.Text;
            cmd.Connection = myConnection;
            DateTime dtStart = DateTime.Now;
            for (int i=0;i<100000;i++)
            {
                cmd.CommandText = "INSERT INTO SIMPLE_TBL " +
                    "(SIMPLE_DESC) VALUES ('ODBC INSERT');";
                cmd.ExecuteNonQuery();
            }

            DateTime dtEnd = DateTime.Now;
            Console.WriteLine("Insert Run time: " +
                            (dtEnd-dtStart));
            cmd.Connection.Close();
        }
        catch (OdbcException odbc_e)
        {
            Console.WriteLine(odbc_e.Message);
        }
        catch (Exception e)
        {
            Console.WriteLine(e.Message);
        }
    }
  }
}
```

Inserts performed by a single thread tend to run faster against MyISAM tables than InnoDB tables. In fact, if each row inserted into the InnoDB table is controlled by a transaction, the performance of the MyISAM tables will seem dramatically better. But if there is a need to insert a large number of rows into an InnoDB table from a single thread, those inserts should probably be aggregated into larger transactions. That will, in turn, make the performance of the InnoDB tables much closer to the performance of the MyISAM tables. Nevertheless, as the number of threads increases, the overhead of transaction management begins to be outweighed by the lock contention and concurrency issues of MyISAM. So, if there will be a significant number of threads updating a table, performance will be better with InnoDB tables.

TRANSACTION CONTROL

For many applications, transaction control is essential, and InnoDB provides that control for MySQL. So, here we examine transaction management with InnoDB. As previously mentioned, MyISAM tables do not support transactions. However, some transactional language can be used without causing any errors, and that is illustrated here as well. In addition, MySQL only supports local transactions, and then only with InnoDB or Berkeley DB tables. Here, the sample code was written to use transactions with InnoDB tables. In either case, the transaction syntax is the same for all MySQL tables. The following transaction-related commands are available:

- SET TRANSACTION ISOLATION LEVEL

- SET AUTOCOMMIT

- BEGIN

- COMMIT

- ROLLBACK

By default the transaction isolation level is READ COMMITTED, and MySQL runs with AUTOCOMMIT set to true (1). The transaction isolation level can be set to any of the four ANSI isolation levels, and AUTOCOMMIT can be turned off. Any of these commands can be run against non-transaction-safe tables, but only ROLLBACK will result in an error that indicates that the rollback was incomplete. Listing 13-9 demonstrates the use of transactions performing a set of inserts against an InnoDB table.

Listing 13-9: Transaction Management with InnoDB and the C API

```
// This is the main project file for VC++
// application project generated using
// an Application Wizard.

#include "stdafx.h"

#using <mscorlib.dll>
#include <tchar.h>

#include "\mysql\include\config-win.h"
#include "\mysql\include\mysql.h"

using namespace System;

// This is the entry point for this application
int _tmain(void)
```

Continued

Listing 13-9 *(Continued)*

```
{
    // Basic database connection using MySQL API
    MYSQL *myDB = mysql_init(NULL);

    myDB = mysql_real_connect( myDB, "localhost", NULL, NULL,
                              "myBook", MYSQL_PORT, NULL, 0);
    if (myDB)
    {
        Console::WriteLine(S"Connection Established.");
        Console::WriteLine(S"Server:    {0}",
          new String(mysql_get_server_info(myDB)));
        Console::WriteLine(S"Host:      {0}",
          new String(mysql_get_host_info(myDB)));
        Console::WriteLine(S"Client:    {0}",
          new String(mysql_get_client_info()));


        DateTime dtStart = DateTime::Now;

        mysql_query(myDB,"SET AUTOCOMMIT = 0;");
        mysql_query(myDB,"BEGIN;");

        for (int i=0;i<10000;i++)
        {
            mysql_query(myDB,"INSERT INTO billing_tbl (bill_amt,
                            bill_paid) VALUES (200.00,'N')");
        }

        mysql_query(myDB,"COMMIT;");

        DateTime dtEnd = DateTime::Now;
        Console::WriteLine(S"Run time: {0}",
                        (dtEnd-dtStart).ToString());

        mysql_close(myDB);
    }
    else
    {
        Console::WriteLine(S"Connection Failed.");
    }

    return 0;
}
```

This example is very straightforward. The value of AUTOCOMMIT is set to false, and then a transaction is started using the BEGIN command. A series of inserts is performed — 10,000 in this case — and finally the transaction is committed with the COMMIT statement. When using the API, all of these commands are passed to MySQL using SQL and the mysql_query() function, because the API does not provide any transaction-specific calls. In the following example, shown in Listing 13-10, transaction management is performed using the OdbcTransaction object.

Listing 13-10: Transaction Management with InnoDB and ODBC Using the OdbcTransaction Object

```
using System;
using System.Data;
using Microsoft.Data.Odbc;

namespace mySQLODBCConnectDemo
{
    /// <summary>
    /// Summary description for mySQLODBCConnectClass.
    /// </summary>
    class mySQLODBCConnectClass
    {
        /// <summary>
        /// The main entry point for the application.
        /// </summary>
        [STAThread]
        static void Main(string[] args)
        {
            //
            // TODO: Add code to start application here
            //
            String strConn =
              "DSN=myBookDemo;UID=Administrator;PASSWORD=xxxxx;";
            String strCmd = "INSERT INTO SIMPLE_TBL ( SIMPLE_DESC )
              VALUES ('THIS IS A TEST.');";
            OdbcConnection myConnection = new
              OdbcConnection(strConn);
            OdbcTransaction myTxn;

            try
            {
                myConnection.Open();
                Console.WriteLine("Connection Open.");
                OdbcCommand cmd = new OdbcCommand();
```

Continued

Listing 13-10 *(Continued)*

```
            cmd.CommandText = strCmd;
            cmd.CommandType = CommandType.Text;
            cmd.Connection = myConnection;
            myTxn = myConnection.BeginTransaction();
            cmd.Transaction = myTxn;
            DateTime dtStart = DateTime.Now;
            for (int i=0;i<1000;i++)
            {
                cmd.CommandText =
                  "UPDATE billing_tbl SET bill_paid = 'Y'
                   WHERE bill_id >= " + i.ToString() + " AND
                   bill_id <= " + (i+1000).ToString() + ";";
                cmd.ExecuteNonQuery();
            }

            myTxn.Commit();

            DateTime dtEnd = DateTime.Now;
            Console.WriteLine("Run time: " + (dtEnd-dtStart));
            cmd.Connection.Close();
        }
        catch (OdbcException odbc_e)
        {
            Console.WriteLine(odbc_e.Message);
            if (myConnection.State == ConnectionState.Open)
                myTxn.Rollback();
        }
        catch (Exception e)
        {
            Console.WriteLine(e.Message);
        }
    }
  }
}
```

In this example, transaction control is managed with the OdbcTransaction object myTxn. The object is related to the transaction by the BeginTransaction call on the connection object. This provides a cleaner approach than the issuing of additional SQL commands, as demonstrated with the C++ example. This method also allows transaction exceptions to be caught that would not be noticed using the SQL statements for transaction control.

As mentioned earlier, MySQL does not support distributed transactions, because there is currently no COM+ compensating resource manager for MySQL. However, this doesn't mean that MySQL cannot be enlisted by COM+ components to perform local transactions. In this manner, COM+ components can be used with MySQL in an N-Tier environment to provide object pooling.

MySQL Server Status

Monitoring the status of a server that operates in a critical role is always important, and MySQL provides tools to do the job. The mysqladmin.exe program is a general-purpose administration tool that allows the developer to perform numerous operations quickly without having to log into the MySQL environment. To easily check on the server status, the following four mysqladmin.exe commands are very useful.

- ◆ mysqladmin status
- ◆ mysqladmin extended-status
- ◆ mysqladmin variables
- ◆ mysqladmin processlist

Listing 13-11 shows the execution and results of mysqladmin status. This command provides the basic information about the server. As you can see, this command gives you the top eight pieces of information regarding server status including uptime, active threads, and the ever important average queries per second.

Listing 13-11: Execution and Results of mysqladmin Status

```
C:\MySQL\bin>mysqladmin status
Uptime: 5496  Threads: 3  Questions: 214  Slow queries: 0
Opens: 9  Flush tables: 1  Open tables: 0  Queries per second
avg: 0.039
```

Listing 13-12 shows the execution and results of mysqladmin extended-status. This command provides all the current information about the server. It should be noted that this listing has been greatly truncated. The command actually returns 127 rows of data. This information can also be retrieved using the show status command from the MySQL prompt.

Listing 13-12: Execution and Results of mysqladmin Extended-Status

```
C:\MySQL\bin>mysqladmin extended-status
+---------------------------+-------+
| Variable_name             | Value |
+---------------------------+-------+
| Aborted_clients           | 0     |
```

Continued

Listing 13-12 *(Continued)*

```
| Aborted_connects       | 2     |
| Bytes_received         | 0     |
| Bytes_sent             | 0     |
. . .
| Table_locks_immediate  | 7     |
| Table_locks_waited     | 0     |
| Threads_cached         | 0     |
| Threads_created        | 13    |
| Threads_connected      | 3     |
| Threads_running        | 1     |
| Uptime                 | 5485  |
+------------------------+-------+
```

Listing 13-13 shows the execution and results of mysqladmin variables. This command provides all the current information about the variable settings on the server. Again, this listing has been truncated, because the command will return 116 rows when run. Also, this same information can be retrieved using the show variables command from the MySQL prompt.

Listing 13-13: Execution and Results of mysqladmin Variables

```
C:\MySQL\bin>mysqladmin variables


+----------------------------------+--------------------...------+
| Variable_name                    | Value              ...      |
+----------------------------------+--------------------...------+
| back_log                         | 50                 ...      |
| basedir                          | c:\mysql\          ...      |
| bdb_cache_size                   | 8388600            ...      |
| bdb_log_buffer_size              | 32768              ...      |
| bdb_home                         | c:\mysql\data\     ...      |
...
| tmp_table_size                   | 33554432           ...      |
| tmpdir                           | C:\WINNT\TEMP\     ...      |
| version                          | 4.0.1-alpha-max-nt...       |
| wait_timeout                     | 28800              ...      |
+----------------------------------+--------------------...------+
```

Finally, Listing 13-14 shows the results of running mysqladmin process list. This command provides relevant information about the threads currently running against the server. This table shows all the rows that were returned when this command was executed. The final information field was condensed, resulting in the partial wording found in the third row.

Listing 13-14: Execution and Results of mysqladmin Process List

```
C:\MySQL\bin>mysqladmin processlist
```

```
+----+------+-----------+--------+---------+------+-------+---...--+
| Id | User | Host      | db     | Command | Time | State | In... |
+----+------+-----------+--------+---------+------+-------+---...--+
| 1  | ODBC | localhost |        | Sleep   | 9    |       | ...   |
| 3  | ODBC | localhost | myBook | Sleep   | 39   |       | ...   |
| 4  | ODBC | localhost |        | Query   | 0    |       | sh...t|
+----+------+-----------+--------+---------+------+-------+---...--+
```

Of course, mysqladmin has a multitude of switches and options that aren't covered here, and the MySQL documentation does an excellent job of explaining them. But these four do provide a solid basis for keeping up with activity on the server, and for those new to MySQL, investigating the information contained in the output of these commands will lead to a much greater understanding of MySQL.

Unique Aspects of MySQL SQL

To paraphrase an old saying, the great thing about standards is there are so many to choose from. Each of the databases we've looked at provide some custom extensions and behaviors that don't necessarily conform to a standard version of SQL, and MySQL is no different. It's worth examining some of the unique extensions to MySQL SQL as well as some of the shortcomings.

Common features not found in MySQL

Although MySQL is a good data server, the reality is that it's a long way away from providing anything like SQL-92 compliance, which is often considered a base level for a good relational database management system. Now, it may be that the design goals of the authors were not to produce a heavyweight system, as was explained at the outset of this chapter. Nevertheless, with a name like MySQL, someone new to the system may be surprised to find that the following items are either not supported or only partially supported:

♦ **Stored procedures:** Not supported

♦ **Views:** Not supported but scheduled for 4.1

♦ **Triggers:** Not supported

♦ **Foreign-key constraints:** Currently only supported with InnoDB tables

There are others, but these four are staples in many large database systems. Consider how important they may be to any intended database design.

Extensions found in MySQL

In MySQL, there are also features not found in other databases and put there by MySQL designers looking to solve issues they were dealing with. Here are some of these extensions:

- ◆ ANALYZE TABLE: Used to analyze and store the key distribution of the MyISAM tables specified in the command. This information is then used to optimize JOIN queries.

- ◆ LOAD DATA INFILE: Used to load data from a text file into a database table.

- ◆ REPLACE: Used to insert records into a table. But if a key violation would occur, the existing record is automatically updated.

- ◆ USE: Used to alter the database to which the client is connected.

In short, if you don't have much experience working with MySQL, it's worth reviewing the syntax that is provided by the MySQL documentation before assuming that you know it.

The Driver's Effect on the Application

Each of the three different driver or connection types that we've looked at have advantages and disadvantages. The C API provides the best performance of any of the connection methods. Its only real drawback is that the API has not yet been re-declared for use in Visual Basic .NET or C#. So, if you aren't comfortable in the C++ with managed extensions environment, you'll have to go through the function import process. The MyODBC driver provides good performance, but it isn't the OLE-DB driver that many ADO and ADO.NET components expect. Then there is the MyOLE-DB driver. This driver works satisfactorily with components that expect an OLE-DB provider, but, compared to the other connection methods, the MyOLE-DB driver performs poorly. Nevertheless, there are situations in which you should consider using each of these drivers.

In a typical WinForm application that allows the user to view and update the data in the system, using the MyODBC or the MyOLE-DB driver should be fine. Listing 13-15 shows an example application where a data grid employs an OleDbDataAdapter to display some sample data from the database. The data adapter is using the MyOLE-DB data provider and there was no problem getting it to work.

Listing 13-15: A WinForm Application Using the MyOLE-DB Data Provider

```csharp
using System;
using System.Drawing;
using System.Collections;
using System.ComponentModel;
using System.Windows.Forms;
using System.Data;

namespace mySQLDataGridDemo
{
    /// <summary>
    /// Summary description for Form1.
    /// </summary>
    public class Form1 : System.Windows.Forms.Form
    {
      private System.Data.OleDb.OleDbDataAdapter oleDbDataAdapter1;
      private System.Data.OleDb.OleDbCommand oleDbSelectCommand1;
      private System.Data.OleDb.OleDbConnection oleDbConnection1;
      private mySQLDataGridDemo.DataSet1 dataSet11;
      private System.Windows.Forms.DataGrid dataGrid1;

        /// <summary>
        /// Required designer variable.
        /// </summary>
        private System.ComponentModel.Container components = null;

        public Form1()
        {
            //
            // Required for Windows Form Designer support
            //
            InitializeComponent();

            //
            // TODO: Add any constructor code after
            // InitializeComponent call
            //
            this.oleDbDataAdapter1.Fill(this.dataSet11);
        }

        /// <summary>
        /// Clean up any resources being used.
```

Continued

Listing 13-15 *(Continued)*

```csharp
/// </summary>
protected override void Dispose( bool disposing )
{
    if( disposing )
    {
        if (components != null)
        {
            components.Dispose();
        }
    }
    base.Dispose( disposing );
}

#region Windows Form Designer generated code
/// <summary>
/// Required method for Designer support - do not modify
/// the contents of this method with the code editor.
/// </summary>
private void InitializeComponent()
{
    this.dataSet11 = new mySQLDataGridDemo.DataSet1();
    this.oleDbDataAdapter1 = new
      System.Data.OleDb.OleDbDataAdapter();
    this.oleDbSelectCommand1 = new
      System.Data.OleDb.OleDbCommand();
    this.oleDbConnection1 = new
      System.Data.OleDb.OleDbConnection();
    this.dataGrid1 = new System.Windows.Forms.DataGrid();
    ((System.ComponentModel.ISupportInitialize)
      (this.dataSet11)).BeginInit();
    ((System.ComponentModel.ISupportInitialize)
      (this.dataGrid1)).BeginInit();
    this.SuspendLayout();
    //
    // dataSet11
    //
    this.dataSet11.DataSetName = "DataSet1";
    this.dataSet11.Locale = new
      System.Globalization.CultureInfo("en-US");
    this.dataSet11.Namespace =
      "http://www.tempuri.org/DataSet1.xsd";
    //
    // oleDbDataAdapter1
```

```
//
this.oleDbDataAdapter1.SelectCommand =
  this.oleDbSelectCommand1;
//
// oleDbSelectCommand1
//
this.oleDbSelectCommand1.CommandText = "SELECT " +
  "SIMPLE_ID, SIMPLE_DESC FROM SIMPLE_TBL WHERE " +
  "SIMPLE_ID < 100;";
this.oleDbSelectCommand1.Connection =
  this.oleDbConnection1;
//
// oleDbConnection1
//
this.oleDbConnection1.ConnectionString =
  "Provider=MySqlProv;Data Source=myBook";
//
// dataGrid1
//
this.dataGrid1.DataMember = "";
this.dataGrid1.DataSource = this.dataSet11._Table;
this.dataGrid1.HeaderForeColor =
  System.Drawing.SystemColors.ControlText;
this.dataGrid1.Location =
  new System.Drawing.Point(8, 32);
this.dataGrid1.Name = "dataGrid1";
this.dataGrid1.Size = new System.Drawing.Size(352, 80);
this.dataGrid1.TabIndex = 0;
//
// Form1
//
this.AutoScaleBaseSize = new System.Drawing.Size(5, 13);
this.ClientSize = new System.Drawing.Size(376, 181);
this.Controls.AddRange(
  new System.Windows.Forms.Control[] {
    this.dataGrid1});
this.Name = "Form1";
this.Text = "Form1";
((System.ComponentModel.ISupportInitialize)
  (this.dataSet11)).EndInit();
((System.ComponentModel.ISupportInitialize)
  (this.dataGrid1)).EndInit();
```

Continued

Listing 13–15 *(Continued)*

```
            this.ResumeLayout(false);

        }
        #endregion

        /// <summary>
        /// The main entry point for the application.
        /// </summary>
        [STAThread]
        static void Main()
        {
            Application.Run(new Form1());
        }
    }
}
```

The MyOLE-DB driver performs adequately with a .NET component expecting an OLE-DB data provider. However, the developer should note that when the MyOLE-DB driver was used to perform a large number of record inserts, as demonstrated earlier in the chapter, it performed much worse that the MyODBC driver or the API connection. So, be cautious in your use of the MyOLE-DB data provider.

Using ADO

When writing the samples for the book, there were no problems using the MyODBC driver with the ADO.NET data structures, and the performance was acceptable. Here we cover using MyODBC with ADO and ADO.NET.

ADO.NET performance

When the sample code in shown later in this section was compared to other code employing ADO (not included here), the performance was comparable. The code shown here uses the new ADO.NET DataSet object for collecting and accessing data.

DATAADAPTER

Within ADO.NET, the data adapter components are used to manage the flow of data from the server to the client. With ADO, the developer opened a RecordSet on a connection, which provided access to the tabular data immediately. In ADO.NET an adapter is placed between the connection and a DataSet. Using the ODBC provider, the specific component is the OdbcDataAdapter. This adapter is then used to fill a DataSet with data.

DATASET

The DataSet is a more complex component than the RecordSet. A DataSet essentially provides the client with a local database in memory. The DataSet holds a set of Tables that contain the tabular data once accessed via the RecordSet, and the DataSet can maintain relationships between the Tables. The example in Listing 13-16 shows the use of the OdbcDataAdapter and the DataSet.

Listing 13-16: An Application Demonstrating the Use of OdbcDataAdapter under ADO.NET

```
using System;
using System.Data;
using Microsoft.Data.Odbc;

namespace mySQLODBCConnectDemo
{
    /// <summary>
    /// Summary description for mySQLODBCConnectClass.
    /// </summary>
    class mySQLODBCConnectClass
    {
        /// <summary>
        /// The main entry point for the application.
        /// </summary>
        [STAThread]
        static void Main(string[] args)
        {
            //
            // TODO: Add code to start application here
            //
            String strConn =
                "DSN=myBookDemo;UID=Administrator;PASSWORD=xxxxxx;";
            String strCmd = "INSERT INTO SIMPLE_TBL ( SIMPLE_DESC )
                            VALUES ('THIS IS A TEST.');";
            OdbcConnection myConnection =
                new OdbcConnection(strConn);
            OdbcTransaction myTxn;

            try
            {
                myConnection.Open();
                Console.WriteLine("Connection Open.");
                DataSet dsData = new DataSet();
                DateTime dtStart = DateTime.Now;
                for (int i=0;i<10;i++)
```

Continued

Listing 13-16 *(Continued)*

```
        {
                OdbcDataAdapter odbcDA =
                    new OdbcDataAdapter("SELECT * FROM billing_tbl
                                        WHERE bill_paid = 'Y'",
                                        myConnection);
                odbcDA.Fill(dsData,i.ToString());
        }

        DateTime dtEnd = DateTime.Now;
        Console.WriteLine("Run time: " + (dtEnd-dtStart));

        Console.WriteLine("DataSet tables: " +
                                dsData.Tables.Count);
        for (int i=0;i<10;i++)
        {
            Console.WriteLine("Table " + i);
            Console.WriteLine("---------");
            Console.WriteLine("Columns in table " + i + ": "
                + dsData.Tables[i].Columns.Count);
            Console.WriteLine("Rows in table " + i + ": "
                + dsData.Tables[i].Rows.Count);
        }

        cmd.Connection.Close();
    }
    catch (OdbcException odbc_e)
    {
        Console.WriteLine(odbc_e.Message);
    }
    catch (Exception e)
    {
        Console.WriteLine(e.Message);
    }
        }
    }
}
```

Note that in this example the OdbcDataAdapter was used repeatedly to load data from the connection into the DataSet. The result happens to be ten identical tables in memory, but the query could have been different with each loop, which would have resulted in ten different tables in the DataSet. Also, if the second parameter had not been provided to the fill command, the result (because the structure of the results is the same) would be a single table with all ten sets of records in it.

ADO performance

As mentioned earlier, ADO performance was found to be comparable to the ADO.NET performance; so we won't go into any detail here regarding the use of ADO. However, there are a couple of points of interest regarding ADO recordsets and MySQL.

SERVER-SIDE RECORDSET

MySQL does not have support for server-side cursors. Consequently, there is no support for server-side recordsets.

CLIENT-SIDE RECORDSET

This is the only recordset available in MySQL. As mentioned earlier in this book, the developer should be cautious with this tool. A common mistake is to select too much data into a client-side record set, which can hamper both client and network performance. Although using ADO.NET does not prevent this behavior either, the frequency with which this mistake is made leads us to repeat the warning.

Handling MySQL Bottlenecks

As with any database system, bottlenecks in performance can arise with MySQL In this section, the focus is on the bottlenecks that are unique to MySQL and on what should be done to resolve them.

The impact of table-level locking

The table-level locking employed with MyISAM tables can have a dramatic negative impact on concurrency and performance. It's important to consider how MyISAM tables will be used when incorporating them into your design. When performing a series of inserts and a series of updates independently against a single table, performance was very good for each set of operations. But when both of these operations were conducted at the same time against the same table, the run-time for the operations increased 400 percent.

Now, some may say the situation was contrived and does not represent a real-world situation, but it does provide an illustration of what will likely happen in the event of heavy and sustained loads. Also, it's worth comparing this to when the same operations were run against InnoDB tables. With the InnoDB tables the run-time for the insert operations remained level while the run-time for the update operations only increased marginally. So, it's important to avoid using MyISAM tables in this situation and to use InnoDB tables which will scale in this scenario. The advantages of InnoDB tables in this situation are covered in more detail later.

There are two ways to address this issue with MyISAM tables. The first method would be to use MyISAM tables only in situations where they can provide good concurrency. This occurs when they're performing mostly selects and inserts, which MySQL can handle concurrently if there are no gaps in the table data. These gaps can be avoided by using fixed-length formatted tables and performing updates, and not deletes, on the records in the table. These updates will not be handled concurrently, but if they are infrequent they should not have much of an impact. The second method for dealing with the issue would be to use DELAY WRITE, which will queue the write operations to reduce contention with selects.

DELAY WRITE only provides a limited solution to an otherwise poor concurrency situation. If you anticipate potentially heavy requests, inserts, and updates against a single table, the best option would be to use an InnoDB table.

The impact of limited transaction support

It's important to remember that the default table type for MySQL, MyISAM, does not support transactions. So, there is no inherent way to ensure the logical consistency of data operations that affect multiple tables. Again, this is transactional data consistency, which is not the opposite of data corruptibility. If you have multi-table data operations that you perform against MyISAM tables, then you should create some tool that can check that the data in the system is consistent. Also, you should consider the performance impact that running this tool may have on your database.

The better solution for maintaining consistency in multi-table operations is to use InnoDB and employ transactions. This will also result in better concurrency for these tables. Given the quality of performance of InnoDB tables, the only reason that may prevent the use of InnoDB tables would be exceptionally tight storage requirements that may occur in an embedded space. If you don't have any such exceptional requirement, use InnoDB.

The impact of distributed transactions

Currently, there is no mechanism for MySQL to participate in distributed transactions. Although InnoDB does provide transaction support, there is no interface between MySQL and the Distributed Transaction Coordinator (DTC). MySQL does not currently have a COM+ resource manager available, which is responsible for managing the interface between the data store and the DTC. Remember that distributed transactions happen using a two-phase commit process. Each component participating in a distributed transaction performs its work and then calls SetComplete() or SetAbort() in the first phase of the two-phase commit. If all components call SetComplete(), then as the second phase of the commit the DTC notifies all participating resource managers that their transactions participating in this distributed transaction should be prepared and then committed permanently. If any one of the components calls SetAbort(), the resource managers will be instructed to roll back their participating transactions. So, there is no way for the MySQL server to be notified by COM+ about the second phase of the two-phase commit. However, if you're an ambitious developer who would like to contribute to the Open Source community, the specifications for writing a compensating resource manager can be found at www.microsoft.com.

The impact of object pooling

Using pooled objects can reduce the overhead involved with instantiating objects and creating database connections. By removing these overheads from sets of database operations, performance can be enhanced in some situations. However, pooled objects are run from COM+ Services, which can incur other performance penalties. So, once again, benefits must be weighed against costs.

Performance

In the final analysis, how well does MySQL perform? Like the other databases, if the database is designed correctly, and the database is configured correctly, the answer is, "Very well." Conversely, if the database is performing poorly, something is probably set up wrong.

Also like the other databases, performance generally comes down to the two Cs: connectivity and concurrency. These two items will often drive the capacity of the database to scale more than any other factors. Note that the assertion is often and not always. Also characteristic of these two items is the fact that they often drive performance negatively at more than a linear rate. That is, the load may double but the processing time quadruples.

An important difference between MySQL and the other databases is the ability to impact concurrency by choice of the table type. Nevertheless, we can still make some general assertions about the two primary table types:

◆ **MyISAM:** Tends to have better select and insert performance but should be avoided when large numbers of inserts, updates, and deletes will be run against the same table.

◆ **InnoDB:** Tends to have worse select and insert performance but updates run about level with MyISAM. Provides much better concurrency and should be used with tables that have large numbers of inserts, updates, and deletes.

Similarly, with the three primary means of connectivity from .NET, we can make some generalizations:

◆ **C API:** Provides the best connectivity performance and should probably be used for any data connections that support the high data demand.

◆ **MyODBC:** Provides good connectivity and does not need to be shied away from and should be used when the convenience of ODBC will be beneficial to the system development.

◆ **MyOLE-DB:** Provides mediocre performance and should be used only for OLE-DB aware controls that will not perform a high volume of data operations. Adequate for typical WinForm database applications.

As far as any specific statements about performance, there are none to be made in this context. Exactly how fast something will run will depend on numerous factors including the operating system and the type of hardware on which the server is running. This does not mean that you cannot estimate how a system will scale. Before finalizing a database design and building a complete system on top of it, data should be loaded and basic performance testing should be done. Linear changes in response time with load can often be addressed with better and faster hardware, but non-linear changes in performance require great caution and generally a change in design.

To assist in this process, developers should examine the scripts found in the Bench subdirectory in the MySQL distribution. These scripts are written in Perl and require the developer to download a Perl environment for NT (one can be found at www.activestate.com), but they are a useful place to start. Additionally, the developer should write simple programs that will simulate activity on different parts of the system. Whatever you do, don't wait until the database has been implemented, the system has been developed, and the data has started to flow in to discover the performance bottleneck in the database design.

Summary

MySQL is a solid and proven tool. It does lack some significant features found in other systems including stored procedures, triggers, and views. In many database designs this can be an issue. The only solution to this issue is through the use of client-side development, which can lack the semantic clarity achieved by abstracting certain functionality to the database server. Nevertheless, it provides reliable data storage, competitive performance, and a low cost of acquisition (because, as open source, the cost of acquisition is merely the time it takes to download). Also, with the ability to compile the database comes the ability to tailor the database configuration to meet any given need. The tools available to inspect and monitor the database may not be as pretty as the graphical environments found in other major databases, but the MySQL tools are robust and provide the developer with all the information needed.

MySQL consumes far fewer resources than the heavyweights. Most of the time, we think of enterprise systems as large central servers with millions of records, but sometimes enterprise systems are those that are small but ubiquitous like those running on all the sales force laptops in an organization. In that situation, the system needs reliability and efficiency, which MySQL can provide. So, MySQL is truly scalable and can provide the developer with a consistent back-end from mobile to multi-processor computers.

Many people may mistakenly think that MySQL only runs on a Linux or Unix platform, but MySQL runs on Windows as well. And, with MyODBC, MyOLE-DB, and the C API, Windows client connectivity is not an issue. So whether you need to write a WinForm application to collect customer information on a laptop or write an ASP.NET component for a Web application, MySQL will be able to play nicely with the .NET environment.

Appendix A

Overview of the Timesheet Application

THE SAMPLE APPLICATION that we developed for this book is a Web-based Timesheet application. The application is designed for a general Time and Materials billing system. The billable employees at a company are going to input their billable time into the system. These billable entries are made according to the project and employee. Our application implements the following features and design goals:

◆ **Security:** Users are required to log on. The logon uses forms-based authentication and users are validated against a database.

◆ **Business Logic Layer (BLL):** A business logic laycr has been implemented within the application. The front-end part of the application has no knowledge of the underlying database. The front-end application merely calls into the business logic and returns values based on returns from the business logic layer. We have also heard the BLL referred to as a Data Access Layer and the middle-tier of an application. By writing an application with a Business Logic Layer, the application may be modified to support a different database and not require *major* changes to the application. The advantage of the BLL is that by placing the logic that communicates with the database within one location within our application, changes that need to be made with regards to business rules and database access will only be made in one location. It will not need to be necessary to track down all instances of a function throughout all the files that make up the application. Changes need to be made in only one file. This is an excellent way to design an application.

◆ **Ability to use COM+ Services:** In our example application, there is not a lot of need for COM+ Services. For this application, distributed transactions are too complex for a relatively simple application. Object pooling might be beneficial if the time necessary to startup the objects within the BLL were significant. Support for other COM+ Services could be added in. Support for these services may be easily added to the application because the use of a BLL allows for these services to be added without affecting the front-end of the application.

◆ **Implemented in Visual Basic .NET and C#:** The data-entry section has been implemented in C#. The admin section has been implemented in Visual Basic.

A copy of the application is available from our Web site at `www.scalabilitywith.net`.

Underlying Database Tables

Underneath our Timesheet application are the database tables that hold our data. Figure A-1 shows the relationships between the main tables in our system.

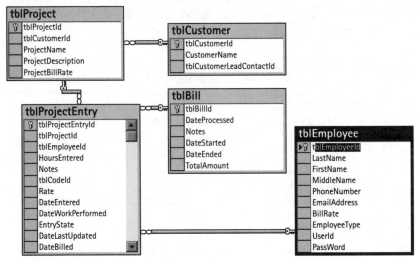

Figure A-1: Table layout for the Timesheet system

Let's look at the tables and what they are designed to hold.

◆ **tblBill:** The tblBill table is designed to hold information specific to a given bill for a customer.

◆ **tblCode (not pictured):** The tblCode table holds the code information pertaining to the work that is performed. For example, an employee may need to bill four hours under a different heading if these hours are spent meeting with a client. These hours would be billed differently or billed under a different heading than hours.

◆ **tblCustomer.** The tblCustomer table holds basic information about the Customer that a project is being done for.

◆ **tblCustomerContact (not pictured):** The tblCustomerContact table holds all project associated contacts. These contacts could be billing contacts, project or section leads, or general contacts at any specific customer.

◆ **tblEmployee:** The tblEmployee table contains a listing of the employees for the service provider. These employees may be either those who may input billable project entries into the system, admin-level users who may perform administrative functions, or those who may be employees with the ability to run reports against.

◆ **tblProject:** The tblProject table describes current projects within the Timesheet system.

◆ **tblProjectEntry:** The tblProjectEntry table contains all billable entries within the system. These entries may be classified as billed, open, and questioned. A billed entry is one that has already been billed. An open entry is an entry that is within the system that has not been billed. A billable employee may only modify an open entry for that employee. A questioned entry is one in which a customer has some type of question regarding that entry.

The Data Entry Section

The data entry section of our application is designed for billable employees of a company to input their billable time on projects. A picture of the project entry screen is shown in Figure A-2.

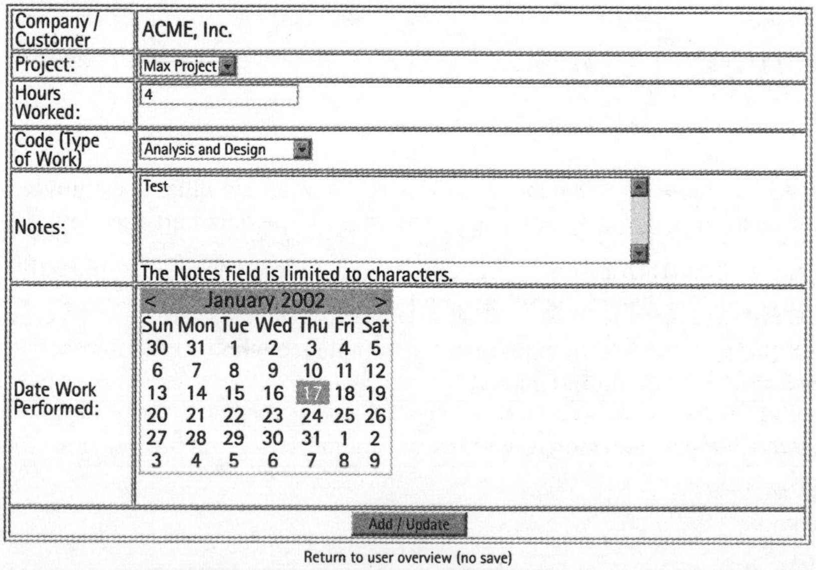

Return to user overview (no save)

Figure A-2: View all billable entries within the system.

The following is a list of the business rules that have been implemented:

♦ **Employees are required to log on.** Employees who are not logged on generate errors and will not be allowed to continue.

♦ **Employees may view only their entries within the listing from the tblProjectEntry table.**

♦ **Employees may only view project entries that have not been billed.** Entries that have not been billed are not viewable. Rows within the table tblProjectEntry have three allowed states:

■ Open (value = 0): An Open entry is one in which an employee has entered information pertaining to a project and that particular entry has not been placed into a bill to send to the customer.

■ Billed (value = 1): A Billed entry is an entry in which an employee has entered information pertaining to a project and that entry has been placed into a bill to be sent to the customer.

■ Questioned (value = 2): A Questioned entry is an entry in which there is a question concerning it, either from the customer or from an admin within the company.

There is currently no interface for handling billed orders, but the ability to handle this state is within the system.

♦ **Project Entries that have been billed not be changed through the user interface.**

Employee Types

There are three levels of employees:

♦ Billable (value = 0): A Billable employee is one who is a billable employee. A Billable employee may enter information onto the data entry section.

♦ Admin (value=1): An Admin employee is an employee who is not directly involved in the generation of income for the company.

♦ Both (value = 2): A Both employee is an employee who is a Billable employee and an Admin employee.

The employee types are stored within an Enumerator structure within the application.

The Admin Section

The data entry section of our application is designed to generate bills based on a set of project entries. Figure A-3 is a screenshot of the bill creation screen.

View Open Entries

Project Name	Customer Name	Hours Worked	Authorized
Max Project	ACME, Inc.	4	☐ Yes

Select All Entries	Process Entries for Billing

Starting Date: 1/5/2002

<		January 2002				>
Sun	Mon	Tue	Wed	Thu	Fri	Sat
30	31	1	2	3	4	5
6	7	8	9	10	11	12
13	14	15	16	17	18	19
20	21	22	23	24	25	26
27	28	29	30	31	1	2
3	4	5	6	7	8	9

Ending Date: 1/19/2002

<		January 2002				>
Sun	Mon	Tue	Wed	Thu	Fri	Sat
30	31	1	2	3	4	5
6	7	8	9	10	11	12
13	14	15	16	17	18	19
20	21	22	23	24	25	26
27	28	29	30	31	1	2
3	4	5	6	7	8	9

Figure A-3: Adding a project entry

The following is a list of the business rules that have been implemented:

◆ Only employees with Admin or Both employee type may logon to the Admin section.

◆ A bill is created by selecting project entries from a list of project entries that have not been already billed.

Summary

The Timesheet application is an ASP.NET-based application that uses a business logic layer (BLL) to allow the front-end application to be managed. It has been designed to be extendible to different databases and to have support for features added to it. There is an underlying database that supports the application. A complete download of the application, including ASP.NET code and database scripts is on our Web site (www.scalabilitywith.net).

Appendix B

Programming and Development Naming Standards

DESIGNING AND DEVELOPING CODE can be a difficult job. There are discussions that must go on with the client, and these discussions should produce requirements documents. From the requirements documents, business rules can be designed and developed. From the business rules, you can then begin writing code that implements those business rules. This book isn't designed to teach you how to interact with customers and write business rules; experience is the best teacher in that area. It is a goal of the book to help developers write better code, and one of the facets of writing better code is to use a set of development standards within your development processes.

Standards are a very important in the development process. Although the use of standards does not directly impact the functionality of a software product, the use of standards contributes to an overall improvement of the understanding of source code and database fields. This improvement allows developers, architects, and database experts to easily move between sections of an application. Standards should not be thought of as an inflexible set of standards. On the other hand, standards should be considered to be a set of guidelines that must change as the database and development tools change. Here are several naming conventions used today:

- **Pascal case:** With Pascal case, the first letter in an identifier and the first letter of each subsequent concatenated word are capitalized.

- **Camel case:** With Camel case, the first letter of an identifier is lowercase. Each subsequent concatenated word is capitalized.

- **Upper case:** All letters in the identifier are capitalized. This convention is used for identifiers that are short, such as two or three letters.

- **Hungarian notation:** Each identifier is prepended by a small set of letters that identify the type of the variable.

In most Windows development today, the Hungarian notation is used as the basis of more development than any other development naming standard notation.

Wally began programming by using Pascal case in the late 1980s. He picked this up from another graduate student. As Hungarian notation became popular, he added that notation as he moved over into Windows-based development. Using the two together has served him very well. However, it is his belief that the use of a development naming convention is *much* more important than the one used. It doesn't matter which one a development project uses, just that it uses one.

General Naming Conventions

The most common standard case and notation used over the past ten years of development is Hungarian notation. This notation scheme has been used since it became popularized in the late 1980s. Over the years, we have used a notation system that is a combination of the Hungarian and Pascal notations. The system basically revolves around prepending a variable with a short set of letters that describe the object type and a variable name that identifies the data held within the object. The one exception to this is in the use of iterators (for example, variables used in a `for` loop). Since the age when dinosaurs walked the Earth, programmers have used the single character term variables i, j, and k as the names of iterators; attempting to change this "historical" standard is the equivalent of attempting to swim up Niagara Falls. Due to this overwhelming support, it's probably a good idea to leave that particular notation as is. Some examples are stored in Table B-1.

TABLE B-1 THE HUNGARIAN/PASCAL NOTATION SYSTEM

Data in Variable	Data Type	Prepended Characters	Example Variable Name
Last name of a person.	String	Str	strLastName
Count of the number of elements within a collection.	Integer	int	intCount
Count of the number of records with a database result set.	Long	Lng	lngCount
Connection to a database. Because an ADO connection allows a program to connect and access a database, rarely is there a need to have more than one connection object in a procedure. In cases where there are, we have used a descriptor for the databases.	Classic ADO 2.x Connection	Cn	cn, cnSql (for multiple database types, cnDataBaseType), cnDataBaseName

Data in Variable	Data Type	Prepended Characters	Example Variable Name
Users within a table.	Classic ADO 2.x Recordset	Rs	rsUsers
Users within a table.	OleDb ADO.NET DataReader	Oledbdr	oledbdrUsers
Datasets tend to be generic across a Database. If there is a need to differentiate between multiple datasets, the differentiator could be a table name or database type if using multiple datasources (SQL Server, Oracle, files, or others).	ADO.NET DataSet, a DataSet is generic and not tied to a specific data technology.	dsData	dsData (when using one Database table), dsDatadbSales (when using a specific database), dsDataOra (when using a specific datasource type, such as Oracle)
Drop-down list of Users.	User Interface element, Drop Down List Box	Ddl	ddlUsers
Calendar listing the meetings in a room.	User Interface element, Calendard	Cal	calMeetings
OLE-DB Connection to a database.	OleDb ADO.NET Connection	oledbCn	oledbCn
DataReader holding a query involving a query of Users.	SQL ADO.NET DataReader	sqldr	sqldrUsers
Connection to SQL Server. SQL Native Provider allows a program to connect and access a database, rarely is there a need to have more than one connection object in a procedure. In cases where there is, using a descriptor for the databases would be appropriate.	SQL ADO.NET Connection	sqlCn	Either sqlCn (a generic SQL Connection) or sqlCnSales (assuming that there is a need for multiple connections within a function)
Message Queue used by an application to communicate with a shipping partner.	Message Queue	Msmq	msmqShip
List of Users.	ListItem	Li	liUsers

Database Objects

When creating a database table, it's also important to use standards when naming objects. In the specific case of a table, there is not much use in defining the data type for each column within a table. It's important to use standards for items like table names, indexes, and other objects within a database. Refer to Table B-2 for some of the standards used within a database table.

Table B-2 DATABASE OBJECT SYSTEM

Database Object	Characters	Example Name
Table	tbl is the prefix.	TblWorkLog
Column holding the primary key	tbl is the prefix; ID is the suffix. Typically, the column name is the name of the table with 'ID' as the suffix.	tblWorkLogID
Column holding the foreign key of another table	tbl is the prefix; ID is the suffix. Typically, the name of a column holding a foreign key value is the same as the primary key column name of the related table.	tblCompanyId (assuming there is a relationship between a table containing Employees and a Company)
Index	idx_TableName_	Idx_TableName_ CompanyName (typically, the format name for an index is 'idx_', followed by the table name, followed by an identifier of the columns contained within the index)
Stored Procedures	sp	spGetSalesData
View	Vw	vwCompanySalesData
Sequence	sq	sqUser (if you aren't familiar with a sequence, it is an Oracle data object that provides a sequence of numbers — the numbers start at the beginning value and continue to the end value)

One word about table design: In many situations, there is some combination of columns within a table that is considered to be unique within a table. Using this combination of tables as a primary key may make sense, however, in general, it is not a good idea to use data columns as a primary key. Why? Business rules change. Data changes. There is a good possibility that the columns that contain the primary key will change. For this reason, it is a good idea to create a column that contains a value that is unique within the table but is not directly associated with any application data. This value could be some type of numeric, such as an integer, or a unique identifier.

Components and Method Calls

Within a component, there are two additional items that are many times used within objects and method development. These are global objects contained within a class/object, properties of class, method calls, and the arguments to a method. These identifiers are listed in Table B-3.

TABLE B-3 OBJECT NAMING

Object Type	Suffix	Example
Global values	g	goledbCn
Method Parameters	p	pstrLastName

Properties and methods are somewhat different. Typically, methods are actions and active terms, so they should be named with verbs and descriptive terms appropriate to the method. Properties of a class are closely related to nouns and specific statements associated with the property, so they should be named with nouns and appropriate associated terms.

Database Access

One of the problems with general client/server and 2-Tier Web development is that the database access may be needed across a number of functions that are spread across a number of different modules, forms, and files. What happens if a logic or business rule change must be made? Programmers will need to look through *all* the files that are a part of the program to make changes. Instead of allowing database access from any location in your programs, how about creating an intermediate layer within your programs. Front-end logic will call into this intermediate layer, which is typically called a Business Logic Layer (BLL) or Data Access Layer (DAL). The intermediate layer then calls the database and returns results. This intermediate layer would be the *only* place within your applications that will access the database. There are several advantages to this approach:

◆ **Changes within the intermediate layer may be made without requiring changes to the front-end/GUI layer.** This includes bug fixes to the database layer and to the business rules.

◆ **Connection string information is not spread out across all the possible forms, modules, and files associated with an application.** The result is less places to make changes. With a BLL/DAL module, connection string information is placed into one.

◆ **By programming to an intermediate layer, it is fairly easy to swap support for one database or database access mechanism for another.** For example, a solution written in Oracle that uses an OLE-DB driver for database access could be changed fairly easily to use a .NET managed provider without having to change a large portion of an application.

◆ **By using an intermediate layer, business logic may be moved into an advanced container, such as COM+ Services, with minimal changes to the whole application.**

Naming Standards for Namespaces

Microsoft's generally suggested approach to creating a name for a namespace is `CompanyName.Technology[.Feature][.Design]`. The suggestions fall into the following items:

◆ `CompanyName`: The name of the company designing the application or the name of a well-established brand. In the case of a system integrator developing a custom application for a single customer, it is also acceptable to use the customer's name.

◆ `Technology`: The technology name used should be a stable technology name. This name may be the general technology used, such as `complus`, or the start of some hierarchy, such as `Data.SqlClient`.

◆ `Feature`: The feature that is being implemented.

◆ `Design`: If the namespace provides support design-time functionality, append the term `.Design` to the namespace.

In addition to these naming conventions, Microsoft has made several other suggestions regarding naming conventions:

♦ Do not use the same name for a namespace and a class.

♦ Use Pascal case for namespaces.

Microsoft's Naming Guidelines

Microsoft, along with companies like IBM, Oracle, and Sun, is one of the largest software development companies in the world. They have extensive experience in developing and maintaining hundreds of millions of lines of software source code. Included within the .NET Framework's SDK Documentation are a set of naming guidelines for your .NET-based applications. They are suggesting extensive use of Pascal naming conventions without the use of the Hungarian notation described earlier.

Summary

Using standard naming conventions throughout your application development is very important. Using a consistent naming convention throughout your applications allows for other developers to come up to speed quickly, for the original developers to quickly come back up to speed in a section that they authored, and improves the overall readability of code that is produced.

Appendix C

Resources

IN THIS APPENDIX, YOU'LL find the online resources that we frequently use. This list is not intended to be comprehensive, given the vast number of resources you may find on any one of these topics. But these have been useful for us, so we hope that they will be useful for you as well.

Scalability.NET

Our Web site, at www.scalabilitywith.net, provides all the source code found in this book, as well as the source code for some utilities not in shown in the book. In addition, on the Web site, you can find all the links shown in this appendix.

.NET Resources

Here are some good links for .NET topics in general:

- ◆ www.microsoft.com/net: Of course, Microsoft provides plenty of .NET information. This site is more product-information oriented, but it provides quick access to downloads and updates as well as recent news from Microsoft.

- ◆ msdn.microsoft.com/net: The MSDN Web site for .NET is focused entirely on .NET development. It is always a good source for technical articles, online documentation, and even more .NET-related links.

- ◆ www.gotdotnet.com: GotDotNet.com is a community site oriented to .NET with articles, code samples, and news. There are also links to .NET downloads and tools as well as other partners' sites.

- ◆ www.dotnetwire.com: .netWire is a site focused on .NET news. It is a clean site with daily updates and a weekly newsletter.

- ◆ www.dotnetjunkies.com: dotnetjunkies is another .NET community site with tutorials, news, and events, along with articles and related links.

ASP.NET

While under the .NET mantle, the following sites focus on ASP.NET:

- ◆ `www.asp.net`: This is Microsoft's ASP.NET Web site providing everything Microsoft can tell you about ASP.NET.

- ◆ `www.aspfriends.com`: ASPfriends.com is a central Web site for a myriad of moderated listserv discussions on topics related to ASP and other topics.

- ◆ `www.123aspx.com`: 123aspx.com is a portal oriented around ASP and ASP.NET.

- ◆ `www.aspnetpro.com`: ASP.netPro is the Web site for the related magazine of the same name. It's a good source for news and articles.

- ◆ `www.learnasp.com/learnasp`: LearnASP is a site focused on tutorials and how-to's. This site also provided a number of listservs.

C#

If you want to learn more about Microsoft's new C# language, here are three places to look:

- ◆ `msdn.microsoft.com/vstudio/nextgen/technology/csharpintro.asp`: This is Microsoft's introduction to and overview of C#.

- ◆ `www.csharphelp.com`: C# Help is a good source for articles as well as question-based help for different C#-related problems.

- ◆ `www.c-sharpcorner.com`: This site is a good source of technical articles not only on C# but also on ASP.NET, Visual Basic .NET, XML, and SOAP.

Visual Basic .NET

If you want to find out more about the changes to VB in Visual Basic .NET or you just want to learn Visual Basic .NET, these sites should be helpful:

- ◆ `msdn.microsoft.com/vbasic`: This is Microsoft's home page for Visual Basic .NET.

- ◆ `www.planet-source-code.com`: This is a site focused on sample programs for many languages including Visual Basic and .NET.

SQL Server

Here are a couple of places to help stay on top of SQL Server information:

◆ `www.microsoft.com/sql`: This is the home page for SQL Server provided by Microsoft.

◆ `www.sqlwire.com`: SQLWire is a news source for information related to Microsoft SQL Server that is updated daily and provides a weekly newsletter.

Oracle Resources

If you're pursuing additional knowledge related to Oracle, check out these sites:

◆ `www.oracle.com`: This is Oracle's home page.

◆ `technet.oracle.com`: This is Oracle's technology network site with online documentation, downloads, technical articles, and sample code.

DB/2 Resources

If Big Blue is of interest, check out these sites:

◆ `www.ibm.com`: This is the IBM home page.

◆ `www-3.ibm.com/software/data/db2`: This is the home page for the DB/2 product family, with immediate links to each DB/2 platform. It also provides links to news, downloads, and developer resources.

MySQL Resources

If you want to benefit from or contribute to the world of open source, hop on over to these sites:

◆ `www.mysql.com`: MySQL.com is the community Web site for MySQL sponsored by MySQL AB. This is a good source for links, documentation, and downloads.

- ◆ `www.innodb.com`: InnoDB.com is the site sponsored by Innobase Oy for information and documentation of the MySQL InnoDB table type, which provides support for transactions, row-level locking, and foreign key constraints.

- ◆ `www.dwam.net/mysql`: This site is a good source of information concerning MySQL on Windows.

- ◆ `www.nusphere.com`: NuSphere.com is the site for NuSphere, which provides Web-development tools based on open-source products, including a distribution of MySQL.

Index

Numerics

A

continued

continued